CONSUMPTION AND THE COUNTRY HOUSE

Consumption and the Country House

JON STOBART
and
MARK ROTHERY

OXFORD
UNIVERSITY PRESS

Great Clarendon Street, Oxford, OX2 6DP,
United Kingdom

Oxford University Press is a department of the University of Oxford.
It furthers the University's objective of excellence in research, scholarship,
and education by publishing worldwide. Oxford is a registered trade mark of
Oxford University Press in the UK and in certain other countries

Published in the United States of America by Oxford University Press
198 Madison Avenue, New York, NY 10016, United States of America

British Library Cataloguing in Publication Data
Data available

Library of Congress Control Number: 2015957362

ISBN 978–0–19–872626–5

Printed in Great Britain by
Clays Ltd, St Ives plc

Acknowledgements

This book is the principal outcome of a two-and-a-half year research project funded by the Arts and Humanities Research Council: AH/H008365/1 'Consumption and the Country House, c.1730–1800', awarded in 2010. This allowed us to explore in depth the archives of three families held at the Northamptonshire County Record Office, the Shakespeare Central Library and Archive, and the Warwickshire County Record Office, and we would like to thank the staff at each for their assistance. We also drew on help and support from the managers and curators at each of the study houses: Caroline Darlington at Arbury Hall, Laura Malpas and Edward Bartlett at Canons Ashby, and Paula Cornwell and Gretchen Ames at Stoneleigh Abbey.

Earlier versions of chapters have been presented at conferences and seminars in Antwerp, Cambridge, Exeter, Hull, Leeds, London, Lyons, Northampton, Norwich, Odense, Oxford, Prague, Rotterdam, Uppsala, Vienna, and Wolverhampton. Our thanks go to the organizers of these events and to all those who participated and helped to shape our ideas and arguments. Particular thanks are due to Briony McDonagh, Kate Smith, and Sara Pennell for reading and commenting on earlier drafts of chapters. Bringing the book to fruition was also assisted by a grant from the Scouloudi Foundation in association with the Institute of Historical Research.

Contents

List of Figures

List of Tables

Introduction

A 1767 correspondent of *The Gentleman's Magazine* wrote that a friend of his in the country had 'beggared himself, and spent the fortunes of three or four children in what he called 'improvements, though it appeared to me that all the money had been thrown away, without either taste or common sense'.[1] In many ways, this conforms to a traditional view of the aristocracy as reckless and feckless spenders, more interested in luxury and expressions of power than in managing resources and spending wisely. The country house is painted as a drain on finances so vast that it could ruin the family for generations to come. Of course, the product of this spending was often superb, both in terms of the house as an architectural and socio-political statement, and its contents, which often spoke of the taste and learning of the owners as well as their considerable spending power. Indeed, it is telling that the correspondent to *The Gentleman's Magazine* was distressed as much by the lack of taste as by the financial imprudence of the exercise. Viewing country houses in this way highlights their importance as part of our cultural heritage: they are key sites to be preserved, celebrated, and visited. But how many people walking through the state rooms at Chatsworth or exploring the kitchens, larders, and laundries at Dunham Massey stop to think about the processes which produced the spaces that they see; the motivations and relationships which lay behind them; or the ongoing work of supply, cleaning, and maintenance that kept the house functioning? Historians also too rarely consider these questions; yet they lie at the heart of the production and reproduction of the country house.

This book addresses some of these issues by focusing on the consumption practices that characterized English country houses and their owners in the eighteenth century. In bridging the divide between analyses of consumption (which are generally focused on the middling sort) and studies of the country house and the elite (often preoccupied with architecture and aesthetics or with high-octane metropolitan social lives), we offer important new insights into the material culture and meaning of the country house. This involves examining the goods being bought and positioned in the house, but we are less concerned with their intrinsic material or aesthetic qualities than with the processes and practices underpinning their acquisition and assemblage: what was bought from whom, where were objects put, and how did they relate to other items already present in the house? People lie at the heart of our study: not just the owners, but also their families, friends, neighbours, and servants. In exploring their consumption practices, we link into a range

---

[1] *The Gentleman's Magazine*, 37 (1767), 287.

of broader themes: from luxury, taste, and comfort to credit relations, trust, and character. In placing it firmly within debates over consumption we reanimate the country house with flows of goods, ideas, and people, and demonstrate its links to wider social and cultural change within a nascent consumer society.

LANDOWNERS AND THE COUNTRY HOUSE

Country houses and their wealthy owners have generated an enormous amount of interest from historians. Many of the pioneering studies of the post-war period, supplied with growing collections of estate papers in the newly established county record offices, focused on the economics of estate ownership and the balance sheet of income and expenditure.[2] Later, in the 1980s, the use of marriage and estate settlements, mortgages, and credit in developing and sustaining elite estates attracted much interest,[3] culminating in Sir John Habakkuk's monumental *Marriage, Debt and the Estate System.*[4] This greatly enriched our understanding of the functioning of landed estates and the legal-structural factors that underpinned continuity in status of early-modern landed elites, land as a source of income being overlain by its significance as the basis of political power. Another strand of research, most notable in the work of F. M. L. Thompson and G. E. Mingay, took wider perspectives on the landed classes as a whole. These studies sought to understand the several social groups of aristocracy and gentry in totality, from social status to political power, along with the economics of estate management.[5] There was some attempt here to understand the outgoings of landowners in supporting and running their households and their lifestyles; but these were brief episodes in studies in which the main focus was on outward projections of power and status, rather than on how this related to and built upon the inner life of consumption within the country house.[6] Indeed, we know far more about the accumulation and distribution of landed wealth through investments and family settlements than we

---

[2] Much of this work can be traced back to Habakkuk's seminal articles: H. J. Habakkuk, 'English landownership 1640–1740', *Economic History Review*, 10 (1940), 2–17; H. J. Habakkuk, 'Marriage settlements in the eighteenth century', *Transactions of the Royal Historical Society*, fourth series, 32 (1950), 15–30.

[3] See, for example, B. English and J. Saville, 'Family settlement and "the rise of the Great Estates"', *Economic History Review*, 33 (1980), 556–8; C. Clay, 'Property settlements, financial provisions for the family and the sale of land by the great landowners 1660–1790', *Journal of British Studies*, 21 (1981), 18–38; J. Beckett, 'The pattern of landownership in England and Wales, 1660–1800', *Economic History Review*, 37 (1984), 1–22.

[4] H. J. Habakkuk, *Marriage, Debt, and the Estate System: English Landownership 1650–1950* (Oxford, 1996).

[5] F. M. L. Thompson, *English Landed Society in the Nineteenth Century* (London, 1963); G. E. Mingay, *English Landed Society in the Eighteenth Century* (London, 1963). See also M. Beard, *English Landed Society in the Twentieth Century* (London, 1981) and for studies of the British landed classes outside of England, see T. Dooley, *The Decline of the Big House in Ireland: A Study of Irish Landed Families* (Dublin, 2001) and P. Jenkins, *The Making of a Ruling Class: The Glamorgan Gentry 1640–1790* (Cambridge, 2002).

[6] For a discussion of the running of households and the expenses incurred, see Mingay, *English Landed Society*, 205–33.

do about the disbursement of that wealth through everyday discretionary spending. If they considered such questions at all, earlier studies tended to assume the nature of aristocratic identity from the wealth, rank, and lifestyle of the owners; they did not attempt the kind of detailed analysis of how the aristocracy chose to spend their money that is necessary to understand more fully the identities of country house owners and how these were produced and performed through consumption.

A great estate meant great wealth, but also considerable influence over the electorate and thus the choice of MPs. In a series of publications, David Cannadine explored the political power of the aristocracy, often focusing in particular on their adaptation to the growing urban context.[7] But others recognized more clearly that this political power was embodied in the country house which, for Girouard, was 'the headquarters from which land was administered and power organized. It was a show-case, in which to exhibit and entertain supporters and good connections...It was an image maker, which projected an aura of glamour, mystery or success around its owner. It was visible evidence of his wealth'.[8] The country house thus became the key area of expenditure, with landowners laying out huge and sometimes ruinous sums on building and decorating halls, and on landscaping parks. An estimated £80,000 was spent on building Wentworth Woodhouse (1723–50), Holkham Hall (1732–66) cost £90,000, and Fonthill Splendens (1757–70) £100,000.[9] As Wilson and Mackley make clear, the cost of fitting out a house could make up a large proportion of the overall cost. Sir John Griffin Griffin, for example, spent £13,424 on furniture at Audley End on top of the cost of the building work, which already came to £73,000.[10] Such vast outlays are usually seen as being financed from loans against the security of land, thus encumbering subsequent generations with debts; others benefitted from endowments brought by propitious marriages. For some, like the Dukes of Chandos, spiralling costs brought serious financial difficulties; but others were able to spread the costs and thus finance extensive building programmes from their income. Sir John Griffin Griffin repaired, rebuilt, and refurnished Audley End over four decades, paying for the work out of income drawn from his estate, military pension, and ownership of lighthouses. And, of course, for every Coke and Beckford, there were hundreds of gentlemen living very comfortably on a few hundred a year in houses

[7] See D. Cannadine, *Lords and Landlords: The Aristocracy and the Towns 1774–1967* (Leicester, 1980); D. Cannadine, *Patricians, Power and Politics in Nineteenth-Century Towns* (Leicester, 1982). See also Cannadine's two studies of the decline of the aristocracy: *The Decline and Fall of the British Aristocracy* (London, 1990) and *Aspects of Aristocracy: Grandeur and Decline in Modern Britain* (Harmondsworth, 1995).

[8] M. Girouard, *Life in the English Country House* (New Haven, CT, 1978), 3. See also L. Stone and J. C. Fawtier Stone, *An Open Elite: England 1540–1880* (Oxford, 1984), 12–14.

[9] C. Christie, *The British Country House in the Eighteenth Century* (Manchester, 2000), 38; R. Wilson and A. Mackley, *The Building of the English Country House, 1660–1880. Creating Paradise* (London, 2000), 393.

[10] Wilson and Mackley, *Building of the English Country House*, 261–5; J. Beckett, *The Aristocracy in England, 1660–1914* (Oxford, 1986), 331.

that cost perhaps £2,000 to build.[11] The wealth, ambition, and financial arrangements of the landowning elite varied considerably.

From the perspective of art history, this investment is taken as a starting point and attention focuses on the resulting architectural and aesthetic development of the country house. Architectural historians have tended to take a linear approach to stylistic development in country house architecture—a tendency seen most clearly in the seminal work of Summerson and Harris.[12] These outline a basic four-stage progression: the grandness of Baroque, dominant at the start of the eighteenth century, was followed by neo-Palladianism, increasingly popular after the publication in 1715 of the first volumes of both Colen Campbell's *Vitruvius Britannicus* and the translation of Palladio's *I quattro libri dell'architettura*. This was gradually superseded by neoclassicism, popularized by the Grand Tour and by the designs of Robert Adam, James Stuart, and others, and then by neo-Gothic styles, which emerged from the mid-eighteenth century as a reaction against Italian-inspired classicism and rose to dominance through their associations with romanticism.[13] With the right knowledge, this approach can tell us much about the political, cultural, and aesthetic values of country house owners, their architectural choices being readable as symbols of their tastes, preferences, and allegiances.[14] Critical in this regard was the choice of architect and the relationship that existed between him and his patron. Not only were the builders making important cultural and political statements; they were also positioning themselves as significant patrons of an important art form.[15] However, some care is needed in interpreting these relationships and, more broadly, the symbolism of architecture. We should be wary of imposing a 'progression' of styles onto the architecture of the past; what architectural historians recognize as classicism was often seen by contemporaries simply as 'modern'. Moreover, these broad shifts are based on key landmark buildings—places like Castle Howard, Wentworth Woodehouse, Keddleston Hall, and Strawberry Hill—whereas the rebuilding and remodelling that characterized many country houses was stylistically much less clear-cut.[16]

[11] H. Chavasse, 'Material culture and the country house: fashion, comfort and lineage' (unpublished PhD thesis, University of Northampton, 2015), 42–59; Wilson and Mackley, *Building of the English Country House*, 242–3; Beckett, *Aristocracy in England*, 26–42.

[12] J. Summerson, *Architecture in Britain 1530–1830* (New Haven, CT, 1993; first published 1953); J. Harris, *The Design of the English Country House* (London, 1985). See also J. Summerson, H. Colvin, and J. Harris (eds), *The Country Seat: Studies in the History of the British Country House* (London, 1970).

[13] Summerson, *Architecture in Britain*, esp. 296, 384–409, 452–4.

[14] Girouard, *English Country House*, 180; D. Arnold, *The Georgian Country House: Architecture, Landscape and Society* (Stroud, 2003), 40; R. MacArthur, 'Material culture and consumption on an English estate: Kelmarsh Hall 1687–1845' (Unpublished PhD thesis, University of Northampton, 2010), 10–11.

[15] Wilson and Mackley, *Building of the English Country House*, 109–44.

[16] Arnold, *Georgian Country House*, 12. See also Christie, *British Country House*, 32; J. Black, *Culture in Eighteenth-Century England: A Subject for Taste* (London, 2006), 51.

Interior decoration was an integral part of the architectural scheme and is often seen as progressing in parallel with that of the building.[17] As with architecture, the country house owner can be seen as a patron of the arts, employing skilled craftsmen and artists to create elegant or magnificent interiors. The best stuccoists, carvers, gilders, and cabinetmakers enjoyed international reputations and were employed at considerable cost to add lustre to interiors through their reputation and the quality of their work. At Lowther Hall, for example, Viscount Lonsdale paid £430 to the Italian Antonio Verrio for painting the hallway and at Blenheim the French decorative artist, Louis Laguerre, was engaged to paint the walls and ceilings of the state rooms.[18] These highly decorated spaces frequently formed the backdrop to collections of paintings and sculptures, sometimes housed in specially constructed galleries such as the Pantheon at Ince Blundell and the Gallery at Corsham Court.[19] Portraits have always been an essential part of country house decoration and the works of a new generation of artists (Lely, Kneller, Reynolds, and Gainsborough) were an expected part of elite collections, alongside the more established corpus of Old Masters, both Italian and Dutch. Increasingly, these were complemented by landscapes, hunting scenes, history paintings, and allegorical scenes so that country houses became 'temples to the arts'.[20]

This reinforces a view of the country house as a preconceived and stable environment—a 'representation of space', planned by the architect and created by the owner to communicate messages of power, wealth, and taste.[21] It links to what might be termed a *Country Life* view of the house: an assemblage of unique and precious objects brought together by discerning owners who were noted aesthetes and key patrons of the arts.[22] Such conceptions overlook the country house as a lived space that contained owners, families, servants, and visitors, and one that was constantly in process, being made and remade in response to social, cultural, and technical change. Girouard highlights some of these processes in his pioneering work and also discusses some of the utilitarian functions of the country house, such as the accommodation of kitchens and servants. Others have followed this

[17] See, for example, G. Beard, *Georgian Craftsmen and their Work* (London, 1966); M. Wilson, *The English Country House and its Furnishings* (London, 1977); C. Saumarez Smith, *Eighteenth-Century Decoration: Design and the Domestic Interior in England* (London, 1993); J. Cornforth, *Early Georgian Interiors* (New Haven, CT, 2004).

[18] Beckett, *Aristocracy in England*, 331.

[19] J. Feijfer and E. Southworth, *The Ince Blundell Collection of Classical Sculpture* (Liverpool, 1998); F. Ladd, *Architects at Corsham Court* (Bradford-on-Avon, 1978), 34.

[20] Christie, *British Country House*, 179–231. See also F. Russell, 'The hanging and display of pictures, 1799–1850', in G. Jackson-Stops, G. J. Schochet, L. C. Orlin, and E. B. MacDougall (eds), *The Fashioning and Functioning of the British Country House* (New Haven, CT, 1989), 133–53; K. Retford, *The Art of Domestic Life: Family Portraiture in Eighteenth-Century England* (New Haven, CT, 2006).

[21] The idea of 'representations of space' is formulated in H. Lefebvre, *The Production of Space* (Oxford, 1991). For more discussion in the context of eighteenth-century England, see J. Stobart, A. Hann, and V. Morgan, *Spaces of Consumption. Leisure and Shopping in the English Town, c.1680–1830* (London, 2007), 21–2, 59–70.

[22] For recent examples of this genre, see M. Miers, *The English Country House. From the Archives of Country Life* (New York, 2009); C. Phillips and G. Wilson, *The Stately Houses, Palaces and Castles of Georgian, Victorian and Modern Britain* (London, 2011); D. Cruikshank, *The Country House Revealed: A Secret History of the British Ancestral Home* (London, 2011).

lead; Sambrook for example discusses the domestic offices of the country house and the lives of servants.[23] But it is only recently that social and cultural historians, such as French and Rothery, Vickery, and Whyman, have begun to lead the historiography of the landed classes into new areas, by considering issues such as gender identities and roles, and the influence of sociability and social networks.[24] As a result of studies like these, we have a far more nuanced picture of the landed classes as rounded people and of the country house as a dynamic and living space, the latter being a theme developed in particular by historians interested in the role of women in the construction of the domestic environment.[25]

Part of this reorientation has involved a growing awareness of the country house as a site of consumption set within local, national, and global systems of supply. In the past, much has been made of European connections and the impact of the Grand Tour, but recent studies have focused more on the links between country houses and Empire. These link in to discussions of an open elite, with nabobs in particular being seen as a threat to the existing social order; they also tie the country house into cultures and material cultures of imperialism. As Barczewski argues, British country houses abound with the 'physical representations of empire'.[26] Even here, the focus has remained largely on the luxurious and the permanent with relatively little attention being given to the full breadth of the elite's changing material culture; the mundane consumption practices through which their ambitions and tastes were brought to fruition; or the everyday systems of supply that serviced their demands. In this respect recent work by Vickery and by Whittle and Griffiths is particularly important in fleshing out our understanding of elite material culture and spending, but this kind of systematic and comparative analysis remains rare in studies of the country house.[27] Several historiographical issues make these lacunae all the more striking. A central preoccupation for historians of the landed classes from the eighteenth century onwards has been their position in relation to the 'rising' middling sorts, part of which has focused on the 'openness'

---

[23] Girouard, *English Country House*; P. Sambrook and P. Brears (eds), *The Country House Kitchen, 1650–1900* (Stroud, 1996); P. Sambrook, *Keeping their Places: Domestic Service in the Country House* (Stroud, 2009).

[24] See A. Vickery, *The Gentleman's Daughter: Women's Lives in Georgian England* (New Haven, CT, 1997); H. French and M. Rothery, *Man's Estate: Landed Gentry Masculinities, 1660–1900* (Oxford, 2012); S. Whyman, *Sociability and Power in Late-Stuart England: the Cultural Worlds of the Verneys, 1660–1720* (Oxford, 2002).

[25] These include J. Lewis, 'When a house is not a home: elite English women and the eighteenth-century country house', *Journal of British Studies*, 48 (2009), 336–63; A. Vickery, *Behind Closed Doors. At Home in Georgian England* (New Haven, CT, 2009); K. Smith, 'In her hands. Materializing distinction in Georgian Britain', *Cultural and Social History*, 11:4 (2014), 489–506.

[26] S. Barczewski, *Country Houses and the British Empire, 1700–1930* (Manchester, 2014), 137. See also the various case studies published as part of the project 'East India Company at Home' available at <http://blogs.ucl.ac.uk/eicah/>.

[27] Vickery, *Behind Closed Doors*; J. Whittle and E. Griffiths, *Consumption and Gender in the Early Seventeenth-Century Household. The World of Alice Le Strange* (Oxford, 2012). For an earlier study of this type, see J. D. Williams, 'The noble household as a unit of consumption: The Audley End experience, 1765–1797', *Essex Archaeology and History*, 23 (1992), 67–78. Two important recent studies are MacArthur, 'Material culture and consumption' and Chavasse, 'Material culture and the country house'.

of the aristocracy to other elite groups.[28] Yet work on the British aristocracy as an open elite failed to recognize the important part played by the transformation of consumption practices in the growing influence of the middling sorts. The focus instead has been on the purchase of landed estates by wealthy merchants, politicians, nabobs, or planters.[29] The emphasis in the history of consumption has been on the middling sorts, with the proviso that great importance has been accorded to the elite as the engine of consumer transformation in the eighteenth century.[30] Few would now agree with John Cannon that the eighteenth century was 'the aristocratic century'; yet we still know very little indeed about the behaviour, attitudes, and impact of the landed elites during this important social and economic transformation.[31]

APPROACHING CONSUMPTION

Consumption has become one of the key metanarratives of historical enquiry, especially for the eighteenth century, where it has eclipsed production and industrialization as the dominant explanatory framework for social, cultural, and economic transformation. Quite apart from its contemporary resonance in our post-industrial society, the broad and malleable nature of consumption makes it useful as an organizing framework for historical enquiry into anything from

---

[28] On the rise of the middling sorts, see P. Langford, *A Polite and Commercial People: England 1727–1873* (Oxford, 1992); M. Hunt, *The Middling Sort: Commerce, Gender and the Family in England, 1680–1780* (London, 1996); H. R. French, *The Middle Sort of People in Provincial England* (Oxford, 2007). The main protagonists arguing for a relatively 'closed' elite and the relevant publications are Stone and Stone, *Open Elite*; J. Cannon, *Aristocratic Century: The Peerage of Eighteenth-Century England* (Cambridge, 1984). These publications sought to critique studies revealing openness in areas such as marriage, put forward most comprehensively in T. H. Hollingsworth, 'A demographic study of the British ducal families', *Population Studies*, 11/1 (1957), 4–26, and T. H. Hollingsworth, 'The Demography of the British Peerage', *Supplement to Population Studies*, 18/2 (1964), 20–46, in which he proposed a gradual reduction of endogamy in aristocratic marriage. The relatively closed nature of marriage has recently been reaffirmed by K. Schutte, *Women, Rank and Marriage in the British Aristocracy, 1485–2000* (Basingstoke, 2014).

[29] For the argument that this occurred frequently, see J. Habakkuk, *Marriage, Debt and the Estate System* and F. M. L. Thompson, *Gentrification and the Enterprise Culture: Britain 1780–1980* (Oxford, 2001). For the alternative perspective, see W. D. Rubinstein, 'New men of wealth and the purchase of land in nineteenth-century Britain', *Past and Present*, 92 (1981), 125–47. On the rise of nabobs and planters as country house owners, see Barczewski, *Country Houses and the British Empire*.

[30] On middling sort material culture, see L. Weatherill, *Consumer Behaviour and Material Culture in Britain 1660–1760* (London, 1988); M. Finn, 'Men's things: masculine possessions in the consumer revolution', *Social History*, 25:2 (2000), 133–55; W. Smith, *Consumption and the Making of Respectability, 1600–1800* (London, 2002); M. Berg, *Luxury and Pleasure in Eighteenth-Century Britain* (Oxford, 2005); J. Stobart, *Sugar and Spice. Grocers and Groceries in Provincial England, 1650–1830* (Oxford, 2013), 240–63. On the importance of elites in consumer change, see N. McKendrick, 'The consumer revolution of eighteenth-century England', in N. McKendrick, J. Brewer, and J. H. Plumb (eds), *The Birth of a Consumer Society* (London, 1982), 9–33.

[31] Cannon, *Aristocratic Century*.

political protest, to imperialism, to the family.[32] Consumption allows us to think about individuals and groups; norms, behaviours, and practices; relationships with goods and spaces; ideas of agency and identity; and local and global links. As Trentmann puts it, 'consumption is a mirror of the human condition'.[33] Peering into this mirror, historians of the eighteenth century have particularly looked for a clear image of the causes and consequences, and indeed the very existence, of a nascent consumer society.[34] One of the key aspects of this has been the attempt to uncover consumer motivations, both at an individual and group level. To an extent, choices about consumption are attributable to price relative to income; as things became cheaper, a wider set of people could consume them in larger quantities. Even at a base level, however, de Vries demonstrates that this involved households reorienting their spending around the market supply of a new set of goods, including colonial groceries and imported textiles, but also more traditional objects of desire: clothing, bedding, and alcohol.[35] When it came to those with greater disposable incomes, choices were more complex and often oriented towards the need for social differentiation.

For Veblen, the social status of what he called 'the leisured classes' was cemented and communicated through their conspicuous consumption of goods and display of personal accomplishments. In the context of late nineteenth-century America, Veblen highlighted the knowledge of 'dead languages', the correct handling of grammar, and an understanding of the proprieties of dress. He also emphasized the conspicuous employment of male servants as symbols of 'waste' or unnecessary expenditure, a feature that also characterized the liveried manservant of elite eighteenth-century families.[36] Most important, however, were positional goods, the inherent scarcity of which meant that consumption by one group or individual necessarily denied them to others. The character of these goods changed over time and with it the character of the domestic environment: pewter was replaced by earthenware and porcelain, turkey work by mahogany, and tapestry by damask or paper wall hangings. The emphasis for elite consumers remained on magnificence and luxury, defined in terms of cost, complexity of acquisition, and association

---

[32] See, for instance, M. Hilton, 'Consumer movements', in F. Trentmann (ed.), *The Oxford Handbook of the History of Consumption* (Oxford, 2012), 505–20; T. Bickham, 'Eating the empire: intersections of food, cookery and imperialism in eighteenth-century Britain', *Past and Present*, 198 (2008), 71–109; J. de Vries, *The Industrious Revolution. Consumer Behaviour and the Household Economy, 1650 to the Present* (Cambridge, 2008), 186–237.

[33] F. Trentmann, 'Introduction', in Trentmann, *Handbook of the History of Consumption*, 1.

[34] For key studies, see McKendrick, 'Consumer revolution'; G. McCracken, *Culture and Consumption. New Approaches to the Symbolic Character of Consumer Goods and Activities* (Bloomington and Indianapolis, IN, 1988), 3–30; J. Brewer and R. Porter (eds) *Consumption and the World of Goods* (London, 1993); Smith, *Consumption and the Making of Respectability*; Berg, *Luxury and Pleasure*.

[35] De Vries, *Industrious Revolution*, 122–85. See also A. McCants, 'Poor consumers as global consumers: the diffusion of tea and coffee drinking in the eighteenth century', *Economic History Review*, 61 (2008), 172–200; S. Horrell, J. Humphries, and K. Sneath, 'Consumption conundrums unravelled', *Economic History Review*, 68 (2015), 830–57.

[36] T. Veblen, *The Theory of the Leisure Class: an Economic Study of Institutions* (Basingstoke, 1912), 25, 57, 75.

with exclusive systems of knowledge.[37] In practice, this often linked elite consumption with imported goods and transnational cultures of consumption. The precise blend of objects and influences varied across time and space, but drew influence from different parts of Europe and the wider world—the latter in the form of colonies and colonial trade, but also through an enduring fascination with the orient, be it the Ottoman Empire or China and India. Combined with transnational travel and networks of family and friends, these varied stimuli created a material and cultural cosmopolitanism that helped to define European elite identity around socially exclusive luxuries, behaviours, and knowledge.[38]

Luxury, though, was a slippery and changing concept, the morality of which was the subject of fierce debate throughout the early-modern period and beyond, not least as the potential to consume luxuries spread to new social groups. Much of the historiographical interest in this debate has focused on a change in attitude, often credited to Bernard Mandeville, which saw luxury shift from being a moral vice to an economic virtue.[39] However, recent interventions have sought to emphasize continuity over the *longue durée*, especially in displays of magnificence and splendour.[40] Taking a socio-economic rather than a moral viewpoint, de Vries argues that a fundamental shift was under way that not only redefined luxury, but also moved cultural precedence and leadership away from traditional elites and onto a new urban elite. What he calls 'old luxury' comprised a material culture that distinguished the aristocratic elite and communicated a 'hegemonic cultural message' through grandeur and 'exquisite refinement'.[41] Importantly, such luxury could only be emulated by inferior copies which, in many ways, served to underline social and cultural distinctions. In contrast, 'new luxury' was open to a broader section of the population and was characterized by moderation rather than excess; it was thus perceived to denote virtue and sensibility rather than corruption and decadence. Moreover, new luxury involved different types of goods: things that were less expensive, more readily replicated and heterogeneous in form, and associated with polite sociability rather than social distinction.[42] The different mentality of new luxury meant that consumers were seen as being more ready to switch resources from consumption to production in order to maximize future income

[37] On the definition of luxury, see A. Appadurai, *The Social Life of Things: Commodities in Cultural Perspective* (Cambridge, 1986), 3–63; Berg, *Luxury and Pleasure*, 21–45. On positional goods, see F. Hirsch, *The Social Limits to Growth* (London, 1977).

[38] See, for example, M. Berg and E. Eger (eds), *Luxury in the Eighteenth Century. Debates, Desires and Delectable Goods* (Basingstoke, 2003); K. L. Cope and S. A. Cahill (eds), *Citizens of the World. Adapting in the Eighteenth Century* (Lewisburg, PA, 2015); A. Clemente, 'Luxury and taste in eighteenth century Naples: representations, ideas and social practices at the intersection between the global and the local' in J. Ilmakunnas and J. Stobart (eds), *A Taste for Luxury in Early-Modern Europe: Display, Acquisition and Boundaries* (London, 2016).

[39] For a useful summary of these debates, see M. Berg and E. Eger, 'The rise and fall of the luxury debates', in M. Berg and E. Eger (eds), *Luxury in the Eighteenth Century*, 7–27.

[40] For example, B. Blondé and W. Ryckbosch, 'In splendid isolation. A comparative perspective on the historiographies of the "material renaissance" and the "consumer revolution"', *History of Retailing and Consumption* 1:2 (2015), 105–24.

[41] De Vries, *Industrious Revolution*, 44.

[42] Berg, *Luxury and Pleasure*, 117–92; de Vries, *Industrious Revolution*, 44–5, 55–6.

and more willing to delay gratification than the aristocratic elite. Both the material culture and motivations underpinning new luxury were therefore distinct; they challenged the cultural and social pre-eminence of the elite.[43]

De Vries's concept is not without its problems, not least of which are the historical and geographical specificity of the point at which leadership of material culture transferred from traditional elites to a new urban middle class, and subsequent marginalization of the elite from the dynamics of consumer change. This may have been true of seventeenth-century Holland, but the situation was much less clearcut elsewhere. In eighteenth-century Naples, for example, the conflict took place within the elite, between a new educated and humanist group and an established military and conservative group.[44] This highlights the variable and often ambivalent position of traditional elites within our understanding of eighteenth-century consumption. On the one hand, we can see them increasingly marginalized by cultures of consumption that reflected the values and priorities of the middling sorts—part of the 'new luxury' emphasis on prudence, restraint, and respectability.[45] Taken further, this involved a growing critique of aristocratic excess and decadence. Their taste for luxury, wasteful use of resources, and studied idleness was parodied in satirical prints, plays, and essays, and was portrayed as a sign of moral degeneracy and of their lack of fitness to govern.[46] On the other hand, however, these same tastes were seen as trickling down to those of lower social status. Indeed, for McKendrick, emulation held the key to the consumer revolution which he identified in eighteenth-century England because 'In imitation of the rich the middle ranks spent more frenziedly than ever before, and in imitation of them the rest of society joined in as best they might.' Novelty and fashion were the engines powering this apparent frenzy of consumption, with men and women 'spurred on by social emulation and class competition'.[47] Significantly, the elite were seen both as leading the charge and setting the standard. Allan Ramsay, the portraitist, understood this perfectly. He mused that

> let man of ordinary rank or figure appear in publick in a coat whose cuffs are triangular, when the mode is square; and there is no doubt he will meet with many to despise, but none to imitate him. Let the same be tried by a man blest with title, riches, youth, and all the trappings of prosperity...the triangle will then be found to meet with a quite different reception...will receive a share of respect for being part of him and will soon become the object of imitation.[48]

---

[43] See, for example, B. Blondé, 'Conflicting consumption models? The symbolic meaning of possessions and consumption amongst the Antwerp nobility at the end of the eighteenth century', in B. Blondé, et al. (eds) *Fashioning Old and New, Changing Consumer Patterns in Western Europe, 1650–1900* (Turnhout, 2009), 65–71.

[44] Clemente, 'Luxury and taste in eighteenth century Naples'.

[45] See Vickery, *Gentleman's Daughter*, 127–60; K. Harvey, *The Little Republic: Masculinity and Domestic Authority in Eighteenth-Century Britain* (Oxford, 2012), 167; Smith, *Consumption and the Making of Respectability*, esp. 189–222.

[46] See Berg and Eger, 'The rise and fall of the luxury debates'.

[47] McKendrick, 'Consumer revolution', 11.

[48] A. Ramsay, *A Dialogue on Taste* (London, 1762), 35.

Notwithstanding critiques of this emulation model, which emphasize that the trickle-down of goods and practices should not be read as necessarily emulative, it is apparent that, even within the elite, aspirational spending was important.[49] This is evident from Greig's analysis of the Straffords and their attempts to infiltrate London's beau monde. Lady Strafford observed her peers and inspected their homes, writing to her husband with news about a range of fashionable material objects that would help to project them into this elite world.[50] Yet this reveals the complexity of fashion: it was not simply defined by what was modish, but could also signal refined taste and a set of goods and practices which connoted rank and dignity. As Simmel argued, fashion signalled membership or allegiance—in this instance to a self-defining 'brilliant vortex'. Lord Chesterfield recognized this, noting that members of the beau monde were characterized by a certain 'je ne scay quoy... which other people of fashion acknowledge'.[51]

Refinement of taste and the codes of politeness were a means of tempering the excesses of both fashion and luxury. Berg argues that 'new wealth had to be educated, and the choice, display, and use of the variety of goods had to be cultivated'—a sentiment that echoes Veblen's understanding that the manners, deportment, and good taste that formed 'the voucher of a life of leisure' had to be learned.[52] This same idea lies at the heart of Bourdieu's thesis that taste is the key to social distinction, and to cultural and social reproduction. His focus was on France in the 1960s and 1970s, where the metropolitan elite perpetuated their privilege through the educational opportunities afforded by the *grandes écoles* and through the cultivation of cultural capital.[53] This involved the construction of a set of tastes that were very different from those of the lower orders and often involved a preference for 'difficult' things that were less immediately accessible and pleasurable: the so-called Kantian aesthetic. For Bourdieu, the importance of this process was that it was a conscious strategy of social reproduction through cultural distinction—an idea that resonates with many eighteenth-century elite practices, including attending university and undertaking a Grand Tour; the cultivation of polite attributes; assembling and reading a gentlemanly library; and gaining an understanding of architecture and the classics. This can be seen as a form of defensive consumption, intended to bolster social standing against incursions by the lower orders, and is echoed in attempts by the middle ranks to secure respectability through the material culture and social practices discussed by Smith.[54] The extent to which cultural capital resulted in a distinctively aristocratic material culture is less clear. Bourdieu,

[49] See C. Campbell, 'Understanding traditional and modern patterns of consumption in eighteenth-century England: a character-action approach', in J. Brewer and R. Porter (eds), *Consumption and the World of Goods* (London, 1993), 40.

[50] H. Greig, *The Beau Monde. Fashionable Society in Georgian London* (Oxford, 2013), 36–47.

[51] Greig, *Beau Monde*, 3.

[52] Berg, *Luxury and Pleasure*, 41; Veblen, *Theory of the Leisure Class*, 49.

[53] P. Bourdieu, *Distinction: A Social Critique of the Judgement of Taste* (London, 1984). For a useful critique, see M. Savage, 'Status, lifestyle and taste', in Trentmann (ed.), *Handbook of the History of Consumption*, 557–67.

[54] Smith, *Consumption and the Making of Respectability*. See also Berg, *Luxury and Pleasure*, 199–246. On politeness and consumption, see Langford, *Polite and Commercial People*, 68–99; Stobart, Hann, and Morgan, *Spaces of Consumption*, 4–8, 70–8, 179–85.

amongst others, has drawn on the idea of *habitus* to understand the relationship between social structures (such as gender and class) and individual lifestyle, tastes, and preferences. It is a structured and structuring system, but has clear links across to materiality in the domestic environment—the setting which Bourdieu sees as critical in shaping *habitus*.[55]

The pleasure derived from consumption is rarely considered in these discussions of its rational use in social differentiation. Indeed, pleasure as an emotion plays surprisingly little part in our understanding of consumption. Sombart denounced the sensuality of consumption as 'a pathology of aristocratic wealth', but Berg makes clear that physical and sensual qualities of manufactured items made them attractive to many social groups: the glistening of crystal glass, the gleam of silver, and the warm softness of amber and tortoiseshell snuff boxes.[56] Moreover, novelty itself gives pleasure as it arouses the senses and alleviates the boredom that arises from the satiation of bodily needs. This links closely to Campbell's argument for a shift in values and attitudes during the eighteenth century towards a Romantic ethic marked by 'a distinctive form of hedonism, one in which the enjoyment of emotions as summoned through imaginary or illusory images is central'.[57] For Campbell, the longing for new goods and experiences was just as important as their actual consumption, although the sensory gratification—the pleasure—of drinking tea or chocolate, or smoking tobacco, should not be overlooked.[58] Pleasure might also be drawn from the usefulness of objects. Pepys, for example, was very pleased by some lamp glasses which he saw in the shop of the noted scientific instrument maker, Ralph Greatorex, noting that they 'carry the light a great way, good to read in bed by'.[59]

Part of this utility might come in terms of making the user more comfortable. This sense that comfort meant something physical, and involved making people's lives easier and more convenient, marks a departure from earlier understandings of the term which saw it as connoting support and consolation. Crowley has focused on this change in meaning, arguing that 'physical comfort—self-conscious satisfaction with the relationship between one's body and its immediate physical environment—was an innovative aspect of eighteenth-century Anglo-American culture'.[60] He sees

[55] Bourdieu, *Distinction*, 169–75.

[56] Berg, *Luxury and Pleasure*, 250. See also T. Scitovsky, *The Joyless Economy: An Enquiry into Human Satisfaction and Consumer Dissatisfaction* (New York, 1976).

[57] Campbell, 'Understanding consumption', 48. See also C. Campbell, *The Romantic Ethic and the Spirit of Modern Consumerism* (Oxford, 1987).

[58] B. Cowan, *The Social Life of Coffee. The Emergence of the British Coffeehouse* (New Haven, CT, 2005), 11–14; Smith, *Consumption and the Making of Respectability*, 161–2; Stobart, *Sugar and Spice*, 30–9.

[59] Quoted in N. Cox, *The Complete Tradesman. A Study of Retailing, 1550–1820* (Aldershot, 2000), 138. See also M. Berg, 'New commodities, luxuries and their consumers in eighteenth-century England', in M. Berg and H. Clifford (eds), *Consumers and Luxury. Consumer Culture in Europe, 1650–1850* (Manchester, 1999), 69.

[60] J. Crowley, 'From luxury to comfort and back again: landscape architecture and the cottage in Britain and America', in M. Berg and E. Eger (eds), *Luxury in the Eighteenth Century* (Basingstoke, 2007), 135–50. See also J. Crowley, *The Invention of Comfort. Sensibilities and Design in Early-Modern Britain and Early America* (Baltimore, MD, 2001); Chavasse, 'Material culture and the country house', 123–69.

this search for comfort in the growing use of candles, mirrors, stoves, and lamps, but acknowledges that the search for comfort was tempered by displays of fashion and sometimes sacrificed on the altar of genteel taste. However, such concerns might also be interpreted as meeting a need for social comfort, that is, the feeling of being at ease in polite company. Moreover, ideas of emotional comfort remained important, as even a superficial reading of Jane Austen's novels makes clear. Women in particular valued the sentimental associations carried by certain objects and frequently bequeathed such items to particular friends.[61]

This tells us much about the role that material possessions played in the construction of self-identity, as markers of character rather than status. Indeed, it is possible to see consumption as a process through which the meanings of goods are sorted into a coherent system that constructs and communicates the identity and character of the consumer: as Campbell puts it, 'the self is built through consumption [and] consumption expresses the self'.[62] Individuals thus have agency to exploit the growing array of goods, particularly novelties, in constructing their own identities, sometimes in conscious opposition to social or cultural groupings, but more often to signal their belonging to a broader group, for example gender, class, collector, or dandy.[63] Vickery focuses much attention on the ways in which women created and deployed material objects, drawing on their utility and semiotics, to construct identity and define their position and purpose in life. Smith links the consumption of a range of colonial products to the construction of respectability amongst an expanding middling sort—a process which might be seen as part of the broader project of politeness, which attempted to shape society and social status on virtue and manners, bolstered by material goods and consumption practices. More specifically, Nenadic notes how Glasgow's arriviste colonial merchants engaged in a 'spectacular form of self-invention' through their 'conspicuous consumption and acquisition of elaborate and symbol-laden possessions'.[64] The last of these is particularly significant, as Nenadic argues that these wealthy merchants were carving out a new identity, more akin to the elite than to their middling-sort origins. Two things are important here. First is the idea that identity could be consciously constructed and performed—an echo of Goffman's assertion of the performed self—rather than emerging performatively through the routines of everyday life.[65] Second is the suggestion that identity

---

[61] K. C. Phillipps, *Jane Austen's English* (London, 1970), 74–5; N. Page, *The Language of Jane Austen* (Oxford, 1972), 30, 38–9; M. Berg, 'Women's consumption and the industrial classes of eighteenth-century England', *Journal of Social History*, 30 (1996), 415–34.

[62] Campbell, *Romantic Ethic*, 288.

[63] This is the basis of the 'character-action approach' taken in Campbell, 'Understanding consumption'. See also Berg, *Luxury and Pleasure*, 250–1; Cowan, *Social Life of Coffee*, 10–12, 16–47; J. Styles, *The Dress of the People. Everyday Fashion in Eighteenth-Century England* (Newhaven, CT, 2007), 8–16. See also M. Douglas and B. Isherwood, *The World of Goods* (New York, 1979).

[64] Vickery, *Gentleman's Daughter*; Vickery, *Behind Closed Doors*, esp. 207–90; Smith, *Consumption and the Making of Respectability*, esp. 189–222; S. Nenadic, 'Middle-rank consumers and domestic culture in Edinburgh and Glasgow 1720–1840', *Past and Present*, 145 (1994), 127.

[65] E. Goffman, *The Presentation of Self in Everyday Life* (New York, 1956); N. Gregson and G. Rose, 'Taking Butler elsewhere: Performativities, spatialities and subjectivities', *Environment and Planning D: Society and Space*, 18 (2000), 433–52; P. Glennie and N. Thrift, 'Consumers, identities and consumption spaces in early-modern England', *Environment and Planning A*, 28 (1996), 39–40.

construction could be aspirational, and that there was an identifiable elite character and material culture to which one might aspire. This is particularly significant in an age when, as Corfield puts it 'power was resynthesized into active terms, of acquisition, production, and display, rather than of inheritance, formal title, and ancient lineage'.[66] The nature of a specifically aristocratic male character is outlined by Campbell, but neither he nor the many recent studies of masculinity—which broadly confirm the defining features as honour, virtue, independence, morality, and restraint—discuss in detail how these character traits link to consumption and materiality.[67] Indeed, all too rarely is consumption used as a lens through which to scrutinize the character and identity of elites; most often it is seen as a simple reflection of excess, connoisseurship, or power relations. Some of the complexity of consumption and character is therefore lost.

Within this complexity, the mundane and everyday processes of supply are paramount. Traditionally seen as underdeveloped and primitive, eighteenth-century retailing has been recast in recent years as a dynamic and innovative sector. Work by Walsh, Cox, Glennie and Thrift, Stobart, and Mitchell, amongst many others, has revealed shops as sophisticated social and economic spaces which played a key role in shaping as well as responding to shifts in consumer preferences.[68] Window displays, printed advertisements, and showrooms helped to increase knowledge of the growing world of goods; a blending of credit, ready money, and fixed prices provided flexibility and liquidity to the market, and an improved urban environment underpinned the emergence of shopping as a leisure activity, at least for the middling sorts. The emphasis on pleasurable shopping that involved browsing and sociability is important as it carries the construction of identity and the bolstering of status back through the process of consumption; where and how things were acquired could be just as important as the objects themselves, not least because of the networks of friendship and obligation that this type of shopping could create. But shopping was also a serious business which involved carefully selecting goods of the best quality available and often negotiating the best price; it was mundane and arduous as well as pleasant.[69]

Different modes of shopping might involve different people, with servants or housewives being delegated with everyday provisioning, leaving the homeowner or husband to indulge themselves in more discretionary spending. However, shopping

[66] P. J. Corfield, 'Class by name and number in eighteenth-century Britain', in P. J. Corfield (ed.), *Language, History, and Class* (Oxford, 1991), 129–30.

[67] Campbell, 'Understanding consumption', 49–5.

[68] C. Walsh, 'Shop design and the display of goods in eighteenth-century London', *Journal of Design History*, 8 (1995), 157–76; Cox, *Complete Tradesman*, esp. 76–145; Glennie and Thrift, 'Consumers, identities and consumption spaces'; Berg, *Luxury and Pleasure*, 247–78; Stobart, Hann, and Morgan, *Spaces of Consumption*, 123–32, 171–88; I. Mitchell, *Tradition and Innovation in English Retailing, 1700 to 1850* (Farnham, 2014), 37–60, 129–52.

[69] C. Walsh, 'Shops, shopping and the art of decision making in eighteenth-century England', in J. Styles and A. Vickery (eds), *Gender, Taste and Material Culture in Britain and North America* (New Haven, CT, 2006), 151–77; C. Walsh, 'Shopping at first hand? Mistresses, servants and shopping for the household in early-modern England', in D. Hussey and M. Ponsonby (eds), *Buying for the Home: Shopping for the Domestic from the Seventeenth Century to the Present* (Aldershot, 2008), 13–26; Stobart, *Sugar and Spice*, 190–214.

also involved the bundling of time and space. At one level, this can be seen in the movements of the individual through the city during the course of their everyday activities or on the polite social round, following familiar routes and routines.[70] At another, it is manifest in the complex web of supplies that serviced more substantial households and especially the country house; goods came in through established routes and often as part of a regular cycle of provisioning. This might involve long-distance links, but also a dense network of local supplies, including some that took place outside the mechanisms of market exchange. Whittle and Griffiths, for example, show the importance of gifts of food in the provisioning of the Le Strange household in the early seventeenth century, commodity transfers being bundled with notions of patronage and obligation.[71] This links closely to Trentmann's assertion that 'consumption consists of a bundle of goods, practices and representations'. Within the home, de Vries argues, these 'indivisibilities in consumption' linked a whole range of commodities and durable items, of which tea, sugar, and the paraphernalia for polite tea ceremonies form perhaps the most obvious example.[72] Here the association is practical as well as symbolic; but it could also be framed by ideas of the cultural conformity of established sets of goods. This is the essence of the so-called Diderot effect which, in its most straightforward manifestation, worked 'to prevent an existing stock of consumer goods from giving entry to an object that carries cultural significance that is inconsistent with that of the whole'.[73] In theory, this forms a powerful conservative force shaping domestic material culture, one that would be felt especially strongly in elite and middling households where there was a greater proportion of inherited goods. Yet, as the research of Weatherill and Overton makes clear, novel goods were introduced into many homes, a process which gives particular significance to the spatial and mental placement of new and old.[74]

KEY THEMES

The complexities of consumption have made it a revealing lens through which to explore the domestic realm and with it the culture, identity, and socio-economic relations of its occupants. Focusing this lens on the country house offers a new way of looking at elite material culture that takes us beyond the artefacts and architecture, and behind the management of their estates, and into the lives of the owners and their households, connecting perspectives that have formerly focused either on the social life of the country house, on the built environment of the house, or on the rural social, political, and economic context in which these houses were

[70] Walsh, 'Shopping at first hand?'; Vickery, *Behind Closed Doors*, 113–26; Stobart, Hann, and Morgan, *Spaces of Consumption*, 102–9; A. Pred, *Lost Words and Lost Worlds: Modernity and the Language of Everyday Life in Late Nineteenth-Century Stockholm* (Cambridge, 1990).

[71] Whittle and Griffiths, *Consumption and Gender*, 72–84.

[72] Trentmann, 'Introduction', 8; de Vries, *Industrious Revolution*, 31.

[73] McCracken, *Culture and Consumption*, 123.

[74] Weatherill, *Consumer Behaviour*; M. Overton, D. Dean, J. Whittle, and A. Hann, *Production and Consumption in English Households, 1600–1750* (London, 2004).

situated. It offers insights into the construction, character, and supply of the house and its role as a symbol of elite identity and status, but it also connects the house to systems of taste, supply, and sociability, and to ideas of luxury and cosmopolitanism. It thus situates the house in its broad cultural, economic, and social context, and allows us to use the country house and elite consumption as a means of testing wider conceptualizations of consumption. In short, by bringing the country house into contact with the mainstream of consumption studies, our analysis creates a new and productive dialogue between the two. In doing this, we focus on five broad themes.

The first of these is to consider the country house as a site of both conspicuous and everyday consumption, reflecting its material and cultural complexity. In material terms it housed collections of books and art; large amounts and a wide variety of furniture were required to fills its many rooms; it needed lighting, heating, cleaning, and maintenance; and there were dozens of mouths to feed and bodies to clothe. Symbolically, it communicated the wealth, power, and ambition of the owner, but also their taste and learning, and it signalled the status, identity, and permanence of the family. The country house was thus an arena for display, but it was also a place to live, a family home which had to function on a day-to-day basis and required ongoing consumption in the shape of maintenance, heating and lighting, food, and so on. These issues are covered in the first three chapters. The key ideas within Chapters 1 and 2 are luxury, fashion, and taste, and the ways that material objects were used to display the status and character of the owner. Central here is the question of what defined and differentiated aristocratic consumption and material culture. We critically engage with both Bourdieu's idea concerning taste and distinction, and with de Vries's association of the established aristocracy with 'old luxury'. Undoubtedly, the consumption of English landowners carried many of the material and mental trappings of old luxury. However, we also explore the ways in which they engaged with the ideals and practices of 'new luxury', thus challenging the social and cultural distinctions made by de Vries and questioning the usefulness of this distinction in our understanding of shifts in consumption, material culture, and cultural leadership. This focus on display and status is balanced by analysis of everyday consumption (Chapter 3) and of the relationship between income and outgoings (Chapter 1). The former comprised a substantial proportion of spending, but is easily overlooked, despite its centrality to the respectability of the household and to the exigencies of sound financial management. These are often seen as middling or bourgeois ideals, but to what extent did they also define elite consumption? The latter links back to the different priorities inherent in new luxury; it again challenges our understanding of elite spending and, indeed, our ability to identify a particular aristocratic mode of consumption.

Second, and with clear and close links to this, is the changing nature of domestic material culture in eighteenth-century England. As we have already discussed, this has generated enormous interest in the historiography, with the importance of novelty being highlighted in analyses by Weatherill and others that identify this as a period of profound change in the domestic realm. Novelty was important both in terms of a taste for novel goods and in the very idea of newness and change—something which appealed at a practical and psychological level. And yet change was balanced by continuity and by the very real inertia of existing material objects. We might see these operating in the manner described by Diderot, old things resisting new objects that do not conform to the status quo. They might also be viewed at a more pragmatic level: country houses were large and could accommodate a lot of furniture displaced from its original setting. These processes are explored in Chapter 2, with thrift and novelty combining to steer the retention and relocation of goods, and the creation of different assemblages. Thrift emerges again as an important ideal in household management, discussed in Chapter 3, but so too does the centrality of old goods to elite material culture, notwithstanding McCracken's assertion of the decline of patina in the face of novelty. We explore what old things meant for their aristocratic owners, both as symbols of family and pedigree, and, as Lewis and others have argued, for the emotional comfort they offered to their owners. In this, we critically engage with Crowley's arguments about the changing meaning and manifestation of comfort in the eighteenth-century home. Was the growing emphasis on physical comfort really at the expense of emotional well-being? More generally, there is a need to view consumption practices as both the accumulation and divestment of material goods, and to explore how these related to economic expediency, notions of fashion, intra-family relationships, and individualism.

Third is the relationship between consumption and identity, another key idea within the literature. Consumption has long been seen as a core component in the construction of self. It would be mistaken to reduce the human condition to the goods and experiences consumed; yet, as Trentmann has recently argued, we can learn a lot about ourselves and others by looking closely into the mirror of consumption. In an eighteenth-century context in particular, consumer identities have generally been conceived in terms of broad social categories or ideal types: the respectable middling sort analysed by Smith; the aristocrat or dandies identified by Campbell; the distressed or determined women studied by Vickery, and so on. Building on this work, Chapter 4 examines the construction of masculinity—a category overlooked by historians of consumption until recently. Attention centres on both the patterns of consumption and the processes for managing and regulating spending. This reveals the extent to which elite men conformed to an ideal type of masculinity and the ways in which they balanced the competing priorities of moderation and virtue on the one hand and heroism, pride, and independence on the other. We also note how different men responded to these challenges in different ways and the importance of personality in shaping consumption. Gender relations and distinctive female modes of consumption form the focus of Chapter 5. Here we build on Vickery's analysis of husband–wife relations, but go beyond this to think about singleness and thus how gender interacted with status and family to define self. What happened to a woman's spending when she was free from male constraint and when she was faced with the responsibilities of running the estate? More generally, we consider (most directly in Chapter 2) the extent to which elite identity was bound up with a conscious sense of cosmopolitanism, be it European (inspired by continental travel, often as a Grand Tour) or imperial (linked to the growing array of colonial goods that invaded the country house).

The fourth theme centres on the practicalities of supply and the contingent nature of consumption. By virtue of their wealth and their role as tastemakers and fashion leaders, the elite were able to escape constraints that restricted the consumption of many sections of society. Nonetheless, country house owners were dependent upon a huge variety and number of suppliers, the abilities, merits, and stock of whom had to be carefully assessed and constantly reassessed to ensure reliable supplies of good-quality merchandise at acceptable prices. These practical decisions were rarely taken in isolation; nor did country house owners consume only for themselves. The imperatives of practicality and availability, and the blandishments of wives, children, or neighbours are too often neglected; yet the work of Vickery, Berry, and others shows the importance of such influences for consumers and the significance they were accorded by contemporaries. We engage with this work in Chapters 6 and 7, analysing the ways in which elites related to suppliers and exploring in detail the household as a context for elite consumption. This raises questions about the factors influencing the choice of supplier and how this related to ideas and judgements of credit, honour, and reputation. This in turn invites consideration of what an analysis of country house supply might tell us about the retail system of eighteenth-century England and about the place of landed elites within this changing society. It also raises questions about the role of family and household in shaping consumption: how was their influence balanced against personal preference or the advice of craftsmen and professionals? If consumption was contingent, what were the key forces in operation?

Last, is the spatiality of consumption, both within and beyond the country house. Space has been of growing interest to historians in recent years, both as the forum for human action and as an influence on that activity. We have already noted its impact on studies of shopping and leisure by Walsh, Stobart, and Glennie and Thrift, which have highlighted the importance of the shop and street as a context for consumption and the construction of consumer identities. Space was also influential in shaping conceptualizations of the home, in terms of either public–private or front- and back-stage spaces—distinctions drawn and problematized by Vickery and Weatherill respectively. The size of the country house provides scope for complex differentiations of space in terms of access, room use, and decoration, but has yet to be fully explored in terms which are theoretically informed. This issue is addressed in Chapter 2, which also examines the ways in which sets of assemblages of goods both reflected and moulded the function and status of different rooms. We challenge any simple binary of public–private, front–back-stage, developing Vickery's argument that these were contingent and relative categories. Yet this raises the question of how we then make sense of the variation in decor and mutability of rooms and the ways in which they were constructed by and, in turn, shaped consumption practices. Beyond its four walls, the country house is traditionally seen as embedded in its locality; yet it also drew on national supplies and particularly those from London, the locus of social and political activity, the main conduit for international influences, the centre in which fashions were shaped and from which they were disseminated, and the most important source for fashionable goods. Metropolitan values were a powerful influence, especially on elites who spent a significant part of the year in the capital. It is, therefore, surprising that little attention has been paid to London's impact on the consumption practices of the elite in their provincial country houses. Linking the country house to the capital is thus central to our analysis of supply systems (Chapter 8), but we also examine how the (spatial) practices of shopping in London were related to life cycle, residential location, and personal preference. In a broader sense we see the country house as a nodal point transcending the space of its rural setting and connecting regional, national, and international societies and markets.

In addressing these various themes, we place the country house firmly in the context of changing cultures and practices of consumption. This broadens our perspective on the country house and on the elite, adding a new layer to analyses traditionally dominated by art-historical or economic approaches. Just as importantly, we reflect back on what the country house can tell us about eighteenth-century consumption more generally: the balancing of the extraordinary and the everyday; the varied and contingent nature of consumer motivation; the importance of individual agency in relation to household, family, and locale; and the construction and contestation of gender and status identities.

CASE-STUDY FAMILIES

These issues are addressed through detailed analysis of a three landowning families in the English Midlands: the Leighs of Stoneleigh Abbey and Newdigates of Arbury Hall, both in Warwickshire, and the Drydens of Canons Ashby in Northamptonshire. Stoneleigh Abbey, a former Cistercian abbey, was purchased by Thomas Leigh, a London merchant, in 1571. His son, Thomas, was made a Baronet in 1611 and his grandson, also called Thomas, was created Baron in 1643 for his services to Charles I. The family's finances were seriously compromised in 1646, when Thomas was forced to compound for £4,895, but they recovered in the later decades of the seventeenth century, in part as a consequence of the lands worth £900 per annum brought into the family through the 1669 marriage of Thomas's grandson, the second Lord Leigh (1652–1710), to Elizabeth, the daughter of Richard Brown of Kent. This was an unhappy and childless match that generated a great deal of public acrimony and ended in separation, but Thomas's second marriage was more settled and signalled a much quieter phase in the family history. Thomas focused much of his attention on domestic concerns, although he took his seat in the House of Lords, Hearnes describing him as 'an honest debauched Tory'.[75] The value of the estate grew significantly during the eighteenth century. £4,000 of land was settled on Edward, the third Lord Leigh (1684–1738), and

---

[75] Quoted in M. MacDonald, '"Not unmarked by some eccentricities": the Leigh family of Stoneleigh Abbey' in R. Bearman (ed.), *Stoneleigh Abbey: The House, Its Owners, Its Lands* (Stoneleigh, 2004), 142.

Mary Holbech by her father, Thomas Holbech of Fillongley in Warwickshire, and helped to fund the construction of the massive west range at Stoneleigh Abbey. By 1749 rental income from the estate was £6,975 per annum, a sum which grew considerably in 1755, when the death of Edward's sister-in-law, Lady Barbara Leigh, brought her lands in Leighton Buzzard and the personal estate of her late husband Charles Leigh, Edward's younger brother, into the holdings of Stoneleigh Abbey.[76] These raised the Leighs' annual income to almost £10,000, placing the family in the highest bracket of Massie's 1756 typology; but they remained marginal to county and national politics, only occasionally attending Parliament and holding no political office within the county.[77] Thomas, the fourth Lord Leigh (1713–49) married twice. His first wife was Maria Craven, with whom he had four sons and a daughter (although three sons died in infancy); his second was Catherine Berkley—a marriage which lasted little more than a year and produced a daughter, Anne. The death of Thomas, aged just 36, resulted in a period of minority ownership, as his son, Edward, the fifth Lord Leigh (1742–86), was a mere seven years old when Thomas died. Edward was educated at Westminster and Oriel College, Oxford. He came into his majority in 1763 and held great promise, but his mental health deteriorated from the late 1760s onwards and he was declared insane in 1774. At his death the estates were worth £13,643.[78] Edward never married; with an average age of marriage in the high twenties and already afflicted with mental illness by the time he was 26, it is possible that he simply did not have the time to find a spouse. He died without issue and left the estate to his elder sister, the Honourable Mary Leigh (1736–1806). After twenty years as life tenant, she also died unmarried and childless in 1806, whereupon the estates (by then worth around £19,000) were inherited by a junior branch of the family, the Leighs of Adelstrop, although not without a lengthy legal dispute. By the turn of the nineteenth century, the Leighs were amongst the wealthiest of Warwickshire landowners and, in the national context, were one of a select group of around four hundred 'great landlords', with incomes of over £10,000 and a commensurate 'style of living that distinguished them from the inferior ranks of landed society.'[79]

The Dryden family had held Canons Ashby since the sixteenth century and enjoyed titled status from 1619, when Erasmus (1553–1632) was created a Baronet. He had earlier served as High Sheriff of Northamptonshire and was elected MP for Banbury in 1624—a career in local politics mirrored by his son, John, the second Baronet (*c.*1580–1658). Following the death without issue of John's son, Robert (*c.*1638–1708), the Canons Ashby estates passed to Edward Dryden (d.1717), his first cousin once removed, whilst the Baronetcy went to

[76] Shakespeare Central Library and Archive (SCLA), DR18/31/903—Account of the estate and effects of the Honourable Charles Leigh, 1749.

[77] P. Mathias, 'The social structure in the eighteenth century: a calculation by Joseph Massie', in P. Mathias, *The Transformation of England: Essays in the Economic and Social History of England in the Eighteenth century* (London 1979), 171–89. On the fifth Lord Leigh's attendance in the Lords, see his obituary in *Gazetteer and New Daily Advertiser*, Tuesday 30 May, 1786.

[78] MacDonald, 'Leigh family', 149, 151, 153; SCLA, DR18/31/16–37—Rentals of Real and Devised Estates 1762–1806.

[79] Mingay, *English Landed Society*, 19–20.

another cousin, John Dryden (*c*.1635–1710), who became the fourth Baronet. Edward was a successful London grocer and continued to trade even following his inheritance; he made many improvements to the house and may also have enhanced estate income which, at the time of his death in 1717, amounted to £1,100 per annum. Meanwhile, the title had passed briefly to Sir John's cousin, Erasmus Henry Dryden (1669–1710), a priest who died only a few months after John, and then to Edward Dryden's father, another Erasmus Dryden (1636–1718), who became the sixth Baronet. Sir Erasmus and his son's wife, Elizabeth, lived at Canons Ashby following Edward Dryden's inheritance, managing the estates in his name. Following the deaths of Edward and Sir Erasmus, the former's son, another John (*c*.1704–70), inherited both the estates and the title, thus bringing titular honours and landed income back together. Sir John faced a significant challenge in terms of debts on the estates since Edward had left over-generous provision for his younger sons and daughters. This problem was solved through the sale of Edward's London properties; £1,000 and income from the estates of Frances Ingram (Sir John's first wife, who died in 1724); a win on the lottery to the tune of £590; investments in the South Sea Company; and some thrifty spending habits. By the time of Sir John's marriage to his second wife, Elizabeth Rooper, in 1726, the estates were in credit again. The childless seventh Baronet died in 1770, whereupon the title was extinguished. The estate, by then worth about £2,500, passed to his adoptive daughter Elizabeth (1753–1824), who continued living at Canons Ashby with her mother until 1781, when she married John Turner (1752–97) and moved to 10 Upper Seymour Street, off Portman Square, in London. In 1791, the dowager Lady Elizabeth died and Elizabeth moved back to Canons Ashby with her husband, who added Dryden to his name. John Turner Dryden purchased a Baronetcy in 1793, but enjoyed the title for just four years, dying in 1797 and leaving debts of £10,980.[80] Elizabeth maintained control over the estate until her death in 1824, when Canons Ashby passed to her second son, Henry.

The Newdigates came into possession of Arbury Hall in 1586, when John Newdegate, a lawyer, exchanged it for his property in Middlesex, Harefield Place. John's son, Richard (1602–78), was also a lawyer and rose to the position of Chief Justice before resigning his post at the Restoration.[81] His practice was lucrative, allowing him to buy back the Harefield estates and further land in Warwickshire, and he was made a Baronet in 1677. His son, another Richard (1644–1710), was a keen horseman and horse breeder, who owned sixty-seven horses in 1697, some of them being housed in the large stable block he completed at Arbury in 1677. In the late seventeenth century, the estate income was about £4,000, allowing the second Baronet to make further improvements to the house, including a significant remodelling of the chapel.[82] Richard's son, again called Richard (1668–1727), had seven sons by his second wife, Elizabeth Twisden, but he outlived four, being succeeded

---

[80] NRO, D(CA)536—Marriage settlement of Godfrey Scholey and Dame Elizabeth Dryden, 19 March 1805.

[81] G. Tyack, *Warwickshire Country Houses* (Chichester, 1994), 9–15.

[82] G. Tyack, 'Country house building in Warwickshire, 1500–1914' (BLitt thesis, Oxford University, 1970), 204.

by his fourth son, William (1715–34), who died without marrying. At this point, the estate passed to Richard's youngest son, Roger (1719–1806), who became fifth Baronet when he was just 15 years of age. Sir Roger dominates the story of Arbury and the Newdigate family in the eighteenth century. He went to Westminster School and then to University College, Oxford, before undertaking the first of two Grand Tours (1738–40 and 1774–5).[83] He was MP for Middlesex (1741–7) and Oxford University (1750–80), cementing a close relationship with that institution and underlining his reputation as a renowned classical scholar. He also did his duty in other key positions in local society, including a commission as a Captain of the Warwickshire Militia, a role he greatly valued. Sir Roger completely remodelled Arbury Hall in the Gothic style, funding the work from the growing income from his lands in Warwickshire and Middlesex. Inheriting an estate worth perhaps £5,000, he invested heavily in coal mining and transport improvements, including canals, and increased the estate income to £15,000 at its peak in 1789. This placed him alongside the Leighs at the top of landowning wealth in Warwickshire and, indeed, the country, although the volatile costs and profits from coal mining meant that his income had reduced to about £9,000 by the end of the eighteenth century. His politics were conservative and establishment; Horace Walpole described him as a 'half-converted Jacobite' and Thomas Ward called him a 'true English Gentleman of Polished manners & of the OLD SCHOOL'.[84] Sir Roger enjoyed two lengthy and loving marriages, first with Sophia Conyers and then with Hester Mundy, but had no children. The Baronetcy became extinct and the estate passed for life to a cousin, Francis Parker (1751–1835), who took the name Newdigate.

All three families held hereditary titles in the eighteenth century and all formed part of England's ruling class, a group which made up less than 2 per cent of the population;[85] yet they varied considerably in their wealth, their political ambitions, and their social and cultural aspirations. As such, they form a small cross-section of provincial landed society, but one representative of large swathes of that group. It has been estimated that during the eighteenth century there was a discernible distinction between the four hundred or so 'great landlords' and the 'lesser landlords.'[86] The former, with their larger houses and more lavish lifestyles, required a minimum income of £5,000, but to live this life 'comfortably' a larger income of £10,000 was required. By this calculation the Leighs and the Newdigates moved into this more elite group as the eighteenth century progressed. Throughout our period the Drydens inhabited the world of the 'lesser landlords', still wealthy, but lacking the 'great house' available to families such as the Leighs and the Newdigates. Taken together, these families provide the opportunity for comparative analysis and offer insights into the consumption motivations and practices of the eighteenth-century English provincial landowner.

[83] *Burke's Landed Gentry* (London, 1847), 924; A.W.A. White, *The Correspondence of Sir Roger Newdigate of Arbury Warickshire* (Hertford, 1995), xxiv.

[84] Quoted in Tyack, *Warwickshire Country Houses*, 11.

[85] L. Stone, *The Crisis of the Aristocracy* (Oxford, 1965), 51; Whittle and Griffiths, *Consumption and Gender*, 15.

[86] Mingay, *English Landed Society*, 19–20.

1

Anatomy of Elite Spending
Fashion, Luxury, and Splendour

> Thus first necessity invented stools,
> Convenience next suggested elbow-chairs,
> And luxury the accomplished sofa last.[1]

INTRODUCTION

Spending beyond the need to satiate desire, as William Cowper and many other commentators in this period understood, was characteristic of a novel culture of consumption in eighteenth-century Britain, one in which luxury was available to a wider set of people than ever before. Traditionally associated with elites, luxury was often seen as spreading to the middling sorts and undermining the economy of the country and the moral fibre of its citizens.[2] The debates over luxury are familiar enough, but it was a slippery and relative term, contingent on time and space as well as culture and wealth. Thus, we see Adam Smith complaining that 'For a pair of diamond buckles perhaps, or for something as frivolous and useless, they exchanged the price of the maintenance of a thousand men for a year, and with it the whole weight and authority which it could give them.'[3] The use of material objects to underpin status was nothing new, of course: with purchasing power far beyond the wildest dreams of the common sort of people, the elite had long indulged in conspicuous consumption to proclaim their position at the apex of society.[4] In an argument that presaged Elias's assertion of the necessity of aristocratic spending to maintain status, Veblen noted that consumption by the elite 'undergoes a specialisation as regards the quality of the goods consumed. Since the consumption of these more excellent goods is an evidence of wealth, it becomes honorific; and conversely the failure to consume in due quantity and quality

---

[1] W. Cowper, *The Task*, Book 1: 'The Sofa', 1785.

[2] See, for example, C. Berry, *The Idea of Luxury. A Conceptual and Historical Investigation* (Cambridge, 1994); Berg and Eger, 'Luxury debates'; Berg, *Luxury and Pleasure*, 21–45; L. Peck, *Consuming Splendor: Society and Culture in Seventeenth-Century England* (Cambridge, 2005), 152–88.

[3] A. Smith, *Wealth of Nations* (London, 1776; Oxford, 1976), 418–19.

[4] See, for example, R. M. Berger, *The Most Necessary Luxuries: the Mercers' Company of Coventry, 1550–1680* (University Park, 1993); R. Goldthwaite, *Wealth and the Demand for Art in Italy, 1300–1600* (Baltimore, MD, 1993); Peck, *Consuming Splendor*, 10–22.

becomes a mark of inferiority and demerit.' The excellence of these goods was more than a mere reflection of cost: it required discernment on the part of the consumer to identify the right sort of goods, 'to discriminate with some nicety between the noble and the ignoble in consumable goods'.[5]

The ability to spend lavishly, combined with the discernment required to identify and acquire the right type of things, distinguished the elite and marked out the country house as a key site for luxury consumption: a place where no expense was spared to make a very public statement of the wealth, taste, and connoisseurship of the owner. In this sense, luxuries might be seen as 'social valuables', characterized by their high cost, 'the patron–client relations of production and trade, and the protection and reproduction of status systems'.[6] But they also formed material representations of elite culture—what Bourdieu calls cultural capital—carrying messages about knowledge and learning, as well as rank and status.[7] The nature of these luxury goods is central to the materiality of the country house and the identity of the landowning elite. Yet luxury was undergoing significant change during the early-modern period. Writing in 1577, William Harrison noted that in noblemen's houses one would find an 'abundance of arras, rich hangings of tapestry, silver vessel, and so much other plate as may furnish sundry cupboards'; there would also be turkey work, pewter, brass, and fine linen.[8] For the eighteenth century, Sombart highlighted a new set of goods: crystal lamps, busts and medallions, carved marble chimneys, Asian textiles, gilded furniture, and magnificent clocks.[9] Whilst many of these changes took place within a category of goods which might be termed 'old luxury'—goods that distinguished elite consumers through their character and cost—they also incorporated objects more often associated with so-called 'new luxury', including mahogany and japanned furniture, Wedgwood chinaware, cotton curtains, cut glass, and metal toys.[10] This made the relationship between luxury and elite status problematic: it challenged the social and cultural pre-eminence of traditional elites as consumers, a challenge met by the aristocracy with 'defensive consumption', a need to define their status as different from and more meaningful than the newly wealthy urban elites.[11]

This chapter engages with these ideas by exploring the anatomy of aristocratic spending. We begin by mapping out the overall volume of expenditure by the Leighs and the Newdigates across the period, analysing the rhythms of their spending and

[5] Veblen, *Theory of the Leisure Class*, 74; N. Elias, *The Court Society* (Oxford, 1983), esp. 78–116. See also A. Chatenet-Calyste, 'Feminine luxury in Paris: Marie-Fortunée d'Este, Princesse de Conti (1731–1803)' in D. Simonton, M. Kaartinen, and A. Montenach (eds), *Luxury and Gender in European Towns, 1700–1914* (London, 2015), 171–89.

[6] Berg, *Luxury and Pleasure*, 30.

[7] A. Appadurai, 'Introduction: commodities and the politics of value', in A. Appadurai (ed) *The Social Life of Things: Commodities in Cultural Perspective* (Cambridge, 1986), 3–63.

[8] W. Harrison, *The Description of England* (London, 1587), 197.

[9] W. Sombart, *Luxury and Capitalism* (Munich, 1913); (English edition, Chicago, 1967), 105.

[10] De Vries, *Industrious Revolution*, 44–5, 55–6; Berg, *Luxury and Pleasure*, 117–92.

[11] See, for example, B. Blondé, 'Conflicting consumption models? The symbolic meaning of possessions and consumption amongst the Antwerp nobility at the end of the eighteenth century', in B. Blondé, et al. (eds) *Fashioning Old and New, Changing Consumer Patterns in Western Europe, 1650–1900* (Turnhout, 2009), 65–71.

the causes of change in the tempo of spending from one generation to the next. The reasons for surges in spending varied according to a range of personal and familial factors, but expenditure was generally kept within the limits set by income, leading us to argue that aristocratic spending was characterized by the moderation and self-control characteristic of new luxury. Building on this, we analyse the ways in which spending was distributed across different categories of goods and highlight the relative importance of luxury and everyday spending. Of particular note here is the way that resources were often diverted from consumption to production through investments in the estate and in the wider economy. The chapter closes with a discussion of specific types of luxury and fashion exhibited in these consumption patterns; the importance of positional goods as markers of the elite status of these two families; and the level at which they engaged with 'new luxury' and fashion. Overall, we argue that readings of elite consumption as the pursuit of status need to be balanced by recognition of their engagement with a much broader set of social and economic priorities.

RHYTHMS OF SPENDING

Spending by landowning elites, whether on their estates, houses, or persons, seldom ran at an even pace over the years. Rather, it was punctuated by peaks corresponding to key life events or reflecting the changing status of the individual. Marriage is often highlighted in this regard, Vickery arguing that many bachelors engaged in a bout of spending to create domestic environments suitable for a prospective bride. Expenditure was further increased as new wives then furnished and equipped their houses with proper taste and elegance.[12] Conversely, dowries meant that marriage also provided the stimulus of additional income that allowed costly building projects to go ahead. We see this at Kelmarsh Hall in Northamptonshire, where the £30,000 brought by his new wife allowed William Hanbury to rebuild his house to plans by James Gibbs in the 1720s.[13] Indeed, marriage is seen as one of the key ways in which landed estates were kept in long-term equilibrium as the building schemes of ambitious landowners ran way ahead of rental income.[14] However, there were other life events that stimulated and curtailed expenditure, the transfer of estates between generations on the death of an owner being very significant in this regard. Analysis of spending on the part of successive patricians of the Leigh family and of Sir Roger Newdigate illustrates the variety of factors that influenced consumer behaviour; it also reveals the thriftiness and economy practised by these aristocratic families when compared to their overall levels of income and wealth.

A brief comparison of the total spending of the Newdigates and the Leighs shows a consistently higher level of spending at Arbury Hall than at Stoneleigh

---

[12] Vickery, *Behind Closed Doors*, 83–8.
[13] MacArthur, 'Material culture and consumption', 71.
[14] Wilson and Mackley, *Building of the English Country House*, 297–351.

Abbey across this period. Whilst Roger Newdigate's account books record £297,807 across the fifty year period 1747–96 (an average of £5,956 per annum), the Leighs' bills amount to just £68,395 spent (£911 per annum) between 1730 and 1806. These differences are largely down to the nature of the sources, rather than the behaviour of the respective families. Firstly, the Stoneleigh bills do not, by any means, record all outgoings. Comparisons with short runs of accounts suggest that perhaps one third of spending is captured in the bills; wages, purchases of land and stocks, advances of cash, and payments made through the house steward are largely omitted from the bills, and even some purchases of household goods are missing.[15] In contrast, many of these items of spending, particularly wages and investments, are meticulously recorded in Roger Newdigate's accounts. If the short runs of Leigh accounts are representative of longer-term patterns, it would appear that their spending was broadly comparable to that of the Newdigates, but it ran at a much lower annual average of about £3,000. This further discrepancy was partly a product of the more or less uninterrupted nature of Newdigate's spending, which contrasts with two long periods, 1749–63 (the fifth Lord's minority) and 1774–86 (from his declaration as insane to his death), when Stoneleigh Abbey was largely unoccupied by the family, and during which time discretionary spending dropped to a very low level (see Figure 1.1). Equally, although Roger Newdigate married twice and never had children of his own, Arbury was a household more akin to the stable patriarchal family of husband, wife, and servants than Stoneleigh. Neither Edward, fifth Lord Leigh, nor his sister Mary married or had children, so the costs associated with marriage and marital partners were largely absent from their expenditure. Despite their shortcomings, however, the receipted bills for Stoneleigh

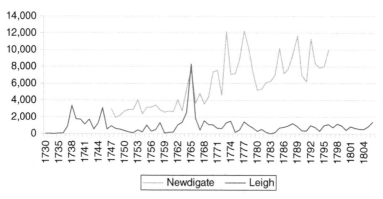

Figure 1.1. Overall spending of the Leighs and the Newdigates, 1730–1806.
Sources: WRO, CR136/V/156, CR136/V/136, Accounts books; SCLA DR18/5/—, Receipted bills.

---

[15] SCLA, DR18/31/22—household accounts, 1778–79; DR18/31/456—Auditor's accounts, 1763–74. See M. Rothery and J. Stobart, 'Inheritance events and spending patterns in the English country house: the Leigh family of Stoneleigh Abbey, 1738–1806', *Continuity and Change*, 27:3 (2012), 387–9.

form a good guide to the overall ebb and flow of discretionary spending and, in combination with Roger Newdigate's account books, provide a useful picture of the variety of family and household forms and processes that shaped the consumption patterns of the landed elite.

At Stoneleigh there were notable peaks in spending in 1738, 1745, and most particularly 1764–5, and troughs in the 1750s and early 1780s (Figure 1.1). All of these related to changes in ownership and the associated settling of accounts and/ or spending by the new owner. When he inherited in 1738, Thomas, fourth Lord Leigh, was faced with the expenses of his father's funeral along with those of a number of other immediate family members (see Chapter 6). Money also had to be found for £367 of legacies to servants.[16] These outgoings, combined with some building work and spending on the estate, largely account for the first spike in spending. That in 1745 is more perplexing, not least because the majority of the bills in this year do not specify the product purchased. However, as discussed in Chapter 4, Thomas Leigh's mother, Mary, continued to reside at Stoneleigh after the death of his father in 1738 and appears to have acted as a brake on his spending, particularly on alterations to the house.[17] Certainly, there was a surge of spending shortly after Mary's death in 1743, at which time Thomas was able to continue work on the house, making this peak effectively a delayed inheritance event. Following his own death in 1749, there was a prolonged lull in spending as the house was effectively closed down during the minority of his children, Edward and Mary, both of whom were cared for by guardians. This lasted for the whole of the 1750s, broken only by smaller peaks of spending in 1755 and 1758 which were associated with the actions taken by Thomas's trustees and executors to settle debts and set the estate on secure financial footing (see chapter 6).

It was the coming of age of Edward, fifth Lord Leigh, in 1763 that produced, through accumulated bills that were finally settled in 1765, the most spectacular peak in spending, amounting to £8,274 recorded in the bills or about £14,500 if outgoings recorded in household and auditor's accounts are also included.[18] This huge upsurge in spending resulted from the need to complete the interiors of the west range built by Edward's grandfather, the third Lord Leigh; fully furnish the upper-floor rooms for the first time; and refurbish or renew interiors of many of the principal rooms which had lain empty for nearly fifteen years. It produced a range of new interiors furnished with high-quality pieces, albeit from craftsmen a notch or two down from the most prominent designers such as Adam, Chippendale, and Linnell, and a splendid collection of books. Again, then, we see expenditure peaking after inheritance, a pattern repeated across Europe as the new owners of substantial estates sought to imprint their own taste onto the country house. At Audley End, for example, Sir John Griffin Griffin made extensive improvements

---

[16] SCLA, DR18/5/2227. The significance of funerals is discussed more fully in Chapter 6.

[17] This is argued by MacDonald, 'Leigh family', 148. Such strong maternal influence was by no means unusual, but it generally encouraged work rather than blocking it—see French and Rothery, *Man's Estate*, esp. 96–106; Vickery, *Behind Closed Doors*, 131–6.

[18] SCLA, DR18/31/22, Household accounts, 1778–9; DR18/31/456, Auditor's accounts, 1763–74.

Figure 1.2. Canons Ashby house. The south front was remodelled by Edward Dryden in the early eighteenth century.

Photograph by Jon Stobart.

after he inherited the property in 1762, including a suite of eight rooms designed by Robert Adam.[19] Almost two generations earlier, Edward Dryden inherited the house and estate at Canons Ashby. Working with a more modest budget, he set about improving and modernizing the house: remodelling the south front, inserting a grand new entrance on the west front (Figure 1.2), and refurbishing many of the rooms, often with pieces ordered from prominent London upholsterers.[20] What is less certain in the case of Edward Leigh is how long the high level of expenditure would have continued had he not begun to suffer mental health problems around 1768, after which his discretionary spending fell dramatically, replaced instead by payments made to various doctors for his care elsewhere in the country.[21] After his formal committal in 1774, spending entered a another lull, most marked in the early 1780s, when the Commission established to oversee the estate (comprising his sister Mary and cousin William Craven) reduced outgoings largely to those necessary for running the estate and maintaining the house.

[19] J. Williams, *Audley End: the Restoration of 1762–97* (Colchester, 1966); Chavasse, 'Material culture and the country house', 61–4.

[20] J. Stobart, 'Inventories and the changing furnishings of Canons Ashby, Northamptonshire, 1717–1819', *Regional Furniture*, xxvii (2013), 1, 7–8.

[21] See MacDonald, 'Leigh family', 150–1.

Inheritance was not the only prompt for upturns in spending by landowning elites, of course: a change in status could also lead to renewed spending on the country house as the owners sought to reflect enhanced social standing in the fabric of their houses. We see this most dramatically in building projects such as those undertaken by Sir Robert Walpole at Houghton Hall and the third Earl of Carlisle at Castle Howard. More typical was the work carried out by Sir John Griffin Griffin, who added a suite of state rooms to Audley End when he was raised to the peerage in 1784. Even at this late date, a state apartment could still be seen as a badge of aristocratic status: despite Girouard's suggestion that, after 1770, 'the concept of state was going out of fashion', Sir John—now Baron de Walden—was assiduous in constructing an appropriate material representation of his newly won title.[22] There is evidence that Sir John Turner Dryden attempted something similar at Canons Ashby following his purchase of a baronetcy in 1795. In this instance, control of the estate following inheritance in 1792 was compounded by his enhanced status. Although the modest proportions of the house prevented any grandiose statement, the wide range of new mahogany, rosewood, and satinwood furniture purchased by Sir John and his wife Elizabeth and their reorganization of room use clearly signalled the new owners' arrival in the lower ranks of the aristocracy.[23]

The overall pattern of Newdigate's spending at Arbury was rather different from that of the Leighs: it lacked the periodic spikes prompted by inheritance, but varied considerably year by year. Sir Roger Newdigate's remodelling of Arbury Hall in the Gothic style took place over several decades, but was interrupted for several years by the death of his first wife in 1774.[24] More generally, however, progress on the house was determined more by Sir Roger's ability and willingness to make it a priority in what was clearly a very busy life. As a Member of Parliament, Justice of the Peace, Grand Tourist, and man of letters, Sir Roger had limited opportunities to plan and direct work—a problem exacerbated by the fact that he supervised much of the work himself.[25] There were bursts of activity in the early 1750s (on the Library), early 1760s (Parlour), around 1770 (Dining Room), early 1780s (Cloisters), and intermittently between 1786 and 1795 (Saloon), but these did not involve notable peaks in Sir Roger's overall spending. Instead there were seven conspicuous years in which Newdigate spent over £10,000 per year, around twice his average spend: 1773, 1777, 1778, 1785, 1789, 1792 and 1796. These peaks were driven principally by borrowing for investments in his estate, mainly through mortgages, and spending on land and bonds, as well as investing in his coal mines,

[22] Girouard, *English Country House*, 230; Chavasse, 'Material culture and the country house', 85–100. For further discussion of the place of state apartments in the country house, see Cornforth, *Early Georgian Interiors*, 13–19; J. Fowler and J. Cornforth, *English Decoration in the Eighteenth Century* (London, 1974), 60; A. Westman, 'A bed in burnished gold', *Country Life* (4 May 2000), 128.

[23] M. Rothery and J. Stobart, 'Merger and crisis: Sir John Turner Dryden and Canons Ashby, Northamptonshire, in the late eighteenth century', *Northamptonshire Past and Present*, 65 (2012), 27–8; Stobart, 'Inventories and Canons Ashby'.

[24] Tyack, 'Country house building in Warwickshire', 214–15.

[25] For example, WRO, CR136/A/582, Diaries: 25 January 1761, 30 October 1761. His involvement in the remodelling of the house is discussed more fully in Chapters 2 and 4.

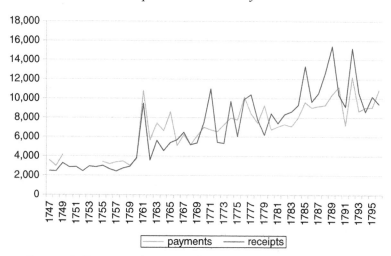

Figure 1.3. Receipts and payments for Sir Roger Newdigate, 1747–96.
Sources: WRO, CR136/V/156, CR136/V/136, Accounts books.

which in turn became a major source of income, particularly into the 1780s (see Figure 1.3). In all but two of these seven years, investments of this type constituted over 70 per cent of total spending. The Leighs also enhanced their estates with purchases of land and the enclosure of existing holdings and by diversifying their investments into stocks and shares; but these investments, which were mainly recorded outside of the receipted bills, did not drive peaks in spending in the way they did for Newdigate.[26] Despite the borrowing and investment exhibited in Sir Roger's accounts, he financed his building work out of current income rather than making recourse to loans. Mortgages are generally seen as underpinning any significant building programme, but at Arbury Hall, Stoneleigh Abbey, and Canons Ashby, there is no evidence that loans were taken for this purpose, despite the extensive remodelling and building work that occurred in each place. As the following section will show, spending of this type, apart from a few bubbles of investment, was kept at a steady pace and work was done gradually rather in rampant peaks of activity. This reveals a deeper current of behaviour amongst both the Leighs and the Newdigates: that of thrift and moderation.

The literature on the aristocracy is replete with examples of heirs spending lavishly, most prominently on extensive building projects. For instance, the first and second Dukes of Chandos, James and Henry, managed to accumulate huge debts through reckless spending and unwise investments during the eighteenth century, and the third Duke, another James, hardly fared any better. However, the penchant that the Dukes of Chandos showed for 'a splendid style of life, whatever it cost', and their 'insouciant attitudes toward debt and an almost heroic financial laxity'

---

[26] See Rothery and Stobart, 'Inheritance events', 388.

was very different from the more measured spending of the kind exemplified by the Leighs and Sir Roger Newdigate, whose average annual expenditure was generally well within the limits set by income.[27] Even if we inflate the totals for the Leighs threefold to accommodate their under-representation of total spending, it is clear that they generally kept their outgoings within reasonable and thrifty limits. For short periods following inheritance Thomas and Edward Leigh spent beyond this limit, but outgoings then returned to more moderate levels. Indeed, whilst income may have imposed an upper limit on their ability or willingness to spend, it seems that the Leighs rarely pushed up against this ceiling. This was especially true in the later years of the century, when Mary Leigh, as tenant for life, had annual outgoings of about £800 recorded in the bills, plus perhaps £3,000 in running costs noted in the household accounts. Compare this with rental incomes of £13,643 in 1786, and a personal fortune of £20,000, and it is apparent that there was a large surplus, at least some of which was invested in stocks and bank annuities that further enhanced the estate income.[28] Sir Roger, meanwhile, spent beyond his income in twenty-two out of forty-five years, mostly in the 1750s and 1760s, after which time income from his collieries rose steadily, supporting levels of spending that had risen from around £3,000 per annum to more than £8,000 per annum (Figure 1.2). Overall, however, his income and expenditure were broadly balanced, his two account books showing a combined surplus of £10,293 over a fifty-year period, 1747–96.

Not all of the subjects of this study followed such a virtuous path, of course, and the spendthrift behaviour of Sir John Turner Dryden and his wife Elizabeth provide an example more closely aligned to the Chandos's, although not on the same kind of scale.[29] In 1791 Elizabeth, the adopted daughter of her otherwise childless uncle, Sir John Dryden (d. 1770) had, with her husband Sir John Turner Dryden, taken full possession of a healthy landed estate. Her adoptive father had, like the Leighs and Newdigates, carefully husbanded his resources, rarely exceeding income with spending, purchasing shares in the East India Company, and making judicious purchases of land along the way.[30] Indeed Elizabeth herself, during her joint stewardship of the estate with her mother, had continued her father's good work. This situation was to change, however, after the death of her mother and her inheritance of the estate with Sir John Turner Dryden. Sir John had spent handsomely whilst a young man, and this behaviour continued after his inheritance of the Canons Ashby estate. Money went on clothing and servants with which to process when he was knighted in 1793, a commission as a captain in the Northamptonshire

---

[27] P. Dickson and J. Beckett, 'The finances of the Dukes of Chandos: aristocratic inheritance, marriage and debt in eighteenth-century England', *Huntingdon Library Quarterly*, vol. 64 (2001), 309–55. For other examples, see G. E. Mingay, *English Landed Society in the Eighteenth Century* (London, 1963), 61–6, 126–9; R. Gemmett, '"The tinsel of fashion and the gewgaws of luxury": the Fonthill sale of 1801', *The Burlington Magazine*, 150 (2008), 381–8; R. A. Kelch, *Newcastle, A Duke Without Money: Thomas Pelham-Holmes, 1693–1768* (London, 1974).

[28] SCLA, DR671/101, Account of the Personal Estate of Mary Leigh, 1822; SCLA DR18/13/7/13–14, Will and codicil of Edward, fifth Lord Leigh, 1767.

[29] For more details, see Rothery and Stobart, 'Merger and crisis'.

[30] NRO, D(CA)/971, Letter from Rev. D. Burton, 1764.

Yeomanry in 1794, and a Baronetcy during William Pitt's first ministry.[31] Correspondence between Elizabeth and their creditors after his death shows that the couple had also spent beyond their means on conspicuous items such as satinwood and mahogany furniture, drapery, and coaches.[32] The cumulative effect of this behaviour, combined with the needs of a large family of nine children, meant that, by the time of his death in 1797, an estate valued at £2,577 was indebted to the tune of £10,680. This left the family to face a period of retrenchment, their finances in 'the most dangerous and embarrassed state imaginable', as Elizabeth herself put it.[33]

It is difficult to assess which characteristic of aristocratic spending was more prevalent: the excess of Elizabeth and John Turner Dryden or the restraint of the Leighs and Newdigates. Certainly Elizabeth and John were an unusual generation within the Dryden family and no doubt an instructive example for later generations. As Harvey argues, good oeconomy was an important part of household management amongst the middling sorts. That it was also important to the landowning elite is apparent from the work of Whittle and Griffiths, and Vickery, who detail some of the ways in which genteel women in particular were involved in careful management of household resources, whether monetary, material, or human. Similarly, French and Rothery have demonstrated how young aristocratic men were trained in the virtues of self-restraint and sound economic management, principles which were central to ideals of masculinity amongst this group.[34] We return to these points in later chapters, but it is important to note at this point that the survival of the family fortune ultimately depended on bringing spending and income into line; the Dryden lifestyle was clearly unsustainable in the long run, and the broader picture of survival of the landed classes suggests the Leighs and the Newdigates were more representative, if less notable.

Perhaps the strongest additional indication of the restraint shown by these families is in their very limited engagement with gambling, a habit often closely associated with the aristocracy. On the evidence we have, it seems neither the Newdigates nor the Leighs spent anything more than the smallest sums on horse racing, cards, or other games of chance. In the early 1750s Sir Roger Newdigate visited the races at Warwick, Rugby, Oxford, and Nuneaton, and placed 1-guinea bets at each event (a total of 16 guineas in 5 years); payments of £1 were made to the race steward at Warwick races in 1764 and 1765, and he purchased a lottery ticket at a cost of £4 in 1753. There are no other entries in his accounts that suggest

---

[31] NRO, D(CA)/1011, Receipt for cost of servants during the award ceremony, no date (1793); D(CA)/219, Commission in the Northamptonshire Yeomanry, 9 May 1794; D(CA)/1021, Letter from W. Chinnery, 26 March 1795; W. Betham, *The Baronetage of England* (London, 1803), 280.

[32] See NRO, D(CA)/903, Inventory, 1791; D(CA)/904, Inventory, 1819; D(CA)/364/37, Letter from Mary Ann Wheatley, 15 March 1804.

[33] NRO, D(CA)/364/2, Valuation of the Dryden estates, no date (1797); D(CA)/364/35, Letter from Lady Elizabeth Dryden, 7 April 1798.

[34] Harvey, *Little Republic*, 33–43; Whittle and Griffiths, *Consumption and Gender*, 26–48; Vickery, *Gentleman's Daughter*, 127–60; French and Rothery, *Man's Estate*, 61–6.

gambling. It is possible that other gambling debts were obscured in the records, but this seems unlikely given the meticulous nature of his account books. It seems much more likely that Sir Roger was visiting and betting on the races as part of a broader process of socializing with polite local company. Similarly, there is very little evidence of reckless spending of this kind by the Leigh family, with just four bills that indicate gambling. The earliest is most significant: a 1748 bill for £64 incurred at Warwick races by Thomas, fourth Lord Leigh, which is probably a cumulative account presented after his death that year. The other three are for gambling on cards and purchasing a pack of cards and a card table by Mary Leigh between 1794 and 1801. Of course, the nature of gambling might militate against its formal recording in the form of a bill, but there is no sign of cash outgoings on a scale that might indicate a serious gambling problem. Whilst higher profile members of the Georgian aristocracy may have been associated with 'gambling craze' of the 1770s, it seems the more sober and refined elite David Spring found in the Victorian period was also flourishing in the eighteenth century.[35]

Both in terms of consumption (spending on goods and services) and production (investments) the Leighs, the Newdigates, and the majority of the Drydens exhibited patterns of behaviour that would be defined, both by contemporaries and historians, as 'new luxury'. In general, their lives were not characterized by the lavish excesses of the 'old luxury' of the aristocracy in the leisure-rich society of previous periods. Rather, they were defined by the virtuous moderation more redolent of the emerging patterns of consumption observed by de Vries and others.[36] In their investments they deferred spending for long-term gain, thereby maximizing income and benefiting the broader economy, behaving in exactly the 'industrious' way expected by theorists of the new luxury, such as Hume and Smith. Such self-control can be found in other types of behaviour and values, not least in gendered ideals of masculinity amongst the eighteenth- and nineteenth-century landed gentry (see Chapter 4).[37] Where peaks of spending did occur, these were related to important moments in the life cycle and the family cycle; restraint and excess were matters of choice for the individual, not a pregiven of middling or aristocratic status. We therefore argue that, whilst new luxury was theorized as a challenge to aristocratic power and distinction, and was indeed a practical means by which lower-ranking groups could secure their status in society, the behavioural tropes of new luxury were far from alien to the Georgian aristocracy. Of course, restraint did not prevent these families from making a mark on society as individuals and families with taste, wealth, and power. Neither, given the huge resources at their disposal, did it mean that they failed to engage in defensive consumption or purchase the traditional signifiers of aristocratic status—points to which we turn next.

[35] D. Spring, 'Aristocracy, Social Structure and Religion in Early Victorian England', *Victorian Studies*, 6, 3 (1963), 263–80.
[36] De Vries, *Industrious Revolution*, 58.
[37] De Vries, *Industrious Revolution*, 67–8; French and Rothery, *Man's Estate*.

PATTERNS OF SPENDING

The aristocracy spent large amounts of money on themselves; on their estates, country houses, and contents; on travel and leisure; and on all the other various aspects of their lives that made them so distinctive. However, they had a certain level of choice to make as to where they would direct their spending: what types of luxuries to buy and which investments to make. The discretionary spending behaviour exhibited by these families can tell us much about their distinctive priorities, interests, and identities, and equally about the values and patterns of behaviour they shared as members of the landed elites. The data in Figures 1.4 and 1.5 represent the total amounts and proportions spent by the Leighs and the Newdigates on groupings of product types. We have not included financial investments, largely because Newdigate's accounts cover this area of spending far better than the receipted bills for Stoneleigh. However, whilst systematic analysis is impossible, there are useful indicators of the relative importance of productive investment in the outgoings of the two families. We know that Newdigate spent a total of £142,617 on developing the estate, investments, taxation, and the like, a colossal sum which amounted to over 50 per cent of his total expenditure across the period. The auditor's accounts for Stoneleigh that run between Edward's inheritance in 1763 and the official declaration of his insanity in 1774 show that just over

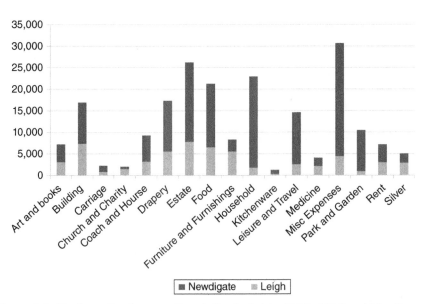

Figure 1.4. Total spending by type of goods for the Leighs (1730–1806) and Newdigates (1743–96).

Sources: WRO, CR136/V/156, CR136/V/136, Accounts books; SCLA DR18/5/—, Receipted bills.

Note: These figures do not include those for investments and taxation, which we comment on above (in the section 'Patterns of spending'): The figure for building work has been extrapolated from our analysis of the account books and from the work of Tyack. See below for further comments.

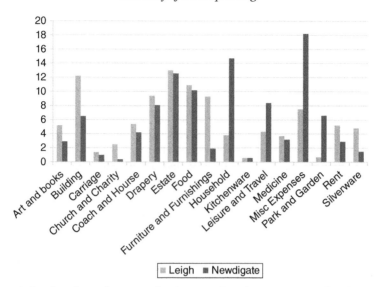

Figure 1.5. Leigh and Newdigate spending by type of goods as percentage of total spending.
Sources: WRO, CR136/V/156, CR136/V/136, Accounts books; SCLA DR18/5/—, Receipted bills.
Note: See note to Figure 1.4.

£20,546 was spent on investments in stocks and shares and purchases of land.[38] The receipted bills for the same period show total expenditure of £22,150, suggesting that the family were matching their spending on investments to discretionary spending on the other categories. In other words, the outgoings of both families were roughly balanced between productive investment on the one hand, and necessary or luxury consumption on the other.

In terms of consumption, there are some striking differences between the two families, although some again are a product of the different data sources, rather than truly divergent behaviour. Sir Roger Newdigate meticulously recorded all his household expenses, including servants' wages. These amounted to £20,198 or 14 per cent of overall spending at an average of £404 each year. The Stoneleigh bills, by contrast, record just £1,751 or 3 per cent of spending in this area, partly because the only wages recorded appear to be those paid to additional servants brought in for special occasions. That this is a gross underestimate is apparent from a set of Stoneleigh household account books, which show spending specifically on the running of the household of £458 in 1774 and of £450 in 1779.[39] These accounts also record cash advances to the house steward, which are generally missing from the bills and go some distance in explaining the differences in the costs of 'miscellaneous expenses' between the two families—the large total for the Newdigates arising from significant cash advances to Sir Roger and his steward. Once these other sources are taken into account, then, it is clear that the two families spent

---

[38] SCLA, DR18/31/461, Auditor's accounts 1763–74.
[39] SCLA, DR18/31/18, Household accounts 1774; DR18/31/22, Household Accounts, 1778–9.

very similar amounts on the running of their households: around £400–450 each year. The longer run of Newdigate accounts reveals inflation in these costs, as should be expected, from an average of £308 between 1747 and 1771 to one of £499 between 1772 and 1796. No doubt earlier household accounts for Stoneleigh would reveal similar inflation.

In some ways, these similarities are unsurprising: a reflection of the spending necessary to maintain a house of a certain size in a manner befitting the lower reaches of the aristocracy. However, expenditure was also comparable across a range of other categories which are much better covered by the Leigh bills: food and drink, drapery, the carriage of goods, and coaches and horses. Taken together these four categories accounted for 28 per cent of spending for the Leighs and 23 per cent for Newdigate, figures which broadly correspond with those which Williams has found for Audley End.[40] This suggests a general correlation between wealth, status, and consumption which overrode differences in family demography and geographical location. Indeed, it stretched beyond national boundaries, Philippe Perrot arguing that, amongst the French nobility, 'rank determined how much you were to spend. The amount of money sent indicated your rank and spending only made sense in relation to your rank.'[41] The provision of food and drink for sociability and entertaining, the adornment of the body with elegant and well-cut clothing, travelling privately in expensive coaches pulled by teams of horses, perhaps kept purely for this function, and the carriage of goods across long distances from London and other urban centres were all indicative of the distinctions of aristocratic life.[42] This rule applies at more detailed levels as well: for instance, of their clothing budgets, the Leighs spent 21 per cent on livery, a figure closely matching the 25 per cent spent by Newdigate. Moreover, despite their very different styles of house, the two families also laid out similar amounts on building work, although this formed a larger proportion of spending by the Leighs, mainly owing to the refurbishment programme undertaken by Edward, fifth Lord Leigh, in the 1760s. Newdigate's expenses in this area were spread more evenly over time and are embedded in a range of different types of outgoings. Tyack calculates that he spent £19,046 on building work between 1750 and 1796, but in reality the total was considerably lower than this, not least because his figure includes considerable building costs not directly linked to the house, such as the construction of a canal to his colliery at Griff.[43] By extracting this spending on the canals from Tyack's overall figure and including what we know from the account books, we have calculated that Newdigate spent £9,593 on building works across the approximately fifty-year period covered here, a substantial sum but one which was quite moderate given his available spending power.

[40] Williams, 'Noble household'.

[41] P. Perrot, *Le Luxe: une richesse entre faste et confort, XVIIe–XIXe siècle* (Paris, 1995), quoted in Chatenet-Calyste, 'Feminine luxury in Paris', 171. There are echoes here of Elias's argument about the spending linked to presence at the French court—see Elias, *Court Society*.

[42] See Whittle and Griffiths, *Consumption and Gender*, esp. 97–105, 117–55, 203–8; J. Stobart, 'Gentlemen and shopkeepers: supplying the country house in eighteenth-century England', *Economic History Review* 64, 3 (2011), 885–904; Williams, 'Noble household'; Greig, *Beau Monde*, 32–62.

[43] Tyack, 'Country house building in Warwickshire', 205–18.

Two categories of spending where there were somewhat surprising differences are furniture and silverware. The former comprised only a small proportion of Newdigate's outgoings (just 2 per cent), purchases being made regularly throughout the period covered by his accounts. This suggests a progressive accumulation and renewal of pieces, partly in line with the ongoing alterations he was making to Arbury Hall. By contrast, the Stoneleigh bills indicate much higher levels of spending (9 per cent) and pronounced bursts of activity linked to inheritance, seen most dramatically in the £4,201 12s. 5d. paid to furniture makers and upholsterers by Edward, fifth Lord Leigh, following his coming of age in 1763.[44] Some pieces and textiles were purchased for the principal reception rooms, but the majority of this spending was to properly furnish, often for the first time, the various bedrooms and dressing rooms on the upper floors of the house. Silverware, including jewellery, was also a much smaller element of Newdigate's expenditure: just 1.5 per cent compared to almost 5 per cent on the part of the Leighs. Some of this additional spending can again be traced to inheritance events, with each new owner of the estate investing heavily in new silver- and plate-ware. In contrast, Newdigate only twice spent more than £100 on silverware in a year, the purchases on both occasions being dominated by jewellery for his second wife, Hester.[45]

These various areas of expenditure might be viewed as the bedrock of the aristocratic lifestyle onto which other things were added, most notably the interests highlighted by Whittle and Griffiths as distinctive elite spending: engagement in political life; literature, music, and science; and travel and leisure.[46] The importance of these varied considerably from one family to another, depending on family circumstances and personal tastes and preferences. The Leighs were largely disengaged from national and even local politics, perhaps reflecting their alleged Jacobite leanings. They thus incurred few expenses of this nature: occasional fees for servants at the House of Lords and treating of tenants at election time, which amounted to a few pounds over the whole study period.[47] By contrast, Sir Roger Newdigate was a highly active MP for thirty-eight years, most of them as the representative for Oxford University. This took up vast amounts of his time and necessitated staying at his London house, in Spring Gardens, during the parliamentary season, which accounted for £6,418 during his career as an MP, if we include rents, taxation, and running costs. Aside from this, however, spending on electioneering is surprisingly modest at just £596. This figure is all the more remarkable when set in the context of his wider spending patterns: a similar sum went on hardware for building (items such as cords, ropes, and locks) and three times this amount was spent on oats, hay, and straw for his horses. The extent to which this was typical of spending by other aristocratic politicians is difficult to assess, but certainly others laid out far more: the contested Chester election of 1732, for

---

[44] The two largest bills were from William Gomm (SCLA, DR18/5/4408) and Thomas Burnett (DR18/3/47/52/15).

[45] WRO, CR136/V136, esp. entry for 1776.

[46] Whittle and Griffiths, *Consumption and Gender*, 185–203.

[47] MacDonald, 'Leigh family', *passim*.

instance, cost the Grosvenors £6,500 to secure.[48] The majority of Newdigate's spending (£480) went on the contested 1747 Middlesex election. Once secured in 1751, his Oxford University seat was only contested in the 1768 general election and he generally spent less than £50.[49] This goes some way to explain the low overall costs of his electioneering, although, as Mingay has pointed out, even uncontested elections could cost hundreds of pounds in entertaining and the like.[50] Moreover, the general cost of electioneering decreased from the early eighteenth century owing to less frequent elections as a result of the Septennial Act and the greater sums the wealthiest families were prepared the deploy. As a result 'lesser' aristocratic politicians such as Newdigate were less likely to fight contested elections and more likely to agree electoral pacts and take safe seats.[51]

Both Newdigate and the Leighs serve as a reminder that, even in an unreformed and corrupt political system, not all landowners were willing to spend large amounts of money to gain power. Newdigate's enthusiasm for politics certainly fluctuated throughout his career, as we show in Chapter 4. In any case, landed hegemony was about far more than the exertion of political power and Newdigate's equivalent spending on horse feed is a reminder of the truth of the importance of such symbols in expressing aristocratic dominance, both in Britain and elsewhere in Europe.[52] Certainly both the Leighs and the Newdigates were more focused on iterating their identities through cultural refinement. The Leighs spent proportionately more than Roger Newdigate on art and books, despite the latter's deserved reputation as a man of letters and a great classical scholar and his considerable purchases of books, medallions, paintings, and sculpture whilst in Italy.[53] This was largely down to the bibliomania of Edward, fifth Lord Leigh, who spent in excess of £1,600 on books between 1763 and 1768, a burst of activity motivated by his enthusiasm as a collector and the lack of a library at Stoneleigh Abbey before his accession.[54] Given that a library was seen as 'an appendage which no man of rank or fortune can now be without if he possesses or wishes to be thought to possess taste or genius', significant spending is entirely understandable.[55] Edward appears to have travelled little beyond Warwickshire, Oxfordshire, and London, perhaps because ambitions for a Grand Tour were thwarted by the onset of his mental illness. His sister Mary spent significant sums hiring coaches in London and in travelling between the capital, Stoneleigh, and Cheltenham, but this was dwarfed by Roger Newdigate's costs in undertaking two lengthy tours of the continent and several others within England. His first Grand Tour, taken as a young man, predated the account books but was undoubtedly a costly venture. During his second tour of

---

[48] Mingay, *English Landed Society*, 124.

[49] White, *Correspondence of Sir Roger Newdigate*, xxix–xliii.

[50] Mingay, *English Landed Society*, 112.   [51] Mingay, *English Landed Society*, 123.

[52] See Thompson, *English Landed Society*, 1; M. Girouard, *Life in the French Country House* (London, 2000), 281–96.

[53] White, *Correspondence of Sir Roger Newdigate*, l–liv; WRO, CR136/B/2638b—Books, marbles, medals, casts, etc. purchased from Italy, July 1774 to Jan 1776.

[54] SCLA, DR18/4/75, List of books at Stoneleigh, 1766 and 1785.

[55] Quoted in Stone and Fawtier Stone, *An Open Elite: England 1540–1880* (Oxford, 1984), 221.

Europe he spent £2,195 on travel alone, a sum which both underpinned and proclaimed his elite status.[56]

The patterns of spending exhibited by these families reveal both the common identities and lifestyles of the aristocracy and their capacity for choice and distinctive behaviour within the group. This was partly a result of demographic and inheritance patterns which lay beyond the control or design of the individual and partly a product of a shared—and arguably Europe-wide—culture of elite consumption; but it was also driven by personal taste and interests. Individual agency was thus set alongside constraints of demography and family, and those imposed by the maintenance of substantial households and an aristocratic lifestyle. However, for all our landowners, luxury played a key role in shaping consumption, as a means of both displaying status and engaging with fashion and elite sociability.

MARKING ELITE STATUS: LUXURY AND FASHION

In 1776, the year of his second marriage, Sir Roger Newdigate spent £1,718, mainly on clothing and jewellery for his new wife, £1,030 of which was paid to the jeweller, Mr Duval. This was equivalent to just over fifty times the annual wages of his highest-paid servant at this time, his new butler, Charles Charlton, who earned £20 each year, and 200 times that earned by his dairymaid, Sarah Palley. It would have taken Charlton several lifetimes to pay for such luxuries. The bill for a china tea service that cost Newdigate 13 guineas would have taken Charlton almost nine months to settle, presuming he had no other aspirations or outlays and that he could even secure such a product from a supplier on credit. Similarly, the £9 paid to Davison and Newman of London for coffee would have been an irrational extravagance, again well beyond Charlton's means.[57] And yet Charles Charlton would have handled his master's china, supervised the serving of his coffee, and observed other wealthy people admire Lady Newdigate's jewellery in polite company at Arbury Hall during the four years that he worked there. These luxuries no doubt gave pleasure to the Newdigates, but they also signalled wealth and status, both to visitors and their own servants, and marked their clear distinction from the lower orders.

This is one way to define luxury: by the cost of the items and the narrow proportion of any given population that can afford to purchase them. Within this, positional goods are particularly significant, as their exclusivity marked out the wealthiest groups as the elite.[58] However, as discussed earlier in the introduction to this chapter, luxury could also take a different flavour: available to a broader section of the population, less expensive, and more 'virtuous'. These 'new luxury' goods were not the most costly: rather, they were marked by novelty and by their use in practices of sociability. Although sometimes posited as

---

[56] WRO, CR136/V/136, Account books, entries for 1774 and 1775: listed under 'casual'.

[57] WRO, CR136/V/136, Account books, entry for 1776.

[58] De Vries, *Industrious Revolution*, 22; Veblen, *Theory of the Leisure Class*; F. Hirsch, *The Social Limits to Growth* (London, 1977).

alternative or competing behavioural frameworks which characterized different social groups and marked an important cultural transition, the reality is that both the Leighs and Newdigates consumed both old and new luxury, markers of status and props to sociability, positional goods and fashionable novelties.

Liveried servants were a luxury that marked out the wealth and status of the individual in a very public manner. Their importance to the aristocracy is apparent from the fact that Sir Roger Newdigate spent almost as much on livery as he did on clothing for himself and his wives across the period of the account books.[59] His annual expenditure on clothing for servants generally varied between £50 and £100, and spending on each servant could easily run into double figures. In 1755, for instance, he purchased leather breeches, a frock suit, a hat, and a box-greatcoat for both his coachman and his groom, at a combined cost of over £20, and in 1763 he spent just over £10 on a hat, a frock suit, and a greatcoat for his under-butler.[60] Mary Leigh's outlay on livery was even greater, although she made a telling distinction between her Warwickshire and her London servants. At Stoneleigh, she provided for the park-keepers, gamekeepers, under-keeper, usher of the servants' hall, and coachman, spending an average of about £7 5s. per servant. This was far outweighed by the £25 per annum that it cost to kit out each of Mary's London servants with four sets of clothes.[61] Like all livery, this clothing was showy, with colours marking out the family by which the servant was employed; as Styles remarks, it was also consciously anti-fashion, with trimmings that spoke of ostentation rather than the refined good taste of a gentleman's wardrobe.[62] Thus, Mary Leigh supplied her four footmen with 'dress livery laced suits', whilst her coachman and postilion each received a 'scarlet cloth laced jacket & waistcoat'.[63]

The link to family that was signalled by livery is surely telling in Mary's case: spending on public displays of rank and dignity kept the Leigh name and title in the public eye, despite the formal demise of the barony with her brother's death in 1786 (see Chapter 5). Much the same was true of her coach, which again carried the family crest and identity into the public domain. Horses and coaches were the *pars pro toto* of an elite lifestyle, merging old repertoires of status consumption with newer concerns for fashionability.[64] The ability to purchase coaches and horses for private travel, and to house, feed, and service horses, clearly demarcated the wealthy elites from the rest of the population. Layered onto this were the style and finish of the coach, and the appearance or gait of the horses, which spoke of taste and discernment. Vickery draws an analogy between the eighteenth-century coach and

---

[59] The actual figures were £3,629 for personal clothing and £3,047 for livery.

[60] WRO, CR136/V/156, Account book, entry for 1755; CR136/V/136, Account book, entry for 1763.

[61] SCLA, DR18/5/6051, DR18/5/6098, DR18/5/6099.

[62] Styles, *Dress of the People*, 295–301.   [63] SCLA, DR18/5/6098.

[64] P. Burke, *The Historical Anthropology of Early Modern Italy* (Cambridge, 1987), 139. Whilst the numerous advertisements for used coaches and carriages found in provincial newspapers from the 1740s onwards might raise questions as to its exclusivity, a substantial and fashionable coach was a key status symbol. See J. Stobart, 'Clothes, cabinets and carriages: second-hand dealing in eighteenth-century England', in B. Blondé, P. Stabel, J. Stobart, and I. Van Damme (eds) *Buyers and Sellers: Retail Circuits and Practices in Medieval and Early Modern Europe* (Turnhout, 2006), 232, 236–7.

the present-day helicopter; yet, in its emphasis on cost and showiness, this perhaps misses some of the nuances of taste and tradition.[65] Indeed F. M. L. Thompson went so far as to suggest that the horse and carriage 'as symbols of social standing' were fundamentally emblematic of the power of the landed classes.[66] It is, therefore, understandable that buyers complained bitterly when their prized new coaches failed to match up to expectations (see Chapter 7). Equally, it is unsurprising to see both Newdigate and the Leighs regularly investing in new coaches and carriages. In total Sir Roger spent £695 on five coaches, a chaise, and a post-chaise purchased in four different periods, between 1747–9, 1755–8, 1765, and 1786–7, a pattern which suggests a regular updating and renewal of his vehicles. The fact that he spent more on low-value mundane items and services such as horse feed, coach repairs, new harnesses, and the hire of horses than he did on the coaches themselves reveals the high ongoing costs of running and maintaining a coach.

Much the same was true of the Leigh bills, which not only enumerate numerous purchases of tack, saddlery, harnesses, and the like, but also provide an insight into the character of the coaches themselves. A 1765 bill from Thomas and James Cope detailed the making of a new coach with 'neat ornament mouldings, painted with a glaz'd ruby colour, and the arms and dignity in very large mantles, and all the framework gilt, and the roof, back and sides japan'd'.[67] The total cost of £130 reflected the workmanship and the very public statement that such a coach would make—essential in signalling the standing of family in both local and metropolitan settings. It is, therefore, telling that, along with details of colours and fabrics, careful mention was made of painting the Leigh family arms. Coaches, horses, and liveried servants are also evocative of de Vries's 'consumption bundles'.[68] Items carried more meaning, he argues, when displayed collectively as groups, an idea that is usually illustrated through the equipage for tea. But the bundling of goods around the coach produced equally powerful meanings and projected a distinctive aristocratic identity.[69]

Cost alone does not provide a precise measure of the significance of these goods, but it can give a fairly good guide to the exclusivity of positional goods. Silverware was particularly important in this regard. Its scarcity and association with coinage had long made it a popular means of investing wealth; but wrought silverware could also be displayed on buffets and used in formal dining to demonstrate wealth to others.[70] The emergence of *service à la française* in the early decades of the eighteenth century opened up an array of new opportunities. A table laid out with sets

---

[65] Vickery, *Behind Closed Doors*, 124.

[66] Thompson, *English Landed Society*, 1. See also: D. Cannadine, 'After the horse: nobility and mobility in modern Britain', in N. Harte and R. Quinault (eds), *Land and Society in Britain 1700–1914: Essays in Honour of F. M. L. Thompson* (Manchester, 1996), 211–35.

[67] SCLA, DR18/5/4350.

[68] De Vries, *Industrious Revolution*, 31. This idea of bundles links closely with the associations between goods that form a central aspect of the Diderot effect, discussed more fully in Chapter 2 (see McCracken, *Culture and Consumption*, 118–29).

[69] See also Blondé, 'Conflicting consumption models?', 65–71.

[70] H. Clifford, 'A commerce with things: the value of precious metalwork in early-modern England', in M. Berg and H. Clifford (eds) *Consumers and Luxury. Consumer Culture in Europe, 1650–1850* (Manchester, 1999), 147–55; Cornforth, *Early Georgian Interiors*, 109–13.

of dishes and plates, arranged according to a careful plan, allowed a silver service to be admired in its entirety and encouraged the acquisition of full and matching sets of silverware, including tureens, dishes, spoons, and candlesticks, the light from which would add to the visual appeal of the silver.[71] As Pepys noted in 1666, 'one thing I reckon remarkable in my own condition is that I am come to abound in good plate, so as at all entertainments to be served wholly with silver plates'.[72] This was probably one reason why the Leighs purchased silverware in large quantities, albeit infrequently: they not only wanted to have complete and coordinated sets, but also needed these sets to allow for dining on a grand scale. The cumulative effect of these purchases was striking. The 1786 inventory of Stoneleigh enumerates 2,102 ounces of plate, including a tea urn, large epergne, handbasin, two large waiters, three large casters, and a coffee pot, plus a variety of other pieces which were not weighed.[73] Subsequent purchases by Mary Leigh augmented the collection so that by 1806 there was a total of 3,340 ounces of silverware.[74] However, in addition to acquiring many new pieces, she also disposed of some unwanted items, the 1788 bill from Robert Makepeace recording over £534 of credit against a bill amounting to £1,031 7s. 3d. This suggests a different motivation for the large-scale purchases made by each generation: the desire to have silverware that was fashionable as well as valuable.[75] Keeping abreast of fashions could also be achieved via the single purchases that characterized Newdigate's spending on silverware. In 1764, for example, he bought a tureen and cover for £80 13s. 6d. from Parker and Wakelin; the following year he purchased a double-branched candlestick at a cost of £28 16s., and two years later a tea vase for £44 6s.[76] His silver table service was thus regularly augmented and updated, responding to the almost endless opportunities for adding new items to existing sets.[77] Indeed, one of Newdigate's final purchases, in 1803, was a fashionable new silver 'Globe Tea Urn with silver marks and mouldings', costing 10 guineas.[78]

To be sure, silverware was both costly and showy; yet it also played an important role in refined social dining. In this, it was augmented by the provision of fine table linen which enhanced the visual display of the dining table, especially when fine damasks and diapers were illuminated by candlelight.[79] Despite a relative decline in the importance of table linen since the seventeenth century, it was purchased in large quantities by Edward, fifth Lord Leigh. Six bills presented by Jordan Heyland Biggar between 1763 and 1766 amounted to a total of over £335 and

[71] B.C. Wees, *English, Irish and Scottish Silver* (Easthampton, ME, 1997), 119, 121; Berg, *Luxury and Pleasure*, 250; MacArthur, 'Material culture and consumption', 192–3.

[72] Quoted in Wees, *English, Irish and Scottish Silver,* 120–1.

[73] SCLA, DR18/4/69, Inventory, 1786.

[74] SCLA, DR18/4/59, Inventory, 1806.

[75] SCLA, DR18/5/5809. We cannot know this for certain, but the style of silverware being made by Thomas Gilpin, the Leighs' main supplier in the 1740s–60s, is very different from that being produced by Makepeace in the 1780s. See Clifford, 'Commerce with things', 148.

[76] WRO, CR136/V/136, entries for 1764, 1765, 1767.

[77] Clifford, 'Commerce with things', 160–2.

[78] WRO, CR136/B/31, Bill for a Tea Urn, 4 November 1803.

[79] D. M. Mitchell, 'Fine table linen in England 1450–1750: ownership and use of a luxury commodity', (Unpublished PhD thesis, University of London, 1999), 256.

included dozens of damask napkins and tablecloths.[80] The cost of these made them luxuries beyond the reach of most households—three large damask tablecloths alone cost Lord Leigh 15 guineas—but their aesthetic and visceral qualities were also important. Their appeal to the senses came in terms of the designs woven into the cloth—small repeat geometrical patterns on diapers and figurative patterns with longer repeats on damasks—and with the fine weave on high-quality imported linens. Quality as well as quantity was thus important, as was the ability to maintain linen in a clean and presentable state.[81] It is unsurprising, then, that elite householders took considerable pride in their linen, Elizabeth Shackleton noting of a cloth first used when guests arrived unexpectedly for dinner: 'Used my handsome, new, damask table-cloth which looks most beautiful for the first [time]. Good luck to it, hope it will do well.' She also notes embroidering initials and symbols onto bed linen to mark both ownership and location.[82]

A rather different rationale lay behind the marking of silverware, much of which was engraved with the family crest or the individual's arms or coronet. Edward Leigh had all his silverware engraved in this manner, as did his sister Mary.[83] As Berg suggests, this stamping of title onto material objects changed anonymous, if splendid, goods into 'signifiers of family and memory'; it also rendered them symbols of pedigree and power, marking the longevity and heritage of the Leigh family as aristocratic landowners.[84] At the same time, engraved silverware linked the individual to that heritage and marked their position in this longer history of patrician power. The message was thus about both collective and individual authority. Family portraits served a similar function: they were a means by which the individual's identity could be placed within a broader family history and the historical claim to power on the part of the family (see Chapter 2).[85] The walls of Stoneleigh Abbey and Canons Ashby were hung with ever increasing numbers of family portraits, and Sir Roger Newdigate sat for several portraits, including one of himself and his wife, commissioned in 1753, for which he paid 10 guineas—a sum dwarfed by the later commission from Romney, which cost £105.[86]

---

[80] Peck, *Consuming Splendor*, 222; SCLA, DR18/5/4028, DR18/5/4193, DR18/5/4345, DR18/5/4346, DR18/5/4347, DR18/5/4478.

[81] Mitchell, 'Fine table linen', 22; B. Lemire, 'An education in comfort: Indian textiles and the remaking of English homes in the long eighteenth century', in J. Stobart and B. Blondé (eds) *Selling Textiles in the Long Eighteenth Century. Comparative Perspectives from Western Europe* (Basingstoke, 2014) 18–20.

[82] Quoted in A. Vickery, 'Women and the world of goods: a Lancashire consumer and her possessions, 1751–81' in J. Brewer and R. Porter (eds) *Consumption and the World of Goods* (London, 1993), 285; Vickery, *Gentleman's Daughter*, 151.

[83] SCLA DR18/5/4251, DR18/5/5695, DR18/5/5809.

[84] Berg, *Luxury and Pleasure*, 242.

[85] See K. Retford, 'Patrilineal portraiture? Gender and genealogy in the eighteenth-century English country house,' in J. Styles and A. Vickery (eds), *Gender, Taste and Material Culture in Britain and North America 1700–1830* (New Haven, CT, 2006), 323–52; O. Millar, 'Portraiture and the country house', in G. Jackson-Stops (ed.) *The Treasure Houses of Britain. Five Hundred Years of Private Patronage and Art Collecting* (New Haven, CT, 1985), 28–39; Cornforth, *Early Georgian Interiors*, 226–9.

[86] WRO, CR136/V/156, entry for 1753; CR135/V/136, entry for 1791. The Romney portrait shows Oxford in the background; a copy by Thomas Kirby now hangs in University College, his alma mater.

Paintings and other forms of artwork also operated as a refined form of conspicuous consumption; they were examples of Veblen's 'more excellent goods' and more specifically 'collectibles' that signalled not simply spending power, but also taste and discernment.[87] At both Stoneleigh Abbey and Arbury Hall, art collections were built up over time, although in both places it is possible to identify key phases of activity. Sir Roger Newdigate's regular accounts record relatively modest levels of spending, including £3 paid to Celeste Regnier in 1750 for watercolours.[88] However, on his second Grand Tour he acquired a large quantity of paintings, statues, medallions, and marble in Italy (see Chapter 8). Some of these were originals, but many were copies or casts of the ancient treasures and Renaissance masterpieces that he encountered on his travels. Quite apart from the impressive spending power represented in a total bill of around £620 (excluding books), this reflected Newdigate's discernment as a man of letters and a classical scholar: he had the means, but also knew what was worth acquiring. Amongst the paintings he had copied were Raphael's *Maria Colonna* and *Maria della Sedia* (both important pieces by a noted master), and he also acquired two landscapes by Gregorio Fidanza, a disciple of Claude Lorrain.[89] A number of Edward Leigh's paintings came from his uncle's house in Leighton Buzzard, including views of Venice and Rome, generally attributed to Canaletto (1697–1768), 'fruit pieces', and two portraits of King Charles.[90] Yet he also acquired several notable pieces: a 'picture by Rembrandt' for 20 guineas and a view of church by 'Stenwick' (most likely Hendrick van Steenwijk, the noted Dutch painter of architectural interiors), which cost £20.[91] Again, we have the discernment of the dilettante as well as the deep purse of the landowner. Surprisingly, then, it was Mary who was more active in acquiring highly regarded painters, both old masters and contemporary artists: two paintings by the Dutch master Cuyp, which cost £153; paintings by Zoffany, Gainsborough, Teniers, Wouwerman, and Van der Meer, amongst others, which were bought 'at the auction of Mr Rigbys Pictures' for a total of £514 10s. 6d.; and a painting by Turner, mentioned in a codicil to her will.[92]

For both men and women, then, art constituted a way of expressing taste as well as wealth. It formed part of the cultural capital of the aristocracy, marking them out from the middling sorts whose purchases centred more on prints and engravings.[93] Even when they bought such items, it was of a type and on a scale beyond

---

[87] Veblen, *Theory of the Leisure Class*, 74; McCracken, *Culture and Consumption*, 113. See also F. Haskell, 'The British as collectors', in Jackson-Stops (ed.) *The Treasure Houses of Britain*, 50–9.

[88] WRO, CR136/V156, Account book, entry for 1750.

[89] WRO, CR136/B2638b, Books, marbles, medals, casts, etc. purchased from Italy, July 1774 to Jan 1776.

[90] SCLA, DR18/18/3/3, Letter from John Franklin, 24 December 1765; DR18/18/3/5, Letter from John Franklin, 26 December 1765; DR18/18/3/4, Inventory of paintings from Leighton Buzzard, no date (1765).

[91] SCLA, DR18/5/4490.

[92] SCLA, DR18/5/5964a; DR18/17/32/186, List of pictures bought at auction, 1788; The National Archives (TNA), PROB 11/1448, Will of Mary Leigh, 1806.

[93] J. Brewer, *The Pleasures of the Imagination: English Culture in the Eighteenth Century* (Chicago, 1997), 201–51.

the scope of the less wealthy. Mary filled a room with over 200 prints, including a set of engravings of David Garrick represented as various characters, from Richard III to Macbeth, which cost her £8 in 1793.[94] The same distinction in quality and quantity was also true of the libraries assembled by the fifth Lord Leigh and Sir Roger Newdigate. At Stoneleigh the vast majority of the book collection had been purchased by Edward Leigh in a surge of spending between 1763 and 1768, during which he laid out in excess of £1,600 on books. This was significantly less than the £1,500 per annum which George III allowed himself for books, but nevertheless represented a substantial outlay—far more than his recorded spending on other luxuries such as carriages (about £687) and silverware (£790).[95]

The speed of acquisition and the quality and price of the books being purchased is remarkable. For example, a single bill from Paul Vaillant, presented on 11 October 1764, includes a number of splendid plate books, most notably *Recueil des peintures antiques* costing £52 10s. and *Herculaneum & Caserta*, in 4 volumes at £50. Such prices put these books on a par with a diamond ring costing £52 10s. or 6 engraved silver candlesticks weighing 111 ounces and costing £49 which Edward bought in 1762.[96] And they were just as impressive, both in their size and appearance. For example, the copy of Basket's *Great Imperial Bible* that he bought in 1766 was 'richly bound in blue turkey with purple ribbons & Gold Fringe'. At the same time, he purchased a copy of Marsaligi's *Cours du Danube*, which he had bound in 'Russia leather, gilt with a border of gold, double headbands'. This work cost him 9 guineas—as much as the book itself. Sir Roger also acquired a substantial number of impressive volumes, including a plate book of the Florentine Museum at 15 guineas; a similar volume for Herculaneum at £19 14s.; a volume of engravings by Piranesi at £30; and Hamilton's *Volcanoes* at 12 guineas.[97] These large folio volumes reflected typical gentry taste for classical architecture and civilization, and would have made impressive additions to any library (see Chapter 4). Books were thus positional goods, the function of which was to project the identity of a refined and virtuous gentleman as much as to inform and educate the owner. However, it is also clear that the libraries of both Newdigate and Leigh were there to be used, a point reinforced by Edward Leigh's decision to bequeath his collection to his alma mater at Oxford.[98] Indeed, books were complex luxuries redolent with messages of wealth and power, but also learning and taste. They reflected the personalities of Leigh and Newdigate as gentlemen of letters, intellectuals keen to collect and digest knowledge and learning. This offers a useful reminder that

[94] SCLA, DR18/5/6049.

[95] J. H. Plumb and H. Weldon, *Royal Heritage. The Story of Britain's Royal Builders and Collectors* (London, 1977), 169–70. For fuller discussion of the book collecting of Edward Leigh and Sir Roger Newdigate, see J. Stobart, 'The luxury of learning: books, knowledge and display in the English Country House', in A. Bonnet and N. Coquery (eds) *Commerce du luxe* (Lyons, 2015).

[96] SCLA, DR18/5/4251. Comparisons might also be made with services of armorial porcelain ware, a whole set of which might cost around £100, including shipping and customs duties—see K. Smith, 'Manly objects? Gendering armorial porcelain wares', East India Company at Home (June 2014), <http://blogs.ucl.ac.uk/eicah/armorial-porcelain/>.

[97] WRO, CR136/B/2638b, Books, marbles, medals, casts, etc. purchased from Italy, July 1774 to Jan 1776; CR136/B/2461e, Bill from Thomas Cadell, 10 April 1771.

[98] SCLA, DR18/13/7/13–4, Will and codicil of Edward, Lord Leigh, 1767.

conspicuous consumption could operate at various different levels and was rarely one-dimensionally 'conspicuous'.

The bills and accounts of the Leighs and Newdigates thus underline the importance of high-end positional goods in the construction of elite identities and lifestyles, but they also demonstrate that elite families engaged in the new fashions of the Georgian period, purchasing goods that linked to changing decorative styles and tastes, and to practices of sociability. New materials, such as mahogany, and the spreading popularity of japanned designs were amongst the most important innovations in furniture during the Georgian period.[99] The Leighs, whilst not at the cutting edge of these innovations, were replacing purchases of walnut furniture with those of mahogany by the early 1740s, when Thomas, fourth Lord Leigh, purchased a range of mahogany pieces, including various tables and a voider, for just in excess of £16.[100] However, it was his son, Edward, who made the most substantial changes to the furniture of Stoneleigh Abbey. He purchased a huge number of pieces, almost all of them mahogany, whilst completing the furnishing of Stoneleigh Abbey in the early 1760s. A bill from William Gomm & Co, paid in 1765, itemizes a remarkable total of £818 9s.' worth of furniture, including 238 mahogany chairs and stools.[101] A related bill from Thomas and Gilbert Burnett shows additional purchases of furniture along with upholstery and indicated where it had been placed. The Library, for instance, was fitted with mahogany chairs, a mahogany stool, and an oval mahogany music table, the last at a cost of £27 10s. In the Green Mohair Room Edward had a pair of 'large mahogany gothick pillars, 9 feet high' fitted to an old bedstead and added eight mahogany back stools, whilst the Great Dining Parlour included a mahogany folding fire screen 'with green sliding pannells'. For most of the bedsteads Edward preferred wainscoting, but with mahogany feet.[102] The Great Apartment retained its walnut furniture (see Chapter 2), but almost everywhere was furnished primarily in fashionable and tasteful mahogany.

Although she spent less on furniture, probably because her brother had spent so much time and money on this aspect of Stoneleigh Abbey's material culture, Mary continued his enthusiasm for mahogany, supplemented with pieces in the newly fashionable satinwood, especially in her Print Room. Perhaps more telling are the bills presented to Mary for japanned furniture and for the rejapanning of existing pieces (see Chapter 3). Chinoiserie of this type was perennially fashionable through the late seventeenth and eighteenth centuries, with black lacquerwork often acting as a foil to other furnishings.[103] Her recorded purchases were quite modest, the most notable being a 'sett of dressing boxes with elegant painted landscapes and gold borders', which cost her £21.[104] The inventories, however, make clear that

---

[99] Cornforth, *Early Georgian Interiors*, 270–2; Barczewski, *Country Houses and the British Empire*, 164–7.

[100] SCLA, DR18/5/2658.   [101] SCLA, DR18/5/4408.

[102] SCLA, DR18/3/47/52/15, Bill from Thomas Burnett, 14 December 1765.

[103] E. de Bruijn, 'Consuming East Asia: continuity and change in the development of chinoiserie', in J. Stobart and A. Hann (eds) *The Country House: Material Culture and Consumption* (London, 2015), 95–104; Cornforth, *Early Georgian Interiors*, 270.

[104] SCLA, DR18/5/5890.

japanned furniture was placed in several rooms: two lanterns on pedestals in the Hall, a white and gold fire screen in the Brown Parlour, and two corner cupboards in the Music Parlour.[105] The significance of such goods is discussed more fully in Chapter 2, but they are more readily seen as statements of elite taste for exotic luxuries than specific links to Empire.[106]

Both brother and sister thus marked their arrival as owners of the estate by purchasing furniture that was fashionable for the period. A similar pattern of behaviour can be discerned at Canons Ashby, although here the uptake of mahogany was very slow. As late as 1756 there were only five pieces of mahogany furniture in the house: one table in the Room over the Great Parlour and another four tables in the Common Parlour, where they sat alongside eight walnut chairs, an inlaid walnut stand, and a walnut settee.[107] This mixture contrasts with the wholesale change seen at Stoneleigh Abbey and characterized the temporal and material eclecticism of the Drydens' home through to the death of Lady Elizabeth in 1791. Thereafter, the new owners, Sir John Turner Dryden and his wife, also called Elizabeth, modernized the furnishings, adding large amounts of mahogany to bedrooms, parlours, dining rooms, and dressing rooms. This influx had a profound impact on the appearance of many rooms, with walnut dominating only in a bedroom known as the White Room. In addition to at least twenty-six new pieces of mahogany furniture, Elizabeth and Sir John further demonstrated their fashionable good taste through the acquisition of a small number of pieces in satinwood. These were principally placed in the Drawing Room and comprised a writing table, a small inlaid work table, three inlaid chiffonier pier tables, and a pair of fire screens.[108] Here, they complemented a number of pieces of inlaid mahogany furniture, and a set of twelve japanned elbow chairs with cane seats. For Sir Roger Newdigate, the march of fashion also moved rather slowly, but at a steady pace. In 1747 he purchased a number of large mahogany tables from John Pardoe and subsequently acquired a mahogany cistern in 1750, a tea board in 1752, eight mahogany chairs in 1758, and a square mahogany table in 1760.[109]

Fashion and taste were also demonstrated through the purchase of large quantities of porcelain. Of itself, this was neither a luxury nor necessarily fashionable: old pieces were frequently mended and there was an extensive trade in second-hand tableware, both porcelain and earthenware.[110] However, there is much to suggest that the chinaware acquired by the Leighs and Newdigates expressed their taste and fashionability as well as their wealth. To explore these various attributes, it is useful to consider different types of porcelain: imported and domestic, useful and ornamental. Until the early eighteenth century, all porcelain was imported from China or Japan. Pieces from the latter increasingly became collectors'

[105] Cornforth, *Early Georgian Interiors*, 270; SCLA, DR18/4/59, Inventory, 1806.

[106] See Barczewski, *Country Houses and the British Empire*, 164–7.

[107] NRO, D(CA)902, Inventory, 1756.

[108] For further discussion, see Stobart, 'Inventories and Canons Ashby', 11–14.

[109] WRO, 136/V/156, entries for 1747, 1750, 1752, 1760.

[110] See R. MacArthur and J. Stobart, 'Going for a song? Country house sales in Georgian England', in J. Stobart and I. Van Damme (eds) *Modernity and the Second-Hand Trade: European Consumption Cultures and Practices, 1700–1900* (Basingstoke, 2011), 175–95; Nenadic, 'Middle-rank consumers'.

items (see Chapter 2), whilst those from the former were gradually replaced by domestically produced wares.[111] References to Chinese porcelain or 'nankeen' ware are notably absent from the Leigh bills and feature just once in Newdigate's accounts when, in 1761, he paid Robert Cartony of London £6 10s. 6d. for a set of 'nankeen tea china'.[112] Although we lack details, it therefore seems that most of the china purchased was produced by the increasingly numerous domestic or European manufacturers.

Newdigate patronized a range of 'chinamen', spending an average of £13 each year, but his most important supplier was Josiah Wedgwood, from whom china was purchased on at least sixteen occasions between 1766 and 1788—the period during which his china rose in fame and fashion. Wedgwood has long been held up as a master of new production techniques and innovative selling practices. As Berg puts it, he 'chose the high road of designer-ware pricing', setting his prices at two or three times higher than prevailing prices; but he also differentiated his products and prices so that he could sell to a wide section of society.[113] To some extent, Newdigate's ongoing purchases reflect the fragile nature of china, which was relatively inexpensive and could be regularly replaced: indeed, his total payments to Wedgwood amounted to about £130 or just over £8 per annum.[114] However, two substantial bills for £21 in 1779 and £38 10s. in 1788 suggest the purchase of complete sets of tableware—perhaps a reflection of changing taste and fashions. This is almost certainly the case for Mary Leigh. Despite the presence at Stoneleigh Abbey of very large quantities of chinaware (see Chapter 3), she acquired a substantial collection of Wedgwood tableware between 1786 and 1790, mostly in the fashionable 'Green Greek Border'.[115] Her first purchase was of 235 pieces of china of various kinds, but forming a complete set of dinnerware and tea-ware; later purchases were apparently directed at augmenting this set with 72 additional pieces. The variety was remarkable—salad dishes, cream bowls, muffin plates, pickle shapes and dishes, whey cups, milk pans, honeypots, sugar dishes, a teapot, soup terrines and fish drainers, amongst many others. Again, though, the cost was a relatively modest £47 10s. 5d. in total—around half the cost of an imported service of armorial porcelain. Wedgwood directed his bills to Mary's London address, Grove House in Kensington Gore, and it seems likely that the whole collection was ordered for that house. The scale of the purchases was remarkable given that Mary

---

[111] Berg, *Luxury and Pleasure*, 127–30; P. Ferguson, '"Japan China": taste and elite ceramic consumption in eighteenth-century England: revising the narrative', in Stobart and Hann (eds) *The Country House*, 113–22.

[112] WRO, 136/V/156, entry for 1761.

[113] Berg, *Luxury and Pleasure*, 148. See also N. McKendrick, 'Josiah Wedgwood and the commercialization of the potteries', in N. McKendrick, J. Brewer, and J. Plumb (eds) *The Birth of a Consumer Society* (London, 1982), 100–45; B. Dolan, Josiah *Wedgwood, Entrepreneur to the Enlightenment* (London, 2004).

[114] China was also mended and sometimes retained, even when cracked. See S. Pennell, '"For a crack or flaw despis'd": thinking about ceramic durability and the everyday in late 17th- and early 18th-century England', in T. Hamling and C. Richardson (eds) *Everyday Objects: Medieval and Early Modern Material Culture and Its Meaning* (Farnham, 2010), 27–40; Stobart, 'Inventories and Canons Ashby', 14.

[115] SCLA, DR 18/5/5684, DR 18/5/5724, DR 18/5/5900.

lived alone and appears to have rarely entertained at Grove House.[116] As a collection of Wedgwood Mary's dwarfed that of Joseph Priestley, whose three sets edged in green, blue, and yellow were valued at just over £13 in 1791.[117] This speaks of the greater purchasing power available to the aristocracy in comparison to the middling sorts; yet Mary Leigh was just as closely engaged with the cultures of new luxury as radicals and dissenters such as Priestley.

Part of the attraction of chinaware, of course, was that it facilitated the sociability of dining and tea drinking; it thus formed part of a deeper consumer culture for the accoutrements of polite and virtuous sociability amongst these two families. Several of the entries in Newdigate's accounts make this explicit, for example the £2 12s. 6d. paid to John Godfrey in 1777 for a range of products including twelve breakfast cups and saucers and twenty-four coffee cups and saucers.[118] Similarly, Mary's purchases from Wedgwood included a diverse equipage for tea. Being able to serve tea from elegant and fashionable china was central to the polite sociability of new luxury. However, Mary's chinaware went further, the black tea pot and two black sugar dishes she had from Wedgwood providing the perfect foil for displays of fine white hands and perfect deportment. As Smith argues, such performances demonstrated the physical attributes of studied leisure: they wove into the act of serving tea signs of distinction and exclusivity that were just as potent as fine silver-ware teapots or sugar tongs.[119]

Black porcelain was also deployed by Wedgwood in the creation of his ornamental ware. As discussed more fully in Chapter 3, there is no shortage of evidence that the Newdigates, Leighs, and Drydens all used china in decorative displays, sometimes placing single or pairs of oriental figures and sometimes assembling plainer domestic ware on mantelpieces or tables. This might be seen as characteristic of new luxury: a form of fashionable decorative motif open to a wide section of society. However, ornamental ware could be exclusive and a marker of status—part of old luxury. Items such as Wedgwood's Portland vase were the acme of this kind of high-end product and ultra-exclusive consumption.[120] Although neither the Leighs nor the Newdigates were in this league, they were both active in acquiring costly decorative pieces. For example, in 1765 Edward, fifth Lord Leigh, spent £26 5s. on two large Chinese figures, although we know little of the detailed form which these took.[121] A little later, Sir Roger Newdigate acquired bespoke pieces from Wedgwood and Bentley; they wrote in 1778 asking him to 'do them the Honour of accepting some of the First Productions, made in Blue & White Jasper, & Black Basalt, from the Casts he was pleased to favour them with'. These comprised a 'Statue of Venus with pedestal ornamented with the Seasons—in Black; Ganymede & the Eagle, A fine Figure with a Seal upon the Lips probably Venus . . .,

---

[116] J. Stobart, '"So agreeable and suitable a place": the character, use and provisioning of a late eighteenth-century suburban villa', *Journal of Eighteenth Century Studies*, (2015).

[117] Berg, *Luxury and Pleasure*, 2.

[118] WRO, CR136/B/2415, Bill, 8 December 1777.

[119] K. Smith, 'In her hands', 495–8. See also W. Smith, *Consumption and the Making of Respectability*, 121–38.

[120] Dolan, *Wedgwood*, 173–80, 349–59.   [121] SCLA, DR18/5/4383.

Ganymede—all in Blue & White Jaspar'.[122] Three things are particularly significant here, all of which mark these as exclusive luxuries rather than fashionable
decoration. First, although basalt and jasper ware was increasingly fashionable at
this time, these were bespoke pieces: Newdigate had commissioned their production
and, indeed, made it possible by providing the original casts. They were later produced in some number for collectors, but remained costly items beyond the reach
of other consumers.[123] Second, the classical figures being portrayed demonstrated
the learning of the owner: an easy familiarity with the classics and the narratives
that attached to each figure which could only be acquired through an expensive
classical education—an idea that links closely to Bourdieu's notion of cultural capital.[124] Third, the casts supplied by Newdigate were brought home from his 1774–5
Grand Tour and thus spoke of his geographical reach as a consumer. Their reproduction as fine porcelain pieces brought the originals to a wider audience, but this
was hardly the democratization of luxury; they remained exclusive collectors'
items. Moreover, their origins were well known, further heightening the prestige
that they brought to Newdigate.[125]

CONCLUSION

Lavish, splendid, and sometimes ruinous spending is often seen as the hallmark of
the aristocracy, their conspicuous consumption being central to their lifestyles and
to the ways in which they distinguished themselves from other social groups. Our
analysis here shows that this is, at best, a partial picture. The rhythms and patterns
of spending in which the Leighs and Newdigates engaged signalled a blending of
identities and behaviour that, in many ways, defies simple and straightforward
social categorizations and typologies. That these families were part of the established 'old elite' did not translate in any straightforward manner to an old luxury
pattern of consumer behaviour aimed primarily at social distinction. Indeed, their
behaviour shows that they were also engaged in modes of consumption characteristic of new luxury, with its emphasis on pleasure, politeness, and sociability.

These families were, of course, part of the wealth elite and they spent huge
amounts of money on luxuries and positional goods in accordance with, and in
order to mark, their rank and status. The sums involved were completely beyond
the means of both ordinary people and most of the middling ranks whose rise
supposedly marks out consumer cultures in eighteenth-century England.[126] Coaches
and liveried servants, and the quality and quantity of silverware, paintings, and

---

[122] WRO, CR136/B/2416, Letter from Wedgwood & Co, 17 April 1778.

[123] On the provenance of Ganymede and the Eagle, see <http://www.bonhams.com/auctions/15270/lot/107/>.

[124] On the importance of cultural capital and education in reproducing the elite class, see Bourdieu, *Distinction*.

[125] The original casts are noted in a list of goods bought by Newdigate whilst on his Grand Tour: see note 47.

[126] These middling ranks are central to McKendrick's vision of a nascent consumer society: see McKendrick, 'Consumer revolution'.

books clearly marked their distinction from such groups; inscribing these goods with crests, coronets, and arms set them apart from even the wealthiest of the newly rich merchants, professionals, and East India men. These groups threatened the established elite in terms of spending power and might be seen as prompting defensive consumption in the form of these traditional symbols of pedigree and social exclusion. But to see the English aristocracy as distinct and isolated from these other groups would be a mistake: in reality they were a permeable group, constantly renewing bloodlines and coffers with the influx of fresh blood and money from the wealthy merchant class. The degree to which the aristocracy were an 'open elite' has been the subject of contentious debate, but most would agree that interactions with other elite groups were significant.[127] Unsurprisingly, then, their consumption patterns reflect this engagement with other social groups and with broader cultures of consumption. In terms of the overall balance of their spending, both the Leighs and Newdigates displayed moderation within their very considerable means: only rarely and for short periods did outgoings exceed income. In this, our analysis offers an important corrective to the widely held view of the aristocracy as reckless and even feckless when it came to money. To be sure, there were individuals who ruined themselves and their families, but this was a choice rather than a structural feature of elite consumption. A certain level and type of spending was undoubtedly necessary to maintain rank and status, but this did not mean ruinous excess: moderation and careful management were more common. An important part of this care came in terms of the productive investment of money in land, industry, and shares. Such outgoings are a defining characteristic of de Vries's reading of new luxury; yet we see them driving the peaks in spending for Newdigate in particular as he developed his estate and coal mines. At the same time, these families also bought the kinds of novel and fashionable goods that denoted taste and virtue rather than merely wealth and status. They equipped themselves for polite sociability and renewed the material culture of their homes in line with changing tastes in furniture and furnishings.

The aristocracy thus engaged in the consumption practices of both old and new luxury. In part, this mixed picture derives from their experience as a 'traditional' landed class living through a period of great social and economic change for consumers, when demands for new products and the supply of those products changed British society in profound ways. Colonial commodities and imported luxuries from the East played an important part in this, but their consumption has been too readily and uncritically seen as part of new consumer cultures driven by the middling sort.[128] Far from being spectators in changes driven by other social groups, landowners and other elites played an important part in leading these transformative processes. They consumed goods and engaged in social practices associated with new luxury and were critical in establishing tastes that were taken up by those lower down the social scale. This is not to argue for a simplistic reading

---

[127] See the Introduction for a broader discussion of debates surrounding the 'openness' of English landed society.

[128] See, for example, Berg, *Luxury and Pleasure*; Smith, *Consumption and the Making of Respectability*.

of emulative consumption; rather, it is to suggest that we should place the country house and its owners back at the heart of eighteenth-century consumer changes. In doing so, we are forced to question the reality of any distinction between old and new luxury.

Our analysis of spending by the Leighs, Newdigates, and Drydens questions the extent to which this binary distinguishes social groups, objects, practices, or underlying motivations in the straightforward manner envisaged by de Vries. This is because, as Blondé and de Laet argue, 'similar consumption and material culture patterns...may serve different social and cultural purposes. Similar objects may function in different consumer models, and they may have a different cultural and social meaning in different social contexts.'[129] In short, these elite families were actively engaged in practices that characterized both old and new luxury. For instance, they purchased and displayed silverware and paintings by old masters, and invested in the splendour of their houses; but at the same time they bought tea services, sought out novel and fashionable goods, and directed large proportions of their resources towards productive investment. Many of the objects they acquired were symbols of old luxury, yet were deployed in the sociability that marked new luxury. Silver tea services form one example: their use both marked social distinction and invited a degree of inclusivity around the tea table. It was the wealth of the landowning elite, of course, that gave them particular scope to engage in these different forms of consumption; but it is significant that they were motivated by both the imperatives of social distinction and those of polite sociability. The size and complexity of their country houses meant that the different and shared material manifestations of these two cultures of consumption were readily accommodated. As we shall see in the Chapters 2 and 3, the material culture of the country house and the spending patterns of its owner reflected continuity and change, social differentiation and integration.

---

[129] B. Blondé and V. de Laet, 'New and old luxuries between the court and the city. A comparative perspective on critical material culture changes in Brussels and Antwerp, 1650–1735', in J. Ilmakunnas and J. Stobart (eds) *A Taste for Luxury in Early-Modern Europe: Display, Acquisition and Boundaries* (London, 2016).

2

Constructing the Country House

Habitus, Performance, and Assemblages of Goods

INTRODUCTION

The process of building the country house was often long and tortuous; certainly it was a complex and costly undertaking, as Wilson and Mackley make abundantly clear.[1] Creating the building often took many years, both in planning and execution, and its subsequent furnishing inevitably extended the project and required further planning and more money. It is unsurprising, then, that designs and even architects were sometimes changed between inception and completion. Perhaps most famous in this regard is Kedleston Hall, with its neo-Palladian north front designed by Brettingham and its neoclassical south front by Robert Adam. But such dramatic changes were the exception; more often we see the vision of the patron or his architect as a golden thread running through to the completed house.[2] This is true of interior decoration and furnishing as much as the architectural form of the building. Indeed, art historical perspectives on the country house place great store on the design of interiors, their conception, execution, and furnishing being part of an integrated process. Beard, for example, traces the chronology of interior furnishing through a series of set-piece rooms and the lives of key craftsmen. Cornforth, meanwhile, details the ways in which a set of exemplar eighteenth-century houses were conceived and constructed, linking the designs of luminaries such as Vanbrugh, Gibbs, and Kent to the extant interiors of Blenheim, Ditchley, Holkham, and the like. And Girouard marks the changing physical layout and sequencing of rooms that characterized the formal house, with its succession of increasingly private spaces, and later the social house, with its emphasis on circulatory routes.[3]

These various designs and interiors are deployed as a device for tracing taste; they are seen as archetypes of the processes through which plans were drawn up and executed, and of the changing character and structure of the country house. Whether assembled gradually or ordered *en suite*, the end result is viewed by Cornforth as a series of interior spaces and assemblages of furniture that worked as a unit,

---

[1] Wilson and Mackley, *Building of the English Country House*, esp. 145–98.

[2] Wilson and Mackley, *Building of the English Country House*, 109–44; J. Harris, *The Design of the English Country House, 1620–1920* (London, 1985).

[3] G. Beard, *Upholsterers and Interior Furnishing in England 1530–1840* (New Haven, CT, 1997); Cornforth, *Early Georgian Interiors*, 275–324; Girouard, *English Country House*, 119–62, 181–212.

often to be experienced as the visitor processed from one room to the next. They were, in effect, 'representations of space': conceived and codified by elites and their architects as expressions of power and taste.[4] In this, the influence of the Grand Tour is apparent in many houses and the impact of Empire can be seen in many more. Individually and especially together, these made the English country house a cosmopolitan construct: a blending of European and oriental cultures and objects.[5] Such influences came directly to houses like Holkham Hall, Powys Castle, and Swallowfield Park; yet in these places and elsewhere the example of other owners was also important. News travelled fast in the hothouse of London, but the growing number of country houses visited by elite travellers and illustrated publications such as *Vitruvius Britannicus* provided alternative routes by which information was spread across the elite.[6] The country house might thus be seen as reflecting the spirit of the age, in terms of both aesthetic trends and the layout of its internal spaces.[7] It was, in effect, the *habitus* of the landowning elite: the material manifestation of a particular culture and lifestyle. Historians have tended to shy away from this concept as too deterministic, although Smith outlines a similar idea in the 'cultural contexts' of consumption.[8] However, the wealth and power of landowners meant that they were perhaps uniquely well-placed to shape their *habitus*, often in a conscious manner.

Although revealing of the broad changes in taste that shaped the country house, such perspectives often lose sight of its complexity as an assemblage of spaces and goods, each with potentially different influences and meanings. This has two aspects, which we explore in turn. We begin by critically examining the extent to which the country house can be understood as an integrated and conscious expression of taste and identity: a single habitus. How important was the idea of a 'grand design' or unifying vision, and how did this play out over several generations of owners? More importantly, perhaps, to what extent should we see the country house as being moulded by shared systems of fashionable taste, be it English, European, imperial, or cosmopolitan? Of course, country houses were not simply transposed from the design book onto the landscape, but how important were other factors—family and pedigree, respectability and convenience—in shaping their interior spaces, and how did possibly competing visions and materialities sit alongside each other: was a cosmopolitan interior possible or even desirable in practice? McCracken's reading of Diderot suggests an emphasis on conformity and harmony, which would strongly militate against diversity or the blending of different cultural influences; but how does this square with Barczewski's suggestion that

    [4] Cornforth, *Early Georgian Interiors*, 281, 313–24; Lefebvre, *Production of Space*.
    [5] Wilson and Mackley, *Building of the English Country House*, 66–79; Barczewski, *Country Houses and the British Empire*, esp. 180–8.
    [6] See J. Robinson, *Regency Country House* (London, 2008), 10–11; I. Roscoe, 'The decoration and furnishing of Kirtlington Park', *Apollo*, January 1980, 22–9; Wilson and Mackley, *Building of the English Country House*, 47–108; Greig, *Beau Monde*, 36–47.
    [7] See D. Arnold, 'The country house: form, function and meaning', in D. Arnold (ed.), *The Georgian Country House: Architecture, Landscape and Society* (Stroud, 1998), 1–19.
    [8] Bourdieu, *Distinction*, chapter 3; Smith, *Consumption and the Making of Respectability*. See also Savage, 'Status, lifestyle and taste', 557–60.

'British country houses were always eclectic'?[9] This links to our second theme: the spatial arrangement of goods and how this related to the use and meaning of rooms. The growing specialization of rooms and furnishings is well recognized in the literature, with much attention focusing on the principal rooms and especially the gendering of dining and drawing rooms.[10] We focus, therefore, on exploring how sets of goods were used to construct stages for the performance of elite identity. In particular, by extending analyses of the nature and type of goods that character-ize different levels of public access to encompass the use and status of particular rooms, we can gain a far more nuanced picture of the interior organization of the country house.[11] We draw on Goffman's ideas of front and back stage, but again link this to so-called 'Diderot unities' and to the agency of goods in shaping the meaning of rooms.[12] In doing so, we break the country house and elite *habitus* into a number of related parts, arguing that the house should be viewed as a col-lage of interacting spaces, each with its own meaning. Within this, we argue that the location of key goods (those which might be viewed as emblematic of elite culture and especially those of an exotic or imperial nature) is particularly reveal-ing of the identity of rooms and is explored in detail. In sum, we question the extent to which the country house formed a single *habitus* that was unifying and normative, arguing instead that it was an assemblage of spaces and goods: *habitus* was a collage.

GRAND DESIGNS? TASTE AND LINEAGE

At Arbury Hall, Sir Roger Newdigate provided a clear and unified vision for remodelling his house into what Tyack describes as 'the most impressive 18th-century Gothic houses in England, Horace Walpole's Strawberry Hill not excepted' (Figure 2.1).[13] He was undoubtedly responsible for much of the overall design as well as the details of particular rooms. His diary entry for 25 January 1761 records that he was 'planning the Parlour'; that for 30 October the same year notes him 'drawing the Gothic work for the plaster under the great arch'.[14] In this, Newdigate followed the example of Lord Burlington and, more particularly, his Warwickshire neighbour, Sanderson Miller, who was one of the pioneers of

---

[9] McCracken, *Culture and Consumption*, 118–23; Barczewski, *Country Houses and the British Empire*, 180.

[10] See, for example: Christie, *British Country House*, 243–68; Cornforth, *Early Georgian Interiors*, 11–74; Robinson, *Regency Country House*, 18–23.

[11] For an interesting analysis of this type, see G. Andersson, 'A mirror of oneself: possessions and the manifestation of status among a Swedish local elite, 1650–1770', *Cultural and Social History*, 3 (2006), 21–44.

[12] E. Goffman, *The Presentation of Self in Everyday Life* (New York, 1956); McCracken, *Culture and Consumption*, 118–23. See also Weatherill, *Consumer Behaviour*, 137–65; M. Johnson, *Housing Culture: Traditional Housing in an English Landscape* (London, 1993), 121–35.

[13] Tyack, *Warwickshire Country Houses*, 9. For a fuller discussion of these alterations, see Tyack, 'Country house building in Warwickshire', esp. 196–218.

[14] WRO, CR136/A/582, Diaries, 25 January 1761, 30 October 1761.

Figure 2.1. Arbury Hall, south front. The house was extensively remodelled in the Gothic style by Sir Roger Newdigate between 1750 and 1806.

Reproduced by kind permission of Viscount Daventry.

the Gothic style.[15] Miller made important alterations to his house at Radway Green and had an influence over the early changes at Arbury Hall, designing the bay windows in the library and parlour. When he and Newdigate fell out in the late 1750s, the latter turned to other outside sources for help, most notably Henry Keene, who was Surveyor to Westminster Abbey. To undertake the actual work, Sir Roger engaged a succession of mostly local craftsmen and, unusually, largely supervised the work himself. The end result can thus be seen as his vision, rather than as the more typical compromise between architect and patron.[16] That said, it was a vision that developed almost organically and there are clear changes in style and execution between the earlier and later rooms, so that each has its own character, despite the overall Gothic aesthetic.[17]

Work began around 1750, when David Hiorn was paid for a 'Dressing Room fitted up Gothic', and continued into the early nineteenth century.[18] Most of the interior work centred on plasterwork to the walls and ceilings, and on chimney

---

[15] On the emergence of Gothic taste in this period, see M. McCarthy, *The Origins of the Gothic Revival* (New Haven, CT, 1987). It formed an increasing focus of the Grand Tour and sparked interest in Batalha in Portugal: see R. Sweet, *Cities and the Grand Tour. The British in Italy, c.1690–1820* (Cambridge, 2012), 236–66; J. Frew and C. Wallace, 'Thomas Pitt, Portugal and the gothic cult of Batalha', *The Burlington Magazine*, 128 (1986), 582–5.

[16] Wilson and Mackley, *Building of the English Country House*, 109–44.

[17] For a summary, see Tyack, *Warwickshire Country Houses*, 12–15.

[18] WRO, CR136/V/156, Account books, entry for 1750: casuals, alterations.

pieces and windows. This is well documented in the account books and forms the principal concern of the literature on Arbury Hall, which links the surviving fabric of the house to a succession of payments made to craftsmen.[19] There is far less evidence about the character of the furniture which Sir Roger placed in each room (the accounts lack this level of detail and few bills for furniture survive); but it is apparent that his taste was broad and inclusive of different decorative styles. In addition to Gothic chimney pieces, there are several references to Gothic stoves or grates designed to make the fire burn more efficiently (discussed more fully in Chapters 3 and 7). The most notable surviving Gothic pieces are a set of chairs and settees, executed by an unknown craftsman probably in the mid-eighteenth century. The style is understated, especially given the increasingly flamboyant plasterwork, and the covers—embroidered by Sir Roger's mother, Elizabeth Twisden—comprise rich floral motifs, suggesting a fairly free interpretation of Gothicism.[20] A further set of Gothic chairs was ordered from Gillows in 1805, a surviving sketch for which shows a rather plain version of the kind of piece advertised by Chippendale in the 1760s.[21]

Alongside this burgeoning Gothic vision, classicism was also much in evidence, and a memorandum from 1775 lists various trophies from the Grand Tour, including four tables made from 'Egyptian granite', two of them placed in the recently remodelled hall; two tables described as 'studio of various marbles'; and another made in Rome from 'a large Plate of Porpheyry', all found in the Saloon.[22] That Sir Roger felt that the two styles could coexist quite happily is evident in his placement of classical statues in the Gothic niches of the Dining Room, completed in the late 1780s. It was carried further in his own design for the ceiling in the library, which, as he noted in his diary on 25 March 1791, was modelled on the Baths of the Empress Livia.[23] This mixing of styles and points of reference was unsurprising, given Newdigate's established status as a classical scholar and was found even in Adam's rigorous neoclassicism. It does not detract from the unity of design, but does reflect the blending of a wide range of cultural influences, filtered by the tastes of one man. It was truly eclectic, drawing inspiration from widely different times and places, but its cosmopolitanism was firmly European. The product was a different kind of unity from that described by Cornforth and Girouard. The aim was not to produce a sequence of rooms the decorative unity of which reflected the progression of the visitor either towards the inner sanctum of the cabinet or through a series of linked spaces designed to display wealth and encourage sociability. Rather, the house is best seen as a number of set pieces, brought together by a unifying aesthetic that was gradually honed as the work progressed. Its success

[19] See G. Nares, 'Arbury Hall', *Country Life* (8 October 1953), 1126–9; (15 October 1953), 1210–13; (29 October 1953), 1414–17; and M. Hall, 'Arbury Hall', *Country Life* (7 January 1999), 30–5, (14 January 1999), 40–3.

[20] Nares, *Country Life* (8 October 1953), 1129.

[21] WRO, CR764/214, Sketch of chair ordered from Gillows, 6 September 1805; T. Chippendale, *The Gentleman and Cabinet-maker's Director* (London, 1762), plate xxi.

[22] WRO, CR136/B/2413i, Memorandum, 1775. This refers to porphyry, a rock often used in sculpture.

[23] WRO, CR136/A/582, Diaries, 25 March 1791.

Figure 2.2. The West Range, Stoneleigh Abbey. Built in the 1720s for Edward, third Lord Leigh, by Francis Smith of Warwick.

Photograph by Jon Stobart.

was built on the remarkably consistent taste system of an owner whose reign at the house lasted for seventy years.

The dynastic situation at Stoneleigh Abbey was very different; yet here too it is possible to see the unifying influence of contemporary taste, albeit heavily tempered by conservatism. Most obvious in this regard was the construction in the 1720s of a massive extension (the west range) by the Warwick architect-builder Francis Smith, and its subsequent decoration by a range of craftsmen from Warwick and London (Figure 2.2).[24] This signalled the wealth, ambition, and taste of Edward, third Lord Leigh (1684–1738), and the ideas that he had picked up on his Grand Tour. Its sheer size made this project a conspicuous show of wealth, but its finished magnificence belies the rather cautious approach taken by Lord Leigh. The outlay was surprisingly modest and its 'aggressively anti-Palladian design' put it add odds with other houses being built in the 1720s, as did the layout, which was rigid and a little old-fashioned, resembling Girouard's 'formal house'.[25] In short, this was not a demonstration of the latest taste: Lord Leigh's choice of decoration in the Great Apartment, whilst fitting for such a badge of aristocratic status, was marked by what Gomme calls 'a conservative but still swagger taste in the 1720s'.[26] The stylar wainscoting, with heavy Corinthian pilasters, was complemented by walnut and gilt furniture, large gilt-framed mirrors, and rich drapery

---

[24] For a fuller discussion of the building work, see A. Gomme, 'Abbey into palace: a lesser Wilton?,' in R. Bearman (ed.) *Stoneleigh Abbey. The House, Its Owners, Its Lands* (Stratford-upon-Avon, 2004), 82–115; A. Gomme, *Smith of Warwick* (Stamford, 2000), 368–75.

[25] Gomme, 'Abbey into palace', 85; Girouard, *English Country House*, 119–62, 181–212.

[26] Gomme, 'Abbey into palace', 87.

in crimson velvet.[27] If this conservatism puts a different complexion on the west range as a statement of taste, so too does the fact that Edward appears to have lost interest in the project once the building was complete and the principal rooms were furnished. Many of the upper-storey rooms and even the hall were left unfinished.

Lengthy delays were not unusual in such building projects, but it was only when Edward's grandson, another Edward, fifth Lord Leigh, came of age in 1763 that the project was finally completed. By this time, tastes had changed and the west range was distinctly dated—something which Edward, fifth Lord Leigh, must have appreciated, especially given the building schemes then being undertaken by his Warwickshire neighbours.[28] In addition to some rather fanciful designs, probably in his own hand, Edward commissioned at least three designs for a new north range, all of which suggest rather conservative taste, as does Edward's choice of decorative scheme for the hall. Rather than adopt the designs put forward by his architect, Timothy Lightoler, which have rococo decorative work and niches containing classical statues, he adopted a scheme depicting the trials of Hercules in a series of wall medallions and in a hugely impressive but unfashionably baroque ceiling panel.[29] This work, then, could hardly have placed the fifth Lord Leigh at the cutting edge of fashion in the sense of the latest taste in interior decoration. Neither does there appear to have been a single clear vision for the house: the hall is very different in style from the Great Apartment and the suite of rooms to the south, where again the fifth Lord Leigh rejected Lightoler's rococo designs.[30] It is only in the first- and second-floor rooms, finished and fitted up between 1763 and 1765, that any unity of design is apparent. Each suite of bedchamber and dressing room was given a unifying colour scheme and furnished with broadly similar sets of furniture, all of it supplied through the London upholsterers Thomas and Gilbert Burnett (see Chapter 7).[31] Yet these were not statements of fashionable good taste: respectability and convenience appear to have been the most important considerations.

Conservatism and convenience were not the only counterbalances to fashionable taste apparent in the fabric of Stoneleigh Abbey. In common with many landowners in Britain and across Europe, they wrote their family status into the decoration and furnishing of the house.[32] In the Great Apartment, Edward, third Lord Leigh, had his coronet and arms incorporated into the capitals of the pilasters. His grandson

[27] SCLA, DR18/4/9, Inventory, 1738.

[28] In 1760, Lord Willoughby commissioned a young Robert Adam to remodel Compton Verney, whilst James West and Sir Roger Newdigate were engaged in Gothicizing Alscot Park and Arbury Hall respectively. Tyack, *Warwickshire Country Houses*, 64–70, 1–5, 9–15.

[29] SCLA, DR671/33, Designs for Stoneleigh Abbey, design for the Great Hall; Gomme, 'Abbey into palace', 103–14. The proposed north range was never built.

[30] SCLA, DR671/33, Designs for Stoneleigh Abbey, design for the Plaid Parlour.

[31] SCLA, DR18/3/47/52/15.

[32] See, for example, L. Worsley, 'Female architectural patronage in the eighteenth century and the case of Henrietta Cavendish Holles Harley', *Architectural History*, 48 (2005), 139–62; Retford, 'Patrilineal portraiture'; J. Cornforth, 'The backward look', in G. Jackson-Stops (ed.) *The Treasure Houses of Britain. Five Hundred Years of Private Patronage and Art Collecting* (New Haven, CT, 1985), 60–9; Girouard, *French Country House*, 94–5, 132–3, 300–1.

included his coat of arms in each of the sketches he made for refronting the west range, and unicorns, central to the family crest, were the key motif of the frieze in the Great Hall. These symbols of titled status were repeated on a range of luxury items, including silverware and coaches, which carried the ecology of signs across the house and beyond.[33] Of particular significance is a set of seven walnut and gilt chairs with seats and backs embroidered with classical figures and the monograms of Edward, third Lord Leigh, and his wife Mary Holbech. As Morrall has argued, such ornamentation was important in shaping the meaning of material objects, forming a 'mode of visual address' which proclaimed definable social and ideological values. They also mobilized luxury items and the fabric of the house more generally as 'signifiers of family' and rendered them symbols of heritance, pedigree and power.[34]

Similar statements of lineage were deployed by aristocrats across Europe. In Holland, Het Loo was replete with symbols of William of Orange and became, in effect, a memorial to the man and his family. In France, coats of arms were emblazoned across many houses and were especially prominent at Vaux-le-Vicomte, along with a wealth of classical allusions and symbolism.[35] A similar mix characterized the homes of many nabobs, including Basildon Park, where griffins feature prominently amongst the broader decorative scheme. Barczewski views the griffin as a subtle reference to India and Sykes's nabob riches, but overlooks its centrality to Sir Francis Sykes's new coat of arms, which was also emblazoned on an impressive armorial porcelain service, completed in the late 1760s.[36] If such pedigrees were sometimes recent and occasionally contrived, this was little different from the practices of apparently more established families. At Canons Ashby, the extensive modifications made by Edward Dryden in the 1710s provided an opportunity to include similar allusions to lineage. The overall aim of the changes was to modernize the house, if not transforming it into a model of Palladian symmetry, then at least giving it a dressing of tasteful classicism. This involved, amongst other things, refacing the south front, installing casement windows, removing a large bay window, and remodelling the Great Hall. But Dryden peppered his improved house with symbols of family. Crests were included on the newly fitted drainpipes and on several firebacks; a painted coat of arms was hung over the chimney in the Great Hall; and on the adjoining wall was placed a 'silk embroidery of the Kings arms on green cloth in gilt frame'.[37] This had come to Edward from his brother-in-law, John Shaw, who was Master of the Board of Green Cloth, the body responsible for law and order in and around the old Palace of Whitehall. It thus signalled his family links to metropolitan authority and, by association, with royal power. Family coats

---

[33] SCLA, DR18/5/2178, DR18/5/2100, DR18/5/4251.

[34] A. Morrall, 'Ornament as evidence', in K. Harvey (ed.) *History and Material Culture* (London, 2009), 47; Berg, *Luxury and Pleasure*, 242.

[35] H. Ronnes, 'A sense of heritage: renewal versus preservation in the English and Dutch palaces of William III in the 18th century', in J. Stobart and A. Hann (eds), *The Country House: Material Culture and Consumption* (Swindon, 2015), 74–83, Girouard, *French Country House*, 127–33.

[36] Barczewski, *Country Houses and the British Empire*, 142; Smith, 'Gendering armorial porcelain wares'.

[37] NRO, D(CA)901, Inventory, 1717.

of arms were placed over the new grandiose entrance inserted in the west front and painted on the panels in the overmantel in the former Great Chamber on the first floor. In the latter he also included a new family motto, 'Antient as the Druids', a link with the past which might help to explain Edward's willingness to retain many earlier decorative features, not least the sixteenth-century overmantel itself.[38] Elsewhere, he was not above creating a bit of family history, the coat of arms and regalia in the Great Hall being complemented by a wide array of weapons which created the impression of a medieval hall and yet had been assembled there only in Edward's lifetime.[39]

The assertion of pedigree amongst the gentry may have been the object of parody by metropolitan critics, but it remained a powerful force amongst the provincial elite. Indeed, they were a central part of what Cornforth calls 'the backward look', that is, the 'thread of historical thinking' that has been so important in shaping English country houses.[40] At Canons Ashby, in particular, this formed an import-ant leitmotif running through the interior decoration of the house, part of Edward Dryden's grand vision for the house. It might also be seen as an attempt to underline his own credentials and those of his family: he was a wealthy and well-connected London grocer who had inherited the estate, but not the baronetcy, which passed to his cousin.

The deployment of overt signs of rank and status was underpinned by collections of family portraits which spoke of lineage and social connections. At Stoneleigh Abbey, there were paintings of several generations of the Leigh family, dating back to Sir Thomas, who acquired the estate in the sixteenth century. These signalled the depth of family lineage whilst others illustrated wider family connections, spreading across the county and beyond. Amongst many others there were por-traits of Thomas Holbech, the father of the third Lord's wife, Mary; Mary Isham, a cousin who married into the Ishams of Lamport Hall, and the Honourable Lady Rockingham, the mother of Eleanor, wife of the second Lord Leigh.[41] The inven-tories of 1749 and 1750 show these hung all together in the Picture Gallery, where they formed the kind of 'pictorial family tree' described by Retford.[42] Similarly, the Dryden portraits comprised several generations of family along with various distant relatives, including Sir Frederick Cornwallis, a Royalist during the Civil Wars and subsequently an MP and Privy Councillor, who marked the fam-ily's political connections. This was a more modest collection, displayed in the

[38] Coats of arms, mottos, and druids also linked Edward to the current fashion for antiquarianism. For a more general discussion, see R. Sweet, *Antiquaries: The Discovery of the Past in Eighteenth-Century Britain* (London 2004).

[39] The 1708 inventory (NRO, D(CA) 49) records few goods in the Great Hall and no collection of weapons at Canons Ashby.

[40] F. Heal and C. Holmes, *Gentry in England and Wales, 1500–1700* (London, 1994), 40; Cornforth, 'Backward look', 60. See also C. Rowell (ed) *Ham House: a History* (New Haven, CT, 2013).

[41] SCLA, DR18/4/27, Inventory, November 1749; DR18/4/66, Valuation of Lady Barbara Leigh's pictures (no date).

[42] Retford, 'Patrilineal portraiture', 327. See also Millar, 'Portraiture and the country house'. This process could sometimes be complicated by a desire to showcase the work of particular painters asso-ciated with the family: see Lewis, 'When a house is not a home', 361.

Great Parlour, but it formed part of the material culture of the country house, anticipated and sought out by visitors.[43] Mrs Lybbe Powys invariably commented on such things, noting at Knole House the richness of the decoration and the treasures recently brought from Rome by the Duke of Dorset, but also placing emphasis on 'portraits of the family for many generations'.[44] The importance of a gallery of family portraits in cementing status was recognized by those returning to Britain from service in India. Writing in 1822 from a house that he was renting from the Burgoyne family, Henry Russell informed a friend that 'they are one of the oldest Families in England: the Hall is lined with the Pictures of their Ancestors'.[45] That this was no idle observation becomes apparent when he and his brother, Charles, were refurbishing the new family home at Swallowfield Park in the 1830s. They engaged in genealogical research and repaired or commissioned numerous family portraits, which were then hung in the house, being joined later by newly acquired portraits of key figures in England's royal history.

Deploying material objects in this way was not an exclusively elite practice: the middling sort, as Harvey notes, also viewed them as markers of time and memory.[46] What distinguished the elite was the character, quantity, and quality of 'family' objects: they had architecture and picture galleries rather than commonplace books through which to communicate messages of family and lineage.[47] In doing so, the priorities and unity of tasteful design were punctuated by objects with complementary or sometimes conflicting frameworks of reference. Edward Dryden's insertion of coats of arms in a 150-year-old overmantel, for example, is incongruous in an overall scheme intent on modernization, but the mixture of old and new is a characteristic of most country houses. It results both from a conscious deployment of the past, in decorative schemes such as that developed by Sir Roger Newdigate, and from the layering of new possessions onto the existing material culture of the house. These juxtapositions and incongruities challenge the unity and harmony of objects posited by Diderot; different tastes and elements could, in fact, readily coexist within the country house. This is because the cultural significance of these different objects was consistent; even when they were no longer fashionable, old goods retained a symbolic significance that encouraged their retention because they all formed part of elite material culture. This in turn highlights the variegated and multifaceted nature of that material culture. This was not so much the geographical blending implicit in cosmopolitanism, but rather a chronological and cultural amalgam which reflected and celebrated heritage. The country house was not simply a reflection of refined taste: it was also layered with the symbolism of family and pedigree, moulded by the imperatives of convenience and respectability, and shaped by the pleasure derived by the individual in their domestic

[43] Retford, 'Patrilineal portraiture', 337–8; A. Tinniswood, *The Polite Tourist: Four Centuries of Country House Visiting* (New York, 1999), 108.

[44] E. J. Climenson (ed.) *Passages from the Diaries of Mrs Philip Lybbe Powys, of Hardwick House, 1756–1808* (London, 1899), 53–4, 149–50. See also Girouard, *French Country House*, 128.

[45] Quoted in M. Finn, 'Swallowfield Park, Berkshire', *East India Company at Home* (February 2013), <http://blogs.ucl.ac.uk/eicah/case-studies-2/swallowfield-park-berkshire/>, 14.

[46] Harvey, *Little Republic*, 119, 172–4.

[47] They also had funerary monuments—a point discussed more fully in Chapter 6.

surroundings—consumption, after all, was about self as well as others, as we shall see in Chapter 6. Each family, each individual, made their own choices about how to combine and balance these different influences, a process that was complicated but given extra scope and meaning by the presence of a series of different spaces within the country house.

ROOM SPECIALIZATION: STAGES AND PERFORMANCES

The differentiation of domestic space can be understood in many different ways, but a broad distinction is often drawn between those rooms intended for public use and those for family use. Cornforth argues that most large houses were divided in this way, the difference being marked by the ways in which they were 'fitted up, decorated and furnished', and Girouard notes a similar distinction in French houses, despite their different overall configuration.[48] These distinctions are very clear at Blenheim Palace, where the suite of family rooms in the east range is spatially discrete and decoratively distinct from the state apartments which run along the full length of the south range; they are repeated on a smaller scale in the distinction between the Great Apartment and the Breakfast Room and Dining Parlour at Stoneleigh Abbey.[49] It is tempting to see these as public and private spaces, but this distinction is too crude. As Vickery has argued, these are relative and contingent terms, depending on who was entering the house, their relationship with the owner, the purpose of the visit, the time of day, and so on.[50]

There is frustratingly little evidence for the actual use of different rooms at Stoneleigh Abbey during the eighteenth century, but a letter written by Jane Austen's mother Cassandra when visiting Stoneleigh with relatives just after Mary Leigh's death in 1806 is revealing. She effectively takes her correspondent on a tour of the house, starting from the main entrance:

> You go up a considerable flight of steps to the door, for some of the offices are underground, and enter a large hall. On the right hand is the dining-room and within that the breakfast-room, where we generally sit; and reason good, 'tis the only room besides the chapel, which looks towards the view. On the left hand of the hall is the best drawing-room and within a smaller one. These rooms are rather gloomy with brown wainscot and dark crimson furniture, so we never use them except to walk through to the old picture gallery. Behind the smaller drawing-room is the state-bedchamber an alarming apartment, with its high, dark crimson velvet bed, just fit for an heroine. The old gallery opens into it. Behind the hall and parlours there is a passage all across the house, three staircases and two small sitting-rooms. There are twenty-six bedchambers in the new part of the house and a great many, some very

[48] Cornforth, *Early Georgian Interiors*, 275; Girouard, *French Country House*, 111–46. See also Robinson, *Regency Country House*, 18–23.
[49] Cornforth, *Early Georgian Interiors*, 276–9; J. Stobart and M. Rothery, 'Fashion, heritage and family: new and old in the Georgian country house', *Cultural and Social History*, 11/3 (2014), 385–406.
[50] Vickery, *Behind Closed Doors*, 25–48. Her discussion of London houses and lodgings is difficult to transfer across into the world of the country house.

Figure 2.3. The Great Hall, Stoneleigh Abbey, completed for Edward, fifth Lord Leigh, in the 1760s, with stuccowork representing the trials and apotheosis of Hercules.
Photograph by Jon Stobart.

good ones, in the old. There is also another gallery, fitted up with modern prints on a buff paper, and a large billiard-room.[51]

Retracing Cassandra's steps allows us to explore the variegated spatiality of the house. We arrive first at the Great Hall. Whilst this lacked the scale and height of those at Houghton, Willey Park, or Ragley, it conformed to the conventions of halls in its rich decoration and relatively sparse furnishing.[52] As noted earlier, the stuccowork was particularly impressive both in style and quality of execution, and the walls were punctuated by a series of scagliola columns topped with Corinthian capitals richly decorated with acanthus leaves (Figure 2.3). Set around the room were four sofas, each with a Brussels carpet set in front; four stools and six japanned chairs; two small mahogany tables and two further carpets.[53] Like other halls, this was a space designed to communicate to visitors the wealth, taste, and classical learning of the owner: for Cassandra Austen at least, it was not somewhere to linger and she quickly moves on to the suites of rooms either side of the hall. There is a sharp distinction drawn between the family rooms to the right and state or public rooms to the left. The former were occupied on a regular basis, whereas the latter were left largely unvisited, their status making them irrelevant to the entertainment

[51] Reproduced in W. Austen-Leigh, R. Austen-Leigh and D. le Faye, *Jane Austen: a Family Record* (London, 1989), 139–40.
[52] Cornforth, *Early Georgian Interiors*, 150–68; Robinson, *Regency Country House*, 116; Girouard, *English Country House*, 136–7.
[53] Gomme, 'Abbey into palace', 93–4; SCLA, DR18/4/59, Inventory, 1806.

of family guests. These distinctions were marked in terms of decor, but equally important is the way in which Cassandra represents these rooms to her sister: the breakfast room is a place to linger and enjoy the views and the company; the best drawing room is gloomy and to be avoided or hurried through. This use of the state rooms as a thoroughfare somewhat undermines their special status, as does the portrayal of the state bed in melodramatic, even Gothic terms. Messages of family pedigree and dignity were not, it seems, something that struck Cassandra Austen.

Her tour continues into the picture gallery beyond the state bedchamber, a room that would form part of the public space of the house and to which visitors would be taken to view the collection of family portraits, paintings, and prints. Yet the room was also filled with an assortment of furniture, including a walnut escritoire desk, glazed bookcase, six walnut chairs upholstered in flowered silk, two writing tables, two card tables, a spinet, a further table, twenty mahogany chairs, and two mahogany elbow chairs.[54] Given the dimensions of this space, much of the furniture must have been arranged along the walls, although the desk, writing and card tables, and spinet suggest the possibility of informal sociability more akin to family rooms. In the absence of a proper library, it is possible that this gallery offered an alternative to the breakfast room as a place to sit.[55] The clear binary of family and state rooms, of spaces for family and those for recollection, was complicated further by the presence at the back of the west range of what Cassandra Austen refers to as two 'small sitting-rooms'.[56] She tells us little about their appearance or use, perhaps because she had little occasion to enter them. Facing onto an inner courtyard, they were undoubtedly rather dark and appear to have been everyday rooms.[57] They were hung with green morine curtains and furnished with mahogany pieces, including chairs and tables, but also japanned cupboards, a bookcase, dumb waiter, music press, and a large number of pictures—a typically eclectic mix of exotic hardwood, oriental-inspired lacquerwork, traditional European styles, and everyday items.

Climbing the main stairs which lie between these two rooms, we come to the twenty-six bedrooms of the west range. A number of these had been furnished and occupied in the 1740s and possibly as early as the 1730s. In memoranda drawn up in September 1762 and April 1763 by Samuel Butler, the steward to Edward, fifth Lord Leigh, there are partial contents lists for several bedchambers.[58] These itemize

[54] SCLA, DR18/4/59, Inventory, 1806.

[55] On the growing use of libraries as family or sitting rooms, see S. Jervis, 'The English country house library: an architectural history', *Library History*, 18/3 (2002), 175–90; Cornforth, *Early Georgian Interiors*, 68–74; M. Purcell, 'The country house library reassess'd: or, did the "country house library" ever really exist?', Library History, 18 (2002), 160, 168–70; Robinson, *Regency Country House*, 18, 127, 157.

[56] For fuller discussion of these different types of space and the problem in drawing firm distinctions between the two, see H. Chavasse, 'Fashion and "affectionate recollection": material culture at Audley End, 1762–1773', in J. Stobart and A. Hann (eds), *The Country House*, 63–73; Stobart and Rothery, 'Fashion, heritage and family'.

[57] SCLA, DR18/4/69, Inventory, 1786; DR18/4/59, Inventory, 1806.

[58] SCLA, DR18/3/47/52/6, Memorandum, 2 October 1762; DR18/3/47/52/7, Memorandum, 13 April 1763.

beds, window curtains, wall hangings, and so on, some of which were to be moved to other rooms as part of the programme of refurbishment discussed in Chapter 7. However, by the time of Cassandra Austen's visit, the bedchambers largely reflected the changes made by Edward, fifth Lord Leigh, albeit with some significant rearrangements subsequently undertaken by his sister, Mary.[59] What Edward produced was a series of rooms, each with its own character, but which contained a largely standard set of furniture comprising the bedstead, a set of mahogany chairs, a dressing table, basin stand, night table, and pot cupboard, sometimes supplemented with a chest of drawers or wardrobe. What distinguished each room was the colour and quality of the bed hangings, window curtains, and wallpaper. Indeed, these were used to identify the rooms in both bills and inventories: blue morine, crimson worsted damask, blue and white cotton, yellow damask, wrought work, and so on.[60] Standardization was thus tempered with qualitative differences, a feature seen most markedly in Lord Leigh's own bedchamber with its chintz hangings and wallpaper, along with gilt leather hangings brought into the room from an older part of the house (see Chapter 3).

This brief walk through Stoneleigh Abbey gives us a feel for the house as a sequence of connected spaces, each with its own function, decor, and atmosphere. State and family rooms were distinct, but they could not be kept entirely discrete from one another. The typical link, as at Stoneleigh, was via a centrally placed hall, although at Blenheim the two sets of rooms were connected through the Duke's bedchamber and dressing room. Once in the state apartment, there was a gradation of privacy that was integral to its form and function. The usual arrangement of great chamber, followed by withdrawing room, antechamber, then bedchamber, and finally the closet or cabinet, is seen most clearly in the biggest houses, such as Chatsworth House, and operated as a filter which progressively restricted access to all but the most favoured visitors in what Giroaurd calls the 'axis of honour'.[61] This archetype is found on a more modest scale at Stoneleigh Abbey, where the Brown Parlour leads into the Drawing Room and thence the State Bedchamber and Dressing Room; but any sense of arriving at an inner sanctum is undermined by the route leading onto the picture gallery and thence the rest of the house. Moreover, such a suite of public rooms is by no means a feature of all country houses. Canons Ashby is perhaps too small to carry such an arrangement, but at Arbury Hall, where there is certainly enough space, Sir Roger Newdigate's remodelling resulted in a series of set pieces in which there is little notion of the flow expected in parade rooms or the self-contained privacy of family rooms. The five main rooms of the house were all accessible from the cloisters, which formed an inner corridor, but they also interlinked. Whilst a parade of sorts is, therefore, possible, there is little notion of progression in terms of decoration or privacy: from the

---

[59] These changes are discussed more fully in Chapter 5. Essentially, Mary moved furniture between bedchambers, but their overall character remained largely unaltered.

[60] See SCLA, DR18/3/47/52/15, bill from Thomas Burnett.

[61] Girouard, *English Country House*, 144. It found its equivalent in aristocratic houses elsewhere in Europe; in France, for example, private cabinets were often separated from public rooms by a gallery—see Girouard, *French Country House*, 113–20.

entrance hall, the first room is the Little Sitting Room, probably best seen as a family room and certainly the least elaborate in its decoration; next is the Saloon, which by contrast has the most elaborate vaulting; this is followed by the Parlour or drawing room, with rather heavier barrel vaulting; then the Dining Room, separated by a narrow hallway; and finally the Library, particularly important given Sir Roger's book collecting (discussed in Chapter 4).

If it is difficult to sustain distinctions of state and family, public and private, it might be more useful to consider these in terms of Goffman's differentiation of front and back stage. This model is built on his assertion that 'the self [is] a performed character', social interaction being seen as an engagement between individuals and audiences in which performances are preconceived and carefully staged.[62] The dramaturgical analogy is continued through the distinction drawn between spaces in which the public self is performed (front stage) and those where preparations are made for such performances (back stage). Although contested, this model has been used in various analyses of domestic material culture to understand differences in the furnishing or decoration of various types of rooms.[63] Its meshes well with conceptions of the country house as a stage for political and social networking, and to its status as a preconceived and planned space of power. Moreover, the multitude of specialist rooms also offers scope for different kinds of performance and for spaces dedicated to preparing for these performances, whether in material or emotional terms.

The most obvious stage for performances of status and wealth were the formal rooms of parade, furnished according to the pocket and rank of the owner, but often following fairly standard conventions.[64] The Great Apartment at Stoneleigh was no exception: panelling to the walls, walnut and gilt furniture, and crimson velvet hangings. Each of these was important in creating the proper setting; the family portraits, added slightly later, heightened the status of the room as a means of demonstrating lineage and connections to neighbouring families. Red was a colour associated with nobility and its variations, especially crimson, were frequently used in royal and state apartments, as at Boughton House, Raynham, and Blickling. These noble associations were underlined by the practical challenges in using red for furnishings, not least because they absorbed light and thus required the use of more candles.[65] Panelling was typical of the great chambers that formed the first room of many state apartments; Smith, as he often did, gave the rooms at Stoneleigh Abbey the additional dignity of a complete order. The furniture principally comprised side tables and chairs, which would generally be set against the walls. Indeed, the most important set of chairs—the embroidered set incorporating the monograms of Edward, third Lord Leigh, and his wife Mary—were clearly intended for

[62] Goffman, *Presentation of Self*, 252.

[63] See, for example: Weatherill, *Consumer Behaviour*, 137–65; Andersson, 'A mirror of oneself'; A. Barnett, 'In with the new: novel goods in domestic provincial England, *c*.1700-1790' in B. Blondé, et al. (eds) *Fashioning Old and New. Changing Consumer Patterns in Western Europe, 1650–1900* (Turnhout, 2009), 84–91.

[64] Cornforth, *Early Georgian Interiors*, 13–18; Girouard, *English Country House*, 194–8.

[65] Retford, 'Patrilineal portraiture'; Millar, 'Portraiture and the country house'; Vickery, *Behind Closed Doors*, 174; Cornforth, *Early Georgian Interiors*, 113–22.

looking at rather than sitting on. Much the same was true of the 'crimson velvet bed and counterpane lined with crimson silk' that formed the centrepiece of the suite of rooms. This was valued in the 1738 inventory at £300 6s., the three rooms of the Great Apartment containing a total of £734 5s. 6d. worth of movable furniture, underlining the importance of these rooms within the country house. In Andersson's terms they were 'public space, front stage'.[66]

This is all very impressive, but if these rooms formed a stage set, we need to consider the nature of the performance being acted out and the character of its audience. Originally conceived as the rooms in which the monarch would stay if they deigned to visit, this function was rendered largely redundant by the marked absence of George I and George II from the country, let alone the country house. Instead, they were increasingly used to communicate the rank and dignity of the owner, operating in effect as a badge of aristocratic status—an association which probably lay behind the decision of Sir John Griffin Griffin to add a state apartment to Audley End in Essex when he was elevated to the peerage in 1784.[67] At the same time, there was a growing recognition that they could also signify the lineage of the family and the permanence of the house. Something of this can be seen in a letter written in 1772 by T. F. Pritchard to the Earl of Powis, suggesting that 'this whole apartment has a most Elegant appearance, and shou'd be preserved to keep up the Stile and Dignity of the Old Castle'.[68] In both cases, they were seldom actually used and only occasionally opened to visitors. As a stage, they were often left empty, as Cassandra Austen noted at Stoneleigh Abbey; rarely was there a performance or an audience that was physically present. Yet their mere existence was sufficient to enact the status, wealth, and lineage of the owner. As Lybbe Powys noted of the state rooms at Houghton Hall, 'the fitting up and furniture very superb; and the cornishes and mouldings of all the apartments being gilt, it makes the whole what I call magnificently glaringly'.[69]

In the absence of a state apartment at Canons Ashby, the Great Parlour provided a stage for muted performances of status and lineage, here in a setting that was used on a regular basis. The room was initially laid out by Edward Dryden, who furnished it as a formal sitting room, somewhat in the form of Humphrey Repton's 'Cedar Parlour'.[70] It contained twelve cane-bottom walnut chairs *en suite* with a settee and marble-topped table, three tea tables, and two lampstands; its panelled walls hung with four looking glasses and two family pictures.[71] Many of these pieces remained in place through the ownership of Sir John, his son, and the long widowhood of Lady Elizabeth's, John's wife, though both added further family pictures. Their adoptive daughter, also called Elizabeth, and her husband Sir John Turner Dryden transformed the room into a Dining Parlour, removing the walnut furniture in favour of mahogany in the form of chairs, a sideboard, dumb waiters,

[66] SCLA, DR18/4/9, Inventory, 1738; Andersson, 'Mirror of oneself', 31.
[67] Chavasse, 'Material culture and the country house', 85–100.
[68] Quoted in Cornforth, *Early Georgian Interiors*, 13.
[69] Climenson, *Diaries of Lybbe Powys*, 6.
[70] H. Repton, *Fragments on the Theory and Practice of Landscape Gardening* (London, 1816).
[71] NRO, D(CA)901, Inventory, 1717.

cases for cutlery, and a large dining table. But they also introduced a large bookcase and two smaller ones, a grand piano, a pair of globes, a Pembroke table, a set of framed prints, and further pictures. What made this room important in dynastic terms was the persistent presence of a group of family portraits comprising Mrs Allen (the wife of Edward Dryden), Sir John Dryden, two of Lady Dryden (née Rooper, Sir John's wife), Mr Puleston (Sir John's brother-in-law), Mr Rooper (Elizabeth's father), and Mrs Dryden.[72] What is particularly intriguing about this list is that the names were clearly added after the inventory had been drawn up; it appears that someone, quite possibly Elizabeth Dryden, intervened to ensure that the inventory accurately recorded these family members. The effect was that on paper as well as in the room the portraits acted as props in the performance of lineage, ancestors looking down on the company as they dined, made music, or read.[73]

In some ways, the Great Parlour also allowed the Drydens to act out performances of polite sociability, but the real setting for this was the first-floor Drawing Room. Elizabeth and Sir John Turner Dryden created this from the rather unprepossessing and sparsely furnished Dining Room from which nothing was carried forward other than the basic structure of the room and an impressive fireplace with its Jacobean overmantel. The furniture assembled represented fashionable good taste: inlaid mahogany and satinwood furniture, a comfortable sofa, light japanned chairs, and display stands for flowers and chinaware. It also encouraged informal sociability around card tables and virtuous feminine pursuits at the work or writing tables.[74] There were even the requisite landscapes, still lifes, and allegorical paintings to add interest and perhaps spark conversation. This was not the equal of the elaborately decorated drawing rooms of Petworth House, Ditchley Park, or Hagley Hall, with their intricate stuccowork, tapestries, and richly upholstered furniture,[75] but it provided a respectable, fashionable, and modestly cosmopolitan setting in which Elizabeth and John could receive guests.

Much the same could be said of the Breakfast Room and Dining Parlour at Stoneleigh Abbey. They too lacked the richness of decoration that might be expected, especially in the principal entertaining rooms of an aristocratic house. In the early 1760s, Edward, fifth Lord Leigh, commissioned designs for what was still called the Plaid Parlour, Timothy Lightoler presenting him with a scheme that included garlands over the windows and a frilly rococo overmantel.[76] The design was not executed and the walls remained plain, but Edward paid Burnett a total of £211 1s. 8½d. for drapery and upholstery work, including 200 yards of rich green silk and worsted damask and 81 yards of deep silk and worsted fringe for the curtains; seven green Italian shades; seven cushions for window seats, covered in green

---

[72] NRO, D(CA)904, Inventory, 1819.

[73] In a similar way, Henrietta Cavendish had names and dates added onto many of the paintings she had hung at Wellbeck Abbey. See Retford, 'Patrilineal portraiture'.

[74] Vickery, *Behind Closed Doors*, 231–56.

[75] See G. Jackson-Stops, 'Petworth House, Sussex, NT', *Country Life* (4 September 1980), 798–9, (25 September 1980), 1030–1; J. Cornforth, 'How French style touched the Georgian drawing room', *Country Life* (6 January 2000), 52–3.

[76] SCLA, DR671/33, Designs for Stoneleigh Abbey, design for Plaid Parlour. See also Gomme, 'Abbey into palace', 97–8.

mixed damask; and covering twenty-four chairs and two French elbow chairs to match.[77] The choice of colour is significant, green being second in the hierarchy of colours, yet often favoured partly because of its associations with Venus and partly because it formed a good backdrop for hanging paintings. Combined with a slew of new furniture and the addition of a large number of landscape paintings, including scenes of Venice and Rome, generally attributed to Canaletto (1697–1768), these soft furnishings created a setting for polite entertainment. Such functions were underscored by the presence of musical instruments and games—a feature reinforced by the changes made by Mary in the final decades of the century. These were classic 'front-stage' spaces, a setting which at once comprised and framed the public performance of the owner as a person of taste and sociability, and one that resembled both Repton's 'Modern Living Room' and Girouard's broader vision of the 'social house'.[78] Cassandra Austen emphasized the views over the river (an important element in performances of aesthetic politeness), but it was the furnishing of these rooms that made them the principal spaces for family and visitors alike. The ongoing changes to the furnishing and decor can thus be seen in part as an attempt to create a tasteful and fashionable space for polite entertaining. Significantly, these drew on a cosmopolitanism that was essentially European, despite the presence of mahogany and chinaware: the landscapes by Canaletto and others by Dutch masters and English artists, in particular, linked Lord Leigh to European cultures of collecting and consumption inspired by the Grand Tour.

Preparations for these varied public performances of self were, according to Goffman, made in back-stage spaces, including both the extensive service areas of the house (kitchens, still rooms, butteries, and the like—discussed in Chapter 3) and more personal spaces, notably bedchambers and dressing rooms. The latter had long been identified as intimate and private spaces. They were, as Vickery puts it, 'venues for elegant relaxation...a response to the stiff-backed awfulness of state-rooms, an antidote to a domestic life "overcharged with ceremony"'.[79] In addition to their use for sleeping, washing, and dressing, they were also places to which the owner might withdraw when unwell, or in which they might read, write letters, sit in the evening, entertain close friends, or even dine. Lady Shelburne's dressing room served all these functions and was 'emphatically not a formal room'; neither was Lady Mary Archer's dressing room at Welford, where a party gathered on a rainy day and rummaged through the books, examined ornaments on the dressing table, stamped crests onto doilies, read, or did their needlework.[80]

This range of functions is reflected in the furnishing of dressing rooms and bedchambers. In the rooms newly fitted up for Edward, fifth Lord Leigh, each suite of bedchamber and dressing room contained furniture for sleeping, washing, and dressing, but also for sitting, either alone or in company.[81] These guest rooms were

[77] SCLA, DR/18/47/52/15.
[78] Repton, *Fragments*; Girouard, *English Country Houses*, 181–212.
[79] Vickery, *Behind Closed Doors*, 147. The quote comes from Elizabeth Montagu during a visit to an overcrowded Bulstrode in 1740.
[80] Vickery, *Behind Closed Doors*, 150; Girouard, *English Country House*, 209.
[81] SCLA, DR18/4/43, Inventory, 1774, with 1806 amendments.

comfortable, but perhaps lacked character. Of more interest in this respect are Lord Leigh's rooms, where a similar set of furniture was supplemented by a japanned dressing glass, serpentine commode, writing table with inkstand, and two family pictures. The very English styles of furniture seen elsewhere were thus joined by a small number of eastern objects, but the real distinction came in terms of the richness of the drapery, for which Burnett charged a total of £205 9s. 4½d.[82] This sum differentiated Lord Leigh's from the other bedchambers and put it on a par with the refurbished breakfast room and dining parlour. In economic terms, then, this room was an important space, receiving investment worthy of the front stage.[83] It was a display of refined taste and comfort, but perhaps also a place of private entertainment: there were ten mahogany chairs in the bedroom and a spinet in the dressing room. Much the same was true of the Wrought Room, just along the corridor, where a pianoforte was installed in the dressing room by Mary Leigh.[84]

Dressing rooms were not the only places into which people could retreat from the formality of the principal rooms. Common parlours were a feature of many country houses and often formed the main living space occupied by the family, especially when they were not entertaining visitors. Lacking the intimate privacy of dressing rooms, Cornforth sees these as central to the running of many houses, being places to eat, sit as a family, and conduct the business of the house.[85] We have already encountered two such rooms on our tour of Stoneleigh Abbey. Situated behind the principal rooms and either side of the main staircase, these were quite literally back stage. In 1737, the combined value of their furniture was just £30 1s. 6d. The Common Dining Parlour was particularly plain in its furnishings (the large oak table, twelve walnut chairs, and small sideboard suggest everyday dining) whilst the Further Back Parlour was a little more elegant (more walnut chairs, an easy chair, baize-covered card table, and a large glass sconce in a gilt frame). These low values and generally plain furniture put them firmly in the private space, back stage of Andersson's typology.[86] Their subsequent status is unclear. Thomas, fourth Lord Leigh, appears to have favoured them as family rooms, hanging twenty-four prints of horses (a passion of his) in what was then called the Common Dining Parlour; yet they were all but stripped after his death, the Dowager Lady Leigh carrying many of their contents to Guy's Cliffe in 1749.[87]

Descent from the centre to the margin of family life was not unusual for such rooms and accords with Cassandra Austen brushing past them in her tour of the house; but they remained sufficiently important to be furnished with several paintings and family portraits throughout the eighteenth century. In contrast, the Common Parlour together with the Withdrawing Room at Canons Ashby suffered a decline in status. The latter was the focus of considerable attention from Edward Dryden, who had the walls painted in *trompe l'œil* panelling and installed an

---

[82] SCLA, DR18/3/47/52/15.
[83] See Andersson, 'Mirror of oneself'; Barnett, 'In with the new', 86–7.
[84] SCLA, DR18/4/43, Inventory, 1774, with 1806 amendments; DR18/4/59, Inventory, 1806.
[85] Cornforth, *Early Georgian Interiors*, 38–40.
[86] SCLA, DR18/4/9 Inventory, 1738; Andersson, 'Mirror of oneself'.
[87] SCLA, DR18/4/27, Inventory, November 1749

impressive set of needlework chairs, bought *en suite* with a sofa and fire screen from Thomas Phill, upholsterer to George I, in 1711.[88] These furnishings remained largely in place through to the succeeding generations, but were supplemented by a bed some time before 1756. From then, the rooms appear increasingly peripheral to the social life of the house, which centred in the Great or Dining Parlour and the upstairs Drawing Room and New White Room, installed by Edward's son Sir John Dryden. It might be possible, then, to see common parlours moving from front to back stage as the spotlight shifted to other domestic spaces.

Two things emerge from this discussion that challenge the usefulness of front- and back-stage distinctions. One is the problematic nature of Goffman's notion of performance—the idea that there is a preconceived self that can be projected to receptive audiences. The impact of identity on elite consumption and the material culture of the country house is explored in more detail in Chapters 4 and 5, but it is important to note here that many of the performances that took place in the country house were about constructing identity as much as projecting it through staged enactments of self. This relates to Butler's argument that 'identities are in some sense constructed in and through social action', that is, through behaviours which are repeated and habitual rather than strategic and knowing.[89] From this perspective, the ways in which owners used dressing rooms and common parlours were just as much performances, and were just as important in the construction of self, as their more obviously 'staged' behaviour in state apartments and drawing rooms. The spaces and the company were more intimate, but the relationship between identity, performance, and stage remained the same. Thus, when Lady Sherburne or Mary Leigh sat in the comfort of their dressing rooms, enjoying the companionship of close friends, they were acting out and constructing their identity just as they were when they entertained company in the drawing room or guided visitors around rooms of parade. Moreover, the rooms themselves can be seen as a product of these performative practices as much as a preconceived stage: they were lived spaces, created by habitual behaviour, as well as preconceived spaces of power and display—an idea discussed in greater detail in Chapter 3. This links to the other difficulty with Goffman's model, and indeed any binary distinction of domestic space: many rooms served a variety of different functions and contained an eclectic assortment of goods, so that public and private, formal and family, front and back stage, are all relative terms.

OBJECTS OF DESIRE? ASSEMBLAGES AND LOCATIONS

Rather than impose a typology of rooms onto the country house, it might be more useful to distinguish rooms, and thus better understand their different roles or relative importance, by mapping the distribution and clustering of key goods.

[88] NRO, D(CA)129, Bill from Thomas Phill, 30 April 1716; D(CA)902, Inventory, 1756.
[89] J. Butler, *Gender Trouble: Feminism and the Subversion of Identity* (London, 2000), 25. See also Gregson and Rose, 'Performativities', 434 and Glennie and Thrift, 'Consumers, identities and consumption spaces', 39–40.

Naturally, such an exercise depends on which objects are defined as 'key' and on reading properly the meanings of any assemblages. The latter links both to understanding how sets of goods came together through polite practices and performances, perhaps creating the kind of eclectic assemblage found in Lady Irwin's dressing room; how they might be seen as conforming in Diderot's harmonious unity; and how they might reflect notions of cosmopolitanism—transnational material cultures drawing together Britain, Europe, and Empire.[90] Tracing the location of goods described as 'Indian' forms a useful starting point, as these give a clear indication of broader geographical horizons, in terms of both supply and, more arguably, direct cultural associations. However, a fuller picture of elite *habitus* is gained by extending the analysis to encompass a broader range of goods: family portraits (as indicators of lineage), other paintings and decorative china (new systems of taste), musical instruments and games (sociability), and old luxuries, such as tapestries, marble tables, and gilt furniture (patina or aristocratic consumption).[91] This is a complex exercise, involving tracing goods across space and time, but one that has the potential to uncover the varied and overlapping distributions of these different aspects of aristocratic consumption.

Mapping the distribution of these types of goods in Stoneleigh Abbey reveals both their presence in a large number of rooms and a clear trend for them to become more widely spread across the house: they were found in fourteen rooms in 1738, rising to twenty-two in 1749, twenty-six in 1786, and twenty-nine in 1806 (Table 2.1). This dispersal meant that no single set of rooms was distinguished as a setting for these objects, although the Breakfast Room and Dining Parlour, and bedchambers and dressing rooms stand out in terms of the range and quantity of key goods they contained.

Barczewski argues that, even country houses without a direct link to the imperial project abound with the 'physical representations of empire'.[92] This might be true in the very broadest sense—there is no shortage of mahogany furniture, chintz fabrics, and chinaware at Stoneleigh Abbey—but more direct allusions to Empire, in terms of goods specifically identified as 'Indian', were comparatively rare. Naturally, the Leighs shared a taste for chinoiserie, seen in the 'Indian' cabinets, screens, prints, and porcelain figures listed in the inventories. In this, they reflected a pan-European fashion, although their adoption of the style is rather more muted than is seen at Saltram, Blickling Hall, and Nostell Priory, for example, or in the Chinese Pavilion at Drottningholm Castle in Sweden.[93] As in these places, overtly

---

[90] Smith, 'In her hands'; Lewis, 'When a house', 353–4; McCracken, *Culture and Consumption*, 118–21; Clemente, 'Luxury and taste in eighteenth-century Naples'; Barczewski, *Country Houses and the British Empire*, 180–8.

[91] Many other goods could be assessed in this way, including books, silks, and scientific instruments. Silverware would also usefully be traced, but is often listed separately on inventories rather than *in situ*.

[92] Barczewski, *Country Houses and the British Empire*, 137.

[93] For discussion of the taste for chinoiserie in Britain, see de Bruijn, 'Consuming east Asia'; O. Impey, 'Eastern trade and the furnishing of the British country house', in G. Jackson-Stops, G. J. Schochet, L. C. Orlin, and E. B. MacDougall (eds) *The Fashioning and Functioning of British Country Houses* (New Haven, CT, 1989), 177–92; Cornforth, *Early Georgian Interiors*, 253–64;

Table 2.1. The distribution of key object types across different rooms, Stoneleigh Abbey

	Picture Gallery & Print Room	Great Apartment	Breakfast/ Dining Room	Common Parlours	Bed & Dressing Rooms	Servants' Rooms	Other
	rooms/ items	rooms/ items	rooms/ items	rooms/ items	rooms/ items	rooms/ items	rooms/ items
Indian							
1738		2/2	1/1	1/1	2/2		
1749		2/2	1/2		3/3		
1786		1/1			3/21		
1806		1/1			3/22		
Portraits							
1738	1/7						1/8
1749	1/19						
1786	1/24	3/7	1/17	2/6	2/3	1/1	
1806	1/24	2/8	1/15	1/6	1/1		
Pictures							
1738	1/26		1/2		1/2		3/22
1749	1/61			2/25	1/4		1/27
1786	1/60		1/26	2/19	2/24	8/14	2/13
1806	1/271		1/36	2/26	2/24	5/6	2/13
China							
1738		2					
1749		2	1		1		
1786		1			5		
1806		2			6		1
Music & games							
1738	1/1						
1749	1/1						
1786	1/1		1/5	1/1			
1806	1/2		1/5	1/1	2/2		
Old luxuries							
1738	1/1	1/10	1/1	1/1	4/9		5/9
1749	1/1	3/15	1/1	1/1	10/16	2/2	1/1
1786	1/1	2/9			4/8		1/1
1806		2/12		2/2	9/11		1/1

Source: SCLA, DR18/4/9, Inventory, 1738; DR18/4/27, Inventory, November 1749; DR18/4/69, Inventory, 1786; DR18/4/59, Inventory, 1806.

'Indian' (Chinese) goods at Stoneleigh Abbey were concentrated into a relatively small number of rooms, most notably the Great Apartment and a few bedchambers and dressing rooms. This clustering, repeated on a much larger scale in the concentration of Indian goods belonging to Sir Lawrence Dundas into just one of his many properties, Kerse House, is significant because it implies only limited

D. Porter, *The Chinese Taste in Eighteenth-Century England* (Cambridge, 2010). On the Chinese Pavilion at Drottningholm, see G. Alm and M. Plunger (eds), *Kina Slott* (Stockholm, 2002).

blending of oriental and Western styles.[94] Such hybridization is central to Barczewski's argument that Empire had a profound impact on all country houses and to broader notions of transnational or imperial identities constructed through material culture.[95] Without denying the importance of these links, it appears at Stoneleigh Abbey that they were spatially contained. Conversely, this meant that these rooms had a discernably different identity. In the Green Damask Room, fitted out for Mary Leigh in the 1760s, there was an India cabinet and seventeen India prints, along with bamboo chairs, a fan glass in a japan frame, seven japan boxes and two large pieces of china. Two further bedchambers, the Wrought and Yellow Damask rooms, were hung with 'Indian' wallpapers, one patterned with birds and flowers and with a chinoiserie ceiling to match; both also contained quantities of Chinese porcelain.[96]

Teasing out the significance and meaning of these decorative schemes is extremely difficult, especially in the absence of family correspondence. Their meanings, after all, are complex and layered. Chinoiserie is sometimes seen as carrying political meanings in the 1730s and 1740s: a critique of the venality of Walpole's administration and a symbol of arguments for active imperialism.[97] The associations were no longer current when the politically disengaged fifth Lord Leigh chose these Chinese decors and there is little to suggest a conscious allusion to Empire. Most likely, they were primarily expressions of taste, aligning the Leighs with fashionable decorative schemes in which the novelty and vitality, and perhaps the cultural illegibility, of the designs were the principal attractions.[98] This makes the location of these goods particularly significant: bedchambers and dressing rooms were important repositories for demonstrations of taste. Moreover, Chinese and especially Japanese porcelain was highly prized both for its aesthetic qualities and as part of collections that reflected the knowledge, discernment, and 'reach' of the owner.[99] Arranged on chimney pieces, shelves, tables, and tea trays, china is a common element of many pictorial representations of bedchambers, although the number of pieces is generally quite modest. The quantity of decorative pieces in the Wrought and Yellow Damask Rooms at Stoneleigh made it much more than an incidental part of the decor and function of the rooms. In the former there was an assortment of thirty-seven pieces of blue-and-white delftware, white embossed

[94] H. Clifford, "'Conquests from North to South': the Dundas property empire. New wealth, constructing status and the role of "India" goods in the British country house', in J. Stobart and A. Hann (eds) *The Country House*, 123–33.

[95] See Barczewski, *Country Houses and the British Empire*, esp. 180–96.

[96] These wallpapers are not itemized in the inventories, but appear in the bill presented by Bromwich and Leigh in 1765: SCLA, DR18/5/4402. Gomme refers to the ceiling of the 'Chinese Room' on the first floor: Gomme, 'Abbey into palace', 113. The porcelain is listed in SCLA, DR18/4/69 1786 inventory. As noted earlier, these 'Indian' goods were prominent amongst the things moved from this room to Lord Leigh's Dressing Room sometime after 1786.

[97] Barczewski, *Country Houses and the British Empire*, 183; S. McDowall, 'Shugborough: seat of the Earl of Lichfield', *East India Company at Home* (April 2013), <http://blogs.ucl.ac.uk/eicah/shugborough-hall-staffordshire/>.

[98] McDowall, 'Shugborough', 10–11; E. Kennedy Johnson, 'The taste for bringing the outside in: nationalism, gender and landscape wallpaper (1700–1825)', in J. Batchelor and C. Kaplan (eds), *Women and Material Culture, 1660–1830* (Basingstoke, 2007), 119–33.

[99] Ferguson, 'Japan China'; McCracken, *Culture and Consumption*, 113;

china, coloured cups, and glassware; in the latter, the assemblage was slightly more practical, the forty pieces of delftware including a coffee pot, cups, and saucers together with chocolate cups, both with and without handles.[100]

These assemblages are important for two reasons. First, the grouping of these items on the inventory suggests a similar clustering in the room itself, an arrangement that would make practical sense in terms of coffee and tea sets, but which also heightened their visual impact.[101] As an assemblage, rather than individual pieces, they had a much greater impact on the identity and meaning of these rooms. Second, not all of these decorative ceramics were oriental in origin. The presence of delftware links the assemblages at Stoneleigh Abbey to an older tradition of owning and displaying majolica that was widespread in early-modern Europe, and yet it also hints at a blending of European and Chinese styles.[102] The inventories are not sufficiently detailed to know the precise character of the delftware, but Dutch manufacturers had been active in producing copies of Chinese styles and in developing their own 'Chinese' ware from the second quarter of the seventeenth century. In this, they paralleled the activities of furniture makers such as Thomas Chippendale, who created designs for Chinese-style furniture, and British and French wallpaper manufacturers, who made cheaper copies of Chinese wallpapers.

These bedchambers and dressing rooms formed important expressions of the fashion for chinoiserie. Fashionable taste was also apparent in the clustering of goods in the main rooms for entertaining, the Breakfast Room and Dining Parlour, but here it took a rather different form. These rooms contained a large number of pictures which, as Cornforth, Retford, and others have argued, were critical in giving character to domestic space.[103] There were a significant number of family portraits, but it was a series of landscapes that made these rooms stand out. At one level, it was the subject matter that counted, Italianate landscapes in particular communicating a link to classicism and the Grand Tour.[104] On another, these were significant pieces, attributed to important artists including Canaletto, Gainsborough, Zoffany, Teniers, Wouwerman, and Cuyp, and costing between £26 5s. and £108 3s. apiece.[105] They added much to the status of these rooms as demonstrations of the owners' appreciation of art and their discernment in collecting work by gifted and sought-after artists—the latter playing a significant part, Lewis argues, in Lady

---

[100] SCLA, DR18/4/69, Inventory, 1786.

[101] See H. Greig, 'Eighteenth-century English interiors in image and text', in J. Aynsley, C. Grant, and H. McKay (eds), *Imagined Interiors: Representing the Domestic Interior Since the Renaissance* (London, 2006), 102–27.

[102] See the various contributions to J. Veeckman (ed.), *Majolica and Glass from Italy to Antwerp and Beyond. The Transfer of Technology in the 16th–early 17th century* (Antwerp, 2003). On the blending of European and Chinese styles, see McDowell, 'Shugborough', 14; Kennedy Johnson, 'Bringing the outside in', 124.

[103] Retford, *Art of Domestic Life*; Cornforth, *Early Georgian Interiors*, 237–50; Haskell, 'British as collectors'; Christie, *British Country House*, 199–215.

[104] J. Hayes, 'British patrons and landscape painting', *Apollo*, 185 (1991), 254–60; Christie, *British Country House*, 199–203.

[105] SCLA, DR18/17/32/186, List of pictures bought at auction, 1788.

Borringdon's rehanging of a set of Reynolds portraits in the library at Saltram.[106] As such, these collections linked Stoneleigh Abbey into Europe-wide cultures of art appreciation and collecting. But paintings also helped to make these rooms lively and interesting spaces in which to entertain guests, a function which was underpinned by their predominance as spaces for informal sociability: there were tables for cards and backgammon, and first an organ, then later a grand piano, offering opportunities to display female virtues and delicate white hands.[107] Just as important, perhaps, was the virtual absence of gilded furniture, heavy panelling, and other 'old luxuries'. Many of the pictures were in gilt frames, but dating from the 1760s; there was no walnut, there were no tapestries, and there was just one pair of white girandoles.[108]

As noted earlier, the Picture Gallery may have offered an alternative place to sit in company, but it is most prominent as a setting for paintings. It was here that the third and fourth Lords hung their family portraits, albeit alongside a growing number of other pictures, including portraits of royalty, landscapes, and even some old prints. Despite this mixture of genres, the Picture Gallery was a key part in Stoneleigh Abbey's ecology of signs, communicating pedigree and family connections through its presentation of a 'pictorial family tree'.[109] Yet its significance in this regard seems to have waned in the later eighteenth century as first Edward, fifth Lord Leigh, and then Mary hung family portraits in the Breakfast Room, common parlours, Great Apartment, and even some bedchambers. The significance of rooms was thus by no means fixed: it changed along with the contents, some meanings and functions being divested and others accrued.

This mutability has already been noted in the case of common parlours, which form perhaps the most surprising rooms in which key goods were concentrated. They did not dominate any particular category, but contained significant numbers of paintings and portraits, musical instruments and games, and even old luxuries. Given the apparent character and function of these rooms as informal family spaces, did the pictures hung there have different meanings and roles? One possibility is that these pictures gave pleasure, making the rooms pleasant and stimulating places in which to be. Lady Dryden's Breakfast Closet and Sitting Room at Canons Ashby had this feel: in addition to tasteful pieces of japanned, mahogany, and rosewood furniture, there were thirty-two paintings, prints, and drawings. This might be read as a cosmopolitan blending of Empire and England, with exotic hardwoods placed alongside British paintings,[110] but traded commodities and taste in furniture cannot be simply read off as indicators of Empire; these rooms are better interpreted as comfortable, personal, and tasteful spaces that drew on colonial supplies and made reference to the wider imperial world. The large number of family portraits hung in the common parlours at Stoneleigh Abbey might also suggest a desire to be surrounded by reminders of family, making the house feel more like

---

[106] Lewis, 'When a house', 361. [107] See Smith, 'In her hands'.
[108] SCLA, DR18/4/43, Inventory, 1774, with 1806 amendments.
[109] SCLA, DR18/4/9, Inventory, 1738; Retford, 'Patrilineal portraiture'; Retford, *Art of Domestic Life*, chapter 5; Lewis, 'When a house', 361.
[110] Barczewski, *Country Houses and the British Empire*, 164–7.

a home. However, unlike Lady Borringdon, who had recently moved into her husband's house at Saltram, the Leighs had no need to feel out of place in their ancestral home.[111] They may instead have been seeking to communicate the same messages of lineage and dignity in a more everyday manner and to different groups of visitors: the tenants and tradesmen who might be invited into the common parlour, but who would never have gained access to rooms of parade.

In stark contrast with this is the Great Apartment, the contents and meaning of which were highly stable throughout the eighteenth century and beyond. It contained the highest concentration of old luxuries of the kind that marked aristocratic consumption, the decorative stability drawing on the patina of the objects in the room. However, the nature of these inherited objects was just as important as their age and pedigree: gilded chairs, tables, and mirror frames were prevalent, whilst tapestries were increasingly relegated to bedchambers and even garrets as early as the 1740s (see Table 2.1).[112] Tapestries could, of course, be a major feature of state bedrooms, as at Boughton House, where the walls are still hung with a set depicting the Acts of the Apostles to designs by Raphael. However, in the major refurbishment of Stoneleigh undertaken in the 1760s, a memorandum notes that tapestries should be removed from many bedchambers and wallpapers hung instead.[113] This same process was seen at Canons Ashby, where, as early as 1717, they were found only on the first floor and mostly away from the principal rooms of the house. By 1819 none at all were listed. Whether they had gone or were simply not thought worthy of note, their relegation is significant, tapestries no longer being seen as useful as displays of status.[114]

As is apparent by now, it was not simply the presence of specific objects that could shape the meaning and identity of rooms within the country house, but also their grouping together into particular assemblages that created a particular aspect of elite *habitus*. We have already seen the impact of different assemblages on the main family and state rooms, especially at Stoneleigh Abbey, but it is worth exploring this relationship in a little more detail through a small number of examples. The Print Room at Stoneleigh Abbey was an innovation introduced by Mary Leigh in the closing decades of the eighteenth century. Its description by Cassandra Austen as a 'gallery fitted with modern prints on a buff paper' suggests a fairly typical arrangement, with most of the 214 prints it contained being pasted in the walls.[115] Such an arrangement was, as Arnold remarks, 'by no means a cheap solution to interior decoration': in addition to the cost of the prints themselves, there was considerable effort expended, usually on the part of women, to create tasteful

[111] Lewis, 'When a house', 356–62.

[112] Table 2.1 underplays these concentrations. Several sets of the walnut chairs were listed in the rooms in successive inventories, but it is not always stated whether they were gilded so they are omitted from the analysis.

[113] Dalkeith et al., *Boughton. The English Versailles* (Derby, 2006), 38–9; SCLA, DR18/3/47/52/7, Memorandum 13 April 1763.

[114] See Stobart, 'Inventories and Canons Ashby'.

[115] Austen-Leigh, Austen-Leigh, and le Faye, *Jane Austen*, 140; SCLA, DR18/4/59, Inventory, 1806.

and pleasing combinations.[116] At Castletown, it was Lady Louisa Connolly who created the famous Print Room around 1768, mixing a collection of images by old masters with contemporary prints of Garrick. A generation later at the Vyne, the Print Room was created in 1804 out of the Little Parlour when Caroline Workman collaborated with her brothers to display on the walls many prints that 'had always been kept in a large portfolio in the gallery'. Perhaps slightly later, a similar room was created at Calke Abbey, although here the emphasis was on caricatures, including those by Rowlandson, Gillray, and Cruikshank.[117] Its use by the family as a private drawing room points to print rooms being spaces for sitting in company rather than simply inspecting the pictures. Mary's was certainly well appointed in this respect: there was a large sofa, three satinwood writing tables, five chairs, and six japanned stools.[118] The assemblage of prints and furniture combined to make this a fashionable, stimulating, and comfortable room; it forms a clear, but rare, example of her (female) taste being imprinted onto the fabric of the house.[119]

A rather different collection was housed in the New White Room at Canons Ashby, which was fitted out by Sir John Dryden sometime before 1756. At that date, its furniture comprised a white damask bed and matching window curtains; eight walnut chairs, the seats of which were upholstered to match the bed; and a dressing table, looking glass, and Indian chimney board. It was decorated with two china candlesticks and five china jars, all arranged along the chimney piece.[120] In this, it resembled many other bedchambers, but it subsequently became the chief setting in the house for decorative china. By 1770, the original white bed furniture and window curtains had been replaced by others in needlework, whilst the collection of ceramics had mushroomed to over fifty pieces, including a red-and-white bowl, two jugs, four bottles, eighteen flower pots in various sizes, ten 'small pieces of decorative china', and a candlestick. Although nothing compared with the collection of Betty Germain, this was a significant assemblage in a house of this size. Moreover, the fact that several items were listed as damaged, including a 'large china jar, cracked' and a 'broken china coffee pot', suggests that chinaware did not have to be in pristine condition to be valued either for its continued utility or more likely its aesthetic or sentimental qualities.[121] From being a small element in a tasteful and coordinated decorative scheme, the set of china had grown to define the room, the assemblage moving beyond what was simply tasteful into something resembling a collection.

[116] D. Arnold, 'Defining femininity: women and the country house', in D. Arnold (ed.), *The Georgian Country House: Architecture, landscape and society* (Stroud, 1998), 93, 95.

[117] Arnold, 'Defining femininity', 93; M. Howard, *The Vyne* (Swindon, 1998), 16; O. Garrett, *Calke Abbey* (London, 2000), 9.

[118] SCLA, DR18/4/59, Inventory, 1806.

[119] On the gendering of space in the eighteenth-century home, see K. Sharp, 'Women's creativity and display in the eighteenth-century British domestic interior', in S. McKellar and P. Sparke (eds), *Interior Design and Identity* (Manchester, 2004); Cornforth, *Early Georgian Interiors*, 203–9; Kennedy Johnson, 'Bringing the outside in'; K. Harvey, 'Men making home: masculinity and domesticity in eighteenth-century England', *Gender and History* 21/3 (2009), 520–41; Vickery, *Behind Closed Doors*, 207–30. See also Chapter 5.

[120] NRO, D(CA)902, Inventory, 1756.

[121] NRO, D(CA)201, Inventory, 1770; Pennell, 'For a crack or flaw despis'd'.

A bedchamber with a very different character was created at Stoneleigh Abbey for Edward, fifth Lord Leigh. The dominant decorative motif was formed by the chintz fabric used for the window curtains and bed furniture, a design picked up in the 'painted paper' supplied to match.[122] Chintzes were, in origin, Indian textiles, but such printed textiles were still prohibited at this time, so the actual provenance and character of the cloth remains uncertain. The hangings were lined with green lustring and trimmed with green silk lace and 'cut fringe', which both added richness to the furnishings and domesticated the orientalism of the chintz in a way that was seen a generation earlier at Houghton.[123] At the same time, the furniture itself was high-quality, but relatively plain: a wainscot bedstead with mahogany posts, a serpentine commode dressing table, a set of mahogany back stools, and so on. All these pieces were supplied new, along with the hangings and papers, but the wallpaper merchant, Thomas Bromwich, also charged for 'additional leather to make out the silver hanging, 12 skins', suggesting the repair of an older gilt leather wall hanging which existed alongside all these novel and fashionable goods.[124] The combination of old and new, and of old-fashioned and novel, is particularly striking in a room so thoroughly and expensively refurnished by Lord Leigh, but was quite common in country houses, linking to particular aristocratic modes of consumption.

Fifty years earlier, Edward Dryden was also interested in combining old and new objects. Entering the house today, the visitor is struck by the collection of armour, guns, swords, heraldic images, and large embroidery of William III's arms in the Great Hall. The room is redolent of a long and glorious past, but it was constructed in this way by Edward Dryden at some point after 1708. The inventory of that year lists nothing more than two long tables and four forms—a layout which suggests its use as a communal dining hall. Edward transformed it into a pseudo-medieval great hall, anticipating later developments at Warwick Castle, Strawberry Hill, and numerous French chateaux in the early nineteenth century.[125] His precise motivations are unknown and seem a little at odds with the manner in which he swept away the Jacobean fabric and furnishings in many rooms. A taste for the historical is apparent, but Edward was probably trying to proclaim the long lineage of the Dryden family, a message repeated in the heraldic devices placed across the interior and exterior of the house. The success of this room is apparent from its largely unchanging character over the following century and is dependent upon on assemblage rather than any single object.

CONCLUSION

Viewing the country house as an expression of the taste and identity of the landowning elite has tended to encourage a unified and normative view of its material culture. Variation is recognized, of course, but is often discussed in terms of adherence

---

[122] SCLA, DR18/5/4402.
[123] Cornforth, *Early Georgian Interiors*, 259.   [124] SCLA, DR18/5/4402.
[125] Cornforth, *Early Georgian Interiors*, 219; Girouard, *French Country House*, 296, 300–1. See also C. Wainwright, *The Romantic Interior. The British Collector at Home, 1750–1850* (New Haven, 1989).

to or departures from standard types or a cosmopolitan eclecticism that itself forms a trope of elite taste.[126] Our analysis here has questioned the overweening influence of fashionable taste, arguing that this was tempered by other influences, including a powerful strand of conservatism and an emphasis on other aspects of elite culture, notably rank and lineage. Even where there is a coherent and consistent vision of design, as at Arbury Hall, this could involve a blending of styles, cultural references, and material forms. This blending linked different times as well as different places: past and present as well as Britain and Empire. Indeed, it is far from clear that Empire or the broader colonial world formed a conscious point of reference at Stoneleigh Abbey. There were many objects whose origin might be traced to the workshops of India and China or the plantations and forests of the Caribbean and Central America; but this did not, of itself, make them emblematic of Empire. Their meanings were complex and multilayered, and they can equally be viewed as expressions of more self-contained elite European taste.

If the country house was indeed the material manifestation of elite cultural capital—that is, elite *habitus*—then its expression was variegated, contingent, and sometimes internally contradictory, symbols of lineage sometimes jarring with statements of fashionable taste. These complexities are, to some extent, both facilitated by and expressed through a series of different spaces within the country house. Distinctions between state and family rooms are familiar enough, their diverse functions and meanings being reflected in sometimes sharply contrasting designs and contents. State rooms were obvious stages for the performance of rank and status, but the distinction between public and private, front and back stage, was never sharply or simply defined. Nor is the performance metaphor straightforward. At one level, there is the question of multiple selves, performances, and audiences. The Great Hall at Canons Ashby, for example, was the setting for performances of self as the wealthy and powerful landowner, the man of taste, the learned antiquary, or the successor in a long line of descent.[127] At another, there is the issue of whether self and space are seen as preconceived and consciously constructed, or the product of the routines of everyday practices—ideas discussed more fully in Chapter 3 in the context of lived space.

Tracing the assemblages of goods found in these different spaces in terms of the location and grouping of key goods underlines the dynamism and mutability of the country house. State rooms were relatively stable in their contents and meanings, but others changed profoundly; clusters of key goods shifted over time and focused attention onto sometimes surprising places. If state rooms and drawing rooms stand out, then dressing rooms and common parlours were also important hot spots. Moreover, whilst these groupings sometimes formed the kind of conformity described by Diderot—most notably in the Breakfast Room and Yellow Damask and Wrought bedrooms at Stoneleigh Abbey—there was often an eclectic mixture of provenance, period, and style. Such variation reflected the easy way in

---

[126] See, for example, Arnold, 'The country house', 1–19; Barczewski, *Country Houses and the British Empire*, 181.

[127] A similar process can be seen at Audley End in the 1820s and 1830s—Chavasse, 'Material culture and the country house', 170–220.

which goods from across the world were incorporated into elite material culture, but also the extent to which their owners were content to renew or retain existing items. Rather than view the country house as a single unifying *habitus*, then, our argument leads us to suggest something less coherent and constant: a collaging of interrelated spaces and objects that reflect the complex and multifaceted nature of elite identities. Different rooms were shaped by different aspects of these identities and, in turn, served to mould and project that identity in material form. Importantly, the multiple spaces of the country house accommodated both the conscious construction of space and identity, and its emergence through everyday practice.

3

Practicalities, Utility, and the Everydayness of Consumption

INTRODUCTION

The country house was not just a product of grand designs and elegant furnishing schemes. It also comprised the routine activities of everyday life and the consumption of mundane goods that supported these practices and the fabric of the house itself. Food was bought, stored, cooked, and eaten; rooms were illuminated and heated; floors were scrubbed and textiles were laundered; windows were mended, woodwork painted, and furniture reupholstered. All the while, country house owners went about their daily lives: reading, sewing, studying, socializing with friends and family, writing letters, managing the servants, and so on. All of these activities were important in an intensely practical sense, not least because of the money and time that they absorbed.[1] But the everyday was also significant in conceptual terms: how we understand the processes through which the country house was produced, and how these related to the needs and wants of the owners, both physical and emotional. In this context, there is growing interest in the ways in which small items and modest changes to the fabric of the building were important in easing everyday life, improving aesthetics, and making the house a place in which people felt at home. Vickery highlights the work of Lady Ailesbury in decorating her house in Fulham, where she ordered an 'additional door to ye young ladies dressing room next ye library' which was intended 'to make ye side of ye room more level'; she also notes the role of women's handiwork in personalizing domestic interiors. Lewis goes a stage further, arguing that such personal goods were central in rendering houses into homes, a process in which women played a central role both in Britain and elsewhere.[2] Many of these goods were decorative rather than practical, but the utility of new goods was important to many consumers. As Berg notes, 'they were frequently ascribed with values of usefulness, civility and ingenuity'—a sentiment

---

[1] Williams, 'Noble household'; Whittle and Griffiths, *Consumption and Gender*, 26–48, 86–116; Vickery, *Gentleman's Daughter*, 127–60; Greig, *Beau Monde*, 42–3.

[2] Vickery, *Behind Closed Doors*, 158, 233–56; Lewis, 'When a house'; M. Finn, 'Colonial gifts: family politics and the exchange of goods in British India, *c.*1780–1820', *Modern Asian Studies*, 40 (2006), 203–31.

that links closely to Scitovsky's division of utility into the search for comfort and the search for pleasure.[3]

Recognizing that goods could be both useful and meaningful is central to understanding the material culture of the country house as a marrying of conceived and lived space, the former planned out by the architect and an expression of power and the latter produced by the routines and behaviours of everyday life.[4] Focusing on the idea of lived space has allowed historians, especially those concerned with the role of women in shaping the domestic environment, to take a rather different view of the country house and its contents, and to think about the ways in which it functioned as a home as well as a showcase of status and power.[5] It has also concentrated attention on the ways in which material objects were valued and deployed within the country house: their ability to make life more convenient and comfortable, and to carry meanings both for house owners and society more generally. The Regency country house was, according to Cornforth and Robinson, a site of 'unprecedented comfort', marked by new technology and a growing emphasis on furniture, especially chairs, being comfortable.[6] In making this assertion, they build on Repton's 1803 observation that 'the present era furnishes more examples of attention to comfort and convenience than are to be found in the plans of Palladio, Vitruvius or Le Nôtre, who, in the display of useless symmetry, often forget the requisites of habitation'.[7] This was the physical ease that Crowley asserts came to dominate understandings of comfort in the later eighteenth century. The provision of such comfort might thus be seen as increasingly central to the *habitus* of the country house: it shaped the choice of furniture, heightened the desire for effective lighting and heating, and underscored demand for food and drink, especially when these were consumed in social settings.[8] Yet this focus on physical comfort needs to be matched with concern for emotional comfort. Jane Austen made frequent use of the word in her novels and correspondence, nearly always referring to emotions and expectations rather than physical attributes. And, as historians such as Lewis have demonstrated, these emotions were central to the everyday consumption practices of many female residents and owners.[9] This refocuses attention away from the (technologically) new and onto older goods that

[3] M. Berg, 'New commodities, luxuries and their consumers in eighteenth-century England', in M. Berg and H. Clifford (eds) *Consumers and Luxury: Consumer Culture in Europe, 1650–1850* (Manchester, 1999), 69; Scitovsky, *Joyless Economy;* de Vries, *Industrious Revolution,* 21–4.

[4] See Lefebvre, *Production of Space;* E. Soja, *Thirdspace* (Oxford, 1996).

[5] Girouard, *English Country House,* was a pioneer of this approach, which has more recently been adopted by historians of women and the country house. See, for example, Vickery, *Behind Closed Doors;* Lewis, 'When a house'; Arnold, 'Defining femininity'; H. Greig, 'Eighteenth-century English interiors in image and text', in J. Aynsley, C. Grant, and H. McKay (eds), *Imagined Interiors: Representing the Domestic Interior Since the Renaissance* (London, 2006), 102–27, and the various contributions to R. Larsen (ed.) *Maids and Mistresses: Celebrating Three Hundred Years of Women and the Yorkshire Country House* (Castle Howard, 2004).

[6] Robinson, *Regency Country House,* 11–12; J. Cornforth, *English Interiors 1790–1848: The Quest for Comfort* (London, 1978). See also Cornforth, *Early Georgian Interiors,* 209–12.

[7] Quoted in Crowley, 'From luxury to comfort', 137.

[8] Crowley, *Invention of Comfort,* esp. 142–9.

[9] Phillipps, *Jane Austen's English,* 74–5; Page, *Language of Jane Austen,* 30, 38–9; Lewis, 'When a house'. See also Chavasse, 'Material culture and the country house'.

held particular significance in symbolizing home, lifestyle, and identity—a shift in emphasis which also fits neatly with a growing awareness of the desire of Anglo-Indian elites to link their lives in England and India through material objects as well as conceptualizations of 'home'.[10]

Here, we build on these ideas to explore three related themes. We begin by assessing the nature of spending on everyday goods and activities, including food and drink, cleaning, and repairs. Of particular interest is the extent to which spending was planned and routine, or responsive to needs as they arose. As such, our analysis links into broader discussions of household management and oeconomy, but it also leads into a consideration of the ways in which 'mundane' spaces (particularly kitchens, storerooms, and servants' rooms) were equipped and furnished: was utility as practicality always the key driver? Next, we broaden the perspective on utility by considering ideas of pleasure and particularly comfort. Here, we take Crowley's analysis as a point of departure, exploring the ways in which ideas of physical comfort were important in shaping consumption and the material culture of the house; but we also emphasize the importance of emotional comfort—of feeling at home—and its link to the country house as lived space. Finally, we consider the particular position of old goods in these processes. How were they viewed and deployed, especially in relation to new goods, and what motivations underpinned their persistent presence in the country house? Overall, we argue that to fully understand consumption and materiality in the country house, we need to engage with the everyday practices and lived spaces which underpinned its social and spatial construction.

HOUSEHOLD MANAGEMENT: SUPPLIES AND STORES

Proper management was central to the sound oeconomy of all households. Amongst the middling sort, such tasks were generally the responsibility of the wife, who would keep separate accounts, sometimes in printed account books which provided a template for good practice in terms of a detailed matrix of daily spending in a range of standard categories.[11] These books reflect long-established practices amongst the gentry, where again it was the wife who was often responsible for managing the household, generally under the watchful eye of her husband.[12] In elite households, it was more usual for such management to be delegated to stewards or their equivalent, but the broad accounting systems remained the same. This is apparent from the structure and detail of Sir Roger Newdigate's account books, which differentiated spending on the household from that on the person,

[10] See, for example: K. Smith, 'Warfield Park: longing, belonging and the country house', *East India Company at Home* (April 2013), <http://blogs.ucl.ac.uk/eicah/warfield-park-berkshire/>; Finn, 'Swallowfield Park'.

[11] For example: *The Housekeeper's Accompt-Book* (Bath, 1797). See Vickery, *Behind Closed Doors*, 108–9; Harvey, *Little Republic*, 77–81.

[12] Vickery, *Behind Closed Doors*, 111–26. Alice Le Strange had much greater autonomy in terms of household management and her areas of responsibility extended rather further. See Whittle and Griffiths, *Consumption and Gender*, 28–36.

Table 3.1. Average annual spending on selected categories of goods at Arbury Hall, 1750–94

	1750–4		1760–4		1770–4		1780–4		1790–4	
	£	%	£	%	£	%	£	%	£	%
Meat & Fish	62.5	19.5	48.8	13.1	62.1	12.5	69.5	11.3	173.5	25.0
Fuel	38.2	11.9	51.5	13.9	89.1	18.0	23.8	3.9	8.1	1.2
Groceries (inc. candles & oil)	112.1	35.0	117.3	31.6	166.2	33.6	221.8	36.2	297.2	42.8
Furniture & household	57.3	17.9	107.5	29.0	143.4	29.0	237.3	38.7	158.2	22.8
Wines & Spirits	50.4	15.7	46.2	12.4	34.1	6.9	60.9	9.9	57.3	8.3
Total	320.5		371.3		494.9		613.3	694.3		

Source: WRO, CR136/V156, Account book; CR136/V136, Account book.

Notes: Fuel includes coal for Spring Gardens, London; consumables and durables are defined in the text.

cellars, stables, gardens, and so on.[13] For the 'House', there were entries for meat (oxen, sheep and lambs, calves, and hogs either delivered by the farm or the butcher), poultry and dovecote, fish, fuel (coals and charcoal), and wheat; 'Tradesmen Bills' from suppliers of consumables (the oilman, grocer, chandler (tallow and wax), saltman, soapman, confectioner, and, and by the 1760s, the tea warehouse); and a further set of tradesmen supplying durable goods (the upholsterer, cabinetmakers, china and glassman, brazier, locksmith, silversmith, copper, clockmaker, turner, dyer and 'scowrer', and linen draper). The Cellar accounts included sections for wines (including port, mountain, Florence Madeira, and claret), spirits (brandy and gin), cider, and verjuice.[14]

The balance of spending between these different categories is revealing of the character of routine and periodic expenditure, and how these shifted over time, although trends were by no means straightforward (Table 3.1). Apart from the steady rise in overall spending, what is most striking is the persistent importance of consumables, which accounted for over one-third of the spending examined here. This chiefly comprised edible groceries, but candles accounted for £20–£30 per annum in the 1750s, rising to £70–£90 in the 1780s, a figure which matches closely the £85 spent on lighting at Audley End in the period 1763–97.[15] Spending on furniture and household goods was more variable, rising overall but fluctuating in accordance with the amount of building work and refurbishment under way at Arbury Hall. It peaked in the 1780s, when work on the cloisters and Saloon was under way: during this time, Gillows presented bills totalling £177 11s., but there were also substantial payments to a brazier called Steane and to Dewsbury, a china merchant.[16] Fuel rose as an area of expenditure into the 1770s, but thereafter declined to insignificant levels, largely because Newdigate was increasingly able to service his needs from his own mines, but also because he rarely used his London

---

[13] WRO, CR136/V156, CR136/V136.

[14] This structure resembles that of the Audley End accounts analysed by Williams, 'Noble household'.

[15] Williams, 'Noble household', 69, 78.   [16] Tyack, *Warwickshire Country Houses*, 14.

house after he retired as an MP in 1780, thus alleviating the need for coal to be purchased in the capital. The reasons for the jump in spending on meat and fish is not so readily explained, as the account books become less detailed in the 1790s, but the relative decline in spending on wine may reflect a decrease in social entertaining in later years.

Despite the careful recording of expenditure, Newdigate's account books lack detail on exactly what was being purchased from these various suppliers. A clearer picture of this can be gained from the bills presented to the Leighs, which reveal purchases of a wide range of groceries and other consumables, from lump sugar to lobsters. Fresh foods were often acquired by the housekeeper and thus appear in the accounts presented to her employers (see Chapter 6). In addition, eggs and butter were bought in to supplement production from the home farm and the dairy—a practice seen in many country houses—whilst the park and garden were vital to the provision of game and fresh vegetables and fruit.[17] The former held symbolic importance: it signalled landowning status and facilitated the kind of dining imagined in the bills of fare published in cookery books, which often included a range of game dishes.[18] More prosaically, it was a regular supply of meat for the table. Something of the volume of game and garden produce generated at Stoneleigh can be seen from the supplies sent to Grove House whilst Mary Leigh was resident there. In 1794, for example, the consignments included 43 rabbits and hares, 59 wildfowl, and 14 deer from the park; and 585 cucumbers, 66 peaches, 45 melons, 29 lettuces, and 22 boxes of French beans from the garden.[19]

Shopkeepers' bills also indicate that the Leighs generally purchased their groceries through a combination of large periodic orders and small regular transactions. Thomas Ballard's bill of 13 June 1789 comprised 36 pounds of tea, 10 pounds of coffee, and 6 pounds of chocolate, and reflected the bulk buying of groceries that would be consumed over the following weeks and months. In contrast, William Leaper's bill of 17 December in the same year incorporated 46 transactions spread over the previous 14 months, the largest of which was £1 8s. for 56 pounds of moist sugar.[20] Combining these and the other grocers patronized by Mary Leigh during this period, it is apparent that she bought groceries once or twice a week: staples such as coarse sugar, dried fruit, peas, and soap were purchased with greater frequency than were more exotic or luxury goods; but, as is clear from Ballard's bill, the latter were sometimes acquired in large batches. This indicates that at least some of these purchases were carefully planned, reflecting the rhythms of consumption

---

[17] Whittle and Griffiths, *Consumption and Gender*, 72–84; L. Bailey, 'Squire, shopkeeper and staple food: the reciprocal relationship between the country house and the village shop in the late Georgian period', *History of Retailing and Consumption*, 1 (2015), 8–28.

[18] See G. Lehmann, *The British Housewife: Cookery Books, Cooking and Society in 18th Century Britain* (Totnes, 1999); S. Pennell, 'Material culture of food in early-modern England, *c.*1650–*c.*1750' (unpublished DPhil thesis, University of Oxford, 1997).

[19] SCLA, DR18/31/655, Account of Sundries from Stoneleigh Abbey, 1793–8. Melons in particular represent a link to the exotic and reflected considerable investment in terms of manpower and infrastructure in the kitchen garden.

[20] SCLA, DR18/5/5851, DR18/5/5866.

and the stocks held in storerooms and larders. This link is made explicit in the accounts kept in the 1750s by the Leighs' cousins at Adlestrop in Gloucestershire.[21] These comprise an opening balance for each type of grocery, a note of any purchases made (arranged by month), a total for goods consumed, and a closing balance for each six-month period. Comparing the timing and size of purchases with the amount of each commodity 'in store' between April 1757 and March 1759 indicates that good supplies of some essential items were always maintained, whilst stocks of others were allowed to dwindle before being replenished. Thus, purchases were made to ensure that a minimum of 92 pounds of candles was held in store, whereas the closing balance for both moist and coarse or brown sugar was zero in three of the four accounting periods, as it was for best and common raisins. It is possible that other types of sugar or fruit might have been substituted when supplies ran out, but there was clearly a policy of buying these goods periodically rather than as needed. In contrast, tea and coffee were bought quarterly to ensure fresh supplies, although this sometimes led to overstocking if purchases ran ahead of consumption, as happened in the winter of 1757–8, when a balance of 4½ pounds of coffee was accumulated against a half-yearly consumption of only 1½ pounds.

A similar management of stores can be seen at Arbury Hall. A notebook, presumably kept by the butler, notes the names of visitors in 1798, the duration of their stay, and whether they dined.[22] It also records the quantity of port, Lisbon, and mountain wine consumed each month, together with opening and closing balances, and any new additions made to the cellar. These indicate that purchases were generally reactive, wines being bought in response to the amount consumed and the stocks remaining. In January, a closing balance of three bottles of port, none of Lisbon and one of mountain prompted the purchase of twenty-four, eighteen, and six bottles respectively on 1 February, whilst a closing balance of seventeen, seventeen, and five bottles meant that no further wines were acquired in March. This pattern was maintained throughout the year, with the butler apparently content to let stocks fall to very low levels before buying more wine. In May, this seems to have caused something of a problem: consumption was a little greater than usual and an additional eight, four, and two bottles were bought on 21 May, plus a further eighteen, eighteen, and two bottles on 1 June. In general, however, the balance of purchases and consumption was maintained with only a relatively small stock being held at a time. This required careful planning and a good relationship with a wine merchant who could supply the necessary stock at short notice. This may have encouraged the kind of 'chummy' relationship described by Vickery, but the evidence here suggests that it was his butler, rather than Newdigate himself, who was dealing with the supplier.[23]

---

[21] SCLA, 18/31/548, Account of stores expended every half year, Adlestrop, 1757–61. On the rhythms of purchasing groceries, see Stobart, *Sugar and Spice*, 199–203; Bailey, 'Squire, shopkeeper and staple food'.

[22] WRO, CR136/A47, Visitors at Arbury, 1798.

[23] Vickery, *Behind Closed Doors*, 114. See also L. Bailey, 'Consumption and Status: Shopping for Clothes in a Nineteenth-Century Bedfordshire Gentry Household', *Midland History*, 36, 1 (2011), 89–114.

MUNDANE SPACES: BELOW STAIRS

The balancing of stores and purchases required careful management and revealed a sound household oeconomy—as Harvey argues for the middling sorts.[24] Yet having a well-run household also meant investment in the infrastructure and equipment for storing and preparing these consumables, and the equipage for serving them at table.[25] At Canons Ashby, the Drydens had a large kitchen and larder, a bakehouse, washhouse, brewhouse, laundry, and dairy, arranged in sequence along the ground floor on the north and east ranges of the house. There was also an ale cellar, a butler's pantry, a housekeeper's room, and a 'cupboard upon the stairs'.[26] In 1791, the kitchen contained many items for preparing and cooking food, and for storing plates and cutlery; but no range is listed, suggesting that all the meals were cooked on the open fire or in the bread oven.[27] Opening off the kitchen, the larder was clearly used for storing and preparing wet food, as there were weights and scales, pickling pans, dripping pots, and tallow tubs. As quite often happened, the housekeeper's room doubled up as a still room and storeroom: a coffee mill and pots for tea, coffee, and chocolate sat alongside galley pots, 'petti-pans' and pickling pots, and china basins and sauce boats. The butler's pantry served as a storeroom for a wide range of tableware, including glasses, punchbowls, candlesticks and snuffers, carving and oyster knives, glass and earthenware decanters, and trays; but the 'stand to brush clothes' indicates that it was also used for cleaning outer garments. More tableware was stored in 'a cupboard upon the stairs': mostly white stoneware, including dishes, platters, and soup plates. The mixture of goods found in each of these rooms reflected their functional nature: they were lived spaces, created through the everyday and routine activities carried out by the Drydens' servants.

The modest size of Canons Ashby led to an overlapping of functions that was less apparent in larger houses where the use of space was more specialized. Indeed, much thought was put into the spatial organization of the service rooms of the country house, with numerous variations being tried around the basic pattern of either a central spinal corridor or a kitchen pavilion.[28] At Stoneleigh Abbey, the 1806 inventory enumerates a total of twenty-one rooms for preparing food and storing goods relating to their consumption, the contents of which reflect the ideals being outlined in advice manuals.[29] The exact spatial arrangement of these rooms is unclear, but the order in which they appear in the inventory suggests their

---

[24] Harvey, *Little Republic*, 33–43. See also Whittle and Griffiths, *Consumption and Gender*, 72–84; Greig, 'Eighteenth-century English Interiors'.

[25] For discussion of the changing character of the kitchen and service areas, see: P. Sambrook and P. Brears (eds), *The Country House Kitchen, 1650–1900* (Stroud, 1996); Weatherill, *Consumer Behaviour*, 145–51; S. Pennell, *Making the British kitchen, c.1600–1850* (forthcoming).

[26] NRO, D(CA)903, Inventory 1791.   [27] Pennell, *Making the British kitchen.*

[28] P. Brears, 'Behind the green baize door', in Sambrook and Brears (eds), *Country House Kitchen*, 30–76; S. Paston-Williams, *The Art of Dining. A History of Cooking and Eating* (Oxford, 1993), 224–5.

[29] See P. Brears, 'The Ideal Kitchen in 1864', in Sambrook and Brears (eds), *Country House Kitchen*, 11–29.

sequencing on the ground. We commence at the kitchen, which housed a range and a fireplace complete with spit racks, smoking and clockwork jacks, hanging irons, a pair of steelyards, and a 'large meat screen lined with tin'. These arrangements were probably put in place during the refurbishment of the house in the 1760s and show a kitchen in line with the latest developments, as does the cast-iron oven listed later in the inventory. Together, these allowed for controlled roasting of meat, the preparation of sauces, the baking of pastries, and so on.[30] The kitchen also contained, amongst other things two large kitchen tables, two cupboards, and a square deal table; chopping blocks, carving knives, toasting forks, a salamander, gridirons, and a cheese toaster; numerous copper pans, pudding moulds, baking dishes, and pattys; and a salt box, sugar dredger, and '14 spice tins in draws'. Timing and control over the use of this *batterie de cuisine* was asserted by a 'dial clock in a wainscot case'. The kitchen might thus be viewed as a carefully planned and controlled space of power; but it was also produced by routine activities and even afforded the possibility for at least a few moments of relaxation and sociability, as there was an oak 'pillow and claw table' with four chairs. The next-door scullery, where wet food was prepared and dishes washed, was unequivocally a working space: it had a large and small copper, lead and copper cisterns, a dish rack, several basins, and dozens of trenchers. After passing through the cook's and man cook's rooms, we arrive at the larder. This was a similar model of carefully appointed efficiency, with a wire safe, shelves, and a dresser for storing dry foods; so too was the neighbouring wet larder, where the presence of '2 large salting weights, 1 smaller D° for hams' indicates that it also doubled up as a salting room—preserving meat being an essential practice in all houses.[31]

Following the inventory, we move out of the realm of the cook and into that of the butler, and then the housekeeper. As at Canons Ashby, the butler's pantry contained an array of equipment for storing and caring for tableware. Central to the room's purpose and functioning were two tables on which glasses, decanters, and plates could be laid before being sent upstairs. There were also three glass and china cupboards, a dresser with seven drawers, and a japanned plate warmer (revealingly bracketed with a bath stove on the inventory); mahogany trays for carrying food and drink to the table and two 'foul plate tubs' for returning them below stairs; decanters and glasses; and cork drawers, cucumber slicers, and plate brushes. The organization of the inventory suggests that much of the china and the large quantity of silver plate (discussed in Chapter 1) were stored in 'China Closets' and a secure 'Plate Room' elsewhere in the house; they were brought from there to the butler's pantry immediately prior to being used and returned there afterwards.

Via the 'boot room and lamp hole' we next arrive at the pastry, a room sometimes under the control of a specialist pastry chef, but here more obviously linked

---

[30] SCLA, DR18/17/27/97, Letter to William Craven, 11 February 1764; Paston-Williams, *Art of Dining*, 228. See also P. Brears, 'Kitchen fireplaces and stoves', in P. Sambrook and P. Brears (eds), *Country House Kitchen*, 92–105; Pennell, *Making the British kitchen*.

[31] P. Sambrook, 'Larder and other storeplaces for the kitchen', in Sambrook and Brears (eds), *Country House Kitchen*, 184–6.

to the cook or perhaps the housekeeper, whose own room was apparently next door. Its traditional function is apparent from the flour tubs, sugar and spice boxes, rolling pins, bread graters, and four boxes of pastry cutters listed in the inventory; but it also contained large quantities of pewter dishes and plates, suggesting that it served as a storeroom as well. Moreover, the baking tins, moulds, and baking dishes that might be expected were instead located in the still room—an arrangement which reflects the increasing overlap in function of the two rooms.[32] At Stoneleigh Abbey, the still room appears to have retained its original purpose as a place for distilling; the 'large copper still and 3 small lead D°' are the first items enumerated in the room, although whether they were still being used is hard to tell. However, the room had also taken on its more modern functions as a location for preserving fruit, making confectionery, preparing tea and coffee, and even cooking light meals. There were brass and copper preserving pans, and glass and stone jars; scales and weights, cake tins, baking sheets, jelly moulds, and sugar nippers; and a coffee mill, chocolate and coffee pots, two japanned tea urns, tea trays, and fifteen tea canisters. This set of goods and functions closely resembles that seen at Attingham in the 1820s, and it is likely that the division of labour was similar: the still-room maid being responsible for baking and perhaps preserving, whilst the housekeeper took charge of tea—her own room containing two mahogany tea chests. This layering of functions and material culture into a single room made a great deal of sense in terms of the day-to-day operation of the house. In part this resulted from their changing function over time, but it also reflected the ways in which activities spread across a number of rooms. In this sense, they were lived spaces, created by the routines of everyday life: the labour of numerous servants working to fulfil the ongoing demand for food and drink, but also the myriad items of kitchen- and tableware, furniture, and linen that this was built upon.

The housekeeper would also have been responsible for the linen, purchased in large quantities by Edward, fifth Lord Leigh, and listed separately on the inventory. Tablecloths and napkins came in different grades (damask, diaper, huckaback, and homespun) and there were distinctions made between old and new, and between those for the dining room and servants' hall. In addition, there were supper and breakfast cloths, sideboard cloths, 'layovers', and table covers. Different cloths were also listed as glass, decanter, china, plate, tea, knife, parlour knife, folding, dresser, basket, oyster, and butcher's; towels were made from huckaback, fine diaper, and bird's-eye pattern, and sheets from fine Irish, Holland, Russia, and Yorkshire cloth, or were simply flaxen; there were also pillow cases, and old and new cotton nightcaps. This quantity, variety, and specialist purpose was by no means unusual, but made managing the household linen a complex task, especially given its symbolic as well as practical importance.[33]

---

[32] Paston-Williams, *Art of Dining*, 233–4; C. A. Wilson, 'Stillhouses and stillrooms', in Sambrook and Brears (eds), *Country House Kitchen*, 140–2; P. Brears, 'The pastry', in Sambrook and Brears (eds), *Country House Kitchen*, 144–50; Pennell, *Making the British kitchen*.

[33] See Mitchell, 'Fine Table Linen', 22–3, 213–15; MacArthur, 'Material culture and consumption', 196–9. The symbolism of linen is discussed in Chapter 1.

Laundering was central to effective public displays of status through table linen and to ideas of cleanliness as a virtue that betokened respectability.[34] Soap was, therefore, an important commodity in the country house. At Arbury Hall, the soapman's bill amounted to £6 12s. per annum through the early 1750s, rising to £12 3s. by 1770—a figure which matched closely the £12 per annum spent at Audley End and one that easily exceeded the £9 per annum that Newdigate paid his laundry maid.[35] In terms of infrastructure, the laundry at Stoneleigh Abbey contained the usual range, ironing stove, ironing tables, and flat irons, as well as a mangle, laundry baskets, and clothes horses; in the neighbouring wash house were two coppers and five brass kettles, a variety of washing and rinsing tubs, buckets and bowls, a drying horse, chest, and soap box. The work carried out in these spaces was central to the functioning of the house both as a family home and a projection of status, a significance which underscores the importance of the spending in these seemingly mundane areas.

Other household textiles required rather different forms of cleaning, often undertaken by specialists. Newdigate's accounts include several payments under the heading 'dyer and scowrer', including those in October 1747 to Edward Eyre, 15s. 6d. for cleaning a chintz bed, and to S. Taylor, £1 15s. for cleaning some green worsted hangings.[36] Fifty years later, Mary Leigh was paying the upholsterers Bradshaw and Smith for cleaning a set of blinds at Grove House and another upholsterer, Michael Thackthwaite, for 'cleaning 30 yds of green tammy' at a cost of 4d. per yard.[37] This cleaning took place as part of the broader maintenance of both Grove House and Stoneleigh Abbey. Amongst other things, Bradshaw and Smith charged for: repairing a spring barrel from a set of curtains; 'ripping silk covering from elbows of 6 Cabrick chairs & covering with green Tabaray after japanning', and 'ripping brown linen from your chymny board & new covering with linen dyed on purpose'.[38] Quite apart from the dramatic and visceral descriptions, the last of these is of particular interest, as it suggests the provision of cloth to match an existing scheme, thus renewing yet retaining the decor of the room. At Stoneleigh, Daniel Frost was engaged in the 1780s in altering carpets, restuffing mahogany chairs, silvering mirrors, and mending frames, whilst Mary Leigh's cousins at Adlestrop were paying Thomas Hunt for altering a set of dining tables and two Pembroke tables, and mending a tea chest.[39]

Such repairs and alterations extended the life of furniture and were essential in the maintenance of soft furnishings in particular. They parallel the behaviour of Sir John Griffin Griffin at Audley End, whose bills include numerous payments for repairs to furniture and reflect the importance of the regular business of repair and maintenance to many upholstery and mercery businesses, both in Britain and

[34] Smith, *Consumption and the Making of Respectability*, 60–1, 130–8; Lemire, 'An education in comfort'; Vickery, *Gentleman's Daughter*, 149–51.

[35] WRO, CR136/V/156, Account book, *passim*; CR136/V/136, Account book, *passim*; Williams, 'Noble household', 69.

[36] WRO, CR136/V/156, Account book, entry for 1747.

[37] SCLA, DR18/5/5980, DR18/5/5703.

[38] SCLA, DR18/5/6023.   [39] SCLA, DR18/5/5822, DR18/5/5960.

elsewhere.[40] A similar regime of repair and maintenance was necessary for the upkeep of a wide range of other objects. Newdigate's accounts record regular payments for repairs to clocks, coaches, saddlery, and even portraits, and practically every tinsmith or brazier billing the Leighs included the cost of repairing pots and pans. John Walker was fairly typical; his bill from 1799 includes several new items such as a brass skillet and three tin candlesticks, but mostly comprises charges for repairs (an iron pot, an oil can, a copper in the brewhouse, and a tea urn) and for retinning a total of sixty-nine pieces, from egg spoons to frying pans to gravy pots.[41] At £13 13s. 11d., the total cost was relatively modest, but this still represented an important area of spending, one that was essential to the continued functioning of the kitchen and thus the sustenance of the household.

By far the largest area of spending in this regard was aimed at maintaining the fabric of the building. It is not always easy to tease out spending on repairs from that on new work or alterations: the Newdigate accounts collapse the two into a single category, and bills from tradesmen often comprised both alterations and maintenance. Nonetheless, it is clear that the level of spending could easily run into hundreds of pounds, as is apparent from the 1789 bill from the house painter, Richard Bevan, which itemized work carried out on thirty-two rooms and passages at Stoneleigh Abbey.[42] This appears to have been the first time that these rooms had been painted since 1765 and thus represented a major refreshing of the interior, although there is little indication that colours were changed from those painted by George Downs twenty-five years earlier. In this sense, then, Bevan was undertaking routine maintenance, not least in terms of painting the exterior window frames. He also charged a total of £99 3s. for japanning or gilding of a total of sixty-one picture frames, and for cleaning and repairing an unspecified number of pictures. This formed a significant outlay on maintaining the decorative status quo.

Taken together, cleaning, repairs, and maintenance had an important impact on both domestic space and the domestic economy.[43] The sums involved were large, often on a par with those expended on consumables such as groceries and candles, and they formed a significant element of year-on-year spending in the country house. This work did not transform interior spaces, but rather maintained them in their current state or made subtle changes in terms of colour or texture. Yet it was vital work, both in assuring the physical integrity of the building and creating a comfortable and presentable living environment. The dangers inherent in letting things slip were all too apparent from a note made by Elizabeth Dryden about a set of prints placed in the storeroom for safekeeping: 'from some wet coming thro' the roof, before the compleat repair of it, they are I am sorry to observe somewhat damaged'.[44] Maintenance of the fabric of the house was aligned with maintenance

---

[40] Chavasse, 'Material culture and the country house', 57–60; M. Ponsonby, *Stories from Home. English Domestic Interiors, 1750–1850* (Aldershot, 2007), 80–3; C. Sargentson, *Merchants and Luxury Markets: The Marchands Merciers of Eighteenth-Century Paris* (London, 1996), 32–3.

[41] SCLA, DR18/5/6487.   [42] SCLA, DR18/5/4395.

[43] See Vickery, *Gentleman's Daughter*, 147–9.

[44] NRO, D(CA)903b, Letter, 13 January 1817.

of status because, as Vickery puts it, 'the neatness and order of the house and furniture was a quintessential feature of genteel economy'.[45] However, it was more than defensive consumption and went beyond the respectability of cleanliness to encompass ideas of comfort, patina, and lineage.

COMFORT AND CONVENIENCE

Food and drink are basic human needs, but they also offer comfort in terms of pleasure and sociability.[46] Much has been made of the physiological effects of tea, coffee, and chocolate as stimulants, and of tobacco as a narcotic; they offered new physical and mental sensations to the early-modern consumer, tobacco in particular affording comfort through its calming qualities. Caffeine drinks were also an important vehicle for the consumption of sugar, another commodity that was moving from luxury to decency, and which offered comfort.[47] As noted earlier, in Chapter 1, with the exception of tobacco, these were all goods on which the Leighs and Newdigates spent large amounts of money, as they did on the equipage necessary for their preparation and consumption.[48] In common with many young elite men at the time, Edward, third Lord Leigh, was purchasing tea, coffee, and chocolate, and an array of pots, cups, and saucers, from the start of his days at Oxford University in the early years of the eighteenth century.[49] A clearer picture of the scale and range of necessary chinaware comes from the 1774 inventory at Stoneleigh Abbey, which lists a total of 173 pieces in 6 different sets of cups and saucers (Table 3.2). The Leighs thus had choice about which service to use and could serve tea, coffee, and chocolate to substantial numbers of guests. Importantly, the largest set, in blue and white, also included four large and sixteen small plates in the same pattern, allowing cake or bread and butter to be offered with tea—as Elizabeth Shackleton did for ex-servants, the mothers of tenants and servants, visiting tradesmen, and, of course, her social equals.[50] Furthermore, the Leighs' new and old dinner services, which comprised 152 and 153 pieces respectively, were also blue and white, suggesting the coordination of chinaware between dinner and tea, and the kind of material conformity described by Diderot.[51]

Eating and drinking thus provided opportunities for displays of wealth and discernment, the cultural capital of imported porcelain helping to fix country house dining into transnational frameworks of taste and global systems of supply. In this,

---

[45] Vickery, *Gentleman's Daughter*, 147.

[46] See the discussion of Robinson Crusoe in Crowley, *Invention of Comfort*, 154–7.

[47] W. Schivelbusch, *Tastes of Paradise. A Social History of Spices, Stimulants and Intoxicants* (New York, 1993), esp. 103, 131–2; Cowan, *Social Life of Coffee*, 16–17, 31–40; Smith, *Consumption and the Making of Respectability*, 83–4, 121–4; Stobart, *Sugar and Spice*, 33–9; Crowley, *Invention of Comfort*, 155–7.

[48] The only record of tobacco in the Leigh bills was for workers on the estate.

[49] SCLA, DR18/29/6 Box 1, Pocketbook of Edward, 3rd Lord Leigh, 1702; Stobart, *Sugar and Spice*, 218. Sir John Dryden also made substantial purchases of coffee and chocolate whilst at Oxford in 1721: NRO, D(CA)311, Sir John Dryden's expenses at Oxford, 1719–23.

[50] Vickery, *Gentleman's Daughter*, 208.

[51] See McCracken, *Culture and Consumption*, 123–4.

Table 3.2. Stoneleigh Abbey chinaware for tea, coffee, and chocolate, 1774

	Cups & saucers	Tea cups & saucers	Coffee cups & saucers	Choc. cups & saucers	Sugar pots	Tea pots	Cake dishes/ cream jugs	Basins/ trays	Total
Blue & gold	12				2		4	3	21
Purple & gold	9		3		2	1	3	2	20
White & gold			6			1			7
Blue & white	4	29	30	12	2		3	11	91
White			6	11					17
Scallop-edge	6	8				1		2	17
Total	31	37	45	23	6	3	10	18	173

Source: SCLA, DR18/4/43, 1774 inventory with 1806 amendments.

English elites shared a common experience with their counterparts in the American colonies and elsewhere in Europe.[52] Added to this were the conviviality of shared meals and the physical pleasure derived from the commodities being consumed. Comfort was derived from the meal and the setting, the latter incorporating both the chinaware on which food was served and the wider ambience of the room. Crowley places great emphasis on the luxury of artificial lighting in the early-modern home, both in Britain and America, arguing that the public use of candles—initially at the theatre, but increasingly at pleasure gardens, balls, and coffee houses—spread into the home.[53] Lighting became a mark of respectability, not least as the array of candlesticks, girandoles, and sconces made it more versatile and effective; yet it remained an expensive undertaking, and elaborate lighting was a distinction of elite *habitus*. Sitting at leisure into the dark of the evening was a key sign of the landowner's wealth and lifestyle, and features over and again in Jane Austen's novels.

Candles varied hugely in the quality of light they produced and the smell they generated. Tallow candles were the most widely used in England, but they were frowned on in the best circles, Lady Strafford noting with scorn their use in the St James's Street house of Mr Marshall. He should, of course, have had wax candles, the burning qualities and cost of which acted as a specific symbol of wealth and taste.[54] Bills presented to the Leighs show that they were paying 2s. 10d. apiece for wax candles—a price that held steady through the second half of the eighteenth century.[55] Tallow candles were much cheaper, varying between 7½d. and 10½d. apiece in the 1790s—a difference which may reflect quality as well as size, the cheaper candles coming from a chandler who also collected grease from the kitchen, allowing £3 6s. against a bill of £11 13s.[56] Whatever their drawbacks,

[52] See Barczewski, *Country Houses and the British Empire*, 173–7; Smith, *Consumption and the Making of Respectability*, 171–88; Clemente, 'Luxury and taste in eighteenth-century Naples'.
[53] Crowley, *Invention of Comfort*, 112–15, 130–1.   [54] Greig, *Beau Monde*, 42.
[55] The price was the same from wax chandlers (e.g. SCLA, DR18/5/4619) and from grocers (DR18/5/5849).
[56] SCLA, DR18/5/5991. This reflects an increase over the course of the eighteenth century; in 1738, tallow candles cost 5d. apiece—DR18/5/2188.

then, tallow candles made sound economic sense in a well-managed household and they were used far more than wax: the Newdigate accounts, which contain separate entries for the tallow and wax candles, suggest a ratio of between 10:1 and 20:1. There is also an indication, made explicit in some of the Leigh bills, that rushlights were also being used; despite Crowley's suggestion that they were 'unacceptable in households with any pretension to refinement', they clearly had their place, presumably in the servants' quarters.[57]

The impact of candlelight was heightened through the use of girandoles and sconces, both of which appear in all the principal rooms and many of the bedrooms at Stoneleigh Abbey. These not only amplified the amount of light produced, but added considerable lustre to the room: the 'large glass sconce in a gilt frame' in the drawing room, for instance, was valued at £12 in 1738.[58] Changing technology was also embraced in an attempt to further enhance lighting: both the Leighs and Newdigates were buying lamp oil from the 1750s, and Mary was dealing with Argand & Co towards the end of the century, although she appears to have moved cautiously, ordering a single lamp in 1790.[59] Comfort thus came through the provision of light and the luxury of the fittings—a point brought home by the extraordinary spending of Mary's successor, James Henry Leigh, who laid out a total of £383 in 1813 on 'one handsome 16 light cylindrical sweep lustre', twelve matching lights, and a '4 light Grecian lamp, cut in diamonds'.[60] This reflected a desire for social as much as physical comfort; leisure activities and socializing could extend into the evening, clothing and fittings being chosen to make the most of the shimmering candlelight.[61] One particularly dramatic example of this is a suit of clothing made for Sir John Turner Dryden, the dark crimson velvet being stitched with a series of hanging glass crystals that would have moved with the wearer, catching and shimmering in the light.

The other great physical comfort emphasized by Crowley was heat, which he discusses largely in terms of technological developments.[62] This was certainly an important consideration for Count Axel von Fersen when building his new house at Ljung in Sweden where stoves were installed in all rooms. There were ornate blue-and-white tiled stoves, designed by the architect and supplied by Stockholm craftsmen, for the public rooms and plainer green stoves for the servants' rooms. These were more efficient than open fires in heating the house—a necessity in such a cold climate, but a comfort also seen in French houses especially in the *salle à manger*.[63] Similar concerns preoccupied successive owners of Audley End: Sir John

[57] WRO, CR136/V/136, Account book, *passim*; SCLA, DR18/5/5887; Crowley, *Invention of Comfort*, 113.

[58] SCLA, DR18/4/9, Inventory, 1738. See also Greig, *Beau Monde*, 44.

[59] SCLA, DR18/5/5899.   [60] SCLA, DR18/5/6992.

[61] Berg, *Luxury and Pleasure*, 37; Crowley, *Invention of Comfort*, 130–2.

[62] Crowley, *Invention of Comfort*, 171–90. See also Girouard, *English Country House*, 263–5; J. M. Robinson, *James Wyatt (1746–1813): Architect to George III* (New Haven, CT, 2012), 219, 238; Girouard, *French Country House*, 219–40.

[63] J. Ilmakunnas, 'To build according to one's status: a country house in late 18th-century Sweden', in J. Stobart and A. Hann (eds) *The Country House: Material Culture and Consumption* (Swindon, 2015), 38; Girouard, *French Country House*, 144–5.

Griffin Griffin and Richard Neville. However, whilst the former addressed the need in a similar manner to von Fersen, through the installation of register stoves in the principal rooms and bath stoves elsewhere, the latter expressed it through his correspondence, which frequently commented on *feeling* warm and comfortable.[64] As Chavasse notes, this distinction appears to reflect the different mentalities of the owners, something which is difficult to ascertain with the Leighs given the paucity of correspondence. Nonetheless, it is apparent that they too had a practical concern with the warmth and comfort of their rooms. The 1774 inventory lists stove grates in each of the principal rooms, sometimes ornamented with fretwork; that in the Brown Parlour had the distinction of a compass stove. The precise nature of these is difficult to assess, although the 'moveable stoves' in the drawing room and New Rooms were probably register stoves which had the advantage of an iron plate in the flue that regulated the updraught and thus the intensity with which the fire burned.[65] Rather more basic were the bath stoves found in almost every bedchamber by 1774: a comprehensive distribution that reflects a shift from the 1749 inventory, when around half are listed as containing grates, and an indication of the growing concern for warmth. Yet this is as far as the Leighs went with heating technology; enclosed stoves, favoured in North America and northern Europe, and championed in England by Abraham Buzaglo, were never tried at Stoneleigh Abbey.[66] Newdigate was a little more adventurous: in addition to a variety of fireplace stoves, he ordered a free-standing stove from the Patent Stove Warehouse in Holborn. Although his primary concern here appears to have been aesthetic rather than practical, his diary occasionally hints at a desire for domestic warmth and comfort, as when he noted that he had 'breakfasted, dined and supped in the hall, the warmest room in the house'.[67]

Fires and stoves, of course, required fuel, some of which came from the estate in the form of wood, often burned as faggots in the kitchen or in the tiled stoves used at Ljung.[68] Newdigate bought small amounts of charcoal, but most of the fuel he purchased was coal, on which he spent increasing sums through the third quarter of the eighteenth century (Table 3.1). Spending diminished sharply when production at his own collieries increased in the 1780s, but there is little suggestion that domestic consumption went down, and Mary Leigh was certainly buying coal in considerable quantities around this time, both for Stoneleigh Abbey and Grove House.[69] Although coal was an efficient form of fuel, its use appears to contradict Lady Strafford's haughty condemnation of the practice. That said, there were distinctions to be drawn between different types of coal which appear to link with the chemical content. Thus, Mary wrote with instructions for her servants in London

[64] Chavasse, 'Material culture and the country house', 123–69.

[65] The descriptions differ somewhat from those in the 1749 inventory, which generally refers to grates rather than stoves, but it is unclear whether this reflected new technology or a shift in language. See C. Gilbert and A. Wells-Cole, *The Fashionable Fireplace, 1660–1840* (Leeds, 1985), 22.

[66] Gilbert and Wells-Cole, *Fashionable Fireplace*, 62, 66.

[67] WRO, CR136/A/582, Diaries, 29 December 1773. The purchase of this stove is discussed in more detail in Chapter 7.

[68] Paston-Williams, *Art of Dining*, 233; Ilmakunnas, 'To build according to one's status', 38.

[69] Tyack, 'Country house building in Warwickshire', 204, 214; Stobart, 'So agreeable a place'.

to 'burn up all the Scotch Coal that is now in the House...as fast as they can be wanted, for I certainly will not use any myself'.[70] Again, the physical comfort of heat combined with the social comfort of displaying good taste.

Much the same was true of the growing array of upholstered furniture that characterized country houses through the eighteenth century. Crowley argues that 'the primary purpose of furniture was to express genteel taste' and thus promote social comfort; the key goods of the consumer revolution, he suggests, had 'crucial functions in sociability'.[71] In this sense, elite *habitus* was a construction of taste deployed for others rather than self. However, this emphasis on social comfort seriously underplays the growing physical comfort of furniture and furnishings during this period—as Cornforth argues.[72] The huge sums spent by Edward, fifth Lord Leigh, on upholstered furniture (discussed in Chapter 1) can thus be seen as an attempt to make his house comfortable in both a social and physical sense. Indeed, since much of the spending was on bedroom furniture, the emphasis was perhaps more on a desire to create the kind of convenient domestic environment lauded by Richard Neville at Audley End.[73] The chests of drawers, dressing tables, shaving stands, clothes presses, and pot cupboards supplied by Gomm were clearly intended to make life easier and more convenient for Lord Leigh's guests, whilst the coordinated colour schemes and rich drapery provided by Burnett displayed wealth and taste. More practical, yet still resonant of refined sensibilities, were the bed and bolster supplied for each room.[74] These cost between £5 3s. for a small 'fine' one filled with 'good goose feathers' and £12 16s. for one described as 'superfine large bordered' and filled with 'the best sweet goose feathers'. The distinctions and cost are both significant, marking gradations of comfort according to the quality of the room and thus of its potential occupant; it is telling that the most expensive (albeit only by a small margin) was in Lord Leigh's own bedroom. Moreover, this investment in comfort was not one-off: Mary Leigh paid Bradshaw and Smith for 'ripping your feather bed & bolster from footmans room, taking out all the old feathers driving part of yours & filling with 40lb best seasons feathers in addition', a job repeated on at least one other occasion.[75]

Comfort in the bedroom thus comprised convenient furniture and a soft and well-stuffed mattress, plus the provision of good-quality sheets and quilts, and, increasingly, bedside carpets. Richard Neville spent significant sums on carpets at Audley End and noted in 1814 that his daughter's new room was 'carpeted & comforted'—a telling pairing of words and actions.[76] At Canons Ashby, carpets were a feature of the better bedrooms from the 1770s, but do not seem to have spread much beyond these even by 1819; they appear, therefore, to have marked a particular distinction in comfort in what was a fairly modest country house. At

[70] SCLA, DR18/17/31/11, Letter, 24 October 1804.
[71] Crowley, *Invention of Comfort*, 146, 148.   [72] Cornforth, *English Interiors*.
[73] Chavasse, 'Material culture and the country house', 130–48.
[74] SCLA, DR18/3/47/52/15, Bill from Thomas Burnett, 1765.
[75] SCLA, DR18/5/6023a.
[76] Quoted in Chavasse, 'Material culture and the country house', 141.

Stoneleigh Abbey, by contrast, carpets formed part of the minimum requirement of comfort. They were found in most bedrooms as well as the principal rooms following the 1760s refurbishment, during which Burnett routinely supplied one or two Wilton carpets for each room. Thus, it appears that comfort and convenience, just as much as luxury, were relative concepts, even amongst the elite.[77] Also standard Fare at Stoneleigh Abbey were pillows stuffed with goose feathers, fine upper- and under-blankets, and cotton counterpanes—a level of comfort that again addressed both physical pleasures and social display to overnight guests.

Comfort was not simply a matter of satisfying physical and social desires. It was also about 'sensibility and feeling', and emotional resonance; it drove the desire to make the house into a home—something with meaning and personal attachment.[78] This aspect of the country house is too easily overlooked; yet Lewis makes clear that feeling 'at home' was important for country house owners, just as it is central to ideas of *habitus*. What she detects amongst her elite female subjects is the close association between physical and emotional comfort: a sense of home deriving from bodily ease, and the companionship of family and friends. For Lady Borringdon, home was a place of familial intimacy and comfort, ideas captured by Austen in *Emma*, where she writes that 'there is nothing like staying at home, for real comfort'.[79]

Family was important in a diachronic sense because it formed a link with the past, and thus with pedigree and lineage, but also with the future through dynastic continuity. This was especially true of the landowning classes, for whom marriage and children were a natural and necessary part of a man's life course; but marriage also offered emotional comfort.[80] The emotional attachment between husbands and wives is apparent from the simple affection shown in Sir Roger Newdigate's frequent letters to his first wife Sophia, who he referred to as Ba. He was assiduous in writing to her and disappointed when replies were delayed: 'I can't tell why I should have no letter from Bath today,' he wrote on Lady Day 1773. 'Not Ba ill, that I won't believe—not Midge ill. I must have had a word then. No—it is the Post failed, it is the footman fail'd, some nonsense or other that vexes Ba too for my disappointment.' He was greatly distressed during her final illness and by her death in July 1774, grief that was repeated at the death of his sister-in-law Mary Conyers in 1797, and his second wife Hester, in 1800.[81] Mary's passing prompted him to write: 'I am old, & every day takes away some friend that I love, & it is natural for me to endeavour to rally the few I have left around me.'[82] For some, comfort could be found in children. Indeed, writing to Jane Parker in 1795 following the death of her husband, Charles (who was to have been Sir Roger's heir at Arbury),

[77] SCLA, DR18/3/47/52/15; Crowley, *Invention of Comfort*, 149–59.
[78] Smith, *Consumption and the Making of Respectability*, 84.
[79] Lewis, 'When a house', esp. 359–60; J. Austen, *Emma* (1815; London, 1985), 277. See also Chavasse, 'Material culture and the country house', 148–69; Vickery, *Behind Closed Doors*, 207–30.
[80] French and Rothery, *Man's Estate*, 191, 232.
[81] WRO, CR136/B/4046/e, Letter, 25 March 1773. White, *Correspondence of Sir Roger Newdigate*, xxxix, l–li.
[82] WRO, CR136/B/1970, Letter, 27 November 1797.

Sir Roger argued that her 'little smiling brood' of five children 'will every day add more & more joy and comfort'.[83]

The comforts associated with family can also be seen at Canons Ashby, where the childless Sir John and Elizabeth Dryden adopted the daughter of his younger brother Beville. Their clear affection for the girl, also called Elizabeth, comes out in their correspondence with her natural parents, where she is described as 'amiable', 'as fine as a princess', and 'a child after our own hearts'.[84] They doted on the girl, but were wary of spoiling her, and balanced presents with care for her health: 'she sat in her Ants lap and had two loose Teeth drawed, it was don with some difficulty, the lady says she sufferd a good deal her self'.[85] Even when they were grown, the departure of children could prompt considerable distress, Lady Irwin writing, 'I cannot bear to have my creatures taken away and be left by my poor self forlorn and solitary'.[86] Such notions of care, companionship, and comfort are leitmotifs in the correspondence between parents and children, and underline the importance of syncretic family as the principal source of emotional support, although letters could often admonish as well as encourage.[87]

Children were incorporated in the lived spaces of the country house: whilst details from Canons Ashby are scarce, the 1749 inventory from Stoneleigh Abbey lists 'Miss Leigh's Room' as well as a nursery—the former presumably for the 13-year-old Mary and containing decorative elements such as tapestries and china jars, and the latter a less richly decorated room which may have lately housed her younger brother Edward.[88] More general in their impact on the spaces of the country house were the routines of amiable sociability with friends. Chavasse highlights the ways in which the company of friends was central to Richard Neville's feeling of comfort and well-being at Audley End: 'Miss Forrest or Harriet generally stay in the Saloon till two & we never want for conversation, & from two till dinner, I have as you know plenty of occupations.'[89] Similar sentiments were expressed by Mary Leigh, who wrote with enthusiasm of being 'wonderfully engaged in receiving and paying visits', but more generally the Leighs had a reputation for being somewhat reclusive, and there is limited evidence that her brother Edward entertained large numbers of guests at Stoneleigh Abbey.[90] In contrast, Sir Roger Newdigate was highly gregarious: he socialized with many of the landed families in the surrounding area during his early years and was still entertaining a regular stream of guests in his eightieth year. The notebook listing guests at Arbury Hall in 1798 records a total of sixty-five visits by twenty-nine different people, including family and friends. Many came on just one or two occasions and only a handful

[83] WRO, CR136/B/2014, Letter, 29 April 1795.

[84] NRO, D(CA)/1032, Letter, 6 April 1761; D(CA)/1035, Letter, 18 June 1761; D(CA)/1037, Letter, 6 October 1761.

[85] NRO, D(CA)/1035, Letter, 18 June 1761.   [86] Quoted in Lewis, 'When a house', 352.

[87] See French and Rothery, *Man's Estate*, 56–9; S. Whyman, *The Pen and the People: English Letter Writers 1660–1800* (Oxford, 2009).

[88] NRO, D(CA)201, Inventory, 1770; SCLA, DR18/4/27, Inventory, November 1749.

[89] Quoted in Chavasse, 'Material culture and the country house', 157.

[90] SCLA, DR671, Letter, 12 September 1791. Edward Leigh did, however, keep up connections with friends made during his time at Oxford—see MacDonald, 'Leigh family', 153–4.

stayed overnight.[91] The most frequent visitors were Dr Bartley, who came twenty times, dining on each occasion, followed by the three Miss Ludfords, his great-nieces, who visited seventeen times between them, sometimes staying for a night or two.[92] But the most important, in terms of their duration, was Francis (Parker) Newdigate, who, as the new heir apparent to the estate, made frequent and often prolonged visits, although he declined to move from his home in Kirkhallam in Derbyshire to be closer to Sir Roger, despite the latter's clear manoeuvring on this front.[93]

The emotional comfort afforded by family and friends helped to make the country house into a home, a process facilitated by and feeding into the creation of informal social settings such as those discussed in Chapter 2. Something of this can be seen in Mary Leigh's correspondence about her Kensington house: 'my wish would be to continue it exactly the same it now is, any alteration would much lessen it in my estimation . . . it is impossible for me to have so agreeable and suitable a place as is the Grove House in every particular'.[94] Pleasure was derived from physical comfort and from associations with shared experiences, associations discussed in detail by both Lewis and Chavasse. However, they focus on events in the past or present: the pleasure of lively company, memories of visits by friends, or the heirlooming of family possessions.[95] These were certainly important, but Mary Leigh appears to have looked forwards as well as backwards in articulating and perhaps constructing her feelings. Writing in August 1790 to her man of business, Joseph Hill, she noted that 'my garden is in perfection, & my new rooms pretty & I think worth seeing & a still more prevailing inducement I really believe the journey and change of air is always of service to Mrs Hills health'.[96] Pleasure came from the nature of her physical surroundings, the anticipation of sharing these with friends, and the benefit in terms of their well-being that this would afford. Physical and emotional comfort were thus combined and mutually reinforced.

OLD THINGS AND FAMILY CONNECTIONS

Old objects were important in creating emotional comfort, especially when they had particular personal or family associations. As McCracken argues, they formed 'a world rich in attachments'.[97] This is clearly seen in the ways that returning officials of the East India Company often brought with them a range of goods that they had accumulated whilst in India. Robert Clive shipped home a huge

[91] A. Wood, 'Diaries of Sir Roger Newdigate, 1751–1806', *Birmingham Archaeological Society*, 78 (1960), 40–1; WRO, CR136/A/47, Notes of persons coming to dinner; beer and ale brewed; and wines ordered, 1798.
[92] The visits of the Ludfords suggests some warming of family relations following a bitter dispute between Sir Roger and his brother-in-law John Ludford which raged through the 1740s and 1750s—White, *Correspondence of Sir Roger Newdigate*, xxx–xxxi, 321–4.
[93] See WRO, CR136/B/1970, Letter, 27 November 1797.
[94] SCLA, DR671, Letter, 27 March 1791.
[95] Lewis, 'When a house'.   [96] SCLA, DR671, Letter, 22 August 1790.
[97] McCracken, *Culture and Consumption*, 52.

range of goods, including a 'very fine dimity chintz bed' and, on a more modest
scale, Richard Benyon was accompanied on his journey back to Englefield House
by, amongst other things, a lacquered Chinese tea chest, a range of porcelain, and
a consignment of tea.[98] Of course, these goods held monetary value and were
signifiers of taste and a cosmopolitan aspect in their owners; but they also carried
personal associations of family and of other homes, far away in India. They were
old things that carried personal meanings. Much the same was true of many
objects that had been given by friends or passed down from parents or other family members. However, the comfort of old and familiar things was often in ten-
sion with the pleasure of the new. On the one hand, Lewis highlights how the
Duchess of Marlborough assiduously noted the biography of numerous items
when drawing up an inventory of Blenheim following the Duke's death in 1722.
On the other, Campbell argues that modern consumption is based on an endless
search for novelty; within the shift he detected towards a Romantic ethic, a longing
for new goods and experiences was just as important as their actual consumption.[99] Linked to this is a countervailing aspect of the Diderot effect: the way in
which a new item within an assemblage induces restless dissatisfaction and the
progressive renewal of the domestic environment.[100] Diderot's essay *Regrets on
Parting with my Old Dressing Gown* begins with the author replacing his old gown
with a new one and then feeling that his desk seems shabby in comparison: changing this makes his wall hangings appear worn, and so on until the whole room has
been renewed. The irony is that, at the end of the process, the writer has a fashionable new room in which everything is again in keeping, but feels that it is no
longer *his* study.

A common problem with many material objects is that they wore out, despite the
regimes of maintenance that formed a central part of household oeconomy.[101] Such
objects were problematic and sometimes unwanted, as is apparent from a memorandum written in 1817 by Elizabeth Dryden as a commentary on an inventory of
the goods in Canons Ashby taken at her aunt's death in 1791. The circumstances
were somewhat fraught and Elizabeth was anxious to downplay the value of the
estate as she sought to protect herself from creditors. She argued that most of
the good furniture belonged to her, either by gift or purchase, and that most of the
other things in the house were old and worthless:

Many articles have been completely worn out, broken, & thrown away having been
very old & decayed in 1770, of course when I succeeded after 21 years they must
many of them be gone and those remaining have but little wear in them. The
Linen...is reduced to mere rags not worth mentioning...As to the Plate, many of the

---

[98] Barczewski, *Country Houses and the British Empire*, 146–7; K. Smith, 'Englefield House,
Berkshire: processes and practices', *East India Company at Home* (March 2013), <http://blogs.ucl.
ac.uk/eicah/englefield-house-berkshire/>.
[99] Lewis, 'When a house', 346–7; Campbell, 'Understanding consumption', 48. See also McCracken,
Culture and Consumption, 31–44.
[100] D. Diderot, 'Regrets on parting with my old dressing gown', in *Rameau's Nephew and Other
Works by Dennis Diderot* (New York, 1964), 309–17.
[101] See Vickery, *Gentleman's Daughter*, 127–60; Whittle and Griffiths, *Consumption and Gender*,
34–43; Harvey, *Little Republic*, 25–43.

small Tea Spoons I am sorry to say have been stolen by the Servants, also the Sugar Tongs (mentioned in the list of Plate) was never found after my Aunts death: they were small in the old fashioned shape. The Silver pronged forks were worn so as to be useless.[102]

Elizabeth's rhetoric makes clear her view of old things as worn out or unfashionable: either way, they had little place in her vision of the house and her role in creating its current material culture. Indeed, the language deployed for her belongings was often very different: 'all the modern cotton counterpanes belong to me' as did 'two large [china] jars with tops quite perfect'.

Many of the old goods belonging to the house were said by Elizabeth to be in the Storeroom, which the 1791 inventory lists as containing an eclectic mix of pewter, china, and glassware; trunks, tin canisters, and deal boxes; chairs and tea boards; a backgammon table, bird cage, and spice box with drawers.[103] Much the same was true at Stoneleigh Abbey, where unwanted pieces were placed in the lumber room, the changing contents of which tell their own story of the ebb and flow of furniture. In 1786, it contained, amongst other things, six part-gilded walnut chairs with crimson upholstery, ten 'old high back chairs' with yellow silk damask covers, four walnut chairs with needlework seats, seven walnut chairs with matted bottoms, a satin covered easy chair, two japanned tea tables, a gilt-framed cabinet, a pillow and claw table with a painted top, and a 'large new Wilton carpet'.[104] Both of these rooms might be viewed as spaces in which objects were divested of personal associations prior to disposal. By residing out of sight and remaining unused, they were, in Epp and Price's words 'cooled' of the 'singularized meanings' that made them belongings and thus rendered commodities again.[105]

Unwanted goods were most readily returned to the commodity market via auctions of household and other goods. Such sales might arise because of the death of the owner, failure to produce an heir, crippling financial difficulties, the abandonment of a property in favour of another family seat, or, more positively, as a means for an heir to monetize unwanted belongings and replace them with more fashionable goods.[106] Once on the second-hand market, these objects did not necessarily follow a downward social trajectory. In Paris, they formed an important component of the stock of many *marchands merciers*, whilst auctions at British country houses often formed an opportunity to acquire prized luxury goods and were well-frequented by aristocratic buyers.[107] There were two sales at Stoneleigh Abbey,

[102] NRO, D(CA)/903b, Letter, 13 January 1817.
[103] NRO, D(CA)903, Inventory, 1791.   [104] SCLA, DR18/4/69, Inventory, 1786.
[105] A. Epp and L. Price, 'The storied life of singularized objects: forces of agency and network transformation', *Journal of Consumer Research*, 36 (2010), 821.
[106] See MacArthur and Stobart, 'Going for a song?'; Gemmett, 'The tinsel of fashion'; Nenadic, 'Middle-rank consumers'.
[107] Sargentson, *Merchants and Luxury Markets*, 32–3; L. Fontaine, 'The circulation of luxury goods in eighteenth-century Paris: social distribution and an alternative currency', in M. Berg and E. Eger (eds), *Luxury in the Eighteenth Century. Debates, Desires and Delectable Goods* (Basingstoke, 2007), 89–102; A. N. Richter, 'Spectacle, exoticism and display in the gentleman's house: the Fonthill auction of 1822', *Eighteenth-Century Studies*, 41/4 (2008), 543–63.

although both were partial clearances and dominated by purchases made by family members. The first took place following the death of Edward, third Lord Leigh, in 1738. His widow Mary moved to a nearby house at Guys Cliff, taking with her small quantities of goods from two of the family rooms in the west range. From the Common Drawing Room, she took a range of decorative items including china, chocolate cups, a punchbowl and basin, and several 'long images'. The Further Back Parlour was effectively stripped, with 'all taken by my Lady Except two pair of Window Curtains, vallans & rods'.[108] Significantly, the principal rooms remained largely intact, the contents being secured by Edward's son Thomas, fourth Lord Leigh. A second clearance took place little more than ten years later, when Thomas himself died in 1749. An inventory taken the following year of goods 'now remaining at Stoneleigh Abbey' shows that his widow Catherine took all the plate (valued at £936 12s. 7d.) and some furniture, whilst the linen, drinking glasses, and a large quantity of household goods were apparently sold. Much of the furniture being disposed of came from bedchambers and servants' rooms, the inventory noting that there was 'nothing left' or 'all sold' in several such rooms.[109] Again, most of the principal rooms were left largely untouched, despite the fact that the house would lie empty for the next fourteen years until Edward, fifth Lord Leigh, came of age. The sale thus cleared items that were marginal to the material culture of the family or that were specifically useful to or valued by Catherine as she set up house.[110]

Full or partial clearances could thus be cathartic experiences, allowing new owners to imprint their tastes on the family home. The house inherited by Edward, fifth Lord Leigh, was hardly a blank canvas, but it gave him considerable scope as well as putting him to significant expense. The surge of spending that ensued brought huge quantities of new furniture into the house and also resulted in the removal of further furniture and fittings, including old gilt leather wall coverings.[111] And yet, whilst the bedchambers and dressing rooms were furnished anew, in other rooms new pieces were added alongside older ones—a process especially apparent in the Breakfast Room and Dining Parlour. Renewal was therefore far from complete, even in a major redecoration scheme.

Much the same was true at Canons Ashby, where Edward Dryden purchased all the furniture in the house he inherited from Sir Robert Dryden.[112] In his subsequent schemes for modernizing the house, these were supplemented and sometimes replaced by new acquisitions, often of pieces in the latest style, including the needlework chairs bought from Thomas Phill and a set of twelve walnut and cane chairs.[113] The more general fate of older items within the changing material culture of Canons Ashby is revealing. Tapestries were initially spread across the house before becoming confined to bedchambers by 1791 and then disappearing

[108] SCLA, DR18/1/815, Goods bought and remaining at Stoneleigh, 1738. Comparing this list of 'Goods Left' with the 1738 inventory allows us to see which items were removed to Guys Cliff.
[109] SCLA, DR18/4/26, Inventory, 1750.
[110] MacDonald, 'Leigh family', 149.   [111] SCLA, DR18/5/4402.
[112] NRO, D(CA)41, Goods purchased by Edward Dryden, 1 November 1708
[113] Stobart, 'Inventories and the changing furnishings of Canons Ashby', 7–8.

altogether by 1819; turkey-work chairs, with their richly decorated seats and backs, followed a similar trajectory. The pathways followed by walnut furniture were more complex: it grew in volume and distribution up to 1756, but then declined in prominence, being increasingly pushed to the spatial margins of the house. Most telling in this respect is the presence in the Brown Gallery, at the back of the house, of eighteen 'old walnut chairs', ten with 'satin and silver seats' and eight with rush seats.[114] In a manner which echoes the preponderance of walnut in the assortment of unloved objects in the lumber room at Stoneleigh Abbey, it appears that at least some walnut furniture, even when finished with unequivocally luxury materials, was not merely old in chronological terms, but it was also deemed old-fashioned and relegated from the principal rooms. Even here, however, the process of replacing old with new was rarely complete. Sir John Turner Dryden or more probably Elizabeth may have moved the sets of old walnut chairs to a back corridor, but they did not dispose of them entirely; they also retained many of the pieces acquired nearly a hundred years earlier by Edward Dryden. At Stoneleigh Abbey there were similar continuities. In a process repeated across many country houses, new items were incorporated alongside existing pieces in many of the principal rooms.[115]

The motivations underpinning these practices were complex and overlapping. Cornforth and Fowler have argued that the owner was often 'moved by contemporary ideas and fashions, but the concept of continuity of the family and of traditional values was always the vital element'.[116] Looking more generally at consumers' attitudes to change, Campbell, Bianchi and others have argued that novelty was a difficult idea. Bringing new goods into existing systems of consumption or sets of goods made them knowable and thus desirable: they maintain the cultural consistency suggested by Diderot.[117] This can be illustrated in the marketing practices of Josiah Wedgwood, but is more difficult to demonstrate in the context of the country house, although it was common for wallpapers to be matched to existing schemes to complete the decorative set in a room. At Stoneleigh Abbey, for instance, Bromwich and Leigh provided '147 Yards of painted paper to match a Chintz' that was being used for Lord Leigh's bed hanging.[118] This was probably a matter of personal taste, as the bedchamber also included silvered leather hangings retained from an earlier period; but existing objects and decorative schemes could also be retained for reasons of thrift. These ideals were important in elite as well as middling sort households and formed a key element of good household management which encouraged the maintenance, repair, and repurposing of

---

[114] NRO, D(CA)904, Inventory, 1756.

[115] For a detailed discussion of these processes at Audley End, see Chavasse, 'Material culture and the country house', 59–81.

[116] Fowler and Cornforth, *English Decoration in the Eighteenth Century*, 33.

[117] C. Campbell, 'The desire for the new: its nature and social location as presented in theories of fashion and modern consumerism', in R. Silverman and E. Hirsch (eds), *Consuming Technologies: Media and Information in Domestic Spaces* (London, 1992); M. Bianchi, 'The taste for novelty and novel tastes', in M. Bianchi (ed.) *The Active Consumer: Novelty and Surprise in Consumer Choice* (London, 1998), 64–86; McCracken, *Culture and Consumption*, 123.

[118] SCLA, DR18/5/4402.

goods. The Duchess of Marlborough, for example, noted that the valance for her bed at Blenheim had been made from her own clothes—a mark of the frugality in which she took great pleasure. This thriftiness extended to bringing furniture to Blenheim from previous homes, including a 'yellow Damask Bed lined with white Sattin Embroidered and a very old suit of tapestry hangings wch the Queen gave me to furnish part of my lodgings at Windsor Castle which afterwards I sent to St. Albans and afterwards to Blenheim from thence to save buying new furniture for that room'.[119] Similar feelings may have motivated Edward, fifth Lord Leigh, in his decision to rehang the gilt leather hangings that were removed from bedroom Number 11 in another bedroom, Number 19, where Bromwich and Leigh charged for '8 Days work putting up the Old Silver leather and mending'.[120]

In both these cases, however, ideas of thrift were probably overwritten with other motivations. Its extended biography also reveals that the Duchess's bed had picked up many important associations along its route, including links to the Queen, to royal palaces, and to the earlier life of its owner. As with the eastern goods brought home by returning nabobs, this was an object replete with personal meanings. Lord Leigh's gilt leather hangings spoke of patina and lineage—an important link back to earlier generations and to the venerable age of Stoneleigh Abbey. McCracken argues that patina (in the broad sense of older, inherited goods) was of declining importance in the eighteenth century as value systems were reformed around novelty and fashion.[121] At the same time, there was a supposed shift from so-called old luxuries (exclusive markers of elite status) to new luxuries (vehicles for polite and urbane sociability).[122] Combined, these developments would seem to undermine the cultural as well as the economic value of old goods; yet inherited goods remained an important way of distinguishing the established social elite. The eighteenth-century critique of nabobs as lacking true pedigree resurfaces in Dickens's styling of the nouveau riche 'Veneerings' in *Our Mutual Friend* and more recently in Alan Clark's famous dismissal of Michael Heseltine as a man who bought his own furniture.[123] The 'patina glow of history' afforded by inherited goods was therefore central to a distinct aristocratic mode of consumption; it operated in part by communicating status through the possession of old luxuries.[124] At Stoneleigh Abbey these included not just the gilt leather wall coverings, but also the gilded walnut chairs, tables, and pier glasses that furnished the Great Apartment. The latter, however, also illustrates the importance of patina in communicating lineage. Inherited goods or heirlooms were important because they represented in material form the long-standing status of the family; as discussed in Chapter 2, the Great Apartment formed the key assemblage of such goods at Stoneleigh.

[119] Quoted in Lewis, 'When a house', 347. See also Whittle and Griffiths, *Consumption and Gender*, 117–53; Vickery, *Gentleman's Daughter*, 151–8.

[120] SCLA, DR18/5/4402.   [121] McCracken, *Culture and Consumption*, 31–43.

[122] De Vries, *Industrious Revolution*, 44–5. See also Chapter 1.

[123] See Ponsonby, *Stories from Home*, 96–7. 65–71.

[124] Blondé, 'Conflicting consumption models?', 67. See also Christie, *British Country House*, 179–273; Jackson-Stops, *Fashioning and Functioning*.

In an inventory drawn up in 1819, Elizabeth Dryden drew a telling distinction between goods that were hers and those that were 'Heir Looms of the Mansion of Canons Ashby'.[125] The particular circumstances in which she found herself make it difficult to discern her true feelings towards these various goods, her money troubles being compounded by disputatious relations with her son. However, she expressed a stronger connection with the things that were her own possessions. She had already noted in a letter: 'All the family writings which I have are in a long box bound with Hair with my Grandfathers initials, sometimes in the Brown Gallery & sometimes in the Storeroom, but ought to be in Sir Edward Drydens custody, as he has the greatest interest in them, not having any myself.'[126] Although not something that interested Elizabeth personally, she was clearly aware of the significant role of family papers in constructing lineage, seeking to pass on both the material objects and the responsibility to her son. Earlier in the same letter, she reveals her feelings about the wider importance of connections between family members and particular objects, what Epp and Price call object–person biographies.[127] First, she notes the presence of 'Two small Cabinet Pictures purchased by my Uncle [which] are in good preservation & hang on each side of the best Cabinet in the Drawing Room'.[128] Provenance, quality, and location are all recorded: they come together to give these pieces significance as objects with a particular family connection that afforded pleasure. In contrast, some 'Mezzotint Prints after the Titian Gallery (I believe now at Blenheim tho' not publicly shown) are papered up in the storeroom. 9 in number the Subjects being indelicate they were put by.' Although copies of old masters hung in one of the foremost houses in the country, these had little emotional connection for Elizabeth; they were relegated to the Storeroom where none but the servants would see them.

CONCLUSION

The everyday routines of country house living were important in shaping the overall patterns of elite spending and the spatiality of the house. Expenditure on food and drink, lighting and cleaning, and maintenance and repairs amounted to a significant proportion of total spending, the proper organization of which lay at the heart of the well-managed household. The idea of good oeconomy was just as important to the landowner as it was to the urban middling sort; the amounts being spent might be greater, but the moral and financial influences were just as significant. Moreover, these routine costs were often necessary rather than discretionary: as Lady Dryden alluded, to skimp on cleaning or maintaining the fabric of the building was a false economy that would undermine the integrity of the house and the status of the family. Maintenance of material objects was important to the maintenance of status. This encompassed but went far beyond the respectability of cleanliness: it ensured the long-term survival of objects that signalled

---

[125] NRO, D(CA)904, Inventory, 1819.
[127] Epp and Price, 'Storied life'.
[126] NRO, D(CA)903b, Letter, 13 January 1817.
[128] NRO, D(CA)903b, Letter, 13 January 1817.

elite rank and distinguished the titled landowner from the nouveau riche and the rising middling sorts. The practicalities of everyday life thus elided with the priorities of consumption practices aimed at defending status. They also reinforced an emphasis on comfort, both physical and emotional. Too often treated as conceptually distinct, these two aspects of comfort were in reality mutually compatible and often reinforced one another. Being warm was central to much of the discussion of physical comfort found in correspondence, and many country house owners invested in a variety of stoves and fireplaces, or moved doorways, or prioritized south-facing rooms in order to increase their comfort. Yet the fireside was also symbolically important as the seat of familial well-being and comfort. Whilst Robert Sayer's etching highlights the discord of a smoky house and a scolding wife, Thomas Rowlandson portrays a contented scene of husband and wife embracing affectionately in front of a welcoming fire, with their children around them, well fed and warm.[129] The emotional comfort afforded by family has been highlighted by Chavasse and is apparent from the correspondence of Sir Roger Newdigate, who displayed real affection and a desire to have family and friends around him.

This link between family, comfort, and environment again highlights the importance of the country house as a lived space, the meanings and associations of particular spaces being constructed through their everyday use. It also had a material expression which, Lewis and Vickery argue, was especially strongly manifested by women and often involved items with sentimental rather than status value. As Nenadic argues, goods could retain symbolic significance even if their stylistic value was diminished.[130] We see this in Lady Dryden's emotional connection with the miniatures bought by her uncle, but it was also apparent in the long-term survival of the chairs bought to commemorate the marriage of Edward, third Lord Leigh, and Mary Holbech, and the preservation of earlier decorative schemes in some of the bedrooms at Stoneleigh Abbey. Here, emotional attachment was underpinned by recognition that these goods also carried messages of family pedigree and longevity—something that becomes central in Lady Dryden's attitude to family papers. Family thus held complex and overlapping meanings. Overall, it is clear that the lived spaces of the country house were multifaceted and interrelated, encompassing anything from the kitchen to the drawing room, and drawing in material objects as varied as washtubs, stoves, and family paintings. What drew together these spaces and objects was the way in which their meaning and use were shaped, in part at least, through their everyday use; they reflected the daily practices of the owners, families, and servants as well as broader notions of luxury, taste, and status.

---

[129] Robert Sayer, *The Comforts of Matrimony—A Smoky House and Scolding Wife*, 1790 (British Museum, 1985,0119.115); Thomas Rowlandson, *The Comforts of Matrimony—A Good Toast*, 1809 (British Museum, 1871,0812.4497).

[130] Nenadic, 'Middle-rank consumers', 135, 138.

4

Gentlemen's Things
The Masculine World of Goods and
Consumption as Self-fashioning

INTRODUCTION

Country houses have traditionally been seen as the product of male preferences and decisions. The importance of the male line, the settlement of estates, and primogeniture have rightly been highlighted as central to elite attitudes to property and to aristocratic self-identity as well as to the overall survival of the British landed establishment. However, whilst men have dominated discourse on the aristocracy, as they have in every other branch of history, it is only recently that the ideas of manhood, masculinity, and manliness have begun to be problematized and serious consideration given to 'what men are' in a historical context. Since the 1990s there has been a frenzy of activity in this subject area, although inevitably gaps and inconsistencies have emerged.[1] Historians working on different periods have tended to focus on different types of men in different contexts: for the eighteenth century, attention has centred on the 'polite gentleman' in the public sphere of coffee houses and salons, whilst those working on the early nineteenth century have focused on the domestic evangelical father of the middle-class home. Only in the last few years has there been an attempt to engage in a sustained analysis of landed masculinities in a field dominated by studies of the middling sorts.[2]

The most yawning gap, however, has emerged in the history of consumption, material culture, and domesticity in the eighteenth century, despite the importance of this period in the consumer transformation. Scholars in this area have been very slow to integrate these approaches and concepts into their subject area,

---

[1] The list of publications is too extensive to examine comprehensively but the major studies in chronological order include M. Roper and J. Tosh, *Manful Assertions: Masculinities in Britain since 1800* (London, 1991); R. W. Connell, *Masculinities* (Cambridge, 1995); M. Cohen, *Fashioning Masculinity: National Identity and Language in the Eighteenth Century* (London, 1996); E. Foyster, *Manhood in Early Modern England: Honour, Sex and Marriage* (Harlow, 1999); T. Hitchcock and M. Cohen (eds), *English Masculinities, 1660–1800* (Harlow, 1999); J. Tosh, *A Man's Place: Masculinity and the Middle-Class Home in Victorian England* (London, 1999); A. Shepard, *Meanings of Manhood in Early Modern England* (Oxford, 2003); K. Harvey and A. Shepard, 'What have historians done with masculinity? Reflections on five centuries of British history', *Journal of British Studies*, 44 (2005), 274–80; J. H. Arnold and S. Brady, *What is Masculinity? Historical Dynamics from Antiquity to the Contemporary World* (Basingstoke, 2011); French and Rothery, *Man's Estate*; Harvey, *Little Republic*.

[2] French and Rothery, *Man's Estate*.

and the focus has remained overwhelmingly on women. This is partly a product of the ongoing tenacity of separate spheres as a concept in gender history, studies of masculinity in the Georgian period only rarely placing the man at home. Some progress has been made. Margot Finn's innovative study of the masculine possessions of four middling gentlemen revealed the typological range of men's purchases and the significance they attached to consumption. Despite received wisdom on men and consumption, they were just as acquisitive as women and sought out novel goods and luxuries, but also inexpensive purchases of everyday items, all of which in various ways played an important part in their self-identity and self-fashioning, even uber-feminine goods such as china.[3] However, although Finn reflects on the contrasts between male and female consumption, the analysis lacks a problematization of consumption specifically in terms of masculinity. Much the same is true of subsequent interventions from Berg and Hussey.[4] Karen Harvey's more recent study has fixed our gaze more consistently on masculinity and has begun to reveal a more nuanced picture of the distribution of provisioning and management responsibilities according to gender and the ways in which self-fashioning was directed through domesticity.[5] Her focus was on the middling sort; our best view of similar processes amongst landed society remains Vickery's *Behind Closed Doors*.

It is worth summarizing Vickery's argument, since it forms an important comparator to the dual focus on men and women we engage with in this chapter and Chapter 5. She described a quite neat sexual division of consumer responsibilities between men and women: the former were responsible for the overall management of household and estate, whilst the latter saw to the more mundane everyday running of the house and family. Men oversaw major household refurbishments, paid taxes, rents, tithes, and annuities, along with the wages of male servants, and they purchased wines, exotic foods, toys, and gadgets. They patronized tailors and bought wigs and other accoutrements; crucially for Vickery, they also selected the coaches, horses, saddlery, and horse tackle. Women did obtain the raw ingredients of men's clothing in the shape of cottons, linens, haberdashery, and millinery, but they rarely saw the tailor. They paid women's wages, costs associated with children (but not school fees for the boys), and purchased china, glass, everyday groceries, and meat. More blurred lines were observed in the case of furniture, some forms of chinaware, and less elaborate interior decoration, but overall the pattern is quite clear and is played out, with local variations, in the three families examined by Vickery.[6] Illuminating as this analysis is, it should be noted that the case studies deployed are all drawn from married couples and cover quite limited periods of time, ranging from one to eleven years of accounting. Clearly there is scope for further research that engages fully with masculinity and the role of

---

[3] Finn, 'Men's things'.

[4] Berg, *Luxury and Pleasure*, 200–43; D. Hussey, 'Guns, horses and stylish waistcoats? Male consumer activity and domestic shopping in late-eighteenth and early-nineteenth century England', in D. Hussey and M. Ponsonby (eds), *The Single Homemaker and Material Culture in the Long Eighteenth Century* (Aldershot, 2012), 47–72.

[5] Harvey, *The Little Republic*, 139–69.   [6] Vickery, *Behind Closed Doors*, 12–13.

women in a range of different domestic settings and arrangements and across longer periods of time.

Bachelorhood, singleness, and the absence of children had an impact on the gender identities of individuals. Marriage and parenthood were key attributes of masculinity and the patriarchal power of men as the head of a household. There is clear evidence that many gentry men who did not marry and set up their own household felt incomplete and lacking in authority: lesser men in a way. In addition, the lack of a husband or a wife and the absence of children had an obvious impact on the nature of consumption and of the country house as a family home (see Chapter 6). However, as Vickery's study makes clear, not all households took stable patriarchal forms containing a master, mistress, children, and servants—a situation which was repeated in households across Europe.[7] The full patriarchal household, with its fully formed ideals of masculinity and femininity, along with the associated patterns of consumption, may have been the norm, but its was not the whole story. We should be aware of and interested in the more unstable households of single men and women, whether this was through widowhood or through spinsterhood and bachelorhood. Such households were common amongst the landed elites in this period, T. H. Hollingsworth noting that between 1700 and 1724 around one quarter of all aristocratic males and females remained unmarried at the age of 50. This proportion gradually fell across the eighteenth century, but remained at 20 per cent of all men and women in 1800. Infertility followed a very similar pattern, with 24 per cent of marriages of aristocratic men remaining childless in the earlier period, falling to 20 per cent by 1800.[8] Early mortality was a constant threat to the continuation of aristocratic lines: life expectancy at birth was 34 years for men and 36 years for women in 1700. Again, rates had improved by 1800, with the comparative figures of 49 for men and 51 for women; but much of this improvement took place in the later eighteenth century. High mortality rates, coupled with uncertain nuptiality and fertility, made for significant levels of instability in aristocratic households. The Leighs, Newdigates, and Drydens, whose family histories were marked by early deaths, single status, and childless marriages, are thus representative of a significant and important minority within the wider aristocratic population.

In this chapter and Chapter 5, we engage with and build on the key historical debates in this area, emphasizing the ways in which men and women had distinct and sometimes combined roles in shaping consumption practices. We conduct a sustained analysis of spending across long periods to observe shifts and continuities in the spending of men and women across the life cycle, amongst married couples and single men and woman. The analysis here centres on two case studies to explore

[7] Vickery, *Behind Closed Doors*, 49–82, 184–206; Chatenet-Calyste, 'Feminine luxury in Paris'; D. Linström, 'Maids, noblewomen, journeymen, state officials and others: unmarried adults in four Swedish towns, 1750–1855', in J. De Groot, I. Devos, and A. Schmidt (eds), *Single Life and the City, 1200–1900* (Basingstoke, 2015), 93–113; J. Bennett and A. Froide (eds), *Singlewomen in the European Past, 1250–1800* (Philadelphia, 1999).

[8] T. H. Hollingsworth, 'The demography of the British peerage', *Population Studies*, 18/2 (1964), 20–46.

in detail the ways in which masculine identities were constructed through and linked to consumption practices. In the first section we explore the masculine world of goods as they are revealed in the spending patterns of Thomas, fourth Lord Leigh, and his son Edward, fifth Lord Leigh. In particular, we focus on those areas of spending highlighted by Vickery as reflecting particularly male interests (for example, horses and saddlery) and those which might be viewed as dynastic in nature (the fabric of the house, artwork, major items of furniture). In the second section we examine Sir Roger Newdigate and his self-fashioning as a polite and learned gentleman, in part through his public life, but also through his consumption and especially his rebuilding and remodelling of Arbury Hall. We argue that all three men illustrate the nuanced way in which individuals interpreted broader social stereotypes of aristocratic masculinities both materially and discursively.

MASCULINITY AND THE WORLD OF GOODS: THE MEN OF THE LEIGH FAMILY

Thomas Leigh inherited the family estates in 1738 at the relatively young age of 25 years and also died young in his 37th year, leaving the estates in minority until his only surviving son came of age in 1763. This relatively brief reign may have curtailed his dynastic ambitions, but we have enough evidence of his spending to get a measure of the man. As a consumer, Edward Leigh sparkled more briefly and brilliantly than his father (Figure 4.1). When a young man at university in Oxford, his spending comprised mostly the costs he incurred within college, although there were outlays for buying, mending, and cleaning clothes, for books, and for some small luxuries, such as a watch and chain bought at Woodstock.[9] Most of his discretionary spending took place between his inheritance and the onset of his mental illness, which appears to have occurred sometime in 1768, although he was only officially declared insane six years later. We can only guess at the possible outcomes of his spending had he lived longer, but Edward certainly had grand schemes for Stoneleigh Abbey which never got further than a series of designs and plans.[10] As with his father, however, Edward's brief expenditure gives us a clear idea of his character and his gender identity.

In many respects, both Thomas and Edward Leigh conformed to the general parameters of masculine spending. As landowners, they were responsible for the overall management of the estate and for the family finances and investments. Such spending was the responsibility of each generation of landed men and, although individuals could make decisions in terms of how they managed their estates, how much land they purchased, and where they invested surplus capital, they were expected to preserve and, if possible, augment the family's wealth for future generations. These were the obligations of aristocratic status, shared with all

---

[9] SCLA, DR18/5/4017. This type of spending was fairly typical of young men at Oxford, although, as mentioned earlier, young men were expected to control their finances whilst at university. See the several examples of parental advice on this matter in French and Rothery, *Man's Estate*, 85–137.

[10] SCLA, DR631/33, Designs for Stoneleigh Abbey.

Figure 4.1. Edward, fifth Lord Leigh (1742–86), as a boy (unknown artist).
Photograph by Jon Stobart.

European elites.[11] Edward's spending was greater in this area (£2,830 as opposed to
the £1,276 laid out by his father), but this represents only a small fraction of the
total outlays made on land, investments, and the like—most being recorded in
separate account books (see Chapter 1). In terms of their discretionary spending,
however, Thomas and Edward behaved quite differently and, seen through their
consumption habits, they were quite different landed gentlemen. It might be
assumed that each generation would make a substantial mark on the fabric of
the country house, remodelling and refurbishing according to their own taste or
the prevailing fashions of the age. Building, decorating, and furnishing an impressive residence were, of course, an important aspect of elite male spending. It served
to define a man's status within society, the elite, and his family, not least because
architecture was often viewed as the most prestigious branch of the arts and thus
most deserving of elite patronage.[12] Furthermore, such spending was dynastic in
that it made an individual contribution to representations of the male line, a visible imprint of the part each male landowner played in the evolution of the family
house. Despite these imperatives, very little substantial activity of this kind can be
seen in Thomas's bills. In total, building work constituted one of the most significant areas of spending, but each bill was of low value and covered servicing and
maintenance rather than rebuilding and remodelling. For example, in 1740 he
employed Jonathan Reading to paint some sash windows and various passages in

[11] Thompson, *English Landed Society*, 151–83; Elias, *Court Society*, 78–116.
[12] See Campbell, 'Understanding consumption'; Arnold, 'Country house'; Christie, *British Country
House*, 26–30, 84–6.

the house at a cost of £35 7s. 6d.; four years later, he paid Thomas Stanley £62 10s. 4d. for plumbing and glazing work.[13] Such work was vital in the upkeep of the house, but did little to materialize Thomas's masculinity in bricks and mortar.

There may be several practical reasons for the lack of large building projects, especially early in Thomas's reign. Firstly, his father had made very substantial changes to the Abbey, chiefly in the form of the massive west wing, which may have led Thomas to feel that further alterations were unnecessary.[14] Secondly, although he was very wealthy, Thomas had other significant calls on his finances. He was faced with bills for a series of funerals, starting with his father's, but also including those of his brother, son, and wife (see Chapter 6), to which was added the payment of legacies to many of his father's servants.[15] Moreover, although the estates had been enriched by the marriage of Thomas's father to Mary Holbech in 1705 and were worth an estimated £6,975 per annum on Thomas's death in 1749, he had inherited an indebted estate. During his father's tenure (1710–38) the estate had been accumulating rent arrears of £2,000 per annum, a problem that appears to have continued through Thomas's reign, which in part explains the £9,000 debts he left when he died.[16] Whilst these debts were not unusual and were settled by the trustees during the 1750s, they would undoubtedly have weighed on Thomas's mind when planning or contemplating large-scale remodelling and refurbishing of the house. 'Masculine spending' thus took place within the context of cyclical and generational peaks and troughs in income and spending, and not all men had the inclination or the opportunity to make their individual mark on the house.

Thirdly, it appears that Thomas's spending was curtailed by his mother Mary, despite her moving out of the family home when her son inherited the estate.[17] The influence of women on the material culture of the country house is now well known, although the literature has more often focused on women building rather than women stopping men building.[18] French and Rothery demonstrate that the influence of mothers was an inherent and accepted element in the development of masculine identities rather than an anti-patriarchal anomaly. They show the strong influence that mothers held over their sons whilst at public school and university, but also into adult life and even after marriage.[19] A steady stream of letters continually brought gentry men to task and reinforced familial values often at odds with the wider social norms attached to masculinity. One of the key skills they sought to imprint onto their sons was the need for thrift, which was their responsibility as the head of the household, to preserve the family patrimony as well as develop

---

[13] SCLA, DR18/5/2425; DR18/5/2697.

[14] Gomme, 'Abbey into Palace', 83. See also Chapter 2.   [15] SCLA, DR18/5/2227.

[16] MacDonald, 'Leigh family', 144; SCLA DR18/17/4/3, Statement of accounts of Lord Leigh, 10 March 1749.

[17] MacDonald, 'Leigh family', 148; A. Gomme, 'Stoneleigh after the Grand Tour', *The Antiquaries Journal*, 68 (1988), 271. This is discussed more fully in Chapter 6.

[18] See, for example, Vickery, *Behind Closed Doors*, 131–6; Christie, *British Country House*, 71–4; Worsley, 'Female architectural patronage'; Arnold, 'Defining femininity'.

[19] French and Rothery, *Man's Estate*. For examples dealing with the maternal influence on schooling, university, and marriage see 67–74, 95, and 195.

their own sense of social status, taste, and virtuosity. It is not unusual or unmanly, therefore, that Mary would wield such an influence over her son. Equally, the importance of thrift in aristocratic masculinities should serve as a counterweight to the expectation of historians that landed men should have spent extensively on remodelling their houses, a costly and sometimes ruinous business, as Wilson and Mackley make clear.[20] In this, British elite men were no different from their European counterparts: the excesses of Lord Harvey, for example, being paralleled by those of Count Jørgen Scheel of Ulstrop castle in Denmark. However, the practice of limiting spending to reasonable limits was entirely within orthodox notions of gentry masculinities and formed an important counterpoint to this excess.

The precise relationship between Mary and Thomas is uncertain, but it is striking that her death in 1743 coincided with the two significant pieces of building work undertaken by the fourth Lord Leigh. The first of these was the construction by the mason Thomas Pickford of a large dog kennel—an essential item for a landed gentleman interested in hunting. The second was a remodelling of the chapel by George Eborall, who redesigned the gallery and inserted a pulpit and pews at a total cost of £92.[21] At the same time, the Worcester stuccoist, John Wright, undertook extensive plasterwork for which he charged £296 11s. 11d. This included tabernacle frames on the walls, executed in a proto-rococo style: some for the doors and windows and some left blank, perhaps to contain paintings. For the ceiling, he made an elaborate centrepiece, described in his bill as 'a Blaze and Blunt Rays with Nine Cherub heads in the clouds' with two side panels. Gomme is rather dismissive of this work: the perspective is poor and the figures 'look rubbery and are not anatomically very plausible'.[22] Nonetheless, it reveals that Thomas, fourth Lord Leigh, was not entirely uninterested in the possibility of enhancing the ancestral home. The debts left at his death included at least £1,200 owing to a variety of craftsmen, including fairly modest sums for furniture.[23] He also commissioned designs for the Great Hall, left unfinished by his father, the third Lord Leigh: William Smith (son of Francis) noted on a bill submitted in January 1745 that he had 'charg'd Nothing for the designs and Estimates of the Hall', but these were left unexecuted at Thomas's death.[24]

Edward, when he came of age, spent at a different order of magnitude from his father, transforming the interior of Stoneleigh Abbey with new decorative schemes, huge amounts of furniture, and a large number of books. Both in his patronage of craftsmen and retailers and in the material outcome of this spending, Edward made a masculine statement of taste and power, albeit still quite modest in comparison with other wealthy landowners and falling short of a major building project. Much of the decorative work conformed to contemporary tastes for rococo and classical

[20] Wilson and Mackley, *Building of the English Country House*, 233–96.

[21] SCLA, DR18/3/47/55/6, Account of the workmen's bills at Stoneleigh, 12 January 1745.

[22] SCLA, DR18/3/47/55/5, John Wright's bill for plasterer's work done in Stoneleigh Chapel, 29 September 1744; Gomme, 'Abbey into palace', 91.

[23] SCLA, DR18/17/4/7, Robert Hughes's Account to Lord Craven, 1749–528; DR18/17/4/8, Account of Christopher Wright, 1749–53.

[24] SCLA, DR18/3/47/55/7, William Smith's bill for work and materials at Stoneleigh, 12 January 1745. See Gomme, 'Stoneleigh after the Grand Tour', 273–4.

motifs. The main staircase was adorned with a series of trophies which celebrate standard themes of elite male identity, including hunting, the arts, and music. This was the work of Robert Moores, who was paid a total of £605 10s. 6d. in 1765–6 for plasterwork—considerably more than the sum received by his former master, John Wright and perhaps incorporating some of the work in the Hall as well.[25] However, the decoration there was altogether different; we noted in Chapter 2 the style of the plasterwork and the selective narration of the life of Hercules. The theme is telling, *The Choice of Hercules* (between luxury and hard work) being popular in the eighteenth century, combining as it did classical mythology with Protestant Christian morality and the physical athleticism and bravery of Hercules himself. This would have made a powerful masculine statement of Edward's gentlemanly refinement and taste for anyone entering the Hall of Stoneleigh, communicating learning, virtue, and heroism.[26] Gomme considers at length the attribution of wall and ceiling panels, without reaching firm conclusions; but we know that Edward turned to the London carver Devereux Fox for the chimney pieces, over which two of the panels were placed (Figure 4.2). His bill for £130 12s. describes the work in detail, including a cornice adorned with 'Groops of Laurel and Oak Leaves, with Acorns & Berrys tied together with Ribbons; the Tablet with a Lyon laying on a Rock'. The room's theme is picked up in the 'Herculeses Heads, with a Lyon mask'd on the top, with the Skin hanging down over the Shoulders'.[27] Again, the quality of the work reinforces the messages of masculine taste and learning.

For the upper-storey rooms in the west range, Edward opted for wallpaper supplied by the London partnership of Bromwich and Leigh. In total twenty-nine rooms were papered at a cost of £356 10s.: mostly bedchambers and dressing rooms, but also closets (a traditional area for papering) and a water-closet.[28] Each room was adorned with between 100 and 120 yards of paper, along with brown underpaper, paper borders, and, in some rooms, papier mâché cornices or borders. Much of the paper was embossed, stuccoed, and striped with combinations of white and yellow, green, crimson, or Saxon blue, but Chinese papers were hung in three rooms (see Chapter 7). Some rooms stand out in terms of cost, notably those numbered 17 and 18, where Bromwich and Leigh charged £16 10s. and £16 4s. respectively for 'Indian paper', plus £3 12s. and £6 12s. for 'papiermache borders painted in colours'.[29] Given that the paper in most rooms cost £2–£6, it seems that these were intended for high-status guests. Edward's own bedchamber was decorated with a mix of chintz paper and gilt leather hangings, the latter perhaps suggesting a masculine style as well as a taste for old luxury. By contrast, Mary's bedchamber was hung with 'fine pea green' paper with the addition of papier mâché borders and knots in 'party gold' and a total of fifteen 'Indian pictures',

---

[25] Gomme,'Stoneleigh after the Grand Tour', 279.

[26] C. Aslet, 'Stoneleigh Abbey, Warwickshire', *Country Life*, (13 December 1984), 1847–8; Campbell, 'Understanding consumption', 49–51. Aslet suggests Joseph Spence's 1747 poem of this name as a scheme for the Stoneleigh plasterwork.

[27] SCLA, DR18/5/4203.   [28] SCLA, DR18/5/4402.

[29] These were the only rooms where there was a separate charge itemized for putting up the paper and borders: six days in room 17 (charged at £1 4s.) and two men for ten days in room 18 (£3 15s.)— SCLA, DR18/5/4402.

Figure 4.2. Chimney piece in the Great Hall, Stoneleigh Abbey (carved by Devereux Fox). Together with its pair on the opposite wall, this cost Edward Leigh £69 11s. in 1765.
Photograph by Jon Stobart.

framed with the same gold papier mâché. This was a more feminine style, especially as green was traditionally associated with love and pleasure,[30] but there is no
indication that Mary had any hand in choosing this scheme, despite the frequent
involvement of women in the decoration of domestic interiors. The correspondence with the London wallpaper merchants, Trollope & Sons, studied by Vickery
includes many letters from women and others that refer to the opinion of wives.
However, the majority of letters were from men, who bore the main responsibility
for refurbishment in general.[31]

What is significant here is that the homeowner's masculinity (or femininity) did
not need to be equally manifest in all domestic spaces. More specifically, we have a
single man, with no immediate prospect of a bride, showing decorative sensitivity
in a manner seldom discussed in the literature.[32] This was also seen in the furniture
and drapery acquired for the bedchambers being papered by Bromwich and for
several of the public rooms on the principal floor of the house. As noted earlier, in
Chapter 2, the former were furnished en suite, with fairly standard sets of furniture
and with the colour of the paper matching that of the drapery, whilst the latter
were fitted out in a tasteful manner.[33] Both types of room, however, lacked the
ostentatious displays of luxury and taste found in many larger country houses. He
eschewed painted ceilings, damask wall hangings and tapestries, and gilt work of
all types, and had no trophies of the Grand Tour to display to admiring guests.
Indeed, his choice of furnishings appears to reflect gentlemanly rather than aristocratic tastes: individual pieces were 'fine', 'solid', or 'neat', built in the plain style
which marked mainstream English taste at this time.[34]

Yet Edward also had grand ambitions and a larger vision for Stoneleigh Abbey.
In a portfolio of plans and designs assembled by Lord Leigh, there are a series of
five drawings depicting embellishments for the west front, probably in his own
hand.[35] These show a startling range of possibilities: two with hexastyle porticos as
grand entrances, of the type frequently added to aggrandize a house (as James
Wyatt did at Ragley Hall); one with a three domes and another with a single dome,
again creating a grand entrance; and finally a Gothic confection which adds arched
windows and a small vaulted portico. As Gomme notes, these were the work of 'a
dashing draughtsman but a pretty crazy architectural designer' and may indicate the
early stages of Edward's mental illness.[36] However, they reflect a genuine gentlemanly
interest in architecture that is mirrored in Edward's library and an appreciation of
stylistic possibilities, if not the principles of building. He also commissioned plans
for a large and impressive library, a new set of service buildings, including a large

---

[30] Vickery, *Behind Closed Doors*, 174.   [31] Vickery, *Behind Closed Doors*, 170–1.
[32] See Hussey and Ponsonby, *Single Homemaker*, 120–1; Vickery, *Behind Closed Doors*, 94.
[33] On the matching of wallpapers to drapery, see Cornforth, *Early Georgian Interiors*, 196.
[34] See Cornforth, *Early Georgian Interiors*, G. Beard, *Georgian Craftsmen and their Work* (London,
1966).
[35] SCLA, DR631/33, Designs for Stoneleigh Abbey.
[36] Gomme, 'Stoneleigh after the Grand Tour', 274–5. The domes have no structural support and
there is little notion of congruity of design. The Gothic vision may have been inspired by the work
done by Sanderson Miller at Adlestrop, the home of a cadet branch of the family who inherited
Stoneleigh Abbey after Mary Leigh's death in 1806.

brew house and laundry, and a huge new north wing—no doubt with an eye to complementing and perhaps upstaging his grandfather's monumental west wing.[37] That few of these plans came to fruition because of his insanity and early death might be seen as curtailing Edward's masculinity in terms of his dynastic impact. Yet this reflects a much broader tendency for the ambitions of even elite consumers to run ahead of their ability to realize them. Building may have been the ultimate expression of gentlemanly virtue, but it could easily be frustrated by demographic or economic misfortune, or be delayed by other commitments—to family, career, or investment, as was seen in Count Axel von Fersen's delayed construction of a new family residence at Ljung in Sweden.[38] Indeed, we might argue that a failure to follow through lavish building programmes in fact demonstrates appropriate manly restraint—an argument in line with French and Rothery's analysis of elite masculinity.[39] Control and management of the self were believed to be the basis of the projection of power and authority over others, whether family members or the lower orders, and the control of finances was considered to be a particularly important component of elite masculinities throughout the early-modern and modern periods. These imperatives spread across the globe, the Anglo-Indian, Sir Henry Russell, reminding his second son Charles that he must be financially 'on your own bottom' when refurbishing his new house in Hyderabad.[40] It is in this light that we should see critiques of the excessive spending of men like Count Jørgen Scheel in Denmark as being based not just on the financial difficulties that it brought to the family, but also the lack of control it displayed in the individual.

We have already seen that Edward was engaged in large-scale spending in other areas, including his personal interest in books, science, and music. Books formed a typical area of elite male spending—communicating taste, discernment, and learning—although it is surprisingly missing from Vickery's sample of gentry families.[41] Thomas, fourth Lord Leigh, was no bibliophile: according to the bills he spent a measly £17 on books across his twelve-year reign and a later memorandum from Edward records just twenty-one 'of my Father's books taken into my Library'.[42] In his attempts to assemble a gentleman's library worthy of the name, Edward therefore had to start from scratch. It is not just the sums laid out and the speed of acquisition that are impressive (around £1,600 in just five years): the variety and quality of his collection are equally striking.[43] This would appear to bracket him with collectors who valued rarity and completeness, priorities seen in tomes such

---

[37] SCLA, DR671/33, Designs for Stoneleigh Abbey; DR18/5/4291, Architectural designs by Giovanni Battista Cipriani, 1 April 1765.

[38] Ilmakunnas, 'To build according to one's status', 34–5.

[39] French and Rothery, *Man's Estate*.

[40] Quoted in Finn, 'Swallowfield Park', 7. For studies of other social groups, see A. Shepard, 'Manhood, credit and patriarchy in early-modern England *c*.1580–1640', *Past and Present*, 167 (2000), 75–106; A. Fletcher, 'Manhood, the male body, courtship and household in early-modern England', *History*, 84 (1999), 419–36; H. Berry, 'Soul, purse and family: middling and lower-class masculinity in eighteenth-century Manchester', *Social History*, 33 (2008), 12–35.

[41] Vickery, *Behind Closed Doors*, 106–29; Brewer, *Pleasures of the Imagination*, 167–97.

[42] SCLA, DR18/4/75, List of books at Stoneleigh Abbey, 1766 and 1785.

[43] For detailed discussion of the collection, see M. Purcell, '"A lunatick of unsound mind": Edward, Lord Leigh (1742–86)', *Bodleian Library Record*, 17 (2001), 246–60.

as his copy of *Recueil des peintures antiques*, acquired from Paul Vaillant for the princely sum of £52 10*s*. Printed in Paris in 1757 for the Comte de Caylus, one of the great figures of French neoclassicism, this includes thirty-three hand-coloured plates depicting Roman wall paintings. Only thirty copies were printed, making it a rare as well as a spectacular volume—one that says much about Edward's taste and discernment, but also one that tied him firmly into a culture of European connoisseurship and collecting. Moreover, it was held in a gold-tooled morocco binding from the workshop of the French *relieur du roi*, Antoine-Michel Padeloup, an association which increased its value and its attraction as a collector's item.[44] However, Edward was also alive to other priorities in book collecting, acquiring at least sixteen volumes published by Elsevier, the Dutch publisher whose books were much in demand by collectors in Georgian England.[45] This again provided a link with European scholarship and taste, although he appears to have been less interested in paintings than was seen in the purchases of collectors such as Count Carl Gustaf Tessin, who bought paintings from François Boucher and Jean-Siméon Chardin, amongst others.[46]

Edward's collecting also lacked any notion of excess or imprudence. Tessin could playfully describe his purchases of art as follies, writing to a friend that they should 'close the curtain over other[s], I see you are looking at me with pity'.[47] In contrast, Edward's library included many useful volumes covering law, gardening, parliamentary debates, and algebra. These were organized in a fairly standard system, Edward's memorandum listing volumes under various thematic headings (including 'poetry & plays', 'antiquities, architecture, ruins, &c', but also 'catches', and 'algebra, figures, mathematics, logic & metaphysics') and giving a letter and number reference, presumably corresponding to bookcases and shelves (Figure 4.3).[48] These were spread across a number of rooms at Stoneleigh: the old library contained the majority, but they were also found in the Music Room, Picture Gallery, and Study.[49] This ad hoc arrangement reflects another of Edward's unfulfilled ambitions: the construction of a two-storey library, complete with three reading rooms and a museum, probably designed to house his scientific instruments.[50]

---

[44] SCLA, DR18/5/4202; Purcell, 'A lunatick of unsound mind', 254.

[45] SCLA, 18/4/75, List of books at Stoneleigh Abbey, 1766 and 1785; N. Ramsay, 'English book collectors and the salerooms in the eighteenth century', in R. Myers, M. Harris, and G. Mandelbrooke (eds) *Under the Hammer: Book Auctions since the Seventeenth Century* (New Castle, DE, 2001), 101.

[46] J. Ilmakunnas, 'The luxury shopping experience of the Swedish aristocracy in eighteenth-century Paris', in D. Simonton, M. Kaartinen, and A. Montenach (eds), *Luxury and Gender in European Towns, 1700–1914* (London, 2015), 118.

[47] Quoted in Ilmakunnas, 'Luxury shopping experience', 118.

[48] SCLA, DR18/4/75, List of books at Stoneleigh Abbey, 1766 and 1785. On the importance of the library catalogue, see, inter alia, D. Stoker, 'The ill-gotten library of "Honest Tom" Martin', in R. Myers and M. Harris (eds), *Property of a Gentleman: The Formation, Organisation and Dispersal of the Private Library 1620–1920* (Winchester and Newcastle, DE, 1991), 91–111.

[49] SCLA, DR18/4/43, Inventory, 1774, with 1806 amendments. See also Stobart, 'Luxury of learning'.

[50] SCLA, DR671/33, Designs for Stoneleigh Abbey.

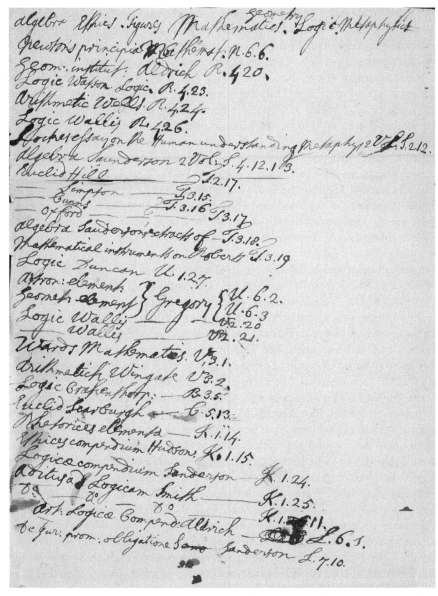

Figure 4.3. Section of a preliminary catalogue of books written by Edward, fifth Lord Leigh, in 1766.

Source: SCLA, 18/4/75. © Shakespeare Birthplace Trust.

Science and music appear to have been particular interests for Edward. His collection of scientific instruments went beyond what was typical of the aristocratic man of leisure. He had the usual globes and barometers, but also bought an air pump, syringes, receivers, cylinder glasses, and other equipment from Edward Nairne, a noted scientific instrument maker of Cornhill in London who patented several electrical machines.[51] Edward's decision to bequeath both his library and his scientific instruments to his alma mater might be seen as further evidence that he wanted these things to be accessible to others—a key aspect in ensuring that collections communicated their owner's taste and distinction, albeit in this case post mortem.[52] That they would also be used was facilitated by his gift of £1,000 to the Vice Chancellor of Oxford University and the Provost of Oriel College to purchase further scientific equipment to illustrate lectures.[53] Edward's passion for music is apparent in the hundreds of scores contained in his library. Of particular note are the numerous volumes of catches by a wide range of composers, which links to Edward's membership of the aristocratic *Catch Club* that sought to encourage the composition and performance of canons, catches, and glees.[54] This practical interest is underlined by his ownership of a volume listed simply as 'violin tutor' and by a 1764 bill from William Hayes which includes £17 8s. 9d. for attending 205 times to give music lessons and tune the harpsichord.[55]

Edward was thus a very different man from his father, who showed no interest in these kinds of objects, either as a 'polite scientist' or, as Edward appears to have been, a more serious scholar. The 1749 inventory, composed after Thomas's death, makes no mention of this kind of equipment: not a barometer to be seen and the only clock, that most basic of scientific instruments, was placed 'under the best stairs'.[56] Instead, Thomas appears to have enjoyed riding and hunting. The construction of the new dog kennel in 1743–6 involved payments totalling £298, suggesting a large pack of hounds was being kept at the house.[57] Around the same time, there were several large accounts from the steward at Warwick races. The details recorded in these are not entirely clear, but the costs appear to reflect Lord Leigh's involvement in organizing the races and the associated junketing, rather than gambling debts. There are, for instance, payments for the 'Trumpet, Rope &c' and two jockeys, and for music and candles at the ball; but there are also receipts for money collected at the ordinary and the ball, and for 'the Warwick contribution' to the overall costs.[58] At home, Thomas acquired a set of twenty-four racing prints, which he hung in private family rooms. Such costs are absent from Edward's bills, but he shared his father's desire for the coaches, horses, and saddlery that befitted his status. In this area, Thomas outspent his son, laying out £719

[51] SCLA, DR18/5/4515, DR18/5/4385.
[52] See Barczewski, *Country Houses and the British Empire*.
[53] SCLA, DR18/13/7/13–4, Will and codicil of Edward, Lord Leigh, 1767.
[54] For example SCLA, DR18/5/4554.
[55] SCLA, DR18/4/75, List of books at Stoneleigh Abbey, 1766 and 1785; DR18/5/4173.
[56] SCLA, DR18/4/25, Inventory of goods remaining at Stoneleigh, 1749.
[57] SCLA, DR18/31/457, Miscellaneous accounts, 1735–44; DR18/31/458, Stoneleigh estate accounts, 1744–6.
[58] SCLA, DR18/5/2381.

compared to £534 by Edward, although none of his bills record a new coach: it seems he preferred to repair and refurbish those inherited from his father, a process which included adding new coronets at a cost of £3 4s.[59] Whilst this may again have reflected his mother's restraining influence, the overall level of spending suggests otherwise, as does the purchase in March 1739 of a 'Leopard Skin Side Sadle & Housing Trimed with Gold fringe & Lace' costing £23 2s. and, just three months later, of another 'Fine Leopard Housing & bags Trim'd with Gold fringe & Lace, very Rich' which cost £26 5s.[60] This display of luxurious exoticism was found across Europe in the eighteenth century (a portrait of Marie Antoinette shows her riding on a leopard-skin saddle), indicating that Thomas was not just a man who liked his horses to be well furnished, but also one in touch with the finest taste. By contrast, Edward acquired a new coach from James Cope in 1765, described in the bill as having 'neat ornament mouldings, painted with a glaz'd ruby colour, and the arms and dignity in very large mantles, and all the framework gilt, and the roof, back and sides japan'd', and another from John Hatchett in 1771.[61] But the spending of neither man was excessive and there is little evidence here of the fetishistic penchant for horse furniture and tackle highlighted by Vickery as a particular feature of elite male spending.[62] In fact, as we discuss in Chapter 5 in more detail, Mary Leigh, Edward's sister, spent more than her brother and father combined on these goods.

This failure to conform to gender stereotypes in purchases of saddlery was repeated, to an extent, in terms of clothing. Thomas again spent more, although some of the £894 10s. laid out to tailors, haberdashers, drapers, and the like was to furnish the bodies of his wife and mother rather than his own. In any case, an annual average of around £82 was very modest and suggests that the £435 spent by Sir John Hynde Cotton was exceptional as well as 'splendid'.[63] Judging from his bills, Edward's outgoings on clothing were even more modest, amounting to an overall total of just £681. Some of the clothing and tailoring he purchased was of good quality and richly decorated. He paid William Fell £9 4d. 4s. for gold embroidered buttonholes for a coat and waistcoat in 1766, for instance, along with two waistcoats, one 'white and gold satin' and the other 'gold and green bordered'.[64] Bills such as this arrived fairly frequently at Stoneleigh and the goods were no doubt valued for their quality, but Edward could hardly be said to be very focused on his clothing. His masculinity was not defined by stylish waistcoats, or by guns and horses for that matter: he represented a different form of masculine identity.[65] He was both typical of elite male practices of collecting and seemingly exceptional in his erudition and intellectual abilities. This same paradox was also seen in his plans for remodelling the west front of Stoneleigh Abbey: they reflect a wider tradition of the gentleman architect, but reveal an individual with extraordinary

---

[59] SCLA, DR18/5/2360.
[60] SCLA, DR18/5/2331; L.-A. Brun de Versoix, *Portrait équestre de la reine Marie-Antoinette* (c. 1783), Musée national des châteaux de Versailles et de Trianon, MV 5718.
[61] SCLA, DR18/5/4350, DR48/5/4893.   [62] Vickery, *Behind Closed Doors*, 124.
[63] Vickery, *Behind Closed Doors*, 114.   [64] SCLA, DR18/5/4483.
[65] See Hussey, 'Guns, horses and stylish waistcoats'.

vision and either a playful or eccentric willingness to experiment with different styles. These characteristics also tie in to his masculine identity as a virtuous scholar, although he was no unworldly aesthete. Thomas's masculinity is more difficult to define. He lacked his son's interest in books and learning, and apparently had few pretensions as a collector, despite undertaking a Grand Tour in 1748 with his second wife, Catherine Berkeley. His enjoyment of hunting and racing might bracket him with the rather boorish country squire frequently mocked in metropolitan journals, but it would be a mistake to dismiss him so easily. He was clearly aware of the dignity of the family and the ancestral home, and invested time and money in improving the house, as well as in public sociability. Indeed, he might be seen as approximating to the stereotype of the polite gentleman, with its concern for display, sociability, and manners.[66] In contrast, Edward's politeness was more akin to the interiority of the virtuous and more 'genuine' gentility found in our next subject, Sir Roger Newdigate.

CONSUMPTION AND SELF-FASHIONING: SIR ROGER NEWDIGATE AND ARBURY HALL

Whilst the receipted bills provide us with a full flavour of the consumption choices made by Edward and Thomas Leigh, in the case of Sir Roger Newdigate we have a far better picture of his character through a series of personal sources, most notably his diaries and his correspondence, both of which cover long periods of his life.[67] They show that his work on Arbury, as well as his lengthy public life as an MP, was critically important to his development and identity as a man. At home, Sir Roger's building projects were sustained over long periods of time, from the 1750s through to the early nineteenth century, reflecting the long-term planning and patience of a gentleman determined to make a statement through architecture. This continuous preoccupation with building was a means to an end, but also an activity reflective of masculine pursuits and identity. Studying architecture, the liberal arts and sciences, and shaping the structure and appearance of his country house were all part of Newdigate's ongoing construction of polite masculinity. At the same time, the meticulous nature of Sir Roger's account books, the regularity and the very form of the entries themselves, reflect his attention to both the detail of the physical works at Arbury and the process of self-fashioning that the works represented. As a politician, Newdigate was a Tory defender of the constitution, the Church of England and the universities, and was rigorously opposed to reform. He greatly valued the independent country tradition in parliamentary politics and detested attachment to party and ideology, often deriding the process of politics both privately and publicly. Writing to the Vice Chancellor of Oxford late in his career, for example, he complained that parliament contained 'only a wretched abuse of talents & a dearth of public virtue. In all of them, majorities implicitly following the

---

[66] See Campbell, 'Understanding consumption'; French and Rothery, *Man's Estate*, *passim*.
[67] WRO, CR136/A/582, Diaries; White, *Correspondence of Sir Roger Newdigate*.

dictates of the Minister of the day, changing their opinions as the Minister was changed.'[68] But Newdigate was no 'backwoods Tory Squire': his individual personality and character transcended stereotypes and he was a complex man in many ways.

Newdigate's experiences in education and on his travels in Europe were quite orthodox: they were seen as central to the development of elite masculinities, adding a 'social polish', instilling the values of independence and self-control, and providing the polite refinements and practical skills in managing one's own affairs that distinguished landed gentlemen from others.[69] As such, they were typical of the European elite and helped to inculcate a shared set of cultural values and aspirations. Newdigate's letters to his mother whilst on his first Grand Tour suggest that he benefited greatly in these ways, although they contain many of the somewhat formulaic ingredients of such correspondence: the 'gaze' of the tourist, the process of understanding the unfamiliar and thereby controlling the experience.[70] He described significant places he had visited, commenting on the architecture and the luxurious material objects they contained. The Duke of Chantilly's castle was 'a fine old building' with stables '600 feet long. In the middle is an opening with a cupola and opposite the door is a cistern adorn'd with the statues of horses as big as life.'[71] At the Palace of Versailles he found the Great Gallery to be 'the finest room I ever saw. It's entirely wainscoted with looking glass and marble of different kinds, and adorn'd with antique statues set in niches.'[72] He mixed in polite circles to add polish to his gentlemanly refinement and commented on the appearance and manners of the company. Lady Vane, for instance, was 'very gentiley dress'd, and painted *à la mode* françoise, the purest vermilion.'[73] But he was also concerned with more practical matters, carefully recording the process of provisioning for and managing the journey as well as his entourage: 'since I began we have agreed for our chaises at 19 guineas each. We have nothing now to do but to buy saddles and jack boots for the servants.'[74] This spoke of dutiful management of his resources, as did his observation in Paris that he had the satisfaction of 'finding my cloaths in the top of the fashion, so sav'd the expens of making any alterations'.[75]

All this was standard fare; unlike many other young men on the Grand Tour, however, these experiences proved to be more than a means to achieve social status and acceptability, a necessary stage on the journey to manliness and training in the practice of authority. Coupled with his later Grand Tour and his experiences as a gentleman builder, they helped to make Newdigate a particular type of polite

[68] WRO, CR136/B/2012, Letter, 1 June 1780.

[69] M. Cohen, 'The grand tour: language, national identity and masculinity', *Changing English*, 8 (2001), 129–41; French and Rothery, *Man's Estate*, 137–54.

[70] C. Chard, 'Grand and ghostly tours: the topography of memory', *Eighteenth Century Studies*, 31 (1997), 101–8.

[71] WRO, CR136/B/4578, Letter, 27 August 1738.

[72] WRO, CR136/B/4579, Letter, 8 September 1738.

[73] WRO, CR136/B/4579, Letter, 8 September 1738.

[74] WRO, CR136/B4577, Letter, 21 August 1738.

[75] WRO, CR136/B4579, Letter, 8 September 1738. In this, he contrasted with Clas Julius Ekeblad, a Swedish aristocrat, who was censured by his father for wastefully buying a new velvet coat in Paris: see Ilmakunnas, 'Luxury shopping experience', 120.

Georgian gentleman. Although politeness provided more social and conversational space for middling sorts of men, acting as a lubricator between traditional elites and urban commercial and professional men, it was also a central reference point for the gentry and the aristocracy.[76] Indeed, the 'polite gentleman' formed an important type within eighteenth-century masculinity that spanned national boundaries.[77] At its most superficial it denoted acceptable forms of social behaviour, ranging from dress and deportment to conversational skills. The ability to interact in polite society in the public sphere, particularly with women, but also in all-male institutions such as coffee houses, was a prized ingredient.[78] Above all politeness was about self-management and the control of emotions. This kind of politeness was focused on the 'outer self', the 'set of attitudes, strategies, skills and devices that an individual could command to gratify others and thus render the social realm truly sociable'.[79] But polite gentility was also about interiority, about virtue and civility gleaned through self-improvement and study, characteristics that had a longer history stretching back to the seventeenth century. This focused on skills and knowledge acquired through learning, self-improvement, and personal accomplishment and applied to cultural activities such as architecture, the arts, and the sciences, the kind of politeness Lawrence Klein found in the third Earl of Shaftesbury.[80]

It was this internal politeness that Newdigate identified with and built his character around. He certainly valued sociability and polite company, as his correspondence shows; but he placed most value on his identity as a polite *learned* gentleman, a serious scholar, historian, and antiquarian with a commitment to the process of learning, and a recognized expert in architecture and literature. His politeness sprang from an interiority of character, a 'genuine' politeness rather than the 'showy' external politeness expressed in dress, manners and deportment, language, and sociability. He encapsulated these values in his perceptions of other men. In 1780, on formally resigning from Parliament, where he had seen 'the lowest baseness', he complimented the virtues of Oxford University, embodied in the Vice Chancellor: 'Long may you flourish, as at present, the firm support and brightest ornament of the establish'd constitution, the source of science & elegant refinement, the school of perfect morality.'[81] In contrast, Newdigate rejected superficiality, jokingly suggesting to his wife Sophia, 'You may expect a very gallant

---

[76] P. Langford, 'The uses of eighteenth-century politeness', *Transactions of the Royal Historical Society*, 6th ser., 12 (2002), 311–31. See also P. Carter, *Men and the Emergence of Polite Society, Britain 1660–1800* (Harlow, 2001); L. E. Klein, 'Politeness and the interpretation of the British eighteenth century', *The Historical Journal*, 45 (2002), 869–98; K. Harvey, 'The history of masculinity, circa 1650–1800', *Journal of British Studies*, 44 (2005), 296–311; M. Cohen, '"Manners" make the man: politeness, chivalry and the construction of masculinity, 1750–1830', *Journal of British Studies*, 44 (2005), 312–29.

[77] Connell, *Masculinities*, 186–99 offers a sociological perspective and Harvey, 'History of masculinity', discusses the shift from the 'Household Patriarch' to the 'Polite Gentleman'. For a re-evaluation of the idea of hegemonic masculinities, see French and Rothery, *Man's Estate*, 3–15.

[78] Harvey, 'History of masculinity'.

[79] L. Klein, 'The third Earl of Shaftesbury and the progress of politeness', *Eighteenth-Century Studies*, 18 (1984–5), 186–214.

[80] Klein, 'Third Earl of Shaftesbury.'   [81] WRO, CR136/B/2012, Letter, 1 June 1780.

Macaroni ready to take you out of your coach' when they next met.[82] In fact, he spent well on clothes for himself, the account books recording £5,933 in this category over a period of fifty-five years—an average of £107 that compares favourably with the outgoings of the Leighs. The details are scant, but purchases in the 1750s included a scarlet frock coat, a blue dress frock coat, a blue satin suit, a brown dress suit, and several black and plain mixed cloth suits. Whilst colourful and expensive dress suits were to be found in his wardrobe (his blue satin suit cost £13 2s. 3d.), these were clearly for special public occasions; Newdigate's usual clothing was sober and more in keeping with his character as a serious man of politics and learning.[83]

Newdigate's particular form of 'inner' politeness was reflected in his correspondence from his second Grand Tour between 1774 and 1775, undertaken at the age of 55. In Florence, he wrote to his friend, John Mordaunt, that he was 'constantly employ'd & engag'd with objects that engage our attention & amuse & please us...Our mornings are spent amongst the statues, paintings, intaglios & cameos, medals, antiquities Roman & Etruscan, of the immense collection call'd the Gallery.'[84] The evenings, however, were taken up with less serious pursuits, including operas, comedies, and masked balls, and he spent a considerable amount of time shopping. Some of this involved the acquisition of significant collector's items. He negotiated in Italian with the antiquary and engraver, Giovanni Piranesi (an indication of his breadth of learning), and sealed in a formal contract the purchase of two candelabra subsequently installed in the Radcliffe Library in Oxford.[85] But a much wider range of goods were within his purview, as is apparent from the last paragraph of his letter to Mordaunt, which reads: 'Can we do anything for you in this country – Books, Music, Perfumes, Sculpture, painting. Send your orders we shall execute them with pleasure.'[86] This kind of proxy shopping was common amongst tourists and was an important mechanism for those remaining at home to acquire some of the material trappings of cosmopolitanism; but it reveals another side of Newdigate, as a man in touch with the growing spirit of consumerism and alive to his potential usefulness to friends at home.[87] Such utility came in the form of connections as well as geographical location. In the mid-1750s, in the process of donating the Arundel Marbles to the University of Oxford, Lady Pomfret sought Newdigate's assistance in recommending them as donations. He wrote to the Vice Chancellor that they were an 'inestimable collection of statues, bustos and other antiquities' that fully merited the time and expense of proper mounting and display

---

[82] WRO, CR136/B/4046e, Letter, 25 March 1773. On the macaroni and the fop as forms of masculinity, see Cohen, '"Manners" make the man'.

[83] WRO, CR136/V/156, Account book, entries for 1750, 1756–60. On the growing dominance of dark and sober clothing for gentlemen, see D. Kuchta, *The Three-Piece Suit and Modern Masculinity: England 1550–1850* (London, 2002), although the dominance of this shift is far from settled.

[84] WRO, CR1368/V/33, Letter, 6 December 1774.

[85] WRO, CR136/B2010, Letter, 6 May 1775, translated in White, *Correspondence of Sir Roger Newdigate*, 206–7. See also M. McCarthy, 'Sir Roger Newdigate and Piranesi', *The Burlington Magazine*, 114 (1972), 468–72.

[86] WRO, CR1368/V/33, Letter, 6 December 1774.

[87] See Ilmakunnas, 'Luxury shopping experience'; Walsh, 'Shops, shopping'.

in Oxford.[88] This forms just one example of Newdigate acting in a manner which consciously shaped the material culture of the university and equally consciously built his reputation as a man of learning. In 1764, for instance, his assistance was sought in renovating and beautifying the Hall of his alma mater, University College, and in raising the necessary finance for the scheme.[89] Some of this, of course, resulted from patronage derived from his position as the MP for Oxford University, but he was undoubtedly considered, both by himself and by others, to be an able scholar and student of antiquities, literature, and architecture.

This reputation coincided with Newdigate's own consumption practices. Along with the candelabra from Piranesi, he acquired a range of medals, vases, and casts that enhanced both his collection at Arbury and his standing as a classical scholar.[90] At the same time, and in common with standard practices of the time, he had copies made of numerous paintings by old masters and acquired a smaller number of contemporary watercolours. These were augmented by the ornamental china-ware produced by Wedgwood from casts supplied by Newdigate (see Chapter 1). Ancient and modern were thus combined in a material sense, but also in Newdigate's connections to networks of supply and knowledge, and through his construction as a learned and polite gentleman. This same interlinking was manifest in his acquisition and deployment of books. As well as laying out over £2,596 with book-sellers in England, he spent £826 on books whilst on his second Grand Tour. The latter included two copies of the twelve-volume set of engravings by Piranesi, one of which he notes as being presented to the Bodleian Library in Oxford, an action which constructed him as an intermediary between European culture and scholarly activity.[91]

As with Edward, fifth Lord Leigh, we see the collector's desire for high-quality and rare volumes. A catalogue drawn up shortly after his death records at least three books printed in the fifteenth century, including Aldus Manutius' 1498 edition of *Aristophanes*, and 261 sixteenth-century books, for example, the 1515 Manutius edition of Dante's *Divine Comedy* and Michele Mercati's 1589 *Degli obelischi di Roma*. There were also numerous multivolume folio works, ranging from a 1742 edition of Johann Albert Fabricius' *Bibliotheca Graeca* in fourteen volumes, through the Comte de Buffon's thirty-five-volume *Histoire naturelle* of 1749–74, to twenty-five volumes of Lords and Commons debates.[92] But Newdigate was a man in less of a hurry; notwithstanding an understandable splurge of spending whilst in Italy, books were acquired slowly over several decades. As his collection grew, so did his reputation. A series of letters between Sir Roger and a London publisher, A. Foulis, showed the esteem in which his taste and knowledge of liter-ature, and also of the market for literature, were held. Foulis asked Newdigate for advice on the layout, price, and number of volumes of an edition of the Greek

---

[88] WRO, CR136/B/2979, Letter, 13 February 1755. In fact, their placement and display remained an unresolved issue at Newdigate's death.

[89] WRO, CR136/B/1860, Letter, 19 October 1764.

[90] WRO, CR136/B/2638b, Books, marbles, etc. See also Chapter 8.

[91] WRO, CR136/B/2638b, Books, marbles, etc.

[92] WRO, CR1841/57, Shelf catalogue of the library at Arbury, *c*.1810.

tragic poets, to which he replied with practical suggestions and an enthusiasm to effectively underwrite the project by subscribing for whatever number was needed to ensure a profit could be made.[93] Such status was endowed in perpetuity in the form of the Newdigate Prize for Verse at Oxford, established by Sir Roger shortly before his death, a lasting memorial to his association with the university and his character as a polite gentleman.[94] Again like Lord Leigh, Newdigate's collection of books was thus not simply an ornament: he was keen for learning to be facilitated whenever possible. His library catalogue shows a systematic and orderly arrangement that was typical of gentlemen's libraries; books were organized by theme and size; his Italian books were shelved together and a note made of their individual provenance; and the publication date and number of volumes in each book were carefully recorded. Sir Roger was clearly a man who liked order as well as books. He extended his reading well beyond the 3,406 books recorded in the catalogue by borrowing from circulating libraries and friends, carefully writing down all the titles in a notebook, along with the date they came to Arbury, and to whom and when they were sent next.[95]

This attention to detail was characteristic of the man, an important part of his identity, but so too was his learning and scholarship. It is no accident that he chose to be painted by Arthur Devis seated in his new Gothic library, leaning on his desk, with plans for Arbury in his hand and surrounded by his books (Figure 4.4). Three things are particularly striking about this: first, Devis painted realistic but generally imaginary settings for his subjects, so including this real-life depiction holds extra meaning; second, an earlier painting by his sister-in-law, Mary Conyers, also places Sir Roger in his library, this time a conventional classical assemblage predating the Gothicization of Arbury; and third, his wife Sophia appears in both images, seated at her needlework in her sister's painting, and as a picture within Devis's portrait, hung behind Sir Roger and in pride of place over the fire.[96] This is clearly no accident and makes apparent the great affection that existed between Sir Roger and Sophia. It also adds another layer onto his masculine identity: that of a devoted husband who wrote to his wife frequently and with real animation, involving her in his public as well as his private life and drawing sustenance from everyday domesticity. Similar affection is apparent for his second wife, Hester Mundy, but neither marriage was blessed with children. Quite apart from the issues this raised with regard to inheritance, he had not been able to practise his patriarchal authority over children, thereby being disavowed of an important element of the masculine self, as fatherhood was a key component of masculinity.[97] He did play out this role as surrogate father to three individuals, to his protégé Charles Parker (discussed in more detail in Chapter 6) and his second wife's protégé Sally Shilton, and briefly

[93] WRO, CR136/B/1687, Letter, 21 August 1786; CR136/B1688, Letter, 4 September 1786.
[94] See WRO, CR136/B/3522b, Letter, 24 January 1805.
[95] WRO, CR136/A/565, Books received at Arbury, from 1783.
[96] On Devis's work, see K. Retford, *The Art of Domestic Life: Family Portraiture in Eighteenth-Century England* (New Haven, CT, 2007); Mary Conyer's watercolour is reproduced in Cornforth, *Early Georgian Interiors*, 70.
[97] For a discussion of the literature on fatherhood and masculinity, see French and Rothery, *Man's Estate*, 185–90.

Figure 4.4. Sir Roger Newdigate in his new library at Arbury Hall (Arthur Devis, *c.*1756).
Note the portrait of his wife, Sophia, hung over the fireplace.
Reproduced by kind permission of Viscount Daventry.

as a godfather to Charles's son, also called Charles. His affectionate and sentimental character comes out clearly in his descriptions of these individuals. Of Charles senior he said: 'how amiable when only a child, how improved by education, how good, how grateful, how pious! As a husband, as a father!'[98] In a letter to a friend he referred to Sally as 'Our sweet siren', but it was Charles's son that received perhaps the most striking adulation. Directly addressing the newly born child in 1793, Sir Roger advised him 'to stretch out your little hands, both of them, remember, & take Papa by the Chin, kiss him & Mamma till they laugh, for no good can come to him—*Cui non risere parentes* [on whom his parents have not smiled]'.[99] Yet even here Newdigate showed his gentlemanly learning, the Latin being drawn directly from the *Carmina* by the Roman poet Catullus, and he assumed it in others, adding that 'I don't explain this, as I conclude your knowledge in all languages is the same.'

The combination of polite learning and family was repeated in the way that Newdigate constructed his masculine identity in and through the material form of Arbury Hall. Sir Roger built according to his own changing tastes but with a view to a grand design for Arbury which, as discussed in Chapter 2, formed a coherent and bold message. The work itself and Newdigate's careful management were also an expression of his patriarchal authority as the head of the household, a unit which, as Harvey has noted, formed a 'prism through which men were viewed'. Moreover, she argues, men's 'household management reinforced their social authority',[100] a responsibility that was writ large in the process of renovation and remodelling at country houses such as Arbury, not least because this involved a close control of costs and designs. The sheer length of time that Newdigate took over the works at Arbury and the intricate planning and implementation in which he engaged speak of the importance of the process as well as the outcome.

Tyack describes how work progressed from one room to another, but it is also possible to see it as a series of concurrent projects within an overall scheme. Some of the earliest work was undertaken on the new library, a telling reflection of its importance in channelling his identity as a virtuous scholar. A bow window was commissioned in 1750 and completed in 1752, at a cost of £50.[101] Work continued with fresh painting in 1755, a brickwork arch in 1769, and a new chimney piece and grate in the 1770s before stalling in the 1780s. Commencing again in 1791 with designs for the ceiling in February and March, the stuccowork was completed in May and, on 1 August, Sir Roger could proudly and perhaps with some relief note in his diary: 'Library finished.'[102] Work on the Hall (now the Dining Room) commenced a little later, but again continued for decades. In 1761 we see Mr Keene taking measurements of the Hall and the front of the house, but

---

[98] WRO, CR136/B/2014, Letter, 29 April 1795. This letter was written to Charles's widow, Jane Parker, shortly after his death. Sir Roger goes on to promise that 'you may depend upon me to be a father to the sweet orphans & Lady Newdigate to be another nursing mother'.
[99] WRO, CR136/B/2439b, Letter, 14 June 1796; CR136/B/2145, Letter, no date, June 1793. In the same letter Newdigate also quotes from Virgil's *Eclogues*—see White, *Correspondence of Sir Roger Newdigate*, 262.
[100] Harvey, *Little Republic*, 134. [101] WRO, CR136/V/156, Account book, entry for 1752.
[102] WRO, CR136/A/582, Diaries, 1 August 1791.

it was not until eight years later that the bow window and then the great chimney were pulled down in readiness for the rest of the works on the window, the ceiling, and chimney piece, which then proceeded more rapidly.[103] By December, Newdigate notes that the Hall is first inhabited and used, as it was the 'warmest room in the house'—the domestic comfort noted in Chapter 3 being underlined by a feeling of self-satisfaction.[104] This short period of rest was then followed by another fifteen years of work, involving the placement of statues in 1778 (the one of Cupid broke as it was being lifted into place and had to be repaired), plastering and glazing in 1780 and 1784, and further plastering and painting in 1787 and 1788. Finally, on 27 May 1788 he reported that he had 'returned to inhabit the hall' and the project was completed, as his often were, with the placement of chandeliers.[105]

The remodelling of the old parlour into a drawing room was a similarly protracted process, as was the creation of the Saloon. It appears that the Newdigates inhabited rooms as and when they could, then moved into other rooms as the next phase of work commenced. At times the complexity of this process and the other demands on Sir Roger produced discernible consternation, as in 1771, when he explained his tardy reply to Nathaniel Wetherell, at Oxford, by reference to 'the incumbrance of a house not yet clear'd of my Churchman friends, the short time left me for the settling of [my] affairs & the necessary preparations for removing my family to Town, the number of workmen in my house and many more out of it'.[106] What heightened both the labour he had to put in and the impact this had on his identity was Newdigate's active involvement in all stages and all aspects of the work. As noted earlier, in Chapter 2, he had a large hand in designing many aspects of the house: in June 1765, he was 'with Mr Keene planning', two days after the designer had travelled from Oxford 'to consult on ... Arbury new front'; in November 1770, he was 'drawing plan of roof of hall logia'; June the following year found him 'planning hall ceiling'; and in August 1781 he was alongside 'Mr Couchman settling the height of the cloister windows'.[107] Sometimes he seems to have inhabited the world of his workmen, for example where he records that he had 'finished the Battlements over the library staircase and tiled the house'.[108] This was more than a figurative expression used in diaries. In a letter to Sophia, written a year after the works on the exterior of Arbury had begun, he described a visit to the house of Lord Edgcumbe. 'The stone of this country', he wrote, 'is too hard and rough to work to a truth, as we masons say.'[109] The physicality of the work of building was as important for Newdigate as his own expertise and knowledge; the work represented a process of crafting both the house and himself.

[103] WRO, CR136/A/582, Diaries, 18 April 1761, 21 June 1769, 11 July 1770, 14 June 1773.

[104] WRO, CR136/A/582, Diaries, 29 December 1773.

[105] WRO, CR136/A/582, Diaries, 21 June 1778, 14 February 1780, 19 May 1784, 12 September 1787, 27 July 1788, 14 July 1778.

[106] WRO, CR136/B/2341, Letter, 11 January 1771.

[107] WRO, CR136/A/582, Diaries, 10 June 1761, 26 November 1770, 16 June 1771, 1 August 1781.

[108] WRO, CR136/A/582, Diaries, 15 September 1770.

[109] WRO, CR136/B/4592, Letter, 17 October 1762.

This reveals some of the complexities of Newdigate's masculine identity that do not precisely map onto stereotypes of 'politeness', which is to be expected when such typologies are studied in detail through an individual. Newdigate jealously guarded and propagated his status as a learned gentleman, as an expert in the polite accomplishments of architecture and literature, and as a gentleman of taste; but he also valued hard work and industry, qualities often more associated with the 'punishing work ethic' of the 'earnest' Victorian middle-class man.[110] Long walks were a favourite form of exercise and, as Anthony Wood has noted, his diaries are replete with entries such as 'Walked to Colliery and canal now cleaning up from the Junction.'[111] Whilst such qualities may seem at odds with the stereotype of leisured country gentleman, recent studies of gentry masculinity have found them to be a common and persistent occurrence across long periods of British history.[112] In a letter of advice to his infant godson, Charles Newdigate Parker, Sir Roger warned him that 'instruction cannot come too soon, and it is never too early to be wise! You have a great deal to do, & the sooner you set about it the better.'[113] The house, for Newdigate, was a labour requiring full commitment and application, as demonstrated by the diaries and the language in which he wrote. He described other aspects of his duties in a similar way. When explaining his resignation as MP for Oxford to the Master of University College in 1780 he referred to the 'laborious duties of Parliament' and emphasized his energetic application to his commitments.[114]

The characteristic and masculine quality that emerges most strongly for Sir Roger Newdigate is that of control and management: of himself, his affairs, and his domestic environment at Arbury Hall. In some ways this is more readily squared off with notions of politeness, although self-management has generally been associated with the conversational and interactional skills of the polite gentleman. Newdigate had learnt the importance of financial self-control early in his life as several of his boyhood letters show. He, like the Leigh men, was not one to allow money to be 'squander'd in riot, extravagance & ambitious views';[115] but his need for control extended further into his role in estate and household management, and he involved himself in the smallest details when it came to these matters. He wrote to his steward about the day-to-day running of the estate, commenting from London about ditching and banking, and sales of livestock.[116] He also monitored the minutiae of the everyday process of implementing his schemes in a way that, as far as we can ascertain, Edward Leigh did not. Thus, he noted in his diary the delay caused by the statue of Cupid being broken; an accident wherein 'Alcott and Docker fell from the scaffold much hurt', and the 'Careless taking down scaffold

---

[110] J. Tosh, 'Masculinities in an industrialising society: Britain 1800–1914', *Journal of British Studies*, 44 (2005), 330–42.

[111] Wood, 'Diaries of Sir Roger Newdigate', 41.   [112] French and Rothery, *Man's Estate*.

[113] WRO, CR136/B/2145, Letter, no date, June 1793.

[114] WRO, CR136/B/1835, Letter, 5 May 1780.

[115] WRO, CR136/B/4640, Letter, 18 March 1750.

[116] WRO, CR691/152/7, Letter, 10 March 1761. This controlling relationship with his steward is discussed more fully in Chapter 6.

from 4th turret a piece fell and broke off the vane'.[117] These entries reflect a mistrust of the craftsmen working on Arbury but also a close supervision, an urge to control the work being carried out, to use his own knowledge and taste to oversee the works, and to industriously apply himself to the task of renovating the house.

The processes by which Newdigate recorded the works carried out on Arbury were themselves a means of self-fashioning and control, important in the construction of self-identity. There has been a growing literature on the rise of self-fashioning literature in the eighteenth century that indicated new forms of identity and a notion of a 'self'. Much of this has engaged with autobiographies, prose that placed the individual at the centre of events in egocentric narratives.[118] Newdigate rarely used 'I' in his diary, but the notes he made reflected his centrality in the activities at Arbury and, indeed, elsewhere: the narrative is centred on self. As Harvey has recently noted, however, 'not all writing is about the self' and she argues that exploring 'a wide range of forms enables us to infer different kinds of identity'.[119] One possibility that has been explored relatively little in this context is the account book (Figure 4.5). Newdigate was an assiduous accountant, paying very careful attention to minute details and often correcting mistakes where he found them in the calculations of others.[120] The household accounts were painstakingly written in Newdigate's own hand, a careful and precise record of all types of spending in the house, from his own clothing and books, to plants and shrubs bought for the gardens, to wine and beer for the cellars, to payments for servants' wages, taxes, and charitable subscriptions. The accounts give an impression of the everyday control and management undertaken by Newdigate.[121] Spending for his wives appears under separate headings in the account books. Purchases from the milliner, mantua maker, mercer, stay maker, shoemaker, haberdasher, linen draper, warehouseman, hoop maker, laceman, and glover form the counterpoint to Sir Roger's accounts with his tailor, draper, peruke maker, hosier, shoemaker, linen draper, glover, hatter, leather breeches maker, and toyman.[122] In addition, the accounts record his wives' spending on jewellery, music lessons, subscriptions, and travel expenses. True discretion was probably exercised only through the ways in which these women disbursed the annual 'miscellaneous' payments to them for their own pin money. That said, as we explore in Chapter 5 through other accounts, Newdigate's wives did have more influence over provisioning for the house, particularly when it came to everyday items for the kitchen and the payment of female servants' wages. This pattern very much reflects the distinction Harvey has noted between the 'global' management of middling men, governing the overall income and spending of the family, whilst women saw to 'local' management, the everyday details of actually keeping the household running.[123] The key point with the household

---

[117] WRO, CR136/A/582, Diaries, 21 June 1779, 29 December 1797, 5 September 1798.

[118] For a useful review of this literature, see Harvey, *Little Republic*, 134–9.

[119] Harvey, *Little Republic*, 138.

[120] For example, see WRO, CR136/C/3298a, Letter, 19 March 1747. See also Chapter 6 for discussion of his checking of accounts kept by his housekeeper.

[121] Harvey, *Little Republic*, 80.

[122] WRO, CR136/V/156, account book, entries for 1755–62.

[123] Harvey, *Little Republic*, 80.

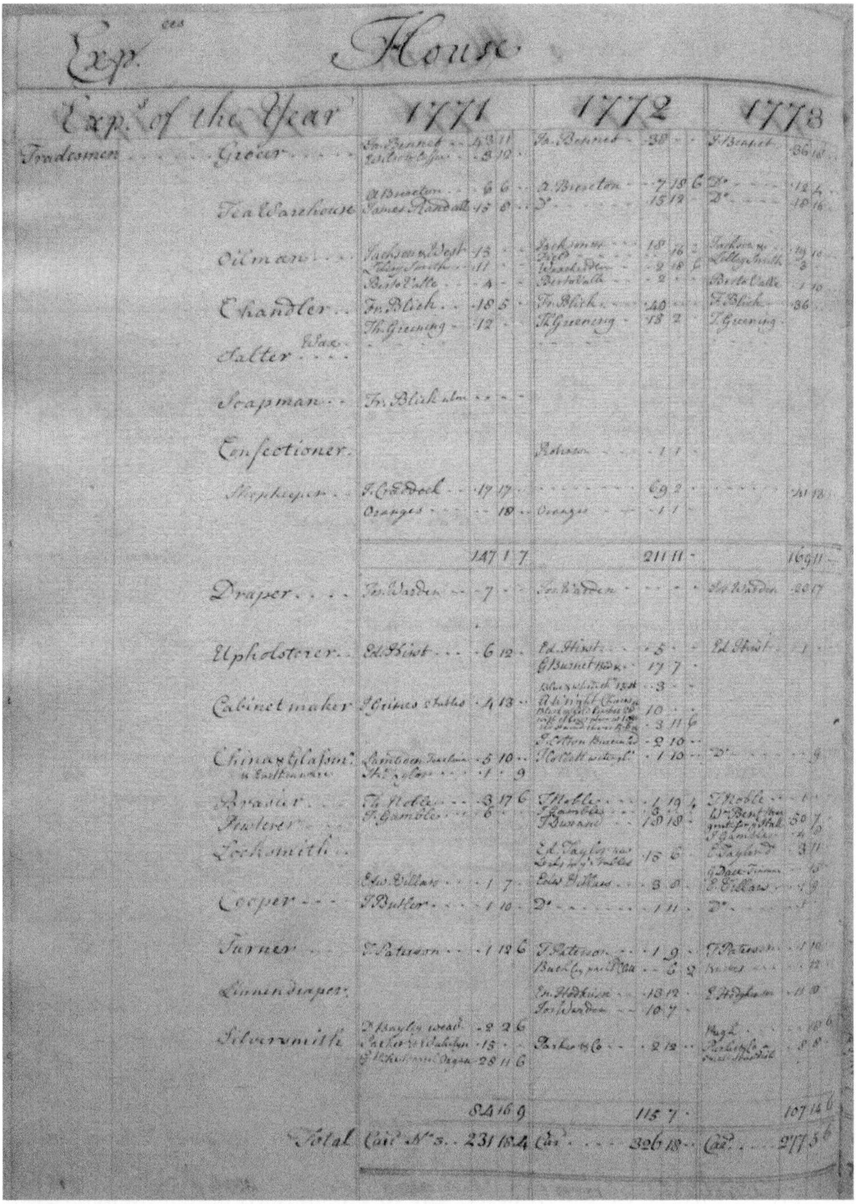

Figure 4.5. Extract from the 1763–96 Account Book for Arbury Hall, showing Sir Roger Newdigate's careful enumeration of outgoings.

Source: WRO, CR136/V/136. © Warwickshire Record Office.

accounts, however, is that by writing them and possessing them Newdigate expressed and exercised his own authority over the household and estate, his oversight of the 'oeconomic household'. They were, then, self-fashioning in a similar way to the diaries.

Above all, Arbury Hall was a domestic environment that Newdigate could shape with his own vision as an escape from the often irritating and disappointing public life he pursued as a politician. Unlike many building projects, it was not a statement of inheritance, or a showcase for trophies from the Grand Tour, or a project undertaken in retirement from public life. Indeed, the remodelling was begun around the time of his election as MP for Oxford University and continued through and beyond his political career. It was, instead, a statement of his character, virtuosity, and moral rectitude that could not be wilfully mistaken or misinterpreted, a testing ground and a record of his intellect, taste, and politeness, and a place where his polite self-fashioning could be played out within tightly defined parameters. He clearly perceived Arbury to be a retreat from the world of politics. On losing his seat as MP for Middlesex in 1847 he told his cousin, George Cooke, that he was relieved to 'have got rid of all the fateague [*sic*], all the mortification that attends the fruitless endeavours to serve one's country'. He looked forward to a life of retirement noting 'that it will be no common temptation in my present way of thinking that will draw me out to sea again'.[124] In the resulting break in his parliamentary career he felt 'in more ease and tranquillity than I ever knew before' and wrote from Arbury that 'my situation here is so easy and delightful that I cannot wish to embark again in publick life'. What ultimately drew him out again was his sense of duty and 'obligations to the University of Oxford'.[125] Just before the election, he was nervous of defeat and wrote to his friend Thomas Burgh that Sophia in particular was anxious for news and 'desires you will despatch a messenger if things go well'; but he continued with apparent sanguineness: 'if he fails to do, we shall draw in our horns and retire again into our comfortable shell'.[126] If defeated, he had Arbury and his beloved Sophia—a reliance on home and family that seems, in some ways, more characteristic of the middle classes than of the aristocracy.

Towards the end of his life Sir Roger Newdigate began, as most people do, to put his affairs in order and to tie up the loose ends of his life, and this was his final contribution to his legacy. Like much of his activity these actions made a specific statement about the man he had been. For instance, he wrote to Josiah Boydell asking that a copy be made of a tapestry, given to him by Lady Pomfret following her donation to the University of Oxford. The tapestry depicted the Triumph of Bacchus, to what Newdigate believed was an unpublished design by Raphael. It was too large and faded to hang at Arbury, but was clearly important to him because of its connection to his first wife's aunt and the Oxford donation. Newdigate clearly had emotional connections to the tapestry; yet he expressed his

[124] WRO, CR136/B/5270, Letter, 25 April 1748.
[125] WRO, CR136/B1574, Letter, January 1750; WRO, CR136/B/1874, Letter, 24 November 1750.
[126] WRO, CR136/B1530, Letter, 28 January 1750.

concern in terms of taste and knowledge about art, requesting the copy lest 'any remnant of such a Master [Raphael] should be lost to the Antiquarian & Painter & perish in oblivion'.[127] He also encouraged Boydell to publish the resulting engraving by subscription, thus bringing this 'lost' piece to public attention and linking his name to it in perpetuity. The same mixture of motivations underlay his establishment of the Newdigate Prize and his continued involvement in trying to arrange the permanent exhibition of the Pomfret marbles in the Radcliffe Library.[128] It is no surprise, then, that he gratefully accepted the 'highly flattering and honourable request' for his portrait to be hung in the Hall of University College, Oxford. Their 'good opinion' of him, he continued, had been 'the ornament and happiness of my youth, & accompanied me during the distinguished honor which the most worthy, most learned and most independent body heaped on me'.[129] Perhaps the most poignant and fitting letter was one that Newdigate had written the previous year. On completion of his work at Arbury—the finale of a life's labour of remodelling and redesigning, imprinting his taste and learning onto the material structure of the house—he wrote to Messrs Parker and Perry, thanking them for supplying a chandelier that marked the completion of his project. 'The lustre', he wrote, 'has been admired by all who have seen it.'[130]

CONCLUSION

The histories of consumption and masculinity have never paid very much attention to each other and yet, as we have shown in this chapter, they have much to discuss. The three men examined in this chapter were, in some ways, quite distinctive and reflect different versions of masculinity that resonated across Britain and Europe. Whilst they all engaged in the masculine enterprise of building, they did so to varying extents and did so with careful reference to the virtue of thrift—an important counterpoint to the usual stories of excess and splendour with which elite men are often associated. Indeed general assumptions about 'masculine domains' of spending are complicated by some of the surprising omissions and inclusions in the spending patterns of Thomas and his son Edward. Comparing their expenditure illustrates that men could select their identities through consumption from a broader palette of masculinity and that family and aristocratic traditions of 'masculine consumption' were not always the main point of reference.

Thomas Leigh seems to have been hesitant in making the 'big statement' about his identity that Edward and Sir Roger Newdigate both achieved. This may have been due to a number of factors, but his greater penchant for personal display and the exhibition of his personal nobility was perhaps indicative of a polite gentleman focused more on outward appearances than inner virtue—a perhaps rather faint

---

127 WRO, CR136/B/3431, Letter, 7 June 1803.
128 WRO, CR136/B/4050b, Letter, 24 May 1805. The scheme was ultimately unsuccessful, and it was only seventy years later that the collection was finally placed in the Ashmolean Museum.
129 WRO, CR136/B/4082, Letter, 5 July 1806.
130 WRO, CR136/B/3576, Letter, 7 November 1805.

echo of the splendid displays of taste and wealth mounted by many aristocrats across Europe. To some extent, both Thomas and Edward conformed to the ortho-dox masculine territories of consumption, but they also expressed their individual personalities through their spending: Thomas, with his emphasis on worldly pur-suits, and Edward, with his apparent lack of interest in the 'dark world' of horses and saddlery, and the splendour of personal display. Indeed, both Edward Leigh and Sir Roger Newdigate illustrate the importance of consumption in the fashion-ing of a politeness focused on inner virtue, learning, and knowledge, again hardly fitting the stereotype of the Georgian aristocrat. Although Thomas seems to have had a penchant for the races at Warwick, none of these three men frittered their family patrimony through gambling or seemed to have expressed any thirst for this habit, thus internalizing their training as landed men, controlling their urges rather than succumbing to temptations in the way that more conspicuous (though less orthodox) examples of profligate gentlemen did.[131] The races were, for Sir Roger Newdigate and Thomas Leigh, a sphere of sociability rather than a source of serious financial speculation. Similarly in terms of politics, neither Thomas nor Edward Leigh seemed to have engaged in their 'duties' as politicians, in contrast to Sir Roger's long career in Parliament. Masculinities were embedded in political discourse and activity in the eighteenth century. The 'independent gentleman' formed the bedrock of the political system in Georgian England and political service was a fundamental duty of elite men, albeit one that was increasingly chal-lenged by radicals such as John Wilkes.[132] Were, then, Thomas and Edward less 'manly' than Sir Roger? We would argue that this question itself belies the wider truth about masculinity, that it was part of the privilege of elite men that they had more autonomy in choosing from the kaleidoscope of masculine attributes than the lower orders. All three constructed their masculinities in different ways, draw-ing on a variety of masculine attributes, an insight strongly supported by their differential spending patterns.

None of the men in this chapter spent beyond their means on their various masculine projects and the importance of self-control, whether by necessity or inclination, comes through strongly in all three cases. In this sense they conformed to deeper values surrounding masculinity: those of thrift and self-control. Such values are seldom to the fore in studies of elite male spending, which generally emphasize external displays of cosmopolitan taste, discernment, and luxury as the touchstones of aristocratic identity. In our analysis, the restraining factors of demography and economic fluctuations are also in evidence: only one of these men became a father and Edward's ambitious plans for Stoneleigh were thwarted by his early mental incapacity. Consumption thus reveals the unfinished and incomplete

---

[131] French and Rothery, *Man's Estate*, 108. For an example of the ruinous consequences of gambling for landed families see the example of Sir Vincent Cotton in J. D. Pickles, 'Cotton, Sir Vincent, sixth Baronet (1801–1863)', in B. Harrison (ed.), *The Oxford Dictionary of National Biography* (Oxford, 2004), <http://www.oxforddnb.com/view/article/6427>, accessed 5 Jan. 2016.
[132] M. McCormack, 'A Man's Sphere?: British politics in the eighteenth and nineteenth centuries', in S. Brady, C. Fletcher, R. Moss and L. Riall (eds), *The Palgrave Handbook of Masculinity and Political Culture in Europe: From Antiquity to the Contemporary World* (forthcoming).

nature of their masculinities and hints at the deeper potential and complexity within all three men. Male spending reflected masculine identities, but it also shaped them. The processes of imagining, designing, provisioning, and implementing plans for the redesign of Arbury Hall were a lifelong task for Sir Roger Newdigate and were closely interwoven with his development as a polite landed gentleman. The process of keeping accounts and diaries was a method by which he tracked and negotiated this development.

The country house and the consumption that provisioned for and shaped its material culture were central to the masculine identities of Georgian aristocrats. Of course, the inheritance practice of primogeniture, the importance of the male line, and the emblems of patriarchy in the governance of servants, farmers, and labourers, along with the wider political and administrative roles of landed men, were a strong statement of masculine authority that was projected beyond the household and onto the surrounding estate, county, and wider British and European society. They formed a bedrock of aristocratic dominance and hegemony in this period. To a large extent the training of landed men and the exertion of their authority was something that took place away from their homes, in the public sphere of schools, universities, parliamentary chambers, and gentlemen's clubs; but this authority and the masculine identity that underpinned that authority began at home. It was expressed in the very fabric of the buildings inhabited by men such as Edward, fifth Lord Leigh, and Sir Roger Newdigate, buildings in which they communicated their character and gender identities. These messages were complex and layered. They communicated, at one and the same time, learned politeness, heroic exertion, and domestic comfort, illustrating the dangers of oversimplifying the gendering of male consumption. This complexity derived partly from the sheer scale of country houses. The masculine identities of the aristocracy as expressed through the country house were writ larger than those of men of the middling sorts; they had larger canvasses to paint on and, in all kinds of ways, their status and authority were more secure, more palpable than those of the lower orders. However, this should not distract us from the significance of practices of consumption in shaping politeness and masculinities amongst this social group. Country houses, as has often been noted, were bold statements of power and ambition;[133] but they were also the homes of men, places where they negotiated and expressed their masculine identities through the goods they purchased and material culture they imprinted on their homes, and spaces in which they worked through their relationship to other members of the family and society. It is to the other members of the family, to the consumption practices of women, wives, female owners of estates, and their influence on the country house that Chapter 5 turns.

---

[133] Girouard, *English Country House*, 1–12.

5

Gentlewomen's Things
Women and Country House Consumption

INTRODUCTION

Landed women were practically invisible in the early studies of the aristocracy and the gentry, apart from fleeting appearances in chapters on social life and home life.[1] In these mainly economic histories it was thought that 'landed families revolved around their menfolk';[2] gentility equated to 'the gentleman'; the landed interest was a 'group of men'. Just as they did in family genealogies, women played a cameo role as marriage fodder, important in terms of the wealth and survival of each family, but of secondary importance in terms of status, rank, and identity. After all, theirs was a 'humdrum existence'.[3] Questions of the 'openness' of landed society to other social groups similarly tended to ignore the varied inputs women made to the group.[4] The perception that landownership was men's business had barely changed by the time David Cannadine came to write his study of the aristocracy in 1990. In its introduction he noted that, because he was concerned with 'wealth, status, power, and class consciousness', which were 'preponderantly masculine assets', there would 'not be many women in this book'.[5] He did, at least, recognize the urgent need for more studies of upper-class women, although there was scarcely a rush to fill the void.[6] Since the late 1990s, however, the history of landed and upper-class women has flourished, catching up with the previous focus in women's history on middling and labouring sorts. Kimberley Schutte's book on the marriages of noblewomen is the most recent and sustained study to place women at the centre of aristocratic identities and status, counterbalancing previous studies.[7] More importantly for our purposes there has been a growing recognition of the important impact of elite women on the material culture of the country (and town) house and their centrality in the construction of elite identities through consumption practices. Amanda Vickery's *The Gentleman's Daughter* was the first to do this in detail for the lesser gentry and it has been followed by a flurry of

---

[1] See, for example, Mingay, *English Landed Society*.

[2] F. M. L. Thompson, *English Landed Society*, 18.

[3] Mingay, *English Landed Society*, 15.   [4] Stone and Fawtier Stone, *An Open Elite*.

[5] D. Cannadine, *The Decline and Fall of the British Aristocracy* (London, 1990), 7.

[6] A rare example from the early 1990s is J. Gerard, *Country House Life: Family and Servants* (Oxford, 1994), esp. 115–42.

[7] K. Schutte, *Women, Rank and Marriage in the British Aristocracy, 1485–2000: An Open Elite?* (Basingstoke, 2014).

further research.[8] Increasingly questions are being asked of the traditional view inherited from Sombart and propagated by McKendrick and de Vries that women, although they were the active agents of the eighteenth-century consumer revolution, were unthinking and imprudent consumers. Instead, women of a variety of different classes are now assigned agency, self-control, and thrift; they are seen as responsible shoppers deeply embedded in networks of exchange and credit, reflecting some of the same virtues as their husbands, albeit in a feminine way.[9]

Aristocratic families are fertile ground for investigations of gender and consumption, not least because of the wealth of sources available; yet Vickery has noted the problems involved in understanding the spending of married women whose choices were often hidden amongst those of their husbands in family accounts.[10] We have obtained a much clearer picture of the individual choices of the four women who form the focus of this chapter and use this to explore the role of gender in the consumption habits of women in a variety of different familial situations. We begin with Hon. Mary Leigh, the sister of Edward Leigh, who inherited after his death in 1786 because of the absence of male heirs. Her consumption practices illustrate the interactions of social and gender status as her life progressed from orphaned child to unmarried estate owner, and highlight the impact of single status—her wealth allowed her to break free of the constraints often seen as binding single women in this era.[11] This example, although by no means unique, is set against the more conventional positions of Sir Roger Newdigate's two wives, Sophia Conyers and Hester Mundy. Spending on and by both of these women was, in some ways, hidden in Sir Roger's accounts, an expression of his overall control of the family wealth. However, some aspects of their consumption are itemized clearly enough, and other sources provide us with a truer impression of their discretionary spending and notions of taste, revealing both as women who had their own tastes, responsibilities, and some independence. Our final example, Elizabeth Dryden, forms another contrast. We focus on her life as an impoverished widow and the problems this produced in terms of her status, but

---

[8] Vickery, *Gentleman's Daughter*. Other examples include M. Vaizey and C. Gere, *Great Women Collectors* (London, 1999); R. Baird, *Mistress of the House. Great Ladies and Grand Houses, 1670–1830* (London, 2003); Lewis, 'When a house'; Grieg, *Beau Monde*, 36–47.

[9] For the 'standard model' of female consumers, see Sombart, *Luxury and Capitalism*; McKendrick, 'Consumer revolution'; de Vries, *Industrious Revolution*, 47. For recent studies questioning this perspective, see Vickery, *Gentleman's Daughter*, 183–94; Berg, *Luxury and Pleasure*, 234–42; H. Berry, 'Prudent luxury: the metropolitan tastes of Judith Baker, Durham gentlewoman' in R. Sweet and P. Lane (eds), *Women and Urban Life in Eighteenth-Century Britain: 'On the Town'* (Aldershot, 2003), 130–54; Walsh, 'Shops, shopping'; Vickery, *Behind Closed Doors*, 106–28, 184–207; Whittle and Griffiths, *Consumption and Gender*; Harvey, *Little Republic*, 33–5, 65–76; A. Shepard, 'Minding their own business: married women and credit in early eighteenth-century London', *Transactions of the Royal Historical Society*, 25 (2015), 53–74.

[10] For example, see Vickery, *Behind Closed Doors*, 5; Vickery, *Gentleman's Daughter*, 141.

[11] P. Sharpe, 'Dealing with love: the ambiguous independence of single women in early modern England', *Gender and History*, 11 (1999), 209–32; R. Larsen, 'For want of a good fortune: elite single women's experiences in Yorkshire, 1730–1860', *Women's History Review*, 16/3 (2007), 387–401; Vickery, *Behind Closed Doors*. 49–82, 188–93; A. Duncan, '"Old Maids": family and social relationships of never-married Scottish gentlewomen, *c*.1740–*c*.1840' (PhD, Edinburgh 2013), esp. 57–87.

also her attempts to bring the finances back into good order. Overall, we present elite women's gender as part of their broader identity; its impact on their consumption and identity was contingent on their marital and social status, and their economic means.

GOVERNING IDENTITIES: THE HONOURABLE MARY LEIGH

Born in 1736, Mary was 13 at the time of her father's death and, like her brother, she was raised from this point by a guardian, in her case a cousin, Elizabeth Verney (Figure 5.1).[12] She emerges in the Stoneleigh Abbey bills in the early 1750s, living in the vicinity of Hanover Square, London, where she remained through much of the 1760s, although she also had a room at Stoneleigh Abbey. When her brother was declared insane in 1774, her life moved into a different phase, as she took on joint responsibility for the estate. It shifted to a third phase when she inherited as a life tenant twelve years later and took ownership of the estate for the remaining twenty years of her life, from 1786 to 1806. These shifts bookmarked changes in Mary's status within the family and in society more generally. As we

Figure 5.1. The Honourable Mary Leigh (1736–1806), as a young woman (unknown artist).
Photograph by Jon Stobart.

[12] MacDonald, 'Leigh family', 148, 153–5.

would expect they also signalled changes in *her* spending patterns. The receipted bills record total spending of £16,339, but this was unevenly distributed across the three phases of her life. Between 1750, when she first appears in the accounts, and her brother's coming of age in 1763, she spent a total of £1,498 (an average of £107 per annum); from then to her inheritance in 1786 she spent a similar sum (£,1465) at an average of £122 per year, although there are no surviving bills for the period 1774–86. However, from the point of her inheritance to her death in 1806 she spent the far larger total of £13,375 (£668 per annum), reflecting the greater responsibilities, spending power, and autonomy she possessed as the life tenant of the Stoneleigh estates. These shifts in levels of spending were significant, but the nature of Mary's spending and the types of goods she purchased also changed according to her shifting status as the relationship between her gender and social identities was altered.

As a young woman, Mary's spending centred on millinery, drapery, silver jewellery, and dressmaking. Through the 1750s and 1760s, these accounted for an average of about £50 per annum—a relatively modest sum, which suggests moderation on the part of a very wealthy young woman. At the same time, there were also bills for music and language lessons; entertainments, such as trips to the opera and Ranelagh Gardens;[13] tableware, tea, and mineral water; hiring coaches and making charitable contributions. There was a more substantial purchase on Mary's 'coming of age' in 1757 that spoke of her status in a different way. That year she acquired a post chaise costing £86 12*s*. from Thomas Cope of London, who described the carriage as being 'neatly Run and carved, Painted stone colour with ornaments on the Pannels of China figures, coats of arms and Cyphers lined with light colour cloth, a coach box to take off at pleasure and a Pair of Harness and Bridles'. This made it a striking blend of fashionable orientalism and the traditional signifiers of aristocratic status, a cosmopolitan hybrid that situated the coach and its owner at an interesting cultural intersection.[14]

Coaches and the associated horse tackle were, according to Vickery, 'an utterly masculine, dark brown territory of goods'.[15] This world, rejected by men such as her brother Edward, was embraced more fully by Mary: Cope's bill marks the beginning of a series of purchases of coaches, saddlery, and tackle made across her life. More tellingly, the coat of arms spoke of Mary's position as a gentlewomen and the derivation of her status from family and heritance. So too did the purchase of livery for her footmen and coachman, purchased later in 1762 from Ann Dorrell. The £6 13*s*. 3*d*. spent on this was pretty modest, but the scarlet and silvered coats with 'silk and twist' for the footmen and the 'blue drab cloth' with 'scarlet cuffs' for the coachman also signalled her status in London society as a wealthy aristocratic woman.[16] Dress embodied gender identities, both for her male liveried servants and herself. Mary's focus on her own clothing reinforced her identity as a woman, especially when augmented by her purchases of jewellery, and

---

[13] See, for example, SCLA, DR18/5/3593, DR18/5/4308.
[14] SCLA, DR18/5/3738.   [15] Vickery, *Behind Closed Doors*, 122.
[16] SCLA, DR18/5/3954. See Styles, *Dress of the People*, 295–301.

might be seen as aligning her to Kowalski-Wallace's assertion of female hunger for 'all the commodities that indulged the body and enhanced physical life'. However, there was little sign of the reckless pursuit of fashion imagined by McKendrick: Mary spent freely, but not to excess.[17] Moreover, she may have spent as a woman, but she also did so as the sister of a peer of the realm and in possession of a substantial private fortune. These types of purchases may be seen more as 'investment strategies' and 'asset management' rather than simply spending for spending's sake.[18] The coach spoke of wealth; the livery and coats of arms signified status and rank; and both distinguished her from Shackleton's concerns for clothing and tableware and Purefoy's focus on groceries, clothing, and furniture.[19]

We know little about Mary's spending during the period of the Commission, between 1774 and 1786, after her brother had been declared insane. The surviving bills suggest that she continued to live in London and that her overall pattern of spending remained broadly stable, although she laid substantial sums out on the hire of horses and coaches, indicating a significant amount of travel, perhaps to and from the Warwickshire estate. On becoming owner of Stoneleigh Abbey in 1786, her spending took on a very different character, expanding into a broader portfolio of elite consumption (Table 5.1). This 'life-cycle cascade' in Mary's spending illustrates a problem with interpretations that would straightforwardly define her consumer identity as feminine or womanly. The accoutrements of a gentlewoman were there throughout her life, but shifts in the life cycle, her movement into adulthood as an unmarried woman and, later, her status as an estate owner and head of two households reflect the way that gender interacted with other identities. In the absence of marriage and without the impact of a husband on the bills addressed to Mary we can see the true effect of landownership on an aristocratic woman.

Established female patterns were now overlain with much larger sums relating to those of a wealthy landowner and a minor player in London society. As a landowner, there were costs incurred in running the estate which formed a continuation of the patterns established by her brother and maintained during the time Mary and William Craven ran the estate during Edward's insanity, with spending on enclosure, maintenance of farm buildings, and so on. Many of the everyday concerns of the male landowner appear in the bills for Mary during this period. There are wages for estate workers such as the bailiff, Thomas Wooton, the warrener, Richard Hands, and the steward, Luke West.[20] Mary had work carried out at Stoneleigh Mill in 1796 and 1800 along with more routine work such as fencing and ditching.[21] There are no large-scale and substantial projects evident from the bills and, at £579,

---

[17] E. Kowalski-Wallace, *Consuming Subjects: Women, Shopping and Business in the Eighteenth Century* (New York, 1997), 5; McKendrick, 'Consumer revolution'. For a fuller discussion of the social significance of jewellery, see M. Pointon, 'Women and their jewels', in J. Batchelor and C. Kaplan (eds) *Women and Material Culture, 1660–1830* (Basingstoke, 2007), 11–30.

[18] Shepard, 'Minding their own business', 56.

[19] Vickery, 'Women and the world of goods'; G. Eland (ed.), *Purefoy Letters, 1735–1753* (London, 1931), *passim*.

[20] SCLA, DR18/5/5742, DR18/5/6781, DR18/5/6782.

[21] SCLA, DR18/5/5768, DR18/5/6213, DR18/5/6178.

Table 5.1. Mary Leigh's spending by goods group, 1750–1806 (to the nearest £)

	Masculine Domain			Mixed Domain			Feminine Domain		
	Build	Estate	Coach & Horse	Furniture	Household	Silver	Art & Books	Drapery	Jewellery
1750–9			129	9	21	36	145	567	29
1760–9	4		403	53	23	5	152	439	6
1770–4	3		26		9		2	94	
1786–95	585	234	266	462	462	1005	81	964	
1796–1806	478	345	533	29	571		97	1024	1
Total	1069	579	1357	551	1086	1046	476	3088	36

Sources: SCLA DR18/5—series of bills.

total spending on the estate was far lower than her brother's spending in this area, which amounted to just under £2,000. However, this was probably because the main outlays in enclosing and improving the estate had already been made before she inherited. Many of the extraordinary costs during Edward's time were focused on enclosure and forestry and there was also a large payment for the renewal of a lease. The key point is that Mary inhabited a role generally associated by historians and contemporaries with the male landowner, servicing the estate and making incremental improvements to ensure a continued income and a healthy inheritance for later generations. She was fulfilling her dynastic responsibilities and conducting a 'prudent economy' that historians are increasingly identifying in women in other social classes.[22]

Mary also made her mark on Stoneleigh Abbey in terms of renovation and furnishings. The amounts of furniture were modest in comparison to those bought by her brother, but the volume of work being undertaken was clearly considerable, as was its impact on Stoneleigh Abbey. This was perhaps clearest in the 'new rooms' and print room created by Mary, apparently in the late 1780s. It is likely that some of the work undertaken by the upholsterer, David Frost—probably a Warwick craftsman—involved furnishing and decorating these rooms. In a 1790 letter written to her friend and solicitor, Joseph Hill, Mary described these as being 'pretty', but the 1806 inventory suggests that they were relatively plainly furnished with a range of mahogany and japanned furniture.[23] If these were, indeed, rooms seen as particularly personal to Mary, they were markedly different from her bedroom, which, in 1764, had been lined with pea-green wallpaper and decorated with several Chinese landscapes.[24] This feels a far more feminine space than that apparently created by Mary herself. Of course, it is possible that Mary was describing to Hill her more general improvements to the house. Like those of Lady Irwin at Temple Newsam and Lady Borringdon at Saltram, these produced comfortable and sociable

[22] See, for example, Shepard, 'Minding their own business'.
[23] SCLA, DR671, 22 August 1790; DR18/4/59, Inventory, 1806.
[24] SCLA, DR18/5/4402. See also chapters 2 and 7; Vickery, *Behind Closed Doors*, 166–83.

spaces in which to entertain her friends, including a print room furnished with fashionable satinwood furniture, a room somewhat akin to the 'feminine spaces' recently described by Ruth Kenny.[25] But there was hardly a room in the house left untouched. As well as introducing new items and refreshing the soft furnishing, she moved many items between rooms. In the principal entertaining rooms—the Breakfast Room and Dining Parlour—the turnover was considerable, furniture being brought in to create a more informal atmosphere and serve a range of recreational uses (see Chapter 2).

Mary also made significant changes to the paintings at Stoneleigh and their arrangement. She moved many of these between rooms and purchased others, augmenting the display in the Breakfast Room and Dining Parlour with additional landscapes and conversation pieces by Zoffany, Gainsborough, Teniers, Wouwerman, and Van der Meer, amongst others.[26] These were hung alongside fifteen family portraits left in place whilst these rooms were reworked, a practice which was repeated across the whole house—portraits being left largely where they were. There was no apparent attempt to produce the kind of pictorial family tree created by Henrietta Cavendish at Welbeck.[27] Yet Mary was clearly conscious of her family's lineage, carefully marking all her silverware as well as her coach with the arms, supporters, and coronet that signalled her rank and dignity—a practice, as we have noted, that she had begun earlier as a young woman in London.[28] That said, Mary did more than simply preserve and present the marks of lineage that she inherited, returning unwanted pieces to Robert Makepeace when buying new silverware.[29] In this way she augmented her gendered status as a woman with her social status as a titled and landed gentlewoman and enriched her material family heritage.

Mary's claim on her family's heritage and her place within this lineage served to cement her social status, an aspect of landed women's activities that historians have recently begun to note, both in Britain and elsewhere in Europe.[30] In this way, it might be argued that she conformed to conventions dictating the nature and scale of spending necessary to maintain aristocratic status—especially when its formal title had been lost.[31] However, Mary also struck an importantly independent note, acquiring a house in Kensington Gore from which she could comfortably retain her connections and social life in London. This occupied much of her attention in the early 1790s, a series of bills being paid to builders, carpenters, plumbers,

---

[25] Lewis, 'When a house'; R. Kenny, '"Apartments that are not too large": pastel portraits and the spaces of femininity in the English Country House', in G. Perry, K. Retford, and J. Vibert (eds), *Placing Faces: The Portrait and the English Country House in the Long Eighteenth Century* (Manchester, 2013), 143–61.

[26] DR18/17/32/186 List of pictures bought at auction, 1788. The cost of these (£514 10*s.* 6*d.*) is not included in Table 5.1.

[27] Retford, 'Patrilineal portraiture', 337–8; Tinniswood, *Polite Tourist*, 108.

[28] SCLA, DR18/5/3194.   [29] SCLA, DR18/5/5809. See also Chapter 1.

[30] For example see P. Mandler, '"From Almack to Willis": aristocratic women and politics, 1815–1867', in A. Vickery (ed.), *Women, Privilege and Power: British Politics 1750 to the Present* (Stanford, CA, 2005), 152–67; Retford, 'Patrilineal portraiture'.

[31] For a parallel in France, see Chatenet-Calyste, 'Feminine luxury in Paris'.

painters, glaziers, and plasterers.[32] This work helped to make Grove House a comfortable and pleasant place in which Mary spent up to nine months of the year. Moreover, it is clear that this presence in London was important to her public reputation as well as being a convenient base for her social activities. This is most evident from her purchases of livery—an important marker of rank and status, and one that Mary clearly prioritized; indeed, the surviving bills show that she spent far more on these than had her brother Edward.[33] Besides her impulse to secure her status through heritance and lineage Mary was also focused on her position as a fashionable gentlewoman and Grove House was a useful location for these statements. Between 1786 and 1790 she purchased over 300 pieces of chinaware from Josiah Wedgwood for Grove House,[34] a clear statement of Mary's distinction, not only as a wealthy landowner but as a London woman of fashion, possessed of spending power and taste. There is little indication that she engaged in large-scale entertaining at Grove House—it appears to have been a place to which she invited selected friends, including her man of business, Joseph Hill, and his wife. Stoneleigh appears to have been more important in this respect and she wrote of being 'wonderfully engaged in receiving and paying visits' in Warwickshire.[35] She generally entertained couples or single gentlewomen, her most frequent guests being Mrs Hale and Mrs Herbert, who also accompanied Mary on trips to Cheltenham in the 1790s; but she also mixed with London society, counting the Ladies Sefton, Ormond, and Howard amongst her circle. Even in her fifties and sixties, Mary was by no means socially isolated, despite the absence of siblings and cousins who Duncan suggests formed the usual focus for the lives of wealthy spinsters.[36]

Visiting required a high level of personal mobility. Whilst Mary acquired her first coach in the 1760s, most of her transport needs during that period were met through hiring rather than buying. By the 1790s, she was still hiring coaches, horses, coachmen, and postilions in London, but was also paying for horse feed and for repairs to her own carriage. Moreover, there were regular bills for a bewildering variety of harnesses, whips, combs, and so on, revealing Mary's continued engagement with the masculine world of coach makers' and saddlers' workshops.[37] There is no evidence that Mary herself went to the coach makers to finger or commission these things, but then it is not always clear that elite gentlemen immersed themselves in such worlds—they had servants who could readily bespeak these goods. What is clear is that Mary prioritized them as part of her material culture, incurring a total of thirty-two separate bills for coach repairs and saddlery. This behaviour reflects her desire for a public display of status and dignity which was not defined by gender in a straightforward sense. Just like the family portraits and silverware in Stoneleigh Abbey, servants' livery and the coaches emblazoned with

[32] For example, SCLA, DR18/5/6122–6130. For more detailed analysis of Grove House, see Stobart, 'So agreeable and suitable a place'.
[33] SCLA, DR18/5/6051, DR18/5/6099, DR18/5/6098. This livery is discussed more fully in Chapter 1.
[34] SCLA, DR18/5684, DR18/5/5724, DR18/5/5900.
[35] SCLA, DR671, letter to Joseph Hill, 12 September 1791. For more discussion of her life at Grove House, see Stobart, 'So agreeable and suitable a place'.
[36] Duncan, 'Old Maids', 121–33.   [37] Vickery, *Behind Closed Doors*, 124.

the family arms were a means of maximizing the status that Mary could achieve, whether in London or in the country, the status of a wealthy gentlewoman, part of a long line of honourable landowners.

Despite this, Mary, like her brother, spent well within her means, the improvements being relatively modest and the bills trifling in comparison with her considerable wealth. The repairs to Grove House, for example, amounted to around £350 in total. We might see this self-control as characteristically masculine consumption, as contemporaries often did, but again it is perhaps better understood as part of the expectation placed upon any landowner: that they should foster and manage resources to augment rather than dissipate the family estate.[38] Certainly, we can see the skills of good financial management in other elite women: Alice Le Strange, for instance, managed resources so that her husband was free to invest in and improve the building and estate, and Marie Fortunée d'Este carefully nurtured her resources following her separation from Louis-François-Joseph de Bourbon-Conti, Count of La Marche—a time when she took on responsibility for funding and running her own household.[39] Mary thus conformed to certain norms of the respectable landowner, showing self-control, pride in family and lineage, and oeconomy on a scale beyond the domestic.[40] It is, we argue, the blending of Mary's social and gender identities that produced this composite pattern of consumption. Her wealth and most especially her single status meant that, unlike Alice Le Strange and most of the women studied by Vickery, Greig, Kenny, and others, she was far more the master of her own consumption decisions. Like Jane Innes in her later years, she could express these identities without reference to a husband; her spending unequivocally reflected her choices and shows clearly the interplay between gender and status. She took advice on business matters, mostly from Joseph Hill, but her consumption and material culture were her own.[41] More orthodox gender identities, although still ones with the power to surprise, are evident in the spending of Sophia and Hester Newdigate.

MARRIED GENTLEWOMEN: SOPHIA AND HESTER NEWDIGATE

The relative freedom and authority exercised by Mary Leigh was unusual, if not entirely exceptional. Although failure in the male line and the absence of other suitable cousins or relations to take over the estate could result in female accession, the standard position for an aristocratic woman was as the wife of the male head of the household, attending to the everyday running of the household but subject to the overall governance of her husband. Such women were, of course, very wealthy and privileged, with great spending power and the social status that flowed from this distinction; but their ability to shape the material culture of the country

---

[38] On masculine self-control, see French and Rothery, *Man's Estate*, 61–6, 78–80, 169–71.

[39] Whittle and Griffiths, *Consumption and Gender*, 203–8; Chatenet-Calyste, 'Feminine luxury in Paris', 181–5.

[40] Harvey, *Little Republic*, 24–35, 65–76.   [41] Duncan, 'Old maids', 200–8.

house and to act autonomously as elite consumers was circumscribed by the framework of patriarchy in which they operated. Lineage and heritance were, as strict settlement and primogeniture prescribed, male domains, and the material culture of the country house partly flowed from these prerogatives. Within these confines, however, women played an important role in the spending that emanated from the country house, taking responsibility for the local management of the household: clothing children, provisioning for the kitchens, paying the wages of and overseeing the work of female servants.[42] Separate accounts for Arbury, written by Hester Newdigate, illustrate this local management, but there is also evidence that both wives engaged in judgements of politeness and taste. They went beyond the mundane and everyday, and contributed significantly to status and identity.

As we discussed in Chapter 4, the account books of Sir Roger Newdigate are an expression of his overall control of house and estate; they give the impression that he managed all spending, from the smallest items entering the kitchen to the large and expansive building projects he engaged in throughout our period. As we might expect, then, his wives appear but fleetingly in these books and in a very limited 'feminine' sense: against payments for clothing, music lessons, travel and leisure, jewellery, and so on. But we should be wary of such one-dimensional readings of the account books and the very orthodox picture they give us of the female genteel consumer. Much of their spending and their responsibility for household management was hidden in the accounts and they undoubtedly had far more responsibility for the day-to-day management of Arbury, albeit within a 'framework of masculine oversight'.[43] Indeed it is most likely that a similar situation to that which pertained at another Warwickshire mansion, Coton House, also existed at Arbury. Like Sophia and Hester, Mrs Grimes appeared infrequently in her husband's accounts and only occasionally beyond the annual allowance for her and the children, at quite similar levels to that provided for Hester. However, Vickery argues that, although she was not given the credit for wider spending and broader responsibilities, Mrs Grimes was actually running the household on a day-to-day basis. It may not be entirely irrelevant that both families operated the same non-double accounting system, with the categories of spending divided into 'House', 'Stable', 'Person', and so on.[44] Accounts of this kind, then, represent more the ideal of patriarchal management than the reality of country house life, and it is on this basis that we explore the spending of Sophia and Hester Newdigate.

In aggregate terms, the money allocated to Hester in the accounts amounted to £8,968 for the years 1776–96, a sum which pales in comparison with Sir Roger's £168,634.[45] However, the latter included building projects, the park and gardens, wider investments, and the upkeep of the estate, as well as wages for servants, food and lighting for the house, and so on. Neither Hester nor Sophia took on the

[42] This is the role highlighted by Vickery, *Behind Closed Doors*, 114–22 and Whittle and Griffiths, *Consumption and Gender*, 26–48.

[43] Vickery, *Behind Closed Doors*, 116.

[44] WRO, CR136/V/156, Account book, *passim*; CR136/V136, Account book, *passim*; Vickery, *Behind Closed Doors*, 116–17.

[45] WRO, CR136/V/136, Account book, entries for 1776–96.

broader responsibilities shouldered by Mary Leigh. That most of the entries for them in Sir Roger's accounts comprise expenditure for the 'Person' suggests the main purpose of his system with regards to his wives was to record levels of spending within the overall outlay of the family, rather than worry about the precise itemized nature of that spending, or about observing and supervising them—a finding that supports that of Vickery in relation to the gendering of household accounting.[46] Some of the entries for Hester were clearly allowance payments, since they have no supplier listed and are of fairly regular annual amounts, increasing from £105 in 1779 to £155 in 1782 and eventually to consistent payments of £210 between 1785 and 1796. Added to outlay on her clothing, discussed below, this easily exceeded the £307 given by Abraham Grimes to his wife for her *and* her children's maintenance in 1781.[47] Moreover, it appears that Hester saw this allowance as her own, noting in a letter to Sir Roger written whilst away in Buxton that 'the money you give me is for no other purpose than to fool away as I like'.[48]

Another account book provides us with a much more detailed impression of the role Hester played in the day-to-day management of the household and of the control she exerted over the more 'local' governance of spending at Arbury.[49] The accounts cover the period 1787–97, but not consistently: the receipts and payments going through Hester's hands are logged for 1787, 1791–3, 1795, and 1797. Payments range from £208 in 1791 to £680 in 1793, a small fraction of the overall spending (averaging around £5,000 per annum) recorded in Sir Roger Newdigate's account book, and mostly cover items that fall fairly neatly into the 'female domain' of spending mapped out by Vickery and others.[50] Hester settled the house book on a monthly basis, which generally came to about £5, although a few months seem to have witnessed unspecified expenses upwards of £30. She purchased textiles, haberdashery, cloth and linens, and small amounts of inexpensive chinaware, and paid for inexpensive items of clothing and tailoring—mostly of underclothes. In 1787, for instance, she paid for the cotton for Sir Roger's nightcaps and later, in 1792, making nine shirts for him cost her £1 2s. 6d. Hester also bought items of hardware such as corkscrews, washballs, and oilcloths, the things required for the everyday running of the house, but hardly conspicuous or costly items. Much the same was true of the regular sums paid to the upholsterer Munro for small repairs and various small items of furnishings and furniture, such as 'six matts for the Chappel' costing 12s. 6d. and the 'scarlet binding for carpets', costing 6s. 4d.[51] There were personal items, such as fragrance, jewellery, spectacles, sheet music, and music lessons, and she was also responsible for payments to her companion

[46] Vickery, *Behind Closed Doors*, 106–28. For the alternative argument, that accounting was an expression of patriarchy, see S. Walker, 'Identifying the woman behind the "Railed-in Desk": the proto-feminisation of bookkeeping in Britain', *Accounting, Auditing & Accountability Journal*, 16/4 (2003), 606–39 and S. Walker, 'Accounting histories of women: beyond recovery?', *Accounting, Auditing & Accountability Journal*, 21/4 (2008), 580–610.

[47] Vickery, *Behind Closed Doors*, 116.

[48] WRO, CR136/B/2803, Letter from Hester Newdigate, 5 October 1781.

[49] WRO, CR1841/29, General Account Book for Arbury Hall.

[50] Vickery, *Behind Closed Doors*, 112–13.

[51] WRO, CR1841/29, General Account Book.

Sally Shilton and for the costs of medicine for the household. In 1792, for instance, she accounted for the cost of two courses of leeches for 'Rhodes [the housekeeper], Cook and Nanny'.[52]

All this was entirely in keeping with a wife's duties in managing her domestic realm. Hester's payments of the female servants' wages also fell into the orthodoxy of Vickery's sexual division of labour. She paid housemaids, dairymaids, still-room maids, laundrymaids, and the cook, but never, according to the account book, the male servants of the household. This shows a level of managerial control at Arbury on the part of Hester—indeed there were several entries where she noted the discharge payments for servants who presumably had committed a misdemeanour of some kind—but well within the gendered boundaries of country house life. More significant, in terms of understanding overlapping areas of authority, is the way that wages and other items were often double-accounted, appearing both in Hester's accounts and Sir Roger's. In fact around one-third of all Hester's entries were also individually listed in her husband's account books. As Vickery notes, women's accounts were often a means for their husbands to supervise their spending, but an annual reckoning of the kind carried out by Sir Roger might simply involve paying the balance rather than scrutinizing the accounts.[53] From a different perspective, we might focus on the false impression that can be given by men's accounts of their unremitting control of the household: some elements, it seems, might simply be copied across for the sake of completeness.

Much the same might be said of the entries in Sir Roger's accounts for spending on his wives' 'Person'—that is, clothing and other personal items. These appear separately in the accounts, bills being settled with the mercer, mantua maker, milliner, stay maker, shoemaker, haberdasher, glover, hosier, linen draper, physician, and apothecary, and also for sheet music and musical instruments.[54] More occasionally, there were payments for luxuries, including £1,030 to Duvall the jeweller and £130 to Eborall the watchmaker, both in 1776 and probably in connection with wedding gifts to Hester.[55]

Such were the very feminine limits of Hester and Sophia Newdigate's expenditure, which remained largely unchanged across the periods of their marriages to Sir Roger, unlike the life-cycle shifts seen with Mary Leigh. They appear to conform to the standard portrayal of genteel women as emasculated by their role as wives and their domestic realm. There are, however, several important caveats that suggest a much larger degree of freedom.

First, Hester's accounts provide us with a glimpse of the way she explored other types of spending, making a number of what Vickery terms 'special purchases', including imported fruits.[56] For example, in 1792 she entered into her account book the purchase of '½ chest of oranges' from the greengrocer Heaway. This seems to be part of a bigger order entered in the main accounts for that year, and

52 WRO, CR1841/29, General Account Book.
53 Vickery, *Behind Closed Doors*, 110–11.
54 WRO, CR136/V/136, Account book, entries for 1771–73.
55 WRO, CR136/V/136, Account book, entry for 1776.
56 Vickery, *Behind Closed Doors*, 114.

Heaway had supplied oranges to Sir Roger each year since 1788. However, the entry of this purchase in Hester's books indicates some kind of agency on her part; given the comprehensive bookkeeping by Hester across a long period and the double-accounting method of the two books, it may even have been her overall responsibility. She also purchased anchovies (which were not in the main account book), sugar, peppermint seeds, sugar candy, and brandy. All of these seem to have been single purchases but, again, they indicate a more significant pattern of spending not revealed by either account book. Three other items are also noteworthy. The 1787 entries include the payment of £15 4s. for 'four pieces of blue striped furniture' and Hester also accounted for a payment for new lining for the coach, at a cost of £3 18s. and a miniature of Romney Park provided by Grimaldi.[57] These kinds of products were significant and visible signs of status and taste; appearing as they do in her account book, they suggest that she played a role in selecting them and in dealing with the suppliers. This independence is underlined by the existence of a catalogue of Hester's library, quite distinct from her husband's.[58] Who paid for the books listed therein is less important here than the fact that they are conceived separately from Sir Roger's library: like her clothes and her allowance, they belonged to Hester.

Second, two purchases recorded in Sir Roger's accounts underline this agency and illustrate the important part that women such as Hester played in the broader dynastic identity of the aristocracy. In 1776 the purchase of a 'post coach & post chaise &c' costing £208 6s. and a sedan chair for £24 were assigned to her in the accounts.[59] Undoubtedly emblazoned with the Newdigate coat of arms, they signal one way that women in the public sphere both contributed to the semiotics of wealth and taste amongst landed elites and drew upon those signs in fixing their own status. Like Mary Leigh, Hester was an important part of the heritance and lineage of the family, a role also reflected in the very common practice of using matronymic surnames as middle names for sons and daughters.[60]

Third, although Sophia and Hester purchased a limited range of goods, their level of spending was high, as befitted their status. Both women consistently spent far more on 'Apparel' (clothing and jewellery) than Sir Roger himself—generally over twice as much (Table 5.2). Although well within an orthodox female domain of spending, this kind of purchasing power suggests a high level of autonomy in discretionary expenditure. The embodiment of social status in this way was highly significant, publicly visible, and contributed to the status of the family, not just in the rarified atmosphere of court, but also in provincial society and leisure resorts.[61]

---

[57] WRO, CR1841/29, General Account Book.

[58] WRO, CR136/V/166, Catalogues of Lady Newdigate's Books, 1798.

[59] WRO, CR136/V/136, Account book, entry for 1776.

[60] There is no comprehensive data on this but even the briefest perusal of genealogies such as *Burke's Landed Gentry* shows that the practice was very common.

[61] On the importance of dress at court, see Greig, *Beau Monde*, 99–130; on public appearance more generally and the critique offered of London taste, see Vickery, *Gentleman's Daughter*, 169–83.

Table 5.2. Mean annual spending on clothing and jewellery by Sir Roger Newdigate, Sophia Newdigate (d. 1774), and Hester Newdigate (d. 1796)

	Sir Roger Newdigate	Sophia Newdigate	Hester Newdigate
	£ - s. - d.	*£ - s. - d.*	*£ - s. - d.*
1747–53	33/12/9	80/18/0	—
1754–60	51/5/0	75/8/6	—
1761–7	27/18/3	84/4/2	—
1768–74	28/13/6	70/4/6	—
1775	13/7/3	—	—
1776	57/0/6	—	1718/16/0
1777–83	28/3/5	—	84/3/11
1784–90	42/4/10	—	103/18/7

Sources: WRO, CR136/V/156, Account book; WRO CR136/V/136, Account book.

Fourth, the two women seem to have had a good deal of autonomy in terms of where they purchased goods. Of the suppliers that are listed for Hester's purchases, over half were not patronized by her husband. Whilst these included milliners, mantua makers, and stay makers, of which Sir Roger had no need, they also numbered physicians, apothecaries, glovers, and shoemakers who could have served both husband and wife. Most striking, perhaps, the jeweller Duval appears only once in the accounts, as does William Insley, who sold Hester the sedan chair. These were significant purchases, both in terms of the sums involved and the type of goods being acquired, and they suggest that she moved within a world of consumption, networks of exchange and shopping at least partly of her own making.

Sophia Newdigate (Figure 5.2) also exercised autonomy in matters of taste and spending, as is apparent from her journal of a tour in the south of England and Sir Roger's correspondence.[62] Sophia took the tour in 1748 with her husband, to whom she refers a number of times, and a small party of friends. The journal is an antiquarian work, bound in leather and carefully written, which comments mainly on the landscape and on the architecture and interiors of the many country houses they visited. It is reminiscent of the late-eighteenth-century diaries of Mrs Lybbe Powys, but lacks the commentary on manners and social intercourse that appears in those volumes.[63] The party left Arbury on 25 July 1748, travelling through Oxfordshire, Northamptonshire, Buckinghamshire, Hertfordshire, and Surrey to London and on to Essex, and then back through Surrey and south-westwards to Portsmouth, the Isle of Wight, Southampton, Winchester, and through Gloucestershire before returning home to Warwickshire on 12 September.[64] There are detailed comments on a select number of houses, such as Stowe and Windsor Castle, whilst others, like Hadlington Hall, were observed in passing

---

[62] WRO, CR1841/7, Lady Newdigate's tour in the south of England (1748).

[63] Climenson, *Diaries of Lybbe Powys.*

[64] An addendum covers a further excursion that takes in Leicestershire, Derbyshire (including Chatsworth), and Nottingham.

Figure 5.2. Sophia Newdigate, née Conyers (d.1774), the first wife of Sir Roger Newdigate, whom she married in 1743 (William Hoare, *c.*1750).
Reproduced by kind permission of Viscount Daventry.

and from a distance. It is most likely, then, that this journey was an exploratory one on the part of Sir Roger Newdigate, taken as it was two years before works began on Arbury Hall in 1750 and perhaps building on his first Grand Tour between 1738 and 1740. It is difficult to assess, therefore, the extent to which Sophia's judgements were purely her own: whilst she was undoubtedly an active participant in the journey, it seems most likely that her assessments were part of a shared experience with Sir Roger, as perhaps was the extensive project he undertook at Arbury, despite the impression given in his diaries of masculine control.

As Lybbe Powys stated in her diaries in 1760, although comments on architecture may have been 'quite out of female knowledge...what at first may appear intricate, after quarter of an hour's converse might give entertainment'.[65] Such conversations are apparent from the numerous observations Sophia made on the architecture of many of the aristocratic houses they visited. At Stowe she noted, as she often did, architectural proportions: the Ballroom was '70ft by 25 & 25' and, in another wing of the house, the Gallery, '75ft by 25 & 20'. The Hall at Bulstrode House, the home of the Duke of Portland, was 'a well proportion'd room', but in

---

[65] Climenson, *Diaries of Lybbe Powys*, 75.

contrast Langley Park in Buckinghamshire was dismissed as 'Irregular'.[66] She noted architectural details—in St George's Chapel, Windsor, a 'very well proportion'd Gothick building, the Arches flatter then common ye arms of the Knights of the Garter'—and was always willing to express critical judgement. The 'Noble apartments' at Stowe were admired, as were the 'Noble Gothick building' of Cowdray Castle in Sussex, which was a 'magnificent seat', and the 'beautiful Gothick work' in Winchester Cathedral.[67] Indeed, Gothic buildings were often commended, a preference which may reflect her husband's influence, although Sir Roger was yet to embark on his Gothicization of Arbury. In contrast she felt that Eton College Chapel had 'nothing remarkable worth taking notice of'; Monkey Island at Bray-on-Thames contained only 'two disagreeable buildings' despite the Duke of Marlborough having spent 'eight thousand pounds' on it; Waltham Abbey was 'dark, damp & very unpleasant'; and Claremont House was 'ugly enough on the outside but convenient within'. The conversations that led to these decisions are often indicated by entries such as that for Wooton Farm, where Sophia noted that 'this is upon the whole a pretty place but we agreed rather too much dress'd'.[68]

Where they had an opportunity to do so, the party went into the houses they were visiting, and Sophia frequently commented on their interior design and material culture. She went to great lengths to describe the interior of Stowe:

> There are two noble Apartments newly built... richly furnished, ye pictures extreamly bad, beyond that is a drawing room furnished with Crimson velvet and hung with whole lengths of all ye Grenville family and further on is a large bedchamber & dressing room fitted up very elegantly with Chintz Chinese pictures and Indian cabinets & opens into a Loggia which makes ye Apartment extreamly agreeable. These rooms with ye Chappell which is handsomely fitted up & has a mosaick ceiling of white & gold.[69]

Like Lybbe Powis, she also viewed collections of chinaware and glassware, commenting on both their quality and position. In the Bedchamber at Windsor castle, for instance, she noted, 'We were not suffer'd to go further than the doors of the picture and china closet of the latter of which was fitted up by the late Queen, there is a great deal of good china, each piece stands on a small shelf gilt with looking glass behind it.'[70] These things were firmly in the female domain of consumption, as contemporaries recognized, sometimes in terms of the analogy of fine women and fine china.[71] Sophia expressed confidence in these comments, passing judgement more freely and probably playing more of a leading role in discussions with

[66] WRO, CR1841/7, Lady Newdigate's Tour, ff. 4, 13, 6.
[67] WRO, CR1841/7, Lady Newdigate's Tour, ff. 10, 24, 35.
[68] WRO, CR1841/7, Lady Newdigate's Tour, ff. 7, 11, 18, 21, 15.
[69] WRO, CR1841/7, Lady Newdigate's Tour, ff. 3–4.
[70] WRO, CR1841/7, Lady Newdigate's Tour, f. 10; Climenson, *Diaries of Lybbe Powys*, 266.
[71] D. Porter, 'A wanton chase in a foreign place: Hogarth and the gendering of exoticism in the eighteenth-century interior', in D. Goodman and K. Norberg (eds) *Furnishing the Eighteenth Century* (New York, 2007), 55; Vickery, *Behind Closed Doors*, 271–7; Baird, *Mistress of the House*, 58–9, 129–30.

Sir Roger and their fellow travellers. This is also evident in her comments on furniture and furnishings. At Claremont 'the furniture of the house in general is very indifferent, the Hangings chiefly paper and hardly any good pictures', and Cowdray Castle, despite her positive assessment of the Gothic architecture, she thought the furniture to be 'in general old & indifferent'.[72]

What interested Sophia most seems to have been the unusual, the exotic, and the 'curious'. Cobham Hall was 'not worth seeing' but had, in the garden 'an extreme pretty Chinese building encompassed with a fine plantation. Here are a great abundance of uncommon and beautiful trees & shrubs & several Orange, Lemon & citrus trees placed in a grove larger than I ever saw.'[73] Goodwood was 'old and indifferent', but Sophia had much more positive comments to make again on the gardens, where she found:

> a kind of Chinese Tent with Chintz Curtains drawn up in Festoons placed in ye midst of a beautiful Grove. A Very light pretty building near it is a seat ye Model of one of ye Gothick Tombs in Westminster Abbey. In another part of the garden is a very particular place called the Stone Dell, wch is a sort of Rocky pit near wch is ye ruins of a Church, an Hermit's cave, a Skittle alley with a Chinese House in it, a Lapland House... In the Woods is a building for Maccaws which fly about & add infinitely to the beauty of them... The garden is enriched with abundance of curious shrubs & plants particularly the Magnolia in plenty.[74]

This speaks volumes of her individual taste and interests, given what we know about Arbury Hall: the Gothic sits alongside a wide variety of other points of cultural reference. Indeed, it is telling that she appreciated older houses that had been remodelled and updated. Thorndon Hall in Essex was favoured because it was 'part old part new' and Esher too because 'Mr Pelham has added to the building and fitted up both outside & in, in a gothic taste'.[75]

What emerges from Sophia's journal is a shared reflection and development of taste when it came to the homes of other aristocratic families and architecture more generally. Indeed, correspondence from Sir Roger to Sophia, letters which no doubt built on face-to-face conversations, reflect this shared culture of taste. In 1762 he wrote to Sophia from militia camp at Plymouth with his comments on Mount Edgecumbe House:

> the house being old, with 4 octagons newly added to the angles, makes a better appearance at a distance than near. The inside too is indifferent, & has nothing worth seeing but some fine marble pillars in the hall, which are cut out of the hill itself, & take a fine polish... The taste of gardening as well as building here runs very low.[76]

This is reminiscent of some of the entries in Sophia's journal, suggesting a shared discourse. Sir Roger had the formal education and language to make informed judgements of country house architecture and design, and thus possessed the tools

---

[72] WRO, CR1841/7, Lady Newdigate's Tour, ff. 21, 24.
[73] WRO, CR1841/7, Lady Newdigate's Tour, f. 23.
[74] WRO, CR1841/7, Lady Newdigate's Tour, f. 26.
[75] WRO, CR1841/7, Lady Newdigate's Tour, ff. 19, 21.
[76] WRO, CR136/B/4592, Letter, 17 October 1762.

to fashion this discourse; but he shared these with Sophia as an equal in discernment. She herself was more than capable of making her own judgements, illustrating the way that aristocratic taste and identity as they related to consumption were, in the case of married couples, a congruence of polite conversation between men and women.[77] Indeed, Sophia did act alone, using her own skills to understand and evaluate art and architecture. The final pages of the journal contain a series of fine and detailed sketches of various buildings the couple encountered on their journeys.[78] Many of them are the features and buildings that Sophia made particular note of in the text of the journal, such as the Gothic Church at Wooton Farm, what appears to be the Chinese Tent at Goodwood (Figure 5.3), the Hermitage at Lilliput near Bath (with a plan), and a plan and view of Stonehenge. Drawing and painting were conventional female skills, developed through lessons and regular practice. Yet Sophia's expertise seemingly went further, because, in a letter to his political patron at Oxford, Dr Nathaniel Wetherell, Sir Roger noted that his wife was, as requested by the University, in the process of designing an ornamental shield to be placed in the Hall of University College.[79]

Sophia emerges from the pages of her journal and in her husband's letters as an active agent in her own judgements of taste, far more than a simple cypher for his knowledge and learning. We see this repeated in a notebook, kept by Sophia during the early 1750s, which details the plants and flowers in various parts of the garden at Arbury.[80] Moreover, the journal itself is far more than a record of events, just as Sir Roger's accounts were more than a record of purchases: like them, it was a form of self-fashioning. The journal is written in retrospect and was probably taken from detailed notes Sophia made during their tour. In this sense the journal was a reflective mechanism for Sophia to interpret and consider her experiences, her judgements, and her evaluations of what she had seen. Like many journals of the Grand Tour, it both reflected and constructed her sense of taste and aristocratic status as well as the taste of others, not least in the way that she commented on the homes of other aristocratic families.[81] The entries are written with the authority and confidence we would expect from an aristocrat, confident in her own distinction and her ability to identify distinction in others. Furthermore, the journal was intended to have an external function, to be read by others; this much is clear from a number of entries. On Stowe, Sophia determined only to 'mention those things that are new within these two years' because 'this place is so well known'; of Windsor Castle, she would 'say nothing' because it was 'well known to all who would ever read this'.[82] The journal was probably

---

[77] Conversational skills, particularly with women, have been seen as a significant element of eighteenth-century politeness. See Cohen, '"Manners" make the man', 312–29 and Langford, 'The uses of eighteenth century politeness', 311–31.

[78] WRO, CR1841/7, Lady Newdigate's Tour, pages following 56.

[79] WRO, CR136/B/2331a, Letter, 7 October 1767.

[80] WRO, CR136/A/248, Notebook of Sophia Newdigate, containing a list of trees and shrubs at Arbury, 1753.

[81] M. Cohen, 'The grand tour: language, national identity and masculinity', *Changing English*, 8 (2001), 129–41.

[82] WRO, CR1841/7, Lady Newdigate's Tour, ff. 3, 7.

Figure 5.3. Illustration from the travel journal of Sophia Newdigate (1748). This probably shows the Chinese Tent at Goodwood, described as having 'Chintz Curtains drawn up in Festoons'.

Source: CR1841/7, Lady Newdigate's tour in the south of England (1748). © Warwickshire Record Office.

not intended for publication but it would presumably have been placed in the library at Arbury as a lasting reminder for later generations of her journey and her reflections on other country houses—certainly it carries a bookplate of the kind used by Francis Newdigate in the early nineteenth century. These impressions, of shared experiences and identities in consumption and taste, were produced within marriage; our final example illustrates the way aristocratic widowed women were required to exercise autonomy, in this case in quite straightened circumstances.

THE RESPONSIBILITIES OF THE WIDOW:
ELIZABETH DRYDEN OF CANONS ASHBY

Although thrift was the general rule for landed families, and women such as Mary Leigh were as keen as men to exercise sound oeconomy, not everyone matched up to this ideal. Lady Elizabeth and Sir John Turner Dryden illustrate the difficulties caused by spendthrift landowners, but also the subsequent efforts of Elizabeth, as a single female in a very different position to the one enjoyed by Mary Leigh, to balance the books and revive the family fortune.

Elizabeth Dryden was the adoptive daughter of her uncle, Sir John Dryden, and lived at Canons Ashby from the age of 8 to her marriage to John Dryden in 1781. We know little about her early years, but her new parents were clearly very fond of their ward, buying her presents and writing approvingly of her character.[83] John Turner was the second son of Sir Edward Turner (1719–66), second Baronet of Ambrosden Park in Oxfordshire. He attended Harrow and later embarked on a Grand Tour in 1774 which took him to France and parts of modern-day Germany.[84] Aspects of this journey, recorded in his journal of the tour, provide useful clues to his habits of spending that were to contribute to the problems he and Elizabeth encountered whilst in control of the Dryden estates. He acquired the best cabin on the packet-ship for the journey, paying 6 guineas for the privilege—a significant sum compared with the 2 guineas he paid for a week's stay at Hotel d'Gorch Foucault's in Paris.[85] John's time in Paris was filled with strolls along boulevards, observations of the fine bridges of the city, meals in hotel restaurants, and Italian comedies in the evening. He appears to have stayed there for around three weeks, noting in his journal costs amounting to around £150—not a huge sum, but quite significant in terms of the length of his visit. He continued spending freely on his return, commissioning for his presentation to Queen Charlotte an ornately embroidered dress suit made from dark-blue cut velvet interwoven with white silk (Figure 5.4).[86] Indeed, such was John's ability to spend that Betham reports that he 'dissipated a large sum of money' and 'contracted debts, which the short possession of a large fortune did not enable him intirely to liquidate'.[87] This fortune was the income of the Canons Ashby estate, then worth perhaps £2,500 per annum—a modest sum in comparison with the Leighs and the Newdigates.

We know little about John and Elizabeth's early married life in London, but John clearly maintained his earlier military interests, being commissioned as a captain in the Oxford Militia in 1782 and later as a captain in the Northamptonshire Yeoman Cavalry.[88] They were apparently living well and rented a second house near Margate in Kent, but there are signs that money needed to be raised as early as 1783, when they took out a number of loans against the security of their future estate income, mostly with George Brooks of Green Street, Grosvenor Square.[89]

[83] For fuller discussion of her relationship with her adoptive parents, see Chapter 6 and Rothery and Stobart, 'Merger and crisis', 22–3.

[84] NRO, D(CA) 347, John Turner Dryden's Tour of France, 1774; Betham, *Baronetage of England*, 279; *The Gentleman's Magazine*, 67/1 (1797), 521.

[85] NRO, D(CA) 347, John Turner Dryden's Tour, 22 July 1774, 28 July 1774. This journal departs from the ideal in that it records few observations on architecture, landscape, or local customs—see C. Chard, 'Grand and ghostly tours: the topography of memory', *Eighteenth Century Studies*, 31 (1997), 101–8.

[86] This suit closely resembles that pictured in Greig, *Beau Monde*, 117. Such suits could only be worn at court or for other very formal occasions, being out of line with the prevailing fashion for more sober styles.

[87] Betham, *Baronetage of England*, 280.

[88] NRO, D(CA) 207, Commission as captain in the Oxfordshire Militia, 30 September 1782; D(CA) 219, Commission as captain in the Northamptonshire Yeomanry, 9 May 1794.

[89] Hertfordshire Archives and Local Studies (HALS), AH/2348, Bond of John Turner to George Brooks, 18 February 1783; NRO, D(CA) 222, Memorial enrolled at Chancery of a bond, warrant, and indenture, 22 April 1790.

Figure 5.4. Dress coat in velvet and silk, with silk embroidery and appliqué work, *c.*1775; probably worn by John Turner Dryden for his presentation to Queen Charlotte.
© The National Trust.

The capital was due for repayment on the death of the dowager Elizabeth Dryden and they took out an insurance policy with the Society for Equitable Assurance on Lives or Survivorships 'That Elizabeth, wife of John Turner (aged 30) of Margaret Street, Cavendish Square, will survive Dame Elizabeth Dryden (aged 76) of Canons Ashby for £500 in favour of George Brooks'.[90] Unsurprisingly, they won their bet: the dowager Elizabeth died in 1791, the estate passed into John's possession, and the couple moved into Canons Ashby. Yet this did not spell the end of their financial problems. John's elevation to the baronetage involved significant direct and indirect expenditure, including £108 on servants for the ceremony in which he

---

[90] HALS, AH/2349, Insurance Policy, 2 April 1783.

received his title.[91] He also took advantage of the sale of honours during William Pitt's first ministry and purchased a baronetcy at a cost of £350—an honour linked to his display of loyalty in raising a troop of the Yeomanry.[92] All the while, they retained a London residence in Upper Seymour Street and acquired a large amount of furniture for Canons Ashby where, as we saw in Chapter 2, they significantly reorganized the use of the principal rooms.[93] In almost every room there were new pieces: a billiard table, maces, cue, and balls, a grand piano for the new dining parlour, and a suite of satinwood tables for the drawing room. There were also more pictures hung on the walls and a burgeoning number of decorative items, such as a pair of globes and a bust of Dryden (their poet ancestor). It is hard to put a cost against these things or the more general growth in the number of items within the house, but comparisons across to contemporaneous spending at Stoneleigh Abbey suggests that the satinwood furniture might have cost a total of around £100, depending on its size and quality.[94] Repeating this across the house must have involved Elizabeth and John in laying out hundreds or perhaps even thousands of pounds, although they eschewed large-scale building projects.

These outgoings were by no means ruinous in themselves, but they came on top of the cost of maintaining the household in both Northamptonshire and London. The cumulative effect, perhaps in combination with problems in servicing Sir John's earlier debts, was clearly enough to place considerable strain on the estate. Already in 1792, John was writing to the Rev Thomas Leigh at Adlestrop in Gloucestershire, apologizing for the delay in repaying a loan of £350.[95] Delaying payment to tradesmen was a more common means of extending periods of credit, but there were clearly problems here as well, both before and after Sir John's death in 1797. A letter written to Elizabeth in July 1800 by a lawyer representing a local coal merchant asked for immediate payment of a bill for 'coals delivered in Sir Johns lifetime', indicating that at least some tradesmen's accounts were left unpaid for a long period. This is confirmed by another letter, in which a coach maker called Wheatley asked for the payment of a bill totalling £35 which had been outstanding 'upwards of seven years'.[96]

These debts were to define much of Elizabeth's widowhood, shaping her life-style, compromising her status as a gentlewoman, and restricting her ability to establish her children in society—a point discussed in Chapter 6. In some respects, she fell into the trap of impoverished singleness described for many widows, but she always avoided dependency and fought hard to defend her status and estate.[97] From a letter to Messrs Barclay, Frither, & Bevan in London, written soon after John's death in 1797, it becomes clear that Elizabeth's power over her own estate

[91] NRO, D(CA) 1011, Receipt for cost of servants during the award ceremony, no date (1793).

[92] NRO, D(CA) 1021, Letter from W. Chinnery, 26 March 1795. Betham, *Baronetage of England*, 280.

[93] NRO, D(CA) 903, Inventory, 1791; D(CA) 904, Inventory, 1819. See also Chapter 2.

[94] SCLA, DR/18/5/6999.

[95] SCLA, DR18/8/6/29, Letter from John Turner Dryden, 3 April 1792.

[96] NRO, D(CA) 364/22, Letter from Wheatley, 7 July 1800; D(CA) 364/37, Letter from Mary Ann Wheatley, 15 March 1804.

[97] See Duncan, 'Old maids', esp. 58, 180–90; Larsen, 'For want of a good fortune'.

had been suspended whilst various creditors attempted to recover her late husband's debts, since she was, in her words, 'not liable to be called upon' for them.[98] A second letter, written ten days later, offered a fuller explanation of her situation: she could not hope to repay the debts owed because 'her estates in the County & Lincolnshire are engaged by a Deed & Fine to a Mr Brooks, a partner in a banking firm in Chancery Lane'. In other words, the estates had been used to guarantee a loan, something Elizabeth claimed not to have known. Here the precariousness of Elizabeth's position became clear, at least by her own testimony. She depended on 'Mr Brooks being a man of character & humanity' for a resolution to her difficult situation.[99] The following year Elizabeth explained, in a somewhat desperate manner in response to one of a number of requests for the settlement of her late husband's debts with a Mr Tritton of Lombard Street, London, that her finances were in 'the most dangerous and embarrassed state imaginable'.[100] She continued by expressing her fears that the estate might soon enter chancery proceedings, that her rents might be seized, and that, in the meantime, she had 'hardly a bare subsistence left for herself & a large young family'. She evidenced this parlous state of her affairs as proof that Mr Tritton was acting under the 'erroneous idea' that she was 'in possession of a large income'. Furthermore, she attested that the debts owed to him were not hers at all, but her late husband's. She had been instructed by her solicitor Mr Brookes that she should not sign anything with regards to his debts because she had 'acted entirely by Sir John's absolute command and authority'.

These letters can be read in a number of ways, all of which reflect her strategic exploitation of opportunities available to her within the system of patriarchy.[101] In some senses, it appears that the financial position Elizabeth found herself in had led to her reliance on the masculinity of others; yet at the same time she appealed to formal arguments that female spending took place entirely under the supervision of their husbands—a legal nicety which we have already seen was rarely played out in practice. More subtly, she played on her female naivety but coupled this with the authority that came with her rank and title; as shown by her argument concerning ownership of property at Canons Ashby (discussed in Chapter 3), she was not a woman to simply accept her fate. Indeed, it is clear that Elizabeth made concerted attempts to deal with debts and to put the family patrimony into better order for her children and for later generations. In this, she took on responsibilities normally prescribed to men, although, as Duncan makes clear, there were plenty of women who were called on to manage the affairs of feckless or simply incompetent male relatives.[102] Indeed, the responsibilities held by Elizabeth were essentially those enjoyed by Mary Leigh; the key difference was their level of wealth and their indebtedness. In reality, Elizabeth had much less scope for independent action, in

---

[98] NRO, D(CA) 364/31, Letter, 6 July 1797.
[99] NRO, D(CA) 364/32, Letter, 17 July 1797.
[100] NRO, D(CA) 364/35, Letter, 7 April 1798.
[101] See Shepard, 'Minding their own business' for an example of this lower in the social hierarchy.
[102] Duncan, 'Old maids', 191–9. She focuses on Jane Innes, who showed an independence of mind similar to that of Elizabeth Dryden.

part because of the size of debts owed, but also because she was not in full control of the estate, a trust having been set up in order to deal with her first husband's debts. The trustees appear to have taken the situation seriously, advising Elizabeth to sell timber off the estate and land to sitting tenant farmers, a course of action which raised over £3,000.[103] However, much of her effort was directed at reducing costs whilst maintaining her rank and dignity. This involved compromises in the education of her children and limits to their social and marital horizons, as we discuss in Chapter 6. It also meant living more frugally, a necessity which was partly met through residing for much of the year in Margate or, after she remarried in 1805, in London.[104] This marriage brought no respite from her debts, however: much of the lengthy marriage settlement between Elizabeth and Godfrey Scholey was concerned with protecting Scholey's estate from the debts of £10,980 left by Sir John.[105] Elizabeth was, therefore, concerned with raising estate income as well as maintaining the house. She wrote to Peacock about the collection of rents and taxes, the employment of servants, plans for the park and gardens, hedging and ditching, and minor repairs, including the roofing of the brewhouse.[106] Her attitude to these matters is hard to discern, although she sustained her correspondence over the years and wrote to her sister-in-law, Mrs Steele, that the repairs at Canons Ashby 'amuse me much'.[107] She clearly paid close attention to these issues, although from a distance, and Peacock regularly sent the household bills and accounts by parcel to Elizabeth, thus giving her a global oversight of the incomings and outgoings.[108]

That indebtedness had a direct impact on Elizabeth's ability to run Canons Ashby and maintain her status was readily apparent, Peacock writing in April 1806 to express his regret that 'Your Ladyship's affairs have not turned out so well.'[109] However, in some ways life continued as it would for other aristocratic families. Correspondence between Elizabeth and her sister-in-law, Mrs Steele, reflects the everyday concerns and gossip of an aristocrat, albeit one in straitened circumstances. She complained, in 1810, of her limited resources and that 'my family have a claim to every thing I can spare from my own necessities'.[110] The same year Elizabeth reported that the family had a 'quiet season but have been most of the time without a cook & some time without a footman', caused, she suggested, by a lack of good men.[111] Deprivation was clearly relative to expectations and previous experience, but the absence of male servants is interesting: Mary Leigh clearly valued these as an expression of status, but Jane Innes, possessing £14,000 capital,

[103] NRO, D(CA) 364/13, Letter, 14 April 1805. Timber sales were discussed in letters from her steward, William Peacock: see NRO, D(CA) 360, 26 February 1805, 12 March 1805, 10 May 1808.

[104] NRO, D(CA) 360, Letter, 13 March 1804.

[105] NRO, D(CA) 536, Marriage settlement of Godfrey Scholey and Dame Elizabeth Dryden, 19 March 1805.

[106] Letters sent in reply by Peacock include NRO, D(CA)/360, 14 January 1805, 6 June 1809, 21 March 1809, 28 March 1809, 11 April 1809, 18 April 1809.

[107] NRO, D(CA) 361, Letter, 3 November 1810.

[108] NRO, D(CA) 360, Letter, 20 April 1804.

[109] NRO, D(CA) 360, Letter, 1 April 1806.

[110] NRO, D(CA) 361, Letter, 3 November 1810.

[111] NRO, D(CA) 361, Letter, 3 November 1810.

refused to employ footmen because of the challenge they formed to her authority.[112] That said, even markers of mere respectability were proving problematic for Elizabeth, china and linen being in short supply at Canons Ashby and beyond the limits of her spending power. She thanked Mrs Steele for some linen she had supplied to her and belatedly sent her £1 for it; but she also noted that 'not one cloth is large enough for our Table, so different are modern dining tables from ancient'.[113] She thus managed to thank her sister-in-law and at the same time hint at the superiority of her own dining arrangements and household. Yet her solution was born of thrifty necessity: she first proposed turning one of the table linens into 'supper cloths' and then enquired whether anyone of Mrs Steele's acquaintance had 'any real foreign linen to dispose of... it must be in tolerable condition & strong'. Second-hand china was also proffered, but declined. This was not as a matter of principle—indeed, there is plenty of evidence of wealthy households buying used goods from motives of thrift and perhaps social emulation[114]—but rather because of its nature: 'old desert China is generally small, & a service I do not want having no formal company'. Like the wealthy merchants studied by Nenadic, it was function and utility that took precedence over appearance when acquiring goods second-hand; Elizabeth wrote subsequently asking Mrs Steele to look out for any 'small plate or basons' which would be 'very useful'.[115]

Elizabeth's comments on her children are also instructive in terms of her limited resources as well as her low expectations for them and their inheritance of their father's character. In September 1809 she was attempting to obtain patronage for her son Leopold from James Leigh, a cousin of Mary and Edward, for a clerkship in the 'India House', hardly a respectable occupation even for a younger son.[116] Although Leopold eventually became a clergyman, it appears he had later been apprenticed in some way and she noted that he had returned to her temporarily whilst switching boarding accommodation from Northamptonshire, which was 'too dear', to Buckingham.[117] She held out few hopes for her second son Henry (who eventually inherited the estate as third baronet) because he had become 'very disrespectful to me & his brother... extremely opinionated'. She feared, perhaps with a view to his late father's attitude to money, that he would be 'extravagant & wrong headed' and later went so far as to describe him as a 'Malignant Demon'.[118] He did acquire a curacy under the patronage of James Leigh, and it appears his brother Leopold was occupied in Madeira, apparently as a naval officer.[119] Despite this, Elizabeth bemoaned that 'He [Henry] does not promise to turn out well... [and]... is very ungrateful to me & I believe everyone else, & inclined to extravagance.' The cause of this behaviour, she suspected, was 'that strange Turner Temper that I fear will put him back in everything'.[120] Later she again noted that

[112] Duncan, 'Old maids', 200.   [113] NRO, D(CA) 361, Letter, 20 October 1814.
[114] See Nenadic, 'Middle-rank consumers'; Stobart, 'Clothes, cabinets and carriages'.
[115] NRO, D(CA)/361, Letter, 19 July 1813.
[116] NRO, D(CA)/361, Letter, 26 September 1809.
[117] NRO, D(CA)/361, Letter, 28 December 1816.
[118] NRO, D(CA)/361, Letters, 26 September 1809, 20 October 1814.
[119] NRO, D(CA)/361, Letter, 3 November 1810.
[120] NRO, D(CA)/361, Letter, 26 May 1812.

all her younger children had 'bad Tempers & bad dispositions...They are all complete Turners which is saying enough.'[121] This round condemnation of her own children, even to a close relative, is striking. Although there are plenty of other examples of this kind of criticism, as French and Rothery have shown, parental correspondence generally reveals loving and caring relationships, even where the tone is critical or instructional.[122]

Perhaps unsurprisingly, Elizabeth's situation deteriorated after her eldest son died and Henry inherited, and initially she made plans to leave Canons Ashby and find a house in London. Unlike his elder brother, Henry had married, and normal practice would have been for her, as dowager, to seek alternative accommodation. She informed Mrs Steele in January 1819 that she had 'ordered two floors' and would 'once more go into that dismal house [Canons Ashby] to pick up some clothes & trifles which are to me valuable and useful, and then leave it for ever'.[123] Yet this process was far from straightforward. As the 1819 inventory makes clear, Elizabeth laid claim to the vast majority of goods in the house: the 'heirlooms' comprising mostly old and worn goods (see Chapter 3). Whether she was driven by sentiment, financial worries, or a desire to spite her son, this episode is quite in character with her careful nurturing of resources—claiming what was due to her and deflecting claims against her estate wherever possible—and also with her awareness and constant buttressing of her rank and title.[124] In April, she was still looking for 'a comfortable House in Town and hope all my friends will look out'. However, she insisted that 'the furnishing cannot be arranged but by myself', thus exerting her authority and her desire to impress her needs, rank, and identity onto any future home. In this she was again at one with Mary Leigh's experience of making Grove House into 'so agreeable a place', somewhere that was her own to shape as she sought fit, and even Lady Strafford's attempts to mould a home worthy of the Beau Monde.[125] Elizabeth closed her letter with a more specific indication of her requirements, if rather ambiguously stated: 'I have my health much better here–but I really think a house in Gower Street would remove many objections.'[126] By June 1819 Mrs Steele had found her a house in Gower Street, but Elizabeth declined the opportunity because it was 'too small'. She apparently saw size as a reflection of her rank, writing that 'I want a good sized House with garden & Coach House & Stables adjoining; the House three rooms on a floor or light closet at least...I want also a large Dining Parlour many feet long.'[127] Later the same year she found a house that answered these requirements:

> I believe I am suited, though it is a little too small and ill situated, but a Garden, Coach House & Stable, which is indispensable as I mean to drive my own Horses. It is

[121] NRO, D(CA)/361, Letter, 28 January 1814.
[122] French and Rothery, *Man's Estate*, 212.   [123] NRO, D(CA) 361, Letter, 8 January 1819.
[124] In this, her character and actions reflect those of Elizabeth Shackleton—see Vickery, *Gentleman's Daughter*, passim.
[125] NRO, D(CA) 361, Letter, [no date] April 1819; Stobart, 'So agreeable and suitable a place'; Greig, *Beau Monde*, 36–47. See also Duncan, 'Old maids', 201–2.
[126] NRO, D(CA) 361, Letter, [no date] April 1819.
[127] NRO, D(CA)/361, Letter, 2 June 1819.

also in repair & the furniture may be bought & entered well... it is clean painted and plastered... It is in the worst part of Gower Street—Rogers thinks I shall not like it being a corner house, but he has seen none with Stables & c.—which I cannot settle without.[128]

Her aim was respectable living, gilded with the dignity of a coach and horses. Like Lady Strafford, she was aware of the nuances of address, yet was willing to compromise for the sake of the coach house and stables and the convenience of clean and furnished rooms.[129] In reality, this may all have been bluster: she never moved to London and her correspondence was addressed from Canons Ashby through to her death in 1824.[130] Perhaps her lack of success resulted from a shortage of the funds necessary to acquire a suitable London residence or perhaps she chose to stay at the family home, enjoying the dignity afforded by a country seat, even when it formally belonged to her son.

The impact of John and Elizabeth's unwise and uncontrolled spending was significant and far-reaching, serving to underline the importance of thrift and self-management amongst the aristocracy, the kinds of habits exemplified by the far wealthier Mary Leigh. Much of Elizabeth's behaviour after her husband's death, at least by her account, was focused on limiting the repercussions of earlier extravagances; but the damage had already been done. We can only guess at where the real responsibility for these problems lay. She blamed her husband and, indeed, the character of the Turners, but no doubt both Elizabeth and John were responsible to some extent. Beyond doubt are the problems that indebtedness created for Elizabeth: these distorted and undermined her social status as a gentlewoman. Her immediate solution centred on appealing to the masculinity of others, including her creditors, and on appealing to gendered divisions in consumption and financial management. As the wife of Sir John, she had limited control over the family finances and over spending on the house and the estate, and this was the social norm that lay at the heart of her appeals to her creditors. She played this gender card to some effect, but at other times emphasized her rank and status, and maintained her independence. As with Mary Leigh and Jane Innes, then, she played on both aspects of her status as a gentlewoman; her problem was that she lacked the wealth that would properly underpin this status.

CONCLUSION

Gender identity was an important determinant of consumption habits amongst women, defining the limits of their autonomy and spending power as well as the types of goods they were likely to be purchasing. Elizabeth Dryden was keen to remind her creditors that, for married women, overall control lay with their husbands, who governed the level of spending and determined the character of dynastic consumption. As Vickery, Harvey, and others have argued, wives were responsible for

---

[128] NRO, D(CA)/361, Letter, 22 November 1819.   [129] Greig, *Beau Monde*, 42.
[130] NRO, D(CA) 361, Letter, 14 December 1823—Elizabeth's last letter to her sister-in-law.

the day-to-day management of the household and the spending which came with this: provisioning, paying female servants, clothing the children, and so on. This gender division of labour is seen most clearly in the accounts kept by Hester Newdigate and periodically settled by her husband. Yet, even here, stereotypes rarely describe social realities; Hester exerted control over the money given to her and apparently made her own decisions about the retailers who supplied her personal needs, despite Sir Roger's apparent oversight through his meticulous household accounts. His first wife, Sophia, enjoyed similar independence and also shared in her husband's notions of taste. This is perhaps unsurprising, given women's acknowledged taste and role in shaping interior decorative schemes. But confining a woman's taste to the niceties of wallpaper and fabrics constrains as much as it liberates: it places limits on the scope of their involvement in determining domestic material culture both imaginatively and spatially. Lady Borringdon went beyond these limits at Saltram, impressing her own character on her husband's house;[131] Sophia's clear understanding and appreciation of architectural as well as decorative taste, and particularly her observations on Gothic styles, stretch the boundaries set by social expectations and bring her much more into an area of apparently masculine control.

The absence of a husband, of course, brought much more scope for independent action, notwithstanding the financial constraints and emotional turmoil that dominate much of the literature on single women. Mary Leigh's single status defined her spending throughout the various stages of her life, but growing constraints were laid down by her family role as a wealthy heiress and later a substantial landowner. In matters of business she leant on men's shoulders—most particularly those of her steward Samuel Butler and her lawyer Joseph Hill—but her spending was determined by her own preferences and tastes. Here, her identity as a woman was overlain by her aristocratic and landowning responsibilities, which, as Elias has argued, brought with them obligations to spend in certain ways.[132] Her life thus reveals how gender, rank, and status were mutually contingent. It also reminds us of the importance of money in realizing the potential for independent action. Whilst Mary was free from the constraints faced by many of the women studied by Vickery, Duncan, and others, Elizabeth Dryden was not so fortunate.[133] In many ways, her position and her character were most complex: she played on her feminine status in arguing that the debts she faced were the responsibility of her dead husband; yet she constantly reasserted her rank and status, and her independence from others. Elizabeth's financial problems throw these different aspects of her life into sharper relief and show the resourcefulness of gentlewomen in balancing the different roles expected of them.

This again illustrates the way that gender interacted with social status and position, as well as familial status and stage in the life course, sometimes in complex and surprising ways. Whilst these women's experiences were specifically those of the elite, they are also evocative of the strategies and behaviour employed by those

---

[131] Lewis, 'When a house', 359–62.   [132] Elias, *Court Society*, 42–65.
[133] Vickery, *Behind Closed Doors*; Duncan, 'Old maids'.

lower down the social scale. Like the middling-sort women studied by Alexandra Shepard, these aristocratic women were closely involved in networks of exchange and credit.[134] They drove economic change and employed strategies of saving and accumulation, rather than simply pursuing taste and desire, comfort and emulation, as McKendrick and others would have us believe. We should not confuse the conventionality of their roles (for instance, in household management) with a lack of agency or autonomy: our elite women cleverly and strategically used the opportunities available to them to shape their lives, their homes, and their relationships with others. Of course, women, like men, did not take these actions as individuals, however, and Chapter 6 explores how both genders acted within broader networks of family, friends, and servants.

[134] Shepard, 'Minding their own business'.

6

Consumption and the Household
Family, Friends, and Servants

INTRODUCTION

Much of the literature on the aristocracy is based on their choices, tastes, and desires as consumers: they were the patrons of architects, craftsmen, and retailers.[1] And yet consumption was rarely an individual process; rather, it took place in the context of the household, family, and friends. The importance of these groups in shaping consumption choices is emphasized by de Vries, who puts the economically independent unit of family-household at the heart of his industrious revolution. Their combined labour was deployed to maximize household income, which was pooled and dispersed for the benefit of household members and the unit as a whole, especially in terms of its consumption choices.[2] But he was most interested in ordinary working households and focused particularly on the nuclear family. Indeed, this tightly defined unit has tended to dominate discussion of household consumption, even amongst the middling sorts, where the composition of the household was often complicated by the presence of servants and apprentices.[3] Smith, for example, emphasizes the importance of the family in producing and reproducing respectability, respectable people being the product of a family 'devoted primarily to educating its members in moral behaviour and to sustaining their virtue', often through the consumption of key domestic goods. Finn, meanwhile, sets men's consumption firmly within networks of family and community, whilst Muldrew emphasizes the household as the key unit of credit and reputation—the setting where the morality and economics of good management came together.[4]

For elite families, which often operated like complex corporations in which the husband and wife acted like non-executive directors, we need to take a rather

---

[1] This approach pervades the canonical literature, often in an implicit manner. See Girouard, *English Country House*; Wilson and Mackley, *Building of the English Country House*; Christie, *British Country House*; Cornforth, *Early Georgian Interiors*.

[2] De Vries, *Industrious Revolution*, esp. 14–18, 71–2, 215–16.

[3] For a fuller discussion of the complexities of household and family, see N. Tadmor, *Family and Friends in Eighteenth-Century England: Household, Kinship and Patronage* (Cambridge, 2000); J. Goody, J. Thirsk, and E. P. Thompson (eds), *Family and Inheritance: Rural Society in Western Europe, 1200–1800* (Cambridge, 1976).

[4] Smith, *Consumption and the Making of Respectability*, esp. 181–7, 210–12; Finn, 'Men's things'; C. Muldrew, *The Economy of Obligation. The Culture of Credit and Social Relations in Early-Modern England* (Basingstoke, 1998), 150, 157–72.

broader view of the household.[5] Vickery goes some way in achieving this through her detailed explorations of the sometimes troubled relationships between husbands and wives, and the trials of dealing with servants or coping with widowhood— themes which are echoed in Chatenet-Calyste's study of Marie-Fortunée d'Este.[6] In a rather different context, Finn describes how the formation of Swallowfield Park as the seat for the Russells was a family undertaking; it involved pooling financial resources from both father and sons, and drawing on their collective resources of cultural capital.[7] Whittle and Griffiths extend this in their analysis of the Le Strange family. They place much emphasis on the relationship between Sir Hamon and Alice, but also focus on the household as a unit of consumption and consider the impact of life cycle on consumption patterns, in terms of both child-care and education, and births, marriages, and deaths. Servants play a role in these processes, but appear mostly as objects of consumption—their labour bolstering the status and easing the lives of the Le Strange family.[8]

In this chapter, we want to build on this work by exploring in detail a matrix of influences on consumption, each of which represents a different aspect of the household. We begin with the immediate family, focusing on children and parents of the head of household. Children generated obvious costs in terms of education and establishment in the world and, unlike those in de Vries's households, there was little prospect of their bringing a wage income into the household. A lack of children could thus afford additional opportunities for consumption— as Wilson and Mackley note of Sir John Griffin Griffin at Audley End—but it also opened opportunities for broadening the definition of children through formal or informal adoption, an option seen in the Drydens and Newdigates.[9] Parents, or perhaps more correctly grandparents, are also largely absent from the breadwinner– homemaker household examined by de Vries, but dowagers in particular could be an important influence on elite consumption, a point explored here in the context of the Leighs and Drydens.[10] We next consider the impact on consumption of a key life-cycle event: death and the funeral. This has two aspects: first is the cost and symbolism of the funeral, which provided an important opportunity to project family and familial status to a wider world, not least by drawing on a large number of people from the broadly defined 'household' of the landed estate; second is the use of funerary monuments of various kinds to memorialize family in terms of both personal relations and status. We then turn to the wider household of friends, considered here through the activities of trustees and guardians. The role of the former was less to guide consumption or shape an individual's behaviour, and more to manage the estate through controlling

[5] Vickery, *Behind Closed Doors*, 159. See also I. Tague, *Women of Quality, Accepting and Contesting Ideals of Femininity in England, 1690–1760* (London, 2002), 97–132.

[6] Vickery, *Gentleman's Daughter*, 127–60; Vickery, *Behind Closed Doors*, 106–65; Chatenet-Calyste, 'Feminine luxury in Paris'.

[7] Finn, 'Swallowfield Park', 6.

[8] Whittle and Griffiths, *Consumption and Gender*, esp. 156–83, 210–38.

[9] Wilson and Mackley, *Building of the English Country House*, 313.

[10] De Vries, *Industrious Revolution*, 186–238. For an example of the influence of a dowager, see that of Katherine Windham in French and Rothery, *Man's Estate*, 192–3, 198–9.

expenditure and maximizing income. The latter operated in effect *in loco parentis* and thus were in a position to offer guidance on a much broader range of matters; but they went beyond this, because they were also available when the young person was setting up home—a role denied to most fathers, because they would often of necessity be dead before the young man could inherit the family home and set about making it his own. A better understanding of the relationship between guardians and their wards thus allows us to engage with recent analyses of the parent–child relationship and particularly the ways in which young men learned about estate and financial management.[11] How did learning extend beyond the nuclear family and into a period when the young man had inherited the family seat? Finally, we turn to servants and examine their role in shaping consumption, not least through their duties in dealing with tradesmen and managing the day-to-day running of the house and estate. This was a peculiar feature of the elite household: wives generally undertook these duties in middling families and even in many gentry families, including the Le Stranges.[12] Overall, we argue that this matrix of influences helped to determine consumption choices by setting the individual into a relational world of family and friends.

CHILDREN AND PARENTS: INTERGENERATIONAL RESPONSIBILITIES

All of the three families included in this study experienced childlessness or periods of minority, or both. Sir Roger Newdigate died childless, despite two lengthy marriages. There were sometimes children present at Arbury Hall, either as long-term or more occasional visitors: for example, when he invited a distant cousin, then a widow in reduced circumstances, to stay at Arbury with her children in the 1760s. A longer-term resident was another distant relative, Charles Parker, who gradually emerged as heir apparent to Sir Roger and eventually inherited his Harefield estates in Middlesex. He stayed with the Newdigates on a number of occasions during his childhood and adolescence and was offered considerable financial support.[13] Yet these arrangements were voluntary and selective: Sir Roger never had the ongoing and unavoidable obligations and costs that came with children. Sir John Dryden and his wife Elizabeth were also without children of their own, but in 1760 they chose to adopt the daughter of Sir John's younger brother Beville following his death and the impoverishment of his wife, who was excluded from her mother-in-law's will.[14] Elizabeth junior remained an only child. At Stoneleigh, Thomas, fourth Lord Leigh, and his first wife, Maria Craven,

[11] See P. Jenkins *Making of a Ruling Class: The Glamorgan Gentry 1640–1790* (Cambridge, 1983), 260–3; J. P. Cooper, 'Patterns of inheritance and settlement by great landowners', in J. Goody, J. Thirsk and E. P. Thompson (eds), *Family and Inheritance: Rural Society in Western Europe, 1200–1800* (Cambridge, 1976), 192–328.

[12] Harvey, *Little Republic*, 106; Vickery, *Gentleman's Daughter, passim*; Whittle and Griffiths, *Consumption and Gender*, 26–43.

[13] White, *Correspondence of Sir Roger Newdigate*, xxxiv–xxxv.

[14] Rothery and Stobart, 'Merger and crisis', 22.

had suffered the death of their first three sons in infancy during the late 1730s, their eldest, Thomas, dying of smallpox in 1737. Their fourth son, Edward, was only seven when his father died: the result was a fourteen-year period (1749–63) of minority, when trustees managed the estate. Edward himself died unmarried and childless, as did his older sister, Mary.

As a consequence of these demographic misfortunes, these families escaped many of the considerable costs that having children brought to the aristocratic household. Mingay estimates the cost of private tutors, schooling, and university education for the son of the 'middling' gentleman Richard Grosvenor of Eaton in Cheshire amounted to about £200 per annum. Those of the son of the Duke of Chandos, who went to Balliol College, Oxford, with attendant servants and had a large apartment in college, ran to over £400 a year.[15] Edward Leigh's education in the 1750s and 1760s probably cost something of this order; perhaps even more. In a letter to Edward's uncle and guardian William Craven, Joseph Hill announced that the Lord Chancellor had agreed to £1,000 'for fitting out his Lordship for the University' and to an annual allowance of £1,000.[16] The surviving bills for this period reveal much more modest spending, although it is unclear whether this reflects their incomplete nature or the economy shown by Edward. Notwithstanding his own lack of children, Sir Roger Newdigate also incurred significant schooling costs, the object of his largesse being Charles Parker. Noting in a letter to J. Mills, written in October 1765, that 'every nerve should be strain'd to furnish the young people with the best education', he first contributed £50 per annum towards his schooling at Eton and later paid for him to learn French at the finishing school in Angers that Newdigate himself had attended as a young man.[17]

The education of a lady was much cheaper: the parents of Anne Ferrier, the daughter of a Pembrokeshire landowner, spent around 50 guineas a year to educate her in a fashionable school in Bath during the 1780s.[18] Spending on Mary's education in the 1750s amounted to a modest total of just £120, mostly for lessons in music, languages, and dancing, although to this we should perhaps add the costs of her board and lodging with her guardian Elizabeth Verney, which appear to have been fixed at twice-yearly payments of £50.[19] We know less about the situation of the young Elizabeth Dryden, who was probably educated at home: the only recorded costs were for gifts from a clearly doting Sir John. Elizabeth wrote to her natural mother that 'uncle brought me play things from Northampton and promises me more. I have got a pretty puppy and am to have a fine new Coat and dressed Linnen...Uncle hopes soon to get me a little Horse.'[20] No doubt there were additional costs for music, language, and dancing lessons, but there is no record of these, and it seems likely that the overall costs of raising and educating Elizabeth were relatively modest. When it came to educating and providing for her

---

[15] Mingay, *English Landed Society*, 135.
[16] SCLA, DR18/1/27/52, Letter, 19 December 1761.
[17] WRO, CR136/B/1833, Letter, 23 October 1765; White, *Correspondence of Sir Roger Newdigate*, xxxiv.
[18] Mingay, *English Landed Society*, 141.   [19] SCLA, DR18/5/3175, DR18/5/3617.
[20] NRO, D(CA)/1081, Letter, 4 May 1761.

own children, Elizabeth's options were severely constrained by the considerable debts left by her husband, Sir John Turner Dryden.[21] Despite directions in Sir John's will regarding the 'education and benefit' of their children, we find Elizabeth writing in 1799 to Mrs Hammond, apologizing for the removal of her daughters and the apparent hardship this would cause, but explaining that 'I am in great want of money myself & oweing [*sic*] large sums to several persons both in law expenses & on other accounts'.[22]

To the costs of formal education might be added the expense of sending a son on the Grand Tour—a necessary introduction to broader European society and culture. James Leigh, the eldest son of William Leigh of Adlestrop and a distant cousin of the Stoneleigh branch of the family, toured Europe between 1747 and 1748. The receipted bills for this tour show that he and his guardian General Wentworth spent around £3,000 during this time, mainly on travel and accommodation expenses.[23] This appears broadly typical of an extensive tour, but families lower down the social scale often limited spending. Charles Hotham was provided with only £800 per annum for his three year tour and Edward Weld's father suggested a figure of £500, although his son argued that this would 'neither suffice in France or Italy'.[24] Edward Leigh never toured extensively, although he appears to have travelled to France briefly in 1767, incurring costs of about £200. Both the timing and the brevity of the trip are surprising, taking place some four years after he left university. The delay might reflect a desire to organize affairs at Stoneleigh Abbey before travelling abroad; the brevity of the trip appears to be related to his deteriorating mental health. Unlike many young aristocrats, Edward was funding his own travels, as was Sir Roger Newdigate, who completed two grand tours in 1738–40 and 1774–5. Sir Roger also funded his protégé Charles Parker on a tour of France, Italy, and Germany in 1784. The total cost is impossible to gauge, but in June that year Charles wrote of his dismay in having lost two letters of credit from Sir Roger whilst en route from Rome to Dresden. Later the same month Sir Roger wrote to bankers in Vienna enquiring after several other letters of credit (at least one of which was to the value of £100) that had gone astray in the post. All told, the tour must have cost Sir Roger a considerable sum, the generosity of which prompted Charles to write on his return that 'I shall never regret the time I have spent abroad, nor be insensible I hope of the obligations I owe you for having proposed it, and so handsomely furnished me with the means of performing it.'[25] His gratitude reflected the persistent importance of the Grand Tour in setting up young men with knowledge and experience of European society as well as the key

---

[21] These amounted to £10,980 on an estate worth £2,577 per annum: see NRO, D(CA)/364/2, Valuation of the Dryden estates, no date (1797).

[22] NRO, D(CA)/364/17, Letter, 15 June 1799.

[23] *Burke's Peerage, Baronetage and Knightage* (London, 1852), 601; SCLA DR18/5/2885–2945— bills relating to a Grand Tour, 1747–8.

[24] Mingay, *English Landed Society*, 138; P. Roebuck, *Yorkshire Baronets, 1640–1760* (Oxford, 1980), 101. Edward Weld's letter to his father is reproduced in M. Rothery and H. French, *Making Men: the Formation of Elite Male Identities in England, c. 1660–1900* (Basingstoke, 2012), 96.

[25] WRO, CR136/B/2120, Letter, 17 October 1784.

sites of ancient and Renaissance Europe; despite growing critiques, it helped to integrate them into a cosmopolitan culture.[26]

Most costly of all were the dowries required for daughters. These varied considerably, again reflecting the wealth and ambition of the family: Elizabeth, daughter of the Hon. William Brownlow, received £6,000 in Exchequer Bills upon her marriage to the Earl of Darnley in 1791, whereas Sarah Western brought a dowry of £30,000 to her marriage to William Hanbury in 1736.[27] In comparison with these, Thomas Leigh made only a modest post-mortem provision for his second wife, Catherine Berkeley, and their daughter Anne: Catherine got £300 over and above her jointure, which had provided an annuity of £500, and Anne received £100 per annum.[28] Mary was settled with a generous portion of £15,000, but there is no evidence that this sum was ever transferred out of the Stoneleigh estate. At Canons Ashby, Elizabeth Dryden struggled to establish her children in life when they came of age in the early nineteenth century. In 1810, one of her daughters received a statement of the money she could expect on coming of age: a sum of just £800. This, Elizabeth asserted, should be invested to produce an annuity for life, 'which it is supposed ~~will~~ may be done at 10%...bringing in by that means eighty pounds (or more if the stock yields more)'.[29] Quite apart from this being a risky form of investment for a life's income, the total was acknowledged as insufficient for the young lady to live by herself; Elizabeth therefore proposed that her daughter should be a 'parlour boarder' with a Mrs Marmaris for eight months of the year, staying at her mother's home for the other four months, from summer to Michaelmas. There was no scope here for a dowry, which might help to explain why none of Elizabeth's daughters married. Of her sons, the eldest, John Edward, died unmarried in 1818 before he had received the estates via his mother's will. He was thirty-six, an age by which many landed gentlemen would have married, so perhaps the indebted estate prevented marriage.[30] Two of his younger brothers, Henry and Lempster, entered the clergy and a third, Leopold, married the daughter of a clergyman. All had respectable but modest livings. This was often the fate of younger sons, but their prospects cannot have been enhanced by the retrenchment at Canons Ashby following the death of their father.

[26] For further discussion of this and the problematic relationship between cosmopolitanism and xenophobia, see J. Black, *France and the Grand Tour* (Basingstoke, 2003); Sweet, *Cities and the Grand Tour*; Cohen, 'Grand tour'.

[27] MacArthur, 'Material culture and consumption', 71. See also Mingay, *English Landed Society*, 102; H. J. Habakkuk, *Marriage, Debt and the Estate System: English Landownership 1650–1950* (Oxford, 1994), 117.

[28] SCLA, DR18/13/1/15, Settlement between Thomas, Lord Leigh, and Catherine, 16 January 1747. A 'jointure' is defined as property settled on a husband and wife for their lives in survivorship of their marriage. See J. Goody, J. Thirsk and E. P. Thompson, *Family and Inheritance: Rural Society in Western Europe, 1200–1800* (Cambridge, 1976), 401.

[29] NRO, D(CA)/364/10, Statement of the Affairs of Miss Dryden, 7 February 1810. The word 'will' has been scratched through and replaced by 'may', perhaps indicating uncertainty over the level of return. The same rewording is made in relation to the principal sum to be received.

[30] For a detailed examination of age at marriage and more general demography of the landed elite, see Hollingsworth, 'Demography of the British peerage'; M. Rothery, 'The reproductive behaviour of the English landed gentry, 1800–1939', *Journal of British Studies*, 48 (2009), 674–94.

Overall, then, provision for children had little bearing on the outgoings of the Leighs and Newdigates, whilst the straitened circumstances at Canons Ashby meant that little could be spared to establish children in ways that might be expected amongst the landed gentry. But this does not mean that synchronic family had no bearing on consumption. The accommodation of dowagers was a perennial problem, both in terms of where they should reside and how much control they should exercise over the household.[31] Katherine Windham, for example, was given control of the family's estates at Felbrigg in Norfolk on her husband's death in 1689, whilst her son Ashe lived in Soho Square. She moved out of the family home ahead of Ashe's planned marriage in 1708, yet retained a close interest in the running and domestic arrangements of the household. Katherine wrote frequent and forthright letters, in particular expressing her concerns about Ashe's spending on jewellery for his intended wife and the drain on resources that this would cause: 'I am utterly against Brilliants, & you may tell her these were mine & I am unwilling they should be changed... Consider what expensive things you have to do, yr self is jewel enough.'[32] It appears that Thomas, fourth lord Leigh, was similarly influenced by his mother, Mary (see Chapter 4). Although it is uncertain how long she continued to live at Stoneleigh following the death of her husband Edward, many of the bills in the early 1740s were still being addressed to her. These covered a great variety of expenditure, including the land tax, building materials, candles and provisions, drapery and haberdashery, and livery: together, they suggest that she remained closely involved in the management of the household.[33] When she subsequently moved to nearby Guy's Cliffe, she took with her a range of goods from Stoneleigh, mostly decorative items and furniture from family rooms (see Chapter 3). To render these rooms habitable once again, Thomas was forced to purchase replacement items, although this might also have given him the opportunity to render these rooms more to his taste—an objective apparent in the inclusion there of a set of racing prints in what was then called the Common Dining Parlour.[34] Yet Mary's influence remained strong, both in her presence in the accounts and in the absence of the goods she removed.

The impact of the dowager was greater still at Canons Ashby. Lady Elizabeth retained control of the estates throughout her widowhood and remained at the house until her death in 1824. She clearly viewed the house as her property, and her eventual heir (the Reverend Henry, her second son) resided at one of his livings, Leek Wootton in Warwickshire, until his inheritance. Elizabeth's management of the estate was initially constrained by the existence of a trust set up in order to deal with her first husband's debts. However, her personal authority, as well as her liability for debts, was clearly laid out in the marriage settlement drawn

---

[31] See Habakkuk, *Marriage, Debt and the Estate System*, 79–89.

[32] Norfolk Record Office, WKC 7/21/15, Letter to Ashe Windham 5 May 1708. See also French and Rothery, *Man's Estate*, 192–3, 198–9; Vickery, *Behind Closed Doors*, 134–5.

[33] MacDonald, 'Leigh family', 148 suggests that she remained at Stoneleigh 'for a few years', but a 1739 list of goods remaining at Stoneleigh following the post-mortem sale indicates that she had already removed goods from the house: SCLA, DR18/1/815, Goods bought and remaining at Stoneleigh, 1738. See also Gomme, 'Stoneleigh after the Grand Tour', 271.

[34] SCLA, DR18/4/25, Inventory of goods remaining at Stoneleigh, 1749.

up for her 1805 union with Godfrey Scholey.[35] In practice, the management and material culture of the house was in Elizabeth's hands for a period of nearly thirty years. This is reflected in the 1819 inventory, which clearly itemizes the furniture and household goods which belonged to her (see Chapter 3). These formed the majority of items in many rooms, but were particularly dominant in a first-floor apartment referred to in the 1819 inventory as *Lady Dryden's Breakfast Closet* and *Lady Dryden's Siting Room and Room Adjoining*. Here, the dowager's influence over decor and, no doubt, use was complete. She created spaces that were intimate and snug: a fluted pillar stove in one room and a Rumford stove in the other; carpets and rugs on the floor; a range of rosewood and mahogany furniture, including several tables; and a large number of prints and drawings, some in gilded frames.[36] They represent the outcome of personal choice, but set within the frame of family. As such, these rooms crystallize the way in which family comprised a series of interlocking relationships that each helped to shape consumption and the material culture of the house, despite ultimate control residing with the individual.

DEATH, MEMORY, AND FAMILY

Even in death, family could impact upon lives and consumption patterns, not least in terms of the cost and character of funerals, which represented an obligation to the dead as well as the living. Whilst funerals inevitably focused on the (deceased) individual, this was not, as McCracken suggests, at the expense of the longer-term considerations of family status. Indeed, they marked the social standing of the family as much as that of the individual, not least through the expenditure involved and the symbolism of the material culture deployed.[37] Houlbrooke goes so far as to claim that 'to skimp on one ribbon or one ritual pair of gloves, was a lapse that would be noticed and could mark the survivors for life'.[38] Thomas, fourth Lord Leigh, was faced with the emotional and financial stress of a series of funerals, for his brother (1737), father (1738), son (1738), mother (1743), and wife (1746). The total cost of these ran in excess of £1,582, with much of the expenditure accounted for by the textiles required for mourners and for dressing the chapel and the house. For the funeral of his father, the third Lord Leigh, the Coventry draper Robert Hughes presented a bill totalling £84 7s.[39] This included lengths of rich black velvet and fine broad cloth, plus nine scarves and hatbands, thirty rich silk hatbands, twenty-eight best crape hatbands, one best crape scarf, ninety-five yards of ribbon to tie the scarves, nineteen cloaks, and one pair of men's black hose. As MacArthur notes, silk and velvet were important symbols of luxury and status,

---

[35] NRO, D(CA)/364/11 Statement of Affairs of Lady Elizabeth Dryden as they related to Sir G. D., no date; NRO, D(CA)/536, Marriage settlement of Godfrey Scholey and Dame Elizabeth Dryden, 19 March 1805.

[36] NRO, D(CA)/904, Inventory, 1819.

[37] McCracken, *Culture and Consumption*, 15. See also C. Gittings, *Death, Burial and the Individual in Early Modern England* (London, 1984).

[38] R. Houlbrooke, *Death, Religion, and the Family in England, 1480–1750* (Oxford, 1998), 175.

[39] SCLA, DR18/5/2210.

whilst the gradations of cloth (rich silk or best crape) marked the status of the wearers and their relationship to the deceased and their family.[40]

Some seventy years later, the death of Thomas's daughter, Mary Leigh, generated even greater spending. The total cost of her funeral in 1806 amounted to £757 6s. 2d., to which was added a further £502 for jewellery supplied by Robert Makepeace and given to a wide variety of women as mourning gifts, as directed in her will.[41] These marked the relationship of the recipient to the deceased, Mary making careful distinctions in terms of the status of the individual and their social and familial proximity. They tied her, post-mortem, to London society and a diaspora of friends and family (see Chapter 5). Many of the costs for drapery were related to the elaborate nature of her funeral procession. In a codicil to her will, written in December 1803, she desires that arrangements should be as follows:

> my corpse in a hearse and six horses; immediately following it my chaise and four, drove by my own coachman and postilion in black jackets, and the glasses of my chaise down to shew it empty, my three footmen and groom, two on each side my chaise, in black jackets, made in the same form as their riding jackets; two coaches and six to follow my chaise...I desire the black plumes and velvet may look fresh and good, and that the black hat-bands and gloves be also good. I desire no escutcheons or any shew whatsoever, my chaise will shew who it is.[42]

This arrangement reflected Mary's status and formed a final and very public demonstration of her rank and importance in society. Of particular importance was the insistence on six horses—a distinct step up on the four used in most circumstances and a definite statement of wealth, Mary having enjoyed an estate worth twice that owned by her father. Also significant was the use of black for the clothing and drapery—white was traditional for unmarried women, but the fashion was changing and perhaps she judged that her age and established identity as the Honourable Mrs Mary Leigh made this less appropriate.[43] Finally, there was a noteworthy absence of escutcheons—an interesting choice for a woman who had a clear idea of her family's status, although she herself held no formal title, and one that showed considerable confidence in the empty carriage, already painted with the family crest, of course, as a signifier of status.

In contrast, the arrangements for the 1786 funeral procession for her brother, Edward, focused not just on the body of the deceased, but made direct and obvious reference to his rank through the presence of his coronet and escutcheons (Figure 6.1). The latter were supplied in considerable numbers by James Fisher, who later furnished Mary's funeral, his bill for £124 14s. 6d. enumerating 12 dozen in silk and 12 dozen in buckram. There were also 17 dozen crests on buckram; twelve shields with coronets and a silver border; '3 majesty Escutcheons with supporting Motto Coronet Crest &c' and 'Two atchievements of this Lordships Arms Supporters Mantle Coronet Motto &c' which alone cost £15.[44] There was to be no mistaking that this was a peer of the realm. The scale of the procession and the

---

[40] MacArthur, 'Material culture and consumption', 216–17.
[41] SCLA, DR18/5/6851.   [42] TNA, PROB 11/1448, Will of Mary Leigh, 1806.
[43] Gittings, *Death, Burial and the Individual*, 120.   [44] SCLA, DR18/5/5711.

Four conductors (Mutes) with Staves cover'd with bl^k Silk [these were Labourers]

Principal Artificers employ'd in the Family

--- two & two --- N.B. these were in N°. 8

Fifty Principal Tenants – two & two

Twelve under Bearers [small Tenants]*, on foot & in Suits of mourning*

& Two Conductors with bl^k Staves

The Coronet, on a Crimson Velvet Cushion – the bearer on Horseback, bear headed

2 Pages, Attendants – with Scarffs & bareheaded

The Body

In a Hearse drawn by Six Horses – Escutcheons and Plumes

Four mourning Coaches with 4 Horses each

1st Coach ------- Chief Mourners

2nd D° ---------- Clergy

3rd D° --------- The Faculty

4th D° ------- Principal Domestics

His Lordship's own Coach (empty) 4 Horses – Postillions in full Livery

Remainder of the Domestics

two and two

in N°12

NB –The customary set of Labourers to the No of 26 attended some at the House and some at other places—but when the Funeral set off all that could conveniently be spared were order'd to attend at the Church yard to form and keep open a free passage for the Funeral these had <u>each</u> a
Hatband, Gloves, and Guinea

Figure 6.1. Funeral procession of Edward, fifth Lord Leigh, 3rd June 1786.
Source: SCLA, DR671/43, Directions for Edward Leigh's funeral, 1786.

direct involvement of tenants and domestic servants signalled Edward's power as a landowner; 90 of them formed part of the entourage and accounts presented by the executors indicate that a total of 245 people were supplied with silk hatbands, again with clear social and relational status signalled through the quality of cloth and clothing.[45] Everything was done on an impressive scale: the church in Stoneleigh and the chapel at the house were hung with 162¾ yards of superfine black broadcloth costing a hefty £146 9s. 6d., and a hearse and four mourning coaches, together with the requisite horses, were brought up from London at a cost of £29 15s. 10d. Within this massive expenditure, three things are of particular

---

[45] SCLA, DR671/43, Directions for Edward Leigh's funeral, 1786.

note. The first is that, despite—or perhaps because of—being out of the public eye for many years, Edward's death was marked with due pomp and ceremony at his country seat. This underlines the importance of funerals as a marker of status, but also the obligations that death brought to the landed family. The second is the presence of 'The Faculty' in the third carriage behind the hearse. There is no indication of who this comprised, but it suggests a link to Edward's status as High Steward at Oxford University. His friends and teachers at Oxford were important beneficiaries of his will and at least one, William Hayes, supplied Edward with books and provided music lessons (see Chapter 7); the presence at his funeral of some representatives of the university would thus be appropriate and again a mark of his standing. The third is the placement of eight of the 'Principal artificers employ'd in the Family' towards the front of the funeral procession. Again, no names are given, but looking at the bills and accounts, the most likely candidates are local craftsmen, including the masons Michael Clarke and John Brown, the blacksmith Thomas Howlett, and the brickmaker Thomas Lea, who supplied the Leighs for forty-two, thirty-seven, thirty-two, and twenty-three years respectively. What is so striking here is that these ordinary tradesmen were central to this marking of status: they may not have shaped decisions about consumption in the way that is seen of architects, upholsterers, and booksellers, but they were an important part of Lord Leigh's identity as a landowner, country house owner, and patron of local trade.

Death thus brought considerable and sometimes distressingly frequent expense to the Leigh family, in some ways counteracting the savings made through the absence of children. The funerals and mourning arrangements for five individuals amounted to at least £3,700, the equivalent of a decent dowry or an extensive European tour. Yet death also offered the opportunity to underline rank and dignity; to cement relationships with tenants and servants, and with friends and peers; and to mark the importance of the family and individual. All this was apparent in the processional arrangements for Edward Leigh, which hinted at his personal connections and achievements.

Such post-mortem celebration of family and the individual was also achieved through memorials, which might be nominal, real, or archival. An example of the first comes in the long-term retention of room names which commemorate a particular individual. At Canons Ashby, an upper-floor room was referred to in the 1717 inventory as 'Late Sir Roberts Room'. It contained a bed furnished in yellow silk damask and was presumably that occupied by the predecessor of the late owner, Edward Dryden. What is unusual is that the name was retained all through the eighteenth century, despite the progressive renaming of other rooms; it formed a curious memorial to Sir Robert. At Stoneleigh Abbey, Lord Leigh's bedroom and dressing room retained their place in the inventory and were, to some extent, preserved by Mary in their original state. However, this was not the kind of immutable family 'shrine' which so fascinated Austen's Catherine Morland on her visit to Northanger Abbey: rather than being closed off and left untouched, items were removed and added in a way that made the rooms dynamic and living spaces.[46]

---

[46] J. Austen, *Northanger Abbey* (1817, Oxford, 1998), 148–9.

More conventional are the memorials that the Leighs, Newdigates, and Drydens placed in their local churches—a common practice amongst landowning families. That for Sir John Turner Dryden (d.1797) depicts a woman weeping by a classical pillar and the inscription repeats the usual lamentations of the 'disconsolate widow and affectionate son' who are left to lament 'his loss and to remember with gratitude his Virtues'. The compositional form and classical allusions are fairly typical of the age, although its rendering as a bas-relief wall plaque is perhaps more unusual. Certainly the scale is modest in comparison with the huge structures created by the Marlboroughs at Blenheim and the Earl of Coventry at Croome Park—a reflection of the Drydens' status or perhaps their straitened circumstances. Of course, marking status was a key function of these memorials and comes to the fore in a remarkable funerary achievement for Sir Robert (d.1708) erected by his successor, Edward Dryden. This comprises an assemblage of gauntlets, spurs, helm, sword, tabard, pennants, and standard, which together form the material markers of his status as a baronet (Figure 6.2). Whilst highly unusual in its composition and its emphasis on the actual clothing and trappings of the deceased, this ties closely to Edward's attempts to mark family lineage in the fabric of his house (see Chapter 2) and reflects the character and ambitions of the man. Paired with the presence in the same church of the family vault, these monuments and others made a clear statement of the Drydens' position in local society.

Much the same was true of the Leighs, who filled the village church at Stoneleigh with a series of fairly standard, if large and costly, monuments. These were again supplemented by the presence of a large family vault. Whilst by no means unusual in itself, we have a unique insight into the interior of this vault by virtue of a drawing, dating from the early nineteenth century, which shows the position of twenty-six coffins, ranging in date from 1672 to 1806 (Figure 6.3).[47] This forms a remarkable archival memorial, a celebration of family, reproducing various crests, arms, and coronets which adorned the vault and bringing the hidden crypt in the pages of the archive. It includes detailed descriptions of the appearance of each coffin and identifies whose remains are contained therein. What is striking is the intensely sensuous nature of the coffins: several are covered in black velvet and have silver or brass plates; that of Edward, fifth Lord Leigh, is described as being 'of Crimson Velvet with the richest silver Ornaments'. As with his funeral procession, then, the passing of Edward was marked in the grandest manner: it was a show of splendour not quite in keeping with his character when alive (see Chapter 4). This underlines Houlbrooke's point that funerals were symbolically as well as financially significant. They were just as important as spending on silverware or stuccoed ceilings, because the semiotics of family expressed through funerals helped to define the individual's identity and embed their consumption in its synchronic and dynastic context. But what of wider web of friends and servants: how did they impact on consumption?

---

[47] SCLA, DR18/29/6, Box 1, Vault at Stoneleigh, no date. A similar document exists for the Ishams of Lamport Hall, but lacks the visual drama: NRO, IL/3902.

Figure 6.2. The funerary monument of Sir Robert Dryden (d.1708), erected in Canons Ashby church by his successor, Edward Dryden. The assemblage of material goods marks his status as a baronet.

Photograph by Jon Stobart.

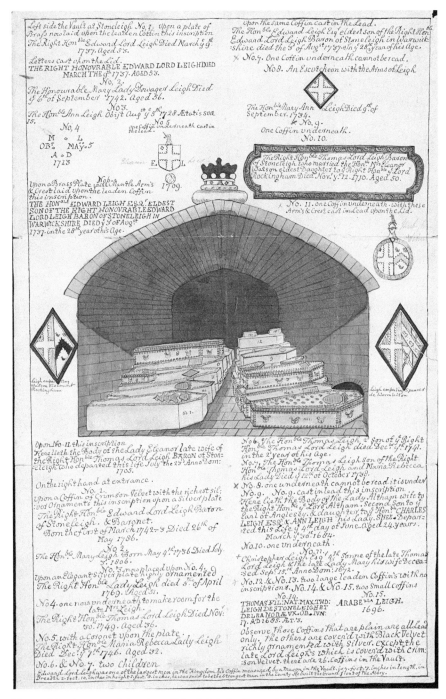

Figure 6.3. Annotated drawing of the Leigh family vault at Stoneleigh (n.d.).

Source: SCLA, DR18/29/6 Box 1 © Shakespeare Birthplace Trust.

FAMILY FRIENDS: TRUSTEES AND GUARDIANS

Trustees and guardians formed a particular set of friends. Whilst their immediate task was the safe custodianship of the estate and/or children, their bonds were primarily to the family rather than the individual, although guardians often developed prolonged and close personal relationships with their wards.[48] The complexities of these responsibilities and relationships are best explored through detailed analysis of a single family, in this case the Leighs. The trustees and executors named in the will of Thomas, fourth Lord Leigh, all had long-standing connections with the Leighs of Stoneleigh—they were, in effect, family friends. William Craven, fifth Baron Craven of Coombe Abbey in Warwickshire, was a cousin of Maria Craven, Thomas's first wife and the mother of Edward and Mary.[49] The association between these families stretched back to the seventeenth century, when Elizabeth Craven, the daughter of Sir William Craven of Worcestershire, had married a cousin of the Stoneleigh Leighs, Theophilus Leigh.[50] Elizabeth Verney, who became the guardian entrusted with the care of Mary Leigh, was the sister of Edward, third Lord Leigh.[51] Sir Charles Mordaunt was a prominent Warwickshire landowner and a Tory MP for the county, and Sir Walter Wagstaffe Bagot was a landowner in Staffordshire, where the Leighs also held estates and with whom they also had historic connections.[52]

As was common for trustees, the most urgent task facing trustees after Thomas's death in 1749 was to make an assessment of the finances of the deceased owner and set the Stoneleigh estates on a surer footing. This involved auditing the accounts of the house steward, Thomas Clarke, and the auditor, Christopher Wright, ordering a full inventory of the contents of Stoneleigh Abbey, and holding sales of livestock and furniture from the house.[53] In total £906 of household goods, including gold plate, drinking glasses, and linen, was sold, with a further £936 of plate being removed by the Dowager Lady Leigh to her house at Guy's Cliff.[54] These actions had a considerable bearing on the immediate financial position, but also on the material culture of the ancestral home, and thus the future consumption of Thomas's heir, Edward, fifth Lord Leigh, who was faced on his inheritance with a large house in which many rooms were essentially unfurnished.

---

[48] On the importance of trustees to estate finances, see Roebuck, *Yorkshire Baronets*, 93–102; G. E. Mingay, *The Gentry: The Rise and Fall of a Ruling Class* (London, 1976), 67–70.

[49] MacDonald, 'Leigh family', 148.

[50] SCLA, DR18/9/1/2, Marriage Settlement of Theophilus Leigh and Elizabeth Craven, 1 December 1679.

[51] SCLA, DR18/17/25/24, Letter from Lord Edward Leigh to Elizabeth Verney, 15 December 1727.

[52] SCLA, DR18/15/11, Indenture Quadripartite between Arden Bagot of Pipe Hall, Esq., and the Hon. Mary Bagot, his wife, 27 May 1678.

[53] SCLA, DR18/17/4/1, Account of Thomas Clarke, 1746–9; DR18/17/4/8, Account of Christopher Wright, 1749–53; DR18/17/4/5, Orders Made by the Trustees of Edward, Lord Leigh, 18 September 1750; DR18/17/4/28, Memorandum relating to Lord Leigh's Affairs, no date, 1749; DR18/4/27, Inventory, November 1749.

[54] SCLA, DR18/4/26, Inventory, 1750.

The trustees' audit, meanwhile, had uncovered the full extent of Thomas's debts, which, in the form of mortgage payments, bonds, unpaid bills, and legacies, amounted to £21,666.[55] Taking into account mortgages lent to other landowners in the local area, rent arrears, and the total value of the household goods and cash at Stoneleigh Abbey, Thomas's personal estate was valued at £11,947, leaving a deficit of £9,719. This level of debt was by no means unusual for landowners during this period and was manageable against an estate income of £7,000 and rising.[56] Nonetheless, the trustees set about assiduously reducing the burden of debt. They recovered some of the accumulated rent arrears, drew in mortgages lent to other landowners, and began repaying mortgages on the estate and clearing outstanding bills and legacies.[57] The way in which bills were settled is of particular interest to us here. In one instance, the trustees were faced with a bill from Thomas Gilpin of London for £1,125 10s. 2d. of silverware supplied to Thomas Leigh in the late 1740s. On 8 February 1750, they began addressing this by returning some of the items, including a breadbasket, tureen, two sauce boats, four salts, and six bottle tickets, and by trading in old plate to the value of £92 12s. 4. A week later, they sent Gilpin four dozen plates and sixteen dishes with a combined value of £489 6s. 7d., the remaining balance being settled with three cash payments in March and October 1750 and February 1751, the first made by Mr Hodgets and the second two by William Craven.[58] Again, these actions had a significant impact on the material culture of the house and arguably deprived the family of important symbols of elite status. However, they closely followed the actions of the Leigh family themselves, who clearly felt little compunction in trading in unwanted silverware when acquiring new items, Mary receiving £534 of credit against purchases of £1,031 7s. 3d. from Thomas Makepeace.[59]

At the same time, the trustees were also engaged in growing the estate income and made investments on behalf of Edward. They bought into the national debt through South Sea Annuities, acquiring £13,349 worth by 1762,[60] but also expressed an interest in buying more land for the Stoneleigh estates, including holdings of the late Corbett Kynaston (d. 1740) in Shevlock, Shropshire, who had left large debts after his death.[61] At the same time, they sought to put controls on spending on the estate and by dependants. This involved setting in place systems for managing and auditing expenditure, most notably by ordering regular accounts

[55] SCLA, DR18/17/4/3, Statement of accounts of Lord Leigh, 10 March 1749.

[56] In comparison, by the early 1740s, the Myddletons of Chirk Castle had accrued debts of almost £30,000 against an estate income of merely £5,000. Although their position was eased in 1761 by a prudential marriage, it deteriorated further in the 1770s and 1780s, resulting in a decision in 1787 to place the estate under the management of a board of trustees. See Mingay, *English Landed Society*, 126–9.

[57] SCLA, DR18/17/4/19, Schedule of bills paid by William Craven, no date, *c.*1754; DR18/17/4/22, Arrears of rent received and unreceived, no date, *c.*1754. For details of the process of clearing these debts, see Rothery and Stobart, 'Inheritance events'.

[58] SCLA, DR18/5/3121.   [59] SCLA, DR18/5/5809.

[60] SCLA, DR18/17/4/10, Account of South Sea Annuities purchased by Mr Hill, 1761–2.

[61] SCLA, DR18/17/4/5, Orders made by the Trustees of Edward, Lord Leigh, 18 September 1750. Such investments mirrored those made by other landowners during this period—see Roebuck, *Yorkshire Baronets*, 32.

to be kept and delivered to them.[62] It also meant reducing the running costs of the house. To this end, the trustees ordered that a very small staff be kept at the house, park, and gardens, including two housemaids, a gardener, a gamekeeper, and a steward.[63] This was to cost no more than £300 a year with the proviso, noted in a later document, that the necessary cleaning and upkeep of the house be maintained, since the house was 'a very large building & great part is very old being the remains of the old Abbey'.[64]

Overall, the trustees operated as important brakes on spending, but also acted to augment income and thus increase the capacity of future generations to spend freely—something which Edward used to full effect in the early 1760s, when discretionary spending peaked at over £8,000 (see Chapter 1). In this way, they acted in a way that parallels de Vries's 'productive household', creating additional wealth that could be spent on material objects and thus driving forward (potential) consumption. These actions, then, mean that the trustees should certainly be viewed as friends of the estate and household, as well as the family and the individual who appointed them. Roebuck has noted their potential to impact positively upon estate finances, in part because spending was taken out of the hands of a single individual—a telling observation in this discussion of the contextualized and contingent nature of individual consumption.[65] Yet friendship went beyond sound financial management and a feeling of obligation to neighbours or distant relatives. Amongst the trustees, William Craven stands out: he had the closest familial relationship with the Leighs and the most extended involvement with the family, since he also acted as guardian to Edward. We know relatively little of his work in this specific capacity through the 1750s, although he received the Lord Chancellor's 'great approbation of the care you had taken of Ld L's Education', as Joseph Hill noted in a letter to Craven in 1761.[66] He certainly built a close relationship with the future Lord Leigh, being a regular presence in the decision-making processes surrounding Edward's refurbishment of Stoneleigh Abbey in the years following his inheritance. Indeed, it appears that he was frequently resident at Stoneleigh during this period, Thomas Burnett's early schedule of work identifying 'Mr Cravens Room' in the south-west corner of the attic storey of the west range.[67]

Craven took on two main roles during this period of heavy spending. The first was to operate as gatekeeper for tradesmen and expenditure, as a kind of surrogate father, carrying Edward into financial maturity by moderating spending and inculcating practices of sound management of the estate. The second was as an arbiter of quality and perhaps taste, a surrogate wife, advising on the decoration of the

---

[62] For example, SCLA, DR18/17/4/8, Account of Christopher Wright, 1749–53; DR18/17/4/7, Robert Hughes's Account to Lord Craven, 1749–52; DR18/17/4/23, Lady Leigh's (Dowager) Accounts to the Executors of Lord Leigh, 1754.

[63] SCLA, DR18/17/4/5, Orders Made by the Trustees of Edward, Lord Leigh, 18 September 1750.

[64] SCLA, DR18/17/4/9, Orders made by the Trustees of Edward, Lord Leigh, 11 October 1754.

[65] Roebuck, *Yorkshire Baronets*, 86–94.

[66] SCLA, DR18/1/27/52, Letter, 19 December 1761.

[67] SCLA, DR18/3/47/52/14, Mr Burnett's Memorandum, no date.

house.[68] Taking these in turn, it was Craven to whom a number of bills were presented, even when Edward had officially reached his majority. For example, in December 1763, Jordan Biggar sent his bill for a variety of sheets and napery, addressing it to 'Wm Craven, Esq., for the Right Honble Lord Leigh'.[69] In some ways, this was a formal nicety, acknowledging the route through which an order came and thus the proper route that the bill should follow. Yet it also signalled the wider influence that Craven carried. It was Craven who authorized the payment of 40 guineas to Mary Leigh for a consignment of china sent down to Stoneleigh in March 1764; and when the steward, Samuel Butler, was increasingly concerned about the possibility of expenditure on improvements to the house mushrooming out of control, it was to Craven that he wrote, no doubt hoping that he would act to caution Edward and perhaps curb the outgoings (see below).[70] Butler also consulted him about hiring a new brewer, giving details of the likely wages and conditions of employment; he ended his letter by noting that, if the two men were not fortunate enough to meet soon, he would be 'obliged to trouble you with more letters as I shall greatly want your advice and directions in many things'. As late as April 1764, Butler was writing to Thomas Burnett in London that he would be able to properly address some of his questions when Craven arrived at Stoneleigh the following week.[71] Craven clearly held considerable sway in the Leigh household—a status recognized by the servants and projected to suppliers.

Questions of taste are more difficult to attribute with precision, but Craven's opinion was again important. Amongst the large quantities of furniture acquired from Thomas Burnett and William Gomm were several pieces judged to be of inferior quality. According to the steward, Samuel Butler, they were:

> universally complained of, the Wood appearing to be (as it really is) very green, & the workmanship very indiff[erent] this prov'd the topic of discourse the next day at Dinner when every person present (without exception to any) agreed in the above relation...Lord Leigh and Mr Craven viewed them, & his Lordship order'd me to write a very severe letter to Mr Gomm upon the occasion.[72]

Craven is thus placed alongside Edward Leigh in adjudicating quality: they inspect the furniture together and discuss its many failings at dinner before agreeing on the best course of action. Further correspondence ensued before Butler wrote again to Burnett, thanking him for his letter and stating, 'I have communicated the contents to Mr Craven who says the Goods may remain at Stoneleigh if you think well at the prices you have sent down, tho' we have many workmen here that will undertake to make better for less money.'[73] Now we see Craven determining that, at a reduced price, the shoddy goods can remain: oeconomy has apparently triumphed over aesthetic concerns. More generally, it seems likely that William

---

[68] See Vickery, *Behind Closed Doors*, 49–53, 83–8; Sharp, 'Women's creativity'; Lewis, 'When a house'.

[69] SCLA, DR18/5/4028. See also DR18/5/4069.

[70] SCLA, DR18/17/27/101, Letter, 25 March 1764; DR18/17/27/97, Letter, 11 February 1764.

[71] SCLA, DR18/17/27/98, Letter, 13 February 1764; DR18/17/27/107, Letter, 21 April 1764.

[72] SCLA, DR18/17/27/84, Letter, 13 October 1763.

[73] SCLA, DR18/17/27/85, Letter, 27 October 1763.

Craven and Edward Leigh would have discussed the necessary improvements to Stoneleigh Abbey and the manner in which they were executed. The generally conservative taste deployed may reflect the fact that Craven's own house, Coombe Abbey, changed little during the first three-quarters of the eighteenth century: it was architecturally the building created in the 1680s by his grandfather.[74]

Historians have tended to overlook the role of guardians in shaping consumption—a surprising omission given the frequency with which they were needed to plug demographic gaps. It is clear that Craven played a key role in this as well as other aspects of Lord Leigh's development. That he acted as a father figure is unsurprising: it reflected the status and responsibilities of the guardian, even if these were being continued beyond the age of majority. His role as a surrogate wife is more contentious and ambiguous: he may well have advised on matters of taste, but never became involved in the day-to-day management of Edward's household. This—and wanting the companionship of a woman—is what drove many widowers to bring unmarried female relatives into their homes.[75] However, it might be argued that landowners with large country houses had less need for this practical support, as much of the everyday business of the household was the responsibility of servants, men and women like the 'most faithful able and Zealous agent' prized by Lady Shelbourne.[76]

SENIOR SERVANTS: MANAGING THE HOUSEHOLD

As the episode with Thomas Burnett and the shoddy furniture reveals, servants could play a significant role in shaping consumption within the country house. This impact was complex and wide-ranging, encompassing the provision of livery, accommodation, and, of course, wages.[77] Consumption for servants marked power and gender hierarchies, and could involve considerable expenditure. As discussed in Chapter 1, wages made up a sizeable proportion of spending at Arbury and marked clear distinctions between the steward, Thomas Hutchins, who received £30 per annum in the mid-1770s, the under-butler, Thomas Docker, who was paid £10, and the housemaids, Hannah and Catherine Bull, who got only £5.[78] Add to wages the cost of board and lodging, and livery, and the costs quickly mounted, as Williams's analysis of the Audley End accounts makes clear. In these situations, the servant might be seen as the object of consumption: certainly they had little influence on what was provided—a point discussed by Styles in the context of clothing.[79] Our purpose here is not to explore this involuntary consumption, important though this is; instead, we focus on the ways in which servants

[74] Tyack, *Warwickshire Country Houses*, 59–61.
[75] K. Glover, *Elite Women and Polite Society in Eighteenth-Century Scotland* (London, 2011), 20–3; Duncan, 'Old Maids', 89–117; Vickery, *Behind Closed Doors*, 49–51.
[76] Quoted in Vickery, *Behind Closed Doors*, 159.
[77] See J. Musson, *Up and Down Stairs: The History of the Country House Servant* (London, 2010); P. Sambrook, *Keeping their Places: Domestic Service in the Country House* (Stroud, 2009).
[78] WRO, CR136/v/136.
[79] Williams, 'Noble household'; Styles, *Dress of the People*, 277–301.

shaped decisions about consumption. To this end, we examine the activities of two types of servant, the housekeeper and the steward.

Housekeepers had many areas of responsibility, but in consumption terms, their key role was in organizing the day-to-day provisioning of the house. This normally involved the housekeeper buying goods from a range of local suppliers and then presenting a 'household account' to her employer, usually monthly but sometimes quarterly. Such arrangements were in place at Stoneleigh. Although the series of bills only occasionally includes household accounts, one example from August 1738 shows the range of goods acquired in this way: peas, besoms, cherries (red and black), turnips, cheese, raspberries, cider, lemons, oranges, newspapers, vinegar, greens, strawberries, beans, carrots, cucumbers, capers, crabs, oil, wooden dishes, fish, eggs, whiting, ducks, and asparagus.[80] A clearer picture of such provisioning comes from two account books kept by Sir Roger Newdigate's housekeepers in the 1770s: Eleanor Walmsley, Hannah Mason, and Mary Cotchett.[81] These recorded payments for a huge variety of individual items, ranging from 5d of birdseed bought on 29 March 1769 to the half salmon costing 5s. acquired on 13 July 1770. They principally comprised fresh foods, including watercress, muffins, butter, eggs, geese, and rhubarb; but there were also groceries such as coffee, currants, and saffron, and small items of kitchenware—a chocolate mill, a mould for jelly, and baskets. Newdigate's housekeepers clearly had scope to choose what was bought and no doubt from whom purchases were made. On occasions, the name of suppliers is noted, most often in the context of those selling poultry and eggs. This underlines the huge number of people with whom the housekeepers were dealing on a daily basis. In December 1770, for example, we see Hannah Mason acquiring chickens from twenty-three different people (only one of whom supplied her on more than one occasion), whilst geese were had from eight individuals, and turkeys from two people. Like those selling or gifting food to the Le Strange family 150 years earlier, these appear to have been tenants and villagers, supplementing their income by supplying the big house; at least eight were women, including 'widow Hollins', and one is referred to as 'Mr Cowrard on the Comon [*sic*]'.[82] In addition, there were regular bills from established, though generally unnamed, tradesmen—the butcher, baker, greengrocer, fishmonger, perfumer, and chandler—plus others for pastry, milk, poultry, and butter.

Housekeepers thus formed a key conduit between the local economy and the big house, a role which shows reliance on their judgement of the quality of goods and on their willingness to negotiate a good price. Walsh argues that such attributes were not always assured in servants, leading many mistresses to shop themselves.[83] This trust went well beyond acquiring provisions for the table to encompass

---

[80] SCLA, DR18/5/2150.

[81] WRO, CR1841/14, Housekeeper's accounts, 1766–70 and CR1841/10, Housekeeper's accounts, 1770–4. The catalogue suggests that these are cook's accounts, but all of these women are identified as housekeepers in the general accounts book (CR136/V/136).

[82] WRO, CR1841/10, Housekeeper's accounts, 1770–4; Whittle and Griffiths, *Consumption and Gender*, 72–83.

[83] Walsh, 'Shopping at first hand?', 13–26.

regular payments for spinning and weaving, and for rat-catching. The last of these was recorded in the accounts as 'rat tails', for which Bob, William or Ellis was paid 1 shilling about twice a month during 1768. In the same year, Eleanor Walmsley also noted her payments to Pheby and Hemsley for spinning. These were frequent, but did not fall into a regular pattern: through the summer months, Hemsley received 6 shillings on 1 July and on 12 July, and 4 shillings on 15 August, whilst Pheby had 4 shillings on 6 and 24 June and 8 July, and 2 shillings on 12 July and 15 August, plus a separate payment of 1 shilling on 15 August and two further payments of 1 shilling on 26 August.[84] These complex arrangements suggest that Walmsley was managing the work of these two women against demand within the household, probably passing the spun yarn to the weaver, whose bills she also paid roughly every quarter.

Walmsley, Mason, and Cotchett were thus responsible for managing much of the day-to-day economy at Arbury—dealing with those areas of consumption that are often overlooked in studies of the country house (see Chapter 3). They kept a running tally of their spending, with overall expenditure in 1768/69 amounting to £18 12s. 7d., to which was added a further £32 13s. 6d. for tradesmen's bills in London, all of them paid in April 1769. These were significant sums for women whose basic wage was only £15 per annum. It was important, then, that the accounts were settled promptly and fully. The former appears to have been more or less the case: a note written by Eleanor Walmsley on 4 November 1768, acknowledged payment by Sir Roger of £15 11s. 2d. 'being the Ballance of Acct in full of all bills & other demands (Wages Excepted) due to me to Michaelmas last'—that is, about two months previously. Characteristically, Sir Roger carefully audited his housekeeper's accounts, sometimes noting deductions in his own hand. Thus, on 30 April 1767 he deducted 13 shillings from an account of £30 8s. 9½d. for a tea kettle, Mr Parker's china, and Miss Palmer's box. Conversely, the housekeeper could supplement her income, Walmsley noting an additional payment of 4s. 9d., received for doing 'washing for Master Newdiget'.[85]

Housekeepers enjoyed considerable power in shaping day-to-day consumption at Arbury, both in terms of managing supplies and payments, and most likely the choice of supplier. Much the same was true of stewards, although here the sums involved and the scope to exercise discretion and power were often much greater. William Peacock was steward at Canons Ashby from at least 1770 into the 1800s. His importance in the household was sufficient to mean that he had his own room, specifically identified in the 1770 and 1791 inventories. This was relatively sparsely furnished, although there were four cane-bottomed chairs, which suggest the ability to have guests sit with him. More telling is the presence of a 'chain for measuring land', a copy of the Militia Act, and three law books: 'Nelson's justice' (1727), two volumes of 'Burns' justice' (1755), and 'Dalton's justice' (1618).[86] These were standard texts, owned by many JPs, and their presence in Peacock's room suggests

---

[84] WRO, CR1841/14, Housekeeper's accounts, 1766–70.
[85] WRO, CR1841/14, Housekeeper's accounts, 1766–70.
[86] NRO, D(CA)/201, Inventory, 1770.

that he needed some knowledge of legal matters in his wider role of estate management. Moreover, he was largely responsible for managing the household at Canons Ashby, as Lady Dryden's Account Book makes clear.[87] These accounts begin in June 1770 following the death of Sir John Dryden in March that year. By this time, Peacock's standing with the family was already established, the second entry in the accounts being a legacy to him of £50, and the following year set the tone for the remainder of the accounts, the steward receiving twelve payments with a combined value of £643 3s. 3d. The precise purpose of many payments is not recorded, but they were undoubtedly to cover his expenses in paying tradesmen's bills as well as his wages and perhaps those of other servants. An entry on 26 June 1783 makes the arrangements explicit, £40 8s. 5d. being paid 'to Ballance Peacocks Accounts with his wages, Abrahams and James'. By this date, several entries each year indicate that he was settling accounts from a variety of named retailers: Mr Ramsay for china, cutlery, and the like; Mr Burton for coffee; Mrs Beech for drapery; and so on. It is unlikely that Peacock was involved in choosing these goods or the people who supplied them, but he was responsible for ensuring that their bills were paid and thus for the oeconomy of the Dryden household.

In some respects, Peacock took on the role of the wife in middling-sort households, as described by Harvey, carefully managing resources and attempting to keep income and outgoings in balance.[88] Lady Dryden, meanwhile, occupied the husband's position, having oversight of the accounts and setting out the parameters of spending. Her accounts include a record of receipts (mostly rental income) as well as payments; although there is no apparent attempt to reconcile the two, it seems that she was seeking to maintain an overall equilibrium between income and expenditure. This further questions the stereotype of the landed classes as reckless spenders, the account book forming a key mechanism for tracking and moderating spending. The lists of outgoings and income, and the periodic totting up of accounts underlined the discipline of financial management and restraint which formed part of the upbringing of landed men and, it seems, women as well.[89]

Peacock continued in his role through the ownership of Sir John Turner Dryden and into the period of Elizabeth junior's widowhood and remarriage to Godfrey Scholey. By the early 1800s and by then probably well into his sixties, he was left in charge at Canons Ashby during Elizabeth's prolonged absences in London and Margate. Although he does not appear to have lived in the house itself, he visited regularly and wrote frequent letters, always addressed from Canons Ashby. As with the correspondence of Will Bishop to Humphrey Morice during the latter's absence from The Grove in Chiswick, these recorded in detail the minutiae of everyday life.[90] Peacock wrote to Elizabeth with news of illness amongst the servants, including the long-term incapacity of James; the well-being of livestock, especially horses

[87] NRO, D(CA)/322, Lady Dryden's account book, 1770–90.

[88] Harvey, *Little Republic*, 86.

[89] French and Rothery, *Man's Estate*, 78–9. These matters are discussed more fully in Chapters 4 and 5.

[90] NRO, D(CA)/360, letters from William Peacock to Lady Elizabeth Dryden, 1804–10; P. Hammond and C. Hammond, *Life in an Eighteenth-Century Country House* (Stroud, 2012).

and dogs; the planting being undertaken in the kitchen garden; the maintenance of ditches, hedges, and fences; and the payment of bills to local tradesmen. On the one hand, it is interesting that Lady Dryden was eager for news of these matters, no doubt in part because she wanted to maintain her control over the business of the estate. On the other, it is striking that Peacock was often unwilling to act without instructions from his employer. He was happy to issue orders to servants about preparing the house for the visit of Sir Edward and Mr Scholey (Elizabeth's son and husband), or to undertake negotiations with tenants about changes to their terms, or to send servants to Towcester and Daventry to enquire after bills sent down from London by carriers.[91] In each case, however, he acted in response to Elizabeth's wishes. More often, his letters seek guidance, for example about whether to sell a mare for which an offer has been received, or whether a £5 bill should be paid, or whether he has correctly understood instructions about the culling of bucks on the estate.[92] Only occasionally does he challenge Elizabeth's judgement and then on matters that involve the practicalities of ditching and hedging.

Peacock emerges from his letters as a trusted servant, responsible for the day-to-day management of the estate at Canons Ashby. His reliability in this role is evident from his long service; yet he appears to have exercised relatively little independent influence over consumption practices at the house, particularly in his later years when money was tight. A similar relationship between employer and servant can be glimpsed through the correspondence of Sir Roger Newdigate, who provided his steward, Richard Jee, with remarkably little scope for personal initiative. In a series of letters written in early 1761 he gave Jee minute instructions about many aspects of his work. Within the house, he suggested covering the 'sashes with oild paper till the inside is done, or, if not, all the lower panes as I don't chuse to hazard the plate glass'.[93] Outside, he gave directions about selling pigs and buying cattle to graze a particular patch of land, sent notice of the arrival of plants and seeds for the garden, ordered abatements to be made to the price of wood being sold from the estate, 'as there is a great deal of very indifferent stuff', and issued instructions about collecting payments for the vicar's stipend and the tithe. He even warned about a potentially troublesome tenant and gave notice of his intention to pursue another 'for the last penny' as an example to others.[94] Such matters would normally lie within the remit of the steward: Sir Roger's close interest matched the attention to detail shown in other aspects of his life, but effectively emasculated his steward. He constantly sought information on the day-to-day business of the estate—'I wrote to you last post & shall be glad to hear a particular account of your goings on'—and only occasionally gave his steward any room for manoeuvre. Moreover, he reminded Jee of his responsibilities for the sound management of the household economy, warning him to take care that the cellars 'are not always open, as when I am at home, for treating and junketing at this time are

[91] NRO, D(CA)/360, 13 March 1804, 27 March 1804, 20 April 1804.
[92] NRO, D(CA)/360, 31 January 1804, 2 April 1804, 27 July 1804.
[93] WRO, CR691/B/152/14, Letter, no date, 1761.
[94] WRO, CR691/152/7, Letter, 10 March 1761; CR691/152/4, Letter, no date, 1761.

out of season, & I hope, & don't doubt, you will maintain the family at as little expense as possible'.[95]

In contrast with this emasculation, Samuel Butler, the steward at Stoneleigh Abbey for over thirty years appears to have enjoyed greater independence of action and had a greater influence over the house and the processes of consumption through which it was serviced and shaped. This influence is most apparent in a series of letters written to William Craven and Thomas Burnett during the period of intense refurbishment in 1763 and 1764. His responsibility in dealing with tradespeople was wide-ranging. He was the chief point of contact for those supplying goods to the house, which, on some occasions, involved communicating instructions to suppliers. Sometimes this meant forwarding details about designs, as when he replied to Burnett's enquiries about the dimensions for the communion table designed by Lightoler, enclosing a sketch provided by the architect.[96] More frequent were letters discussing the readiness of furniture ordered and of the rooms into which this was to be placed. Thus, in April 1763, he wrote to check arrangements for delivery of the first consignments and carefully specified which particular pieces could be sent: 'We have prepared two Rooms No 17 & 18 for the two Crimson Beds whenever they are ready; also the Green Room (No 14) for the Blue damask.'[97] Six months later, he was writing to delay further deliveries until 'the lumber and dust is a little over', and again in February 1764 to say that they could receive chairs, tables, and glasses for the attic floor, but that 'any furniture for the bettermost Rooms will run a great hazard of being spoil'd if sent yet, as we are makeing great alterations in the middle part of the house'.[98]

But Butler's authority went much further. He checked deliveries against his own memoranda of the work to be done and challenged any discrepancies; he also communicated his employers' satisfaction or otherwise with the quality of the furniture being sent to Stoneleigh. In this way, he operated in tandem with William Craven as orbital members of the Leigh family. He wrote to Burnett to complain that 'for want of care in packing up the Inkstand' one of the glasses had arrived broken and the 'black is very much rubb'd off and defaced'.[99] Far more serious was the issue of the poor-quality furniture outlined earlier. This led to a lengthy exchange of letters between Burnett and Butler, the latter being the vehicle through which the displeasure of Leigh and Craven was expressed. However, Butler went beyond this and expressed his own feelings, mostly about the attitude taken by Mr Greenhouse, Burnett's foreman at Stoneleigh. What appears to have irked Butler was that Greenhouse's initial acceptance of the shoddiness of these pieces subsequently turned into attempts to defend their quality and suggest that the best pieces should be retained. As Butler put it, 'I do not blame him for indeavouring to serve his Master as far as he decently may, but S[r] when I have his Lordship's orders how I am to act I shall not submit to have them countermanded by any workman about the

[95] WRO, CR691/B152/14, Letter, no date, 1761.
[96] SCLA, DR18/17/27/91, Letter, 8 January 1764.
[97] SCLA, DR18/17/27/75, Letter, 27 April 1763.
[98] SCLA, DR18/17/27/85, Letter, 27 October 1763; DR18/17/27/96, Letter, 1 February 1764.
[99] SCLA, DR18/17/27/108, Letter, 3 June 1764.

House be he who he will.'[100] His rhetoric drew on the authority of Lord Leigh, but he was also offended that his own authority in the house was being challenged. This re-emerged in other letters written by Butler where he defended himself against accusations that he gave the workmen too much ale, making them incapable of carrying out their work.[101]

Butler, it seems, was very sure of his own authority at Stoneleigh and was equally clear that it incorporated visiting workmen as well as regular servants and transactions. Indeed, he was expressly instructed to do so by Lord Leigh. In a rare surviving memorandum in Leigh's own distinctive hand, he writes that Butler should 'take care that the workmen are as careful as possible, & you must write down the names of the careless ones, if any there be, that they may never do any work for me again'.[102] However, Butler was conscious that there were limits to his knowledge, power, and influence: the kitchen appears to have been a place beyond his remit and perhaps his knowledge. In writing to William Craven on a variety of matters, he included a list of kitchen furniture from Mrs O'Donnell and observed that the old large grate 'is so far worn out, as not to be worth putting into its usual place, yet I did not choose to bespeak a new one, as the Cook perhaps may not like what I should order'.[103] This is an acknowledgement of the distinct spheres of influence of different servants, and the clear boundaries that existed between them: powerful though the steward may have been, he did not stray into the purview of the cook. With a housekeeper and butler also occupying their own roles and physical space (see Chapter 3), the country house was a complex series of interlocking and interacting servant realms.[104]

Conversely, Butler was willing to proffer advice to his employer, as usual via Craven. His warnings about overspending were couched in deferential terms—he did not want it thought that he would 'presume to prescribe rules for his Lordship's conduct'—but they were, nevertheless, clear and direct. He noted in a letter to Craven that Lightoler:

> seems to have cut out a great deal of work for his Lordship, sufficient to take up a good deal of his ready money; If he does not give estimates with his plans, it might be advisable for his Lordship to require it, that he might see how he was going on, for I apprehend it would be a very disagreeable circumstance to his Lordship to be run aground before he was aware…and if his Lordship is inclinable to make any considerable purchases, they will require some ready money.[105]

The impact of this cautionary note is hard to judge, but many of Lightoler's designs for both the interior decorative work and the construction of stables and other outbuildings remained unexecuted. Given that spending during this period ran at an average of about £5,000 per annum, peaking at a cumulative total of

[100] SCLA, DR18/17/27/84, Letter, 13 October 1763.
[101] SCLA, DR18/17/27/88, Letter, 13 February 1764; DR18/17/27/97, Letter, 11 February 1764.
[102] SCLA, DR18/3/47/52/11, Memorandum, 22 July 1764.
[103] SCLA, DR18/17/27/97, Letter, 11 February 1764.
[104] This spatiality comes out through the various contributions to Sambrook and Brears (eds) *Country House Kitchen* and is discussed more fully in Chapter 3.
[105] SCLA, DR18/17/27/97, Letter, 11 February 1764.

c.£14,500 in 1765, it is likely that the warnings were well-founded, at least in terms of cash flow.[106]

For these services, Samuel Butler was well rewarded, not least in terms of the well-appointed rooms he enjoyed at Stoneleigh, itemized on the 1774 inventory as Mr Butler's Bed Chamber & Stewards Rooms & Office. These included a feather bed, complete with furniture; a bath stove and plate warmer; a sconce glass in a gilt frame and a swing glass; a variety of tables in walnut and oak, and eighteen walnut chairs with leather seats (which may have come from elsewhere in the house); a double writing desk and letter box; twelve pictures and a weather glass—a practical tool, but also a mark of his social and gender status. As befitted a senior servant, Butler was both comfortable and well placed to receive guests in his rooms; he could also meet with tenants and tradesmen in the Steward's office, where there were two Windsor chairs.[107] In this sense, he shared some of the accoutrements of the family, but served as a buffer between them and the outside world of commerce and estate. Perhaps most telling is the extensive armoury kept under his care: six pistols, three rifles, two militia carbines, a fowling piece, and a blunderbuss, plus a total of seventeen swords, one described as a 'Coronation sword'.[108] This signified another aspect of the trust placed in him by the family: he kept the house secure as well as feeding into the consumption practices through which it was furnished and maintained.

CONCLUSIONS

Far from being centred solely on the desires and tastes of the individual, consumption in the country house was shaped by a wider matrix of influences defined by the broadly conceived household of family, friends, and servants. These moulded the preferences and decisions of the owner, and thus shaped elite cultures of consumption, whilst at the same time helping to put into practice the exigencies of running a large house and estate. Landowners bore responsibilities to those around them and to the diachronic line of forebears and descendants. Obligations to family were paramount, not least because children were essential for dynastic continuity. The management of succession is often conceived in terms of strict settlement and entailed estates, but our analysis here confirms recent work by French and Rothery in emphasizing how important enculturation was in these processes.[109] Sir Roger Newdigate thus invested heavily in financial and emotional terms to give his chosen heir an appropriately broad education, and William Craven was similarly active in his care of Edward, fifth Lord Leigh. However, the importance of family also comes out very clearly in the arrangements made for funerals: these marked rank and status in a very public manner, but also reminded family members of

---

[106] See Rothery and Stobart, 'Spending patterns', 391.

[107] On the differential furnishing of servants rooms, see A. Elton, B. Harrison, and K. Wark, *Researching the Country House. A Guide for Local Historians* (London, 1992), 138–41.

[108] SCLA, DR18/4/43, Inventory, Inventory, 1774, with 1806 amendments.

[109] French and Rothery, *Man's Estate*, 17, 237–8.

their position in a dynastic line. Moreover, funerals were major consumption events, perhaps not as telling as marriage or inheritance, but still involving significant and varied outgoings. They could be used as instruments of patronage and to mark the position of the landowner in local networks of supply and service—a relational context made explicit in the arrangements for Edward's funeral procession.

Taking Harvey's characterization of middling-rank households as a combination of 'global'-governance (husband's) and 'local'-housekeeping (wife's) roles, it is possible to see the country house as a complex series of interlocking realms and responsibilities, with the owner sitting at the nexus of a web of relations and influences.[110] From our analysis, trustees and guardians emerge as critically important in the global-governance role. They promoted loyalty to the diachronic family and underpinned long-term financial solvency by helping to ensure that the household and estate were productive in the sense that income was enhanced and spending kept in check. As surrogate parents, guardians in particular were also responsible for cultural reproduction in terms of both taste and judgement, and attitudes to financial prudence. Senior servants, meanwhile, were vital in the local-housekeeping role. The size and complexity of the country house often meant that this role was split between several 'wives', rather than the resident wife, daughter, or sister-in-law seen in the middling house. We focused here on housekeepers and stewards, but there were also cooks, butlers, and gardeners, each with their distinct sphere of influence. Whilst the degree of independence and trust, or surveillance and management, varied between families, these servants relieved the wife of many duties, leaving her free to take on a more executive role or to pursue other interests (see Chapter 5). Exploring the activities of these servants reveals their scope of action and the influence which they brought to bear on the full breadth of consumption in the country house, both of which went beyond what Walsh might allow.[111] It also provides a 'grass roots' perspective on the mundane aspects of provisioning which is often missed when attention focuses solely on the owner and the more conspicuous elements of their consumption. Importantly, it was the steward and housekeeper who formed the principal point of contact between the country house and the local and even metropolitan economy—a point to which we return in Chapter 7.

Overall, it is apparent that the landowner and their consumption were influenced by the structure and operation of their family-household, not just in terms of practical day-to-day needs or longer-term financial management, but also in a broader cultural sense. Household provided the relational context in which landowners expressed their identity and spent their money.

---

[110] Harvey, *Little Republic*, 80. See also Muldrew, *Economy of Obligation*, 158–9.
[111] Walsh, 'Shopping at first hand?'.

7

Supplying the Country House
Craftsmen and Retailers

INTRODUCTION

The country house was a physical statement of elite family power, but it was also a nexus of flows, of goods, people, and ideas. Its material culture was the product not just of the owners and their families, but also the many hands which shaped its fabric, furnished its rooms, filled its larders and wardrobes, and supplied its collections. However, the role of the myriad suppliers that produced and serviced the country house is often overshadowed by high-status craftsmen with a national reputation: men like Robert Adam, Thomas Chippendale, and Josiah Wedgwood. Whilst patronage always marked their relationship with landowners, the architecture and decoration of the house are frequently seen as the product of negotiation which drew on the professional expertise and judgement of the architect and craftsman. As Lady Shelburne noted, for example, 'I consulted [Robert Adam] on the furniture for our painted Antichamber & determined that it shou'd be a pea green Satin spotted with white & trimm'd with a pink and white fringe; it was originally my own thought and met with his entire approbation.'[1] Not all craftsmen and retailers could wield this kind of influence, of course; but all held key skills, expertise, and knowledge that were vital to the country house and its owner, and each one had to be chosen from a growing array of options as retailers and professionals proliferated in number through the long eighteenth century.[2]

In Paris, there was a clear understanding of the character and status of suppliers whom French aristocrats and royalty were supposed to patronize in order to maintain their own social standing.[3] Such clarity was largely absent in England, despite the reputation of leading craftsmen, and finding the right architect, bookseller, or grocer was by no means straightforward. This meant that considerable trouble was

---

[1] Quoted in Vickery, *Behind Closed Doors*, 156. For a more general discussion of the influence of craftsmen, see Wilson and Mackley, *Building of the English Country House*, 109–44; C. Edwards, *Turning Houses into Homes. A History of the Retailing and Consumption of Domestic Furnishings* (Aldershot, 2005), 38–74.

[2] The growth of the retail sector is a central theme of McKendrick, Brewer and Plumb, *Birth of a Consumer Society*. See also H.-C. Mui and L. Mui, *Shops and Shopkeeping in Eighteenth-Century England* (London, 1989), 8–29, 106–35; Cox, *Complete Tradesman*, 14–37; Stobart, Hann, and Morgan, *Spaces of Consumption*, 38–49.

[3] Chatenet-Calyste, 'Feminine luxury in Paris', 175. For a more general discussion of high-quality traders in Paris, see Sargentson, *Merchant and Luxury Markets*.

taken to secure a reliable supplier even for mundane and everyday items. Elizabeth Purefoy sometimes wrote speculative letters asking about the availability of goods, for example, in September 1751, when enquiring of a grocer whether he sold pickled mushrooms. Here, she based her enquiry on the hearsay of acquaintances; more usually she drew on the recommendation of friends, as did many provincial consumers, especially when dealing with London retailers, but her clear preference was to deal with known and trusted suppliers with whom she had done business over many years.[4] Much the same was true of the Durham gentlewoman Judith Baker, who used a small set of suppliers for her metropolitan shopping, her choice being 'predicated upon a system of patronage, personal acquaintance and credit'.[5] In this context, credit had both an economic and social meaning, incorporating both financial interdependence and a mutual recognition of honour. Retailer–customer relations were an integral part of the economy of obligation explored by Muldrew, wherein book debts became socialized as personal relationships. The credit of an individual or household was a measure of their economic and social worth—their reputation or standing in the community.[6] Indeed, Finn argues that personal character was central to judgements of credit; yet the relationship was mutable because 'the inherent fluidity of these systems of identity, meaning and exchange thwarted the construction of stable interpretations of consumer characters'.[7] The problem was who to trust: to whom should credit be given? These questions are usually posed from the perspective of the shopkeeper—Defoe dedicated many pages to this in his *Compleat Tradesman*—but how did the buyer know who was reliable and honest or, in other words, a creditworthy supplier? Whilst customers were part of the same webs of credit, character, and honour, their decisions about trust were perhaps also shaped by ideas of knowledge: the trade-related expertise of the retailer or professional and the networks of supply and information to which they had access. These ideas have been explored by Shapin in the context of science, but remain largely ignored in commercial contexts.[8]

In reality, we know relatively little about the ways in which elite consumers related to their numerous suppliers, even in the most basic terms. This chapter therefore begins by laying out some of the parameters that defined the relationship between the Leighs and Newdigates and their suppliers. Attention centres on the number of retailers, craftsmen, and professionals patronized for different types of goods: were some aspects of spending monopolized by key suppliers whilst others were spread across a range of individuals? And how did these relationships vary between generations? Building on this, we identify key suppliers for each house, both in terms of the longevity of their relationship and their overall impact, primarily measured in financial terms. In the second half of the chapter, we focus on

---

[4] Eland, *Purefoy Letters*, no.139. For an example of the provincial elite drawing on the knowledge of metropolitan friends, see Vickery, *Gentleman's Daughter*, 168–72, 180–2.

[5] Berry, 'Prudent luxury', 146.

[6] Muldrew, *Economy of Obligation*, 123–47. See also Shepard, 'Manhood, credit and patriarchy'.

[7] M. Finn, *The Character of Credit. Personal Debt in English Culture, 1740–1914* (Cambridge, 2003), 102–3.

[8] S. Shapin, *A Social History of Truth. Civility and Science in Seventeenth-Century England* (Chicago, 1995).

these key suppliers to establish in more detail the nature of their relationship with the Leighs and Newdigates. This involves analysing the ways in which they extended credit to their customers and the ways in which these credit arrangements were managed in terms of different payment systems. More broadly, we assess the relationship between trust, credit, and reputation in the context of the landowner–supplier relationship; how does it relate to broader conceptions of credit, character, and obligation; were titled landowners part of a distinct aristocratic culture of credit, as Fontaine suggests?[9] Finally, we explore the lives of a small sample of suppliers in some detail, examining in particular their ability to shape consumption decisions, offering advice and anticipating taste. Above all, we explore the nature of trust that existed between wealthy landowners and their suppliers.

SUPPLIERS: PATRONAGE AND LOYALTY

With a sample period stretching over several decades, it is inevitable that there would be considerable turnover in the people supplying Stoneleigh Abbey and Arbury hall, no matter how loyal the family were to particular suppliers. This is reflected in the sheer number of individuals patronized: over 1,800 men and women presented bills to the Leighs, whilst Sir Roger Newdigate's account books enumerate over 1,250 suppliers. As the collection of bills is incomplete and the account books include numerous entries for particular goods without always naming the supplier, both of these figures are undoubtedly under-representations of the supply networks servicing the two families. Nonetheless, they amply illustrate the breadth and variety of professionals, craftsmen, and retailers needed to the supply these substantial country houses—well in excess of the 137 (9 per annum) that serviced the genteel Gibbards at Sharnbrook in the period 1814–29 and more on a par with Parisian elites, such as Marie-Fortunée d'Este, who drew on the services of 414 suppliers over a period of 14 years (30 per annum).[10]

At Stoneleigh, the level of consumption, and with it the number of bills and suppliers, varied considerably over the years. Breaking down the figures into different periods of ownership shows some revealingly different patterns of behaviour between generations (Table 7.1). Thomas, fourth Lord Leigh, and his son Edward, fifth Lord Leigh, both drew on a large number of suppliers—some thirty-five to forty per annum—to provide a wide range of goods and services. Numerically, though, it was those supplying building services, food and drink, and drapery that were dominant, accounting for 51 per cent of suppliers and 39 per cent of bills to Thomas. Edward's suppliers were also varied, but the balance was rather different: booksellers and instrument dealers were more important, accounting for nearly one in ten of his suppliers, and furniture comprised a much larger proportion of

---

[9] L. Fontaine, *The Moral Economy. Poverty, Credit and Trust in Early Modern Europe* (English edition, Cambridge, 2014), 90–4.

[10] L. Bailey, 'Maintaining status: consumption in the nineteenth-century gentry household' (unpublished MA thesis, University of Northampton, 2010), 29; Chatenet-Calyste, 'Feminine luxury in Paris', 175.

Table 7.1. Suppliers to different generations of the Leigh family

	Number	No. p.a.	Spend (£)	Transactions	Transactions p.a.	Transactions per supplier	Spend per supplier (£)	Spend per transaction (£)
Thomas (1738–49)	416	34.7	15,254	787	65.6	1.9	36.7	19.4
Trustees (1750–62)	250	19.2	2,940	456	35.1	1.8	11.8	6.4
Trustees excl. Mary (1750–62)	149	11.5	1,557	231	17.8	1.5	10.4	6.7
Edward (1763–74)	441	40.1	17,763	841	76.5	1.9	40.3	21.1
Committee (1774–85)	222	18.5	6,129	416	34.7	1.9	27.6	14.7
Mary (1786–1806)	421	20.0	15,216	934	44.5	2.2	36.1	16.3

Source: SCLA, DR/18/5—series of bills.

spending (see Chapter 1). With both men, the average size of bills was relatively high, at £37–40 per tradesman and £19–21 per bill, reflecting the fact that both father and son spent handsomely on their house and themselves. However, these similarities are a little misleading, because, as we saw in Chapter 1, Edward's spending was heavily concentrated into the years 1763–66, before his mental illness became evident. This is reflected in his engagement of suppliers, 53 per cent of whom presented bills during this four-year period, whilst many of those from the later 1760s and 1770s were for his sister, Mary Leigh. In reality, then, Edward's patronage of suppliers was brief and highly intense.

Unsurprisingly, the period of Edward's minority and the years following his designation as insane are both marked by low numbers of transactions and a marked reduction in the number of suppliers being drawn on. The effective shutdown of the house between 1750 and 1763 meant that spending was severely reduced, a regime that becomes much clearer if we remove from the analysis the bills presented to Mary Leigh by a range of drapers, milliners, haberdashers, and the like.[11] These comprised 225 bills and 101 individuals in total. Without them, spending was largely restricted to that necessary to maintain the estate, and the suppliers are mostly craftsmen such as carpenters, masons, blacksmiths, and glaziers, although there are also a number of bills for livery. Even so, a range of suppliers was drawn upon: carpentry work, for example, was completed by at least six different individuals and hedging was undertaken by three tradesmen. Overall, however, this was a period during which the number of suppliers servicing Stoneleigh Abbey was much reduced: fewer than twelve tradesmen per annum presented bills. Retrenchment was less severe during the years of the Committee, with bills being presented by a total of 222 individuals (around 18 per annum), but spending narrowed in much the same way as it had during in the 1750s to focus on maintenance of the house and the estate, park, and garden. The work was again spread across a number of tradesmen, bills being presented by nine masons and ten ironmongers, for instance, whilst the eight suppliers of posts and rails reflect the importance of enclosure during this period.

Intermediate between these two, yet rather different from both, were the supply patterns that characterized the period of Mary Leigh's ownership. She drew on a similar number of suppliers to her father and brother; yet these were spread over a much longer period so that the average per annum was more in line with that seen during the Committee's control of the estate. However, the average number of bills presented by each supplier was notably higher, suggesting more sustained relationships over longer time periods—a point to which we return later—whilst the average spend per tradesmen broadly reflected that seen with her male relations. In line with her overall spending patterns, Mary's bills reflected the underlying need for maintenance to the house and estate, but were dominated by those for drapery and especially food and drink.

If patronage of craftsmen and retailers differed from one generation to the next, it also varied considerably between different types of supplier (Tables 7.2 and 7.3).

---

[11] Mary Leigh was resident in London during the 1750s and 1760s—see Chapter 5.

Table 7.2. Suppliers to the Leigh family (by type of goods)

	Number	Spend (£)	Transactions	Transactions per supplier	Spend per supplier (£)	Spend per transaction (£)
Art & books	87	3,115	160	1.8	35.8	19.5
Building	309	7,326	574	1.9	23.7	12.8
Coach & horses	105	3,236	185	1.8	30.8	17.5
Drapery	233	5,572	515	2.2	23.9	10.8
Food & drink	200	6,547	486	2.4	32.7	13.5
Furniture	61	5,578	91	1.5	91.8	61.5
Household	119	1,727	207	1.7	14.5	8.3
Kitchenware	47	427	84	1.8	9.1	5.1
Medicine	58	2,513	115	2.0	43.3	21.9
Park & garden	69	901	113	1.6	13.1	8.0
Silverware	24	2,904	49	2.0	121.0	59.3

Source: SCLA, DR/8/5—series of bills.

Table 7.3. Suppliers to Sir Roger Newdigate (by type of goods)

	Number	Spend (£)	Transactions	Transactions per supplier	Spend per supplier (£)	Spend per transaction (£)
Art & books	127	2,858	389	3.1	22.5	7.3
Building	91	3,607	253	2.8	39.6	14.3
Coach & horses	103	3,760	355	3.4	36.5	10.6
Drapery	307	9,165	1450	4.7	29.9	6.3
Food & drink	206	13,508	895	4.3	65.6	15.1
Furniture	97	2,210	216	2.2	22.8	10.2
Household	348	15,468	1,504	4.3	44.4	10.3
Kitchenware	66	911	138	2.1	13.8	6.6
Medicine	87	1714	336	3.9	19.7	5.1
Park & garden	90	2359	319	3.5	26.2	7.4
Silverware	29	2077	81	2.8	71.6	25.6

Source: WRO, CR136/V/156, Account book; CR136/V/136, Account book.

Note: The transactions for which the supplier's name was not provided (25 per cent of all transactions) have been omitted, making some totals lower than those presented in Chapter 1.

Such variation is to be expected, most obviously because we would expect high-cost goods to be bought from relatively fewer suppliers as these were the purchases that relied more on stable, trusting relationships between customer and retailer. Such arrangements characterized the shopping practices of the Le Strange family in the seventeenth century and the Gibbards in the early nineteenth.[12] Whilst these patterns were broadly true at Arbury Hall and Stoneleigh Abbey, the retailer–customer relationship which emerges was far more complex. At both houses, the ratio of

[12] Whittle and Griffiths, *Consumption and Gender*, 55–72, esp. 68; Bailey, 'Maintaining status', 29–30.

tradesmen per transaction was notably lower than average for those supplying furniture and furnishings, indicating a low level of 'loyalty' to particular suppliers. This reflects the fact that many of these goods, especially larger items of furniture, were purchased only periodically or in bursts of intense spending. This was more pronounced at Stoneleigh Abbey, where each generation engaged with different furniture makers and upholsterers: in 1736, John Taylor supplied Edward, third Lord Leigh, with twelve matted, six carved, and eighteen compass chairs; two years later, John Pardoe presented his bill for a range of parcel-gilt walnut furniture for the Great Apartment; another five years on, H. Hands was supplying Thomas, fourth Lord Leigh, with mahogany tables costing between £2 2s. 6d. and £3 apiece.[13] His son Edward drew primarily on Thomas Burnett and William Gomm; and, in the 1780s and 1790s, Daniel Frost, Michael Thackthwaite, and Bradshaw and Smith undertook upholstery work and supplied a variety of single items of furniture to Mary Leigh, including four mahogany state chairs, a large mahogany Pembroke table, and a crankey mattress, and Henry Clay supplied her with japanned boxes.[14] The continuity of ownership at Arbury Hall brought more sustained relationships with the cabinetmakers W. Yewd and Roger Roe (in the 1750s and 1760s), the upholsterers Edward Hirst, William Lynes, and Thomas Monro (in the 1760s, 1770s and 1780s, and 1790s respectively), and most notably Thomas Gillow, who appears in the account books every year between 1777 and 1795.[15] Bills for upholstery, household linen, and even furniture were generally fairly modest, averaging £28 and only once exceeding £100 in the Newdigate accounts. The figures for Stoneleigh Abbey, by contrast, are skewed by the exceptionally large bills presented in 1765 by William Gomm and Thomas Burnett, which raised the average spend per tradesman and per transaction to levels only matched by purchases of silverware.

The high average size of bills for silverware was a direct consequence of the high value of the goods being supplied. Purchases of watches, snuff boxes, and small items of jewellery could amount to just a few pounds, but buying tableware generally involved a considerable outlay. For example, Sir Roger Newdigate paid the London silversmiths Parker and Wakelin £13 11s. for a tea tub in 1769 and a hefty £80 13s. 6d. for a tureen and cover in 1764.[16] Bills presented to the Leighs often involved the provision of a substantial quantity of silver tableware and so were much larger, the five largest amounting to a total of just over £2,096.[17] These high values were matched by relatively large numbers of transactions per tradesmen, indicating that the Leighs and Newdigates drew on a fairly limited number of suppliers for silverware and jewellery. This can be readily explained in terms of the small number of such high-order tradesmen who were able to serve the needs of these wealthy landowners. Underlining this was the need for trust between silversmith and customer: the latter had to be confident of the quality of the workmanship,

[13] SCLA, DR18/5/2047, DR18/5/2218, DR18/5/2658.
[14] For example, SCLA, DR18/5/5905, DR18/5/5703, DR18/5/6023, DR18/5/5890.
[15] WRO, CR136/V136.
[16] WRO, CR136/V/136, Account book, entries for 1769, 1764.
[17] SCLA, DR18/5/4251, DR18/5/5809, DR18/5/5858, DR18/5/5695, DR18/5/6851.

but also of the intrinsic qualities of the silver, both of which were assured—either directly or indirectly—by the craftsman's hallmark.[18]

A similarly high level of transactions per tradesman was seen for those supplying medical services, drapery, and food and drink. Such tradesmen commanded above-average loyalty from both the Leighs and the Newdigates, despite the lower, albeit highly variable, size of their bills. At Stoneleigh, the overall total for medical bills was greatly inflated by the treatment and care for Edward, fifth Lord Leigh, after he was declared insane: Dr Willis, for example, presented six bills which averaged nearly £160 apiece, much of the cost being for accommodation.[19] At a more mundane level, butcher's bills could easily accumulate to hundreds of pounds, as could those of drapers, wine merchants, grocers, and haberdashers; but there were numerous examples of one-off suppliers. For example, the linen draper Thomas Dobshaw presented a single bill to Mary Leigh in 1795; Thomas Wooton supplied her with peas on a single occasion in 1792; and, much earlier, in 1757, Esther Lowther sold her ass's milk just once.[20] This variability reflects the complex interaction of, on the one hand, consumers being able to choose between a large number of suppliers for these generally lower-order goods and, on the other, the advantages of a stable relationship with particular suppliers; here again, trust and reputation were important in assuring the quality of the product being supplied, be it cloth, lace, wine, tea, or sugar.

Trust lay at the heart of the relationship between tradesmen and their customers in the early-modern period, since it encouraged good service and reduced the transaction costs of shopping. Moreover, Muldrew argues, the interpersonal credit of shop debts encouraged repeat custom and locked retailers and customers into a relationship of mutual dependence.[21] Long-term suppliers are thus significant both in the volume of goods or services provided and the degree of trust that existed between them and their patrons. Much the same might be argued for those suppliers who provided large quantities of goods over shorter time periods. Both groups had the potential to influence purchasing patterns and shape customer preferences. It is hard to fit these key suppliers into any simple typology, not least because tradesmen with the same occupational title could provide very different qualities of goods or services; but they mostly fall into one of three main groups (Table 7.4).

First are those supplying everyday goods on a regular basis. It is unlikely that there was much direct contact between these suppliers and the end consumer, as most transactions were mediated by the steward or housekeeper or made via correspondence (see Chapter 6). There were clearly exceptions to this: some groceries may have been chosen in person and, Vickery argues, saddlery was a personal preoccupation of elite men; but the evidence is equivocal.[22] Whilst Richard Twining wrote to Sir Roger Newdigate to apologize about a consignment of

---

[18] Clifford, 'Commerce with things', 154–63.
[19] There were other payments made to Dr Willis and not recorded in the bills. His total payments were in excess of £3,780. See SCLA, DR18/31/461, Auditor's account, 1763–74 (years 1771–4).
[20] SCLA, DR18/5/6101, DR18/5/5968, DR18/5/3762.
[21] B. Blondé and I. Van Damme, 'Retail growth and consumer changes in a declining urban economy: Antwerp 1650–1750', *Economic History Review*, 32 (2010), 638–63; Stobart, *Sugar and Spice*, 134–5, 144–5, 156–7; Muldrew, *Economy of Obligation*, 123–4.
[22] Reference to people tasting and choosing tea; Vickery, *Behind Closed Doors*, 124.

Table 7.4. Key suppliers to Stoneleigh Abbey and Arbury Hall (number of suppliers)

	Stoneleigh Abbey	Arbury Hall
Everyday goods		
Provisions	5	2
Groceries	3	4
Chandlery	0	5
Building	7	4
Hardware	2	2
Saddlery	0	2
Personal goods		
Wine	2	2
Medicine & law	4	3
Books	2	1
Drapery & tailoring	7	6
Haberdashery & shoes	2	7
High-cost goods		
Architects	(2)	1
Furniture	4	1
Coaches	0	2
Silverware	2	3

Source: SCLA, 18/5—series of bills; WRO, CR136/V/156, Account book, CR136/V/136, Account book.

Note: Key suppliers are defined as those presenting ten or more bills for Stoneleigh Abbey or appearing twenty times or more in the account books for Arbury Hall, or who supplied in excess of £200 of goods or services.

Provisions = butchers, bakers, greengrocers, fishmongers, and greengrocers; Chandlery includes oilmen and seedsmen; Building = masons, carpenters, and turners; Hardware = blacksmiths, locksmiths, and coopers; Medicine = physicians and apothecaries; Furniture = cabinetmakers, upholsterers, wallpaper merchants, and house painters.

souchong tea which was apparently deficient, it is unclear whether the initial complaint came from Sir Roger himself or from his steward or housekeeper: certainly, there is no protracted correspondence of the kind seen between the Purefoys and their suppliers.[23] Similarly, it is doubtful that the goods provided by the wheelwright John Swinnerton and the whittawer William Fortesque involved Sir Roger in lengthy sojourns in their respective workshops. That said, the Gibbards had a close personal relationship with their tea merchant, their correspondence mixing business with family matters. In general, however, the underpinning rationale for long-term relationships with such suppliers is best understood in terms of reliability and convenience. Despite her complaints, Elizabeth Purefoy stuck with Wilson, her chief London grocer, for many years because she could rely on him to provide timely consignments of good-quality provisions.[24]

[23] WRO, CR136/B/2625a, Letter from Richard Twining, 14 February 1803; Eland, *Purefoy Letters*, for example, nos 104, 105, and 106.

[24] For a fuller discussion of these, see Stobart, *Sugar and Spice*, 146–7, 204–7.

It might be argued that these lower-order goods were simply not important enough to make it worthwhile 'shopping around' to obtain the best quality, price, or service: the transaction costs of doing so were too high. However, no single retailer was ever a monopoly supplier to either the Leighs or the Newdigates, suggesting that choices were being made. We have direct evidence of Sir John Mordaunt's servant shopping in this way in London. He wrote to his master detailing prices and qualities of a range of groceries he had been sent to buy.[25] For the Leighs, the evidence is less direct, but is suggestive nonetheless. In 1765, for example, groceries were purchased from five different shops: Blackiston, Myles, & Co.; Hugh Jones; J. Phillips; Lilley Smith; and Thomas Thompson. To an extent, this was a case of specialist sourcing: Thompson appears to have been the main supplier of tea at this date, whilst spices came in greatest number and variety from Blackiston, Myles, & Co. However, there were three grocers supplying tea, three supplying dried fruit, and four selling spices; all of them sold sugar to the Leighs, who were apparently spreading their custom in a manner closely resembling the middle-ranking consumers who patronized Thomas Dickenson's shop in mid-eighteenth-century Worcester.[26] Some choices may have been based on quality, but three of the grocers supplied goods described as 'fine' or 'best', suggesting that other motives, such as price or personal preference, were also important. Indeed, the fact that Blackiston, Myles, & Co. were also patronized by the Leighs' relations at Adlestrop in Gloucester, Sir Roger Newdigate, and the Baker family of County Durham suggests that provincial elites may have shared particular patterns of consumption centring on favoured retailers.[27]

The second category of suppliers, who provided personal goods reflecting the preferences of the individual, is rather different. We have already seen the importance of Thomas Payne in supplying books both to Sir Roger Newdigate and Edward, fifth Lord Leigh, his relationship with the former extending over twenty-five years from the early 1760s. Similar stability was seen with purchases of clothing, medicine, and wine, with both families being more directly involved in the selection and consumption of these goods. Outer clothing, for example, required visits from the tailor or seamstress for fitting, or the provision of templates on which new items could be modelled. On one occasion, a Miss Baker wrote to Mary Leigh from Cheltenham, assuring her that 'Mr Townsend ... promises he will imediately [*sic*] on receiving the pattern shoe make six pair to your order for which with silk heels he must charge twelve shillings per pair.'[28] This appears to have been a one-off transaction with a trusted craftsman, but Mary in particular returned to favoured haberdashers, mercers, and drapers over many years: Carr, Ibbetson, Bigge & Pickard for brocade, silks, and tabbies, Eleanor Brunton for fans and muffs, and Mary Budd for lace, ribbons, stomachers, and

---

[25] WRO, CR1368, Vol. 4/57, Mordaunt Family Letters.
[26] Stobart, Hann, and Morgan, *Spaces of Consumption*, 154–5.
[27] SCLA, DR18/5/3702; WRO, CR 136/V/136, Account book, entry for 1780; Berry, 'Prudent luxury', 148.
[28] SCLA, DR18/17/30/35, Letter from Miss Baker, 19 April 1796. There are parallels here with Henry Purefoy's ordering of a waistcoat discussed in Chapter 8.

caps.[29] Her motivation for doing so was based on the ability of these retailers to match her preferences in terms of style and quality. This was also true of Sabine Winn at Nostell Priory, who enjoyed a very close relationship with a London milliner called Ann Charlton, in large part because she was able to supply a range of French goods, including those only available on the black market, such as French gloves, which were 'too dangerous a thing to deal in'.[30] This ability to meet personal preferences was also important for wine merchants, such as Richard Kilsha and J. Robinson, who each supplied in excess of £350 of wines to Edward, fifth Lord Leigh, and Sir Roger Newdigate respectively. Trust would have been of paramount importance here, because drapers, mercers, and apothecaries in particular were supplying goods that impacted directly on the person: their bodily appearance, health, and character. Ill-fitting clothes, for example, might have a direct bearing on character and reputation, especially in an age when status was increasingly judged from physical appearance.[31] As with grocers, however, none of these suppliers enjoyed a monopoly, although again there was some specialization of provision: Payne tended to supply histories and classic texts, some in Latin, Fletcher sold scientific and religious books, and Vaillant presented his bills for folio editions of prints.[32] And yet there was considerable overlap, and the impression is that Edward at least was acquiring good-quality books as and where he could.[33]

Finally, there was an important group of suppliers providing high-cost positional goods and services. These included the furniture makers and silversmiths discussed earlier (and in more detail below), but also coach makers and architect-builders. Some of these supplied a large quantity of goods in a relatively brief period. In addition to the large bills presented by Burnett, Gomm, and Bromwich, Edward Leigh's refurbishment of Stoneleigh Abbey in the mid-1760s included over £322 of table and bed linen, all of its supplied by Jordan Heyland Biggar. Similarly, in the late 1770s, J. Glover was engaged briefly in providing drapery for the drawing room at Arbury Hall and upholstering furniture in stuff damask for the drawing room, the total cost of which exceeded £240.[34] Others established long-term relationships with their patrons, even if commissions were relatively infrequent. The silversmiths Gilpin and Makepeace fall into this category, as does stone mason William Hiorn, who worked for the third Lord Leigh in the 1730s and again for his grandson in the 1760s.[35] A third set presented substantial bills on a fairly regular basis. Gillow's bills to Sir Roger Newdigate were mostly relatively modest, only three times exceeding £50 (in 1784, 1787, and 1788); but Adkins's regular account

---

[29] For example, SCLA, DR18/5/4441, DR18/5/4248, DR18/5/4331.

[30] Quoted in K. Bristol, 'Between the exotic and the everyday: Sabine Winn and Nostell Priory, West Yorkshire, 1765–1798', in J. Ilmakunnas and J. Stobart (eds) *Taste for Luxury in Early-Modern Europe: Display, Acquisition and Boundaries* (London, 2016), [p.11]. There is little evidence that either the Leighs or Newdigates purchased black-market goods, although, if genuinely Indian, the chintz supplied by Burnett for the fifth Lord Leigh's bedchamber would have been prohibited.

[31] See Finn, *Character of Credit*, 21; P. Borsay, *The English Urban Renaissance. Culture and Society in the Provincial Town, 1660–1770* (Oxford, 1989), 225–32.

[32] See, for example, SCLA, DR18/5/4440, DR18/5/4384, DR18/5/4202.

[33] For fuller discussion, see Stobart, 'Luxury of learning'.

[34] WRO, CR 136/V/136, Account book, entry for 1779.

[35] Gomme, 'Abbey into palace', 87, 85, 97.

for coach repairs was punctuated in 1765 and 1776 by payments of, respectively, £106 9s. 6d. for a new coach and £208 6s. for a post coach and post chaise, the latter coinciding with a surge of spending that marked Sir Roger's second marriage.[36] Coaches appear to be one of the few areas where both families were content to rely on a single supplier. At Arbury Hall, Adkins succeeded James Pinnock, who was the only coachmaker appearing in the accounts between 1756 and 1763, and was followed after 1784 by William Leader, who again operated as the sole supplier. Similarly, at Stoneleigh Abbey, Thomas and then James Cope supplied and repaired coaches from 1757 to 1772 and were succeeded by John Hatchett.

Loyalty to such suppliers reflected a high degree of trust in craftsmen with a good reputation and a track record of supplying high-quality work. The dangers of buying such equipage outside this kind of established and trusting relationship are apparent from the complaints made by the wealthy industrialist Michael Hughes. Despite having placed the order through a friend in London, he was deeply disappointed with the carriage provided, which he described as being 'the most mean paltry thing that ever was sent out of London, & so is deem'd by every Gentleman who has seen it'.[37] The problem was not just the quality of the carriage, but also—and more fundamentally—the breach of trust represented by its shoddy nature. This compromised his social standing and undermined his honour, which was, as Hobbs made clear, the key to trust and reliable dealings.[38] In his complaint, Hughes attempted to turn this around, arguing that the poor quality of the vehicle reflected badly on the character of the coachmaker. In general, therefore, retailers were anxious to protect their reputation as trustworthy; they worked hard to cultivate the custom of wealthy landowners, even when this meant abandoning normal trading practices. Thus, we see Elizabeth Taylor writing to the fifth Lord Leigh in 1764 that she was:

> very sorry to find the Glasses are not such as you approve. I thought the mettal to be very good, theyre not being liked will be a considerable disadvantage to me, as they were order'd on purpose for his Lordship; but if you do not intend to keep them after 12 instant, hope you will send them back by the miller as I have no objection to hireing them for the time, tho' its what I do not very commonly do.[39]

That Taylor was content to have the goods returned is no great surprise; that she was prepared to hire them out after they had been rejected is perhaps more striking, although it might be seen as a means of recouping some of her expense. Certainly, her actions maintained her relationship with the Leighs.

REPUTATION, CREDIT, AND TRUST

Once established, strong relationships with trusted tradesmen were important in assuring quality and service. But this raises the question of how choices of retailer

---

[36] WRO, CR 136/V/136, Account book, entries for 1765 and 1766.

[37] Letter to Messrs Chamberlayne & Co., 23 October 1809, quoted in Stobart, Hann, and Morgan, *Spaces of Consumption*, 162–3.

[38] See Muldrew, *Economy of Obligation*, 148.   [39] SCLA, DR18/5/4122.

were made in the first place. Here, attention usually focuses on customers' assessments of quality and price, and on the ability of retailers to construct and project
a good reputation.[40] The former could be judged in person, most readily by visiting the shop, but also by having samples sent to one's home. Sabine Winn, for
example, received numerous samples from a variety of mercers, drapers, and
milliners, making her choice from first-hand experience of the goods, despite
living in reclusion at Nostell Priory.[41] Sir John Griffin Griffin took this approach
a stage further. His patronage of furniture makers in particular was characterized
by initially smaller orders being followed up by larger commissions, a practice
which suggests that he was testing the supplier before trusting them with important orders.[42] In order to gain attention as a reliable supplier, the trades people
could project their good reputation in a number of ways. Trade cards listing the
range and quality of goods on offer or illustrating these through often stylized
graphic representations offered one possibility, although advertising was viewed
by some as undermining the tradesman's good name. Josiah Wedgwood was most
scathing in this regard, but then practised a wide variety of promotional techniques himself. He was also very conscious of the importance of a prestigious
and exclusive address, famously rejecting Pall Mall as a possible venue for his
showrooms because he thought it too accessible to the common people. However,
Clifford and Berg make clear that trade cards were an important mechanism
for establishing and cementing a tradesman's reputation with his customers.[43]
Personal associations were also important, sometimes in terms of the standing
of previous proprietors, but also through the cachet of patronage by nobility or
royalty.[44] The latter was invariably declared on bill-heads and trade cards, a practice which became increasingly prevalent from the 1780s, as is apparent amongst
the bills presented to Mary Leigh. Amongst her suppliers were silversmiths, booksellers, hatters, china dealers, stationers, whip makers, japanners, lamp makers,
print sellers, and coachmakers, all of whom were able to point to their royal or
noble patrons.

Reputation could also be communicated between (potential) customers on a
more personal basis, either through direct contact or via what Muldrew terms
'community reputation'. The latter involved knowledge of credit being communicated between friends, a process which put great emphasis on words as carriers of
an individual's reputation and worth.[45] Family was important in this context, with
information about retailers and craftsmen being shared both synchronically and

---

[40] For discussion of trust in the customer–retailer relationship, see Blondé and Van Damme, 'Retail
growth'; Walsh, 'Shops, shopping'; Stobart, *Sugar and Spice*, 146–50; Bailey, 'Consumption and
status'.

[41] Bristol, 'Between the exotic and the everyday'.

[42] Chavasse, 'Material culture and the country house', 62–3.

[43] Berg, *Luxury and Pleasure*, 146; M. Berg and H. Clifford, 'Selling consumption in the eighteenth century: advertising and the trade card in Britain and France', *Cultural and Social History*,
4 (2007), 145–70.

[44] J. Stobart, 'Selling (through) politeness: advertising provincial shops in eighteenth-century England',
Cultural and Social History, 5 (2008), 309–28.

[45] Muldrew, *Economy of Obligation*, 151–7. See also Finn, *Character of Credit*, 102–3.

diachronically. At its most elemental, this meant different family members sharing the same supplier—a common practice with husbands and wives, notwithstanding their gender-specific requirements. The Newdigate account books carefully distinguish the tradesmen who were specifically serving Hester Newdigate, but they also note her spending in categories in common with, and with retailers who also served, her husband. For example, both Hester and Sir Roger used Edward Ellicott of Sweetings Alley, London: Hester for silver jewellery and Sir Roger for watches and watch repairs. The purchases were gendered, but their choice of supplier was based on shared knowledge. Sir Roger had patronized Ellicott first, a series of small accounts from 1757 suggesting repairs rather than new goods. He purchased silver jewellery for Hester in the year of their wedding (1776) at a cost of £130 and there were four further purchases accounted to Hester over the next two years, amounting to £67 in total. Sir Roger continued to spend small sums on himself, but also purchased a silver watch in 1786 at a cost of £48 6*s*.[46] It appears, then, that Hester's satisfaction with Ellicott's services may have shaped her husband's choice of supplier for a more significant purchase for himself.

At Stoneleigh Abbey, the widowed Mary remained loyal to many of the tradesmen who had served her husband Edward, third Lord Leigh, after his death in 1738; so too did the trustees who ran the estate from 1750. Amongst these suppliers was Thomas Gilpin, who first served the Leigh family in 1737, when the third Lord paid a bill for some engraving work.[47] His grandson Edward, fifth Lord Leigh, bought jewellery and silver as a boy in 1751 and, when in charge of the estate, made more substantial purchases as well as selling back to Gilpin around £700 of unwanted silver in 1765.[48] Over a similar period, Gilpin also supplied Mary with silverware and jewellery on three occasions, in 1751, 1753, and 1765.[49] Similarly, Edward and Mary's father Thomas, fourth Lord Leigh, made five purchases of clothing and textiles from Robert Hughes of Coventry during the 1740s.[50] Edward, or more probably his guardians, then went to Hughes for livery in 1753, as did Mary in 1753 and 1756.[51] In both cases there appears to be a shared knowledge of the character of suppliers that both Edward and Mary inherited from earlier generations. Since both of them were very young when their father died, we can assume that this information was transferred through their guardians or the steward, underlining their importance to household consumption. These were exceptions, however: in total only thirty-four suppliers continued to serve Stoneleigh Abbey beyond a single generation of the Leigh family, twenty-three of them in trades related to building, maintenance, and estate work. Continuity thus came through the needs of the house and estate rather than the tastes of individual owners—a point which underlines the selection of such tradesmen in Edward's funeral procession in 1786, discussed in Chapter 6.

---

[46] WRO, CR 136/V/156, Account book, entries for 1757–60; CR 136/V/136, Account book, *passim.*
[47] SCLA, DR18/5/1989.   [48] SCLA, DR18/5/3121, DR18/5/4574, DR18/5/3121.
[49] SCLA, DR18/5/3136, DR18/5/3194, DR18/5/4333.
[50] For example, see SCLA, DR18/5/2129.
[51] SCLA, DR18/5/3331 (Edward), and DR18/5/3349, DR18/5/3638 (Mary).

This lack of intergenerational continuity reflects the dynastic problems experienced by the family, with the minority and subsequent madness of Edward, fifth Lord Leigh. It is, nonetheless, remarkable that each generation—and indeed each individual—did so much to construct their own supplier network. Even with the strong thread of continuity provided by Sir Roger Newdigate, there was a marked change in the retailers supplying the needs of his two wives. Sophia, his first wife, patronized a tailor called Pearce, the draper Fairchild, and the linen drapers Spencer and Dyne, and Goodchild up to her death in 1774; his second wife, Hester, used Jones for tailoring, Yeates for drapery, and Blunt or Birchall for linen drapery.[52] This is not to say that every generation started from scratch and that there was no transfer of consumer knowledge between family members. Edward, fifth Lord Leigh and his sister Mary shared at least forty suppliers. These covered a wide range of goods, including clothing, furniture, books, food and drink, coaches and saddlery, silver-ware, and building work. One or two were important suppliers to both, including the apothecary George Hailes and the silversmith Thomas Gilpin, but most were favoured by one and used occasionally by the other—a distinction in part explained by the rather different consumption priorities of the two individuals.

Sometimes, their suppliers were introduced by friends or family. Their respective guardians played a role in this respect (see Chapter 6) and Mary's mother Maria may have introduced her to a number of retailers, making purchases with the haberdasher Mary Kirkpatrick and the glover Joseph Pollard, both of whom were subsequently patronized by Mary.[53] More often, it seems that Edward and Mary exchanged information about suppliers, transmitting knowledge, trust, and repu-tation. The flow of information usually went from Edward to Mary, the latter using tradesmen initially patronized by her brother. At one level, we see William Butler twice supplying livery to Edward before Mary began using him in 1787.[54] More telling, perhaps, when undertaking some small changes to the furnishings of her rooms in London in 1768, Mary turned to Thomas and Gilbert Burnett, the upholsterers who played such a large part in the refurbishment of Stoneleigh Abbey three years earlier. That they were willing to execute such a modest order may reflect the importance of her brother's patronage.[55] Much the same appears true of coaches: Mary followed Edward's lead in going to the same coachmaker, John Hatchett of Long Acre, that he had used in 1771, first to purchase a new coach (1794) and later to have it repaired (1799).[56] As we have seen, Edward spent a lot of money on books in his quest to amass a library befitting a gentleman. Mary was far less of a bibliophile, but again followed Edward's judgement on booksellers, making a small purchase from James Robson—an important bookseller who sup-plied over £400 worth of books to Edward between 1766 and 1768.[57] Perhaps

[52] WRO, CR136/V/136, Account book, entries for the 1760s and 1770s.
[53] SCLA, DR18/5/1929 and DR18/5/3145 (Kirkpatrick); DR185/5/1955 and DR18/5/3757 (Pollard).
[54] SCLA, DR18/5/4657, DR18/5/5062.   [55] SCLA, DR18/5/4620; DR18/3/47/52/15.
[56] SCLA, DR18/5/6054, DR18/5/6446.
[57] SCLA, DR18/5/5000 (Mary's purchase). For examples of Edward's purchases from Robson, see DR18/5/4529.

most striking is the way in which both Edward and Mary drew on two generations of the Fells to provide tailoring and livery from the 1760s to the early 1800s. In some ways, these introductions are unsurprising, especially as many of these goods were often seen as lying in the realm of male spending.[58] Edward's familiarity with these areas of spending put him in a position to provide a personal link to reliable and trustworthy tradesmen.

On other occasions, Mary took the lead, especially when it came to buying textiles and clothing. In 1763 and 1768 Edward made purchases of material from the drapers, Carr, Ibbetson, Bigge, & Pickard, a supplier that Mary had begun using in 1754 and to whom she remained loyal through to the early 1770s.[59] Similarly he made four purchases from Budd and Devall, milliners in Bruton Street, London, following Mary's initial purchase of ribbons and muslin in 1760.[60] In the 1760s they both used Jordan Heyland Biggar, a draper in Leadenhall Street. Again, Mary had made the first contact, in 1762, when she was billed for linen to the value of £1 1s. 8d. Probably on her recommendation, Edward looked to these suppliers when placing a much larger order (worth over £128) for a variety of table and furnishing linens the following year.[61] The lines of communication in operation here resemble those described by Walsh and others, who have demonstrated how provincial elites frequently drew on knowledgeable friends in convenient locations (most often London) to provide information about goods and suppliers, and sometimes to acquire specific items.[62] Mary did this on occasions, a letter from Edward's steward, Samuel Butler, recording the reimbursement of 40 guineas for 'the china sent down to Stoneleigh', and the auditors accounts noting payments to her for books paid for in London, including the 'Baronagium Genealogium'.[63] In this light, we can see Edward drawing on Mary as an experienced metropolitan shopper with first-hand knowledge of retailers and goods.

These common suppliers confirm that Edward and Mary shared information, probably both in terms of quality and reliability, and thus defined *together* the relationships of the Leigh family with their suppliers. Such choices were personal and individual, and to some extent gendered along conventional lines, but they were also embedded in family relationships and in understandings of character and credit. The importance of family in this respect is made clear by the behaviour of Sabine Winn. Rarely leaving Nostell Priory after the birth of her first child, and estranged from her husband's sisters and aunts through disputes over money, she was reduced to combing the newspapers for advertisements in order to identify suppliers appropriate to her needs—which often meant retailers from France or

---

[58] Vickery, *Behind Closed Doors*, 113–26; Hussey, 'Guns, horses and stylish waistcoats?'. See also Chapter 4.

[59] For example, SCLA, DR18/5/4035, DR18/5/4661.

[60] SCLA, DR18/5/3970, DR18/5/4126, DR18/5/4139, DR18/5/4511.

[61] SCLA, DR18/5/3960, DR18/5/4028.

[62] Walsh, 'Shops, shopping'; Vickery, *Gentleman's Daughter*, 168–9.

[63] SCLA, DR18/17/27/101, Letter, 25 March 1764; SCLA, DR18/31/461, Auditor's accounts, entry for 1 July 1766.

those able to supply French goods. Here, reputation was judged through the language of advertising and the lists of goods and services provided.[64]

Reputation and trust were also built through and manifest in the financial credit extended to the Leighs and Newdigates by their respective suppliers—credit which drew the aristocracy into what Fontaine styles an urban mercantile credit system.[65] Credit was central to the operation of business in the eighteenth century; it created great anxiety and considerable amounts of work for shopkeepers, who had to judge the character and creditworthiness of customers, manage accounts and vary credit extended against payments received, and expend time collecting in debts when they came due.[66] The slowness and reluctance of wealthy and especially aristocratic customers to pay artisans' and shopkeepers' bills is a leitmotif of analyses of elite consumption across Europe.[67] In this, the English elite was no exception. Lord Harvey, for example, was a very poor payer, not just of tradesmen, but also his servants, whose wages were often years in arrears.[68] Further down the social scale, Parson Woodforde enjoyed long periods of credit with his suppliers, settling his accounts every December. He took great offence at those who presumed to press him for payment before this date, viewing this as a breach of trust and an attempt to undermine his standing. His recourse was to abuse them in his diaries and refuse to place any further orders with them.[69] However, Elizabeth Purefoy operated in a completely different manner, assiduously asking tradesmen to present their bills along with the goods being supplied and paying promptly, often within a few days or weeks. Her reasons for doing so were made explicit in a letter to the London grocer Wilson: 'I always pay you as ready money because Mr Cossins [Wilson's predecessor] told mee [*sic*] I should be better used for doing so'.[70]

The bills presented to the Leighs reveal three broad types of credit arrangements and thus three different kinds of relationship with suppliers. First, and most straightforward, were bills for single transactions. These were presented by a wide variety of tradesmen, from grocers and mercers to cabinetmakers and stuccoists, and were most common amongst irregular or one-off suppliers. Here, the period of credit was often relatively short and the relationship between tradesmen and customer less strong, each transaction being self-contained and time-limited. For example, in May and June 1767, Edward, fifth Lord Leigh, purchased four wigs from J. Gaest and paid the bill on 15 June; twenty-five years later, Storer and Fisher supplied drapery for the funeral of William Oxlade (a long-standing servant) on

---

[64] Bristol, 'Between the exotic and the everyday'.

[65] Fontaine, *Moral Economy*, esp. 95–127.

[66] For examples of shopkeepers' concerns about credit, see W. Stout, *Autobiography of William Stout of Lancaster, 1665–1752* (Manchester, 1967), 96–120; W. Sachse (ed.), *Diary of Roger Lowe of Ashton in Makerfield, Lancashire, 1663–74* (London, 1938), *passim*. For discussion of managing credit, see Cox, *Complete Tradesman*, 163–96; Stobart, *Sugar and Spice*, 150–7.

[67] See, for example, N. Coquery, *Tenir boutique à paris au XVIIIe siècle: Luxe et demi-luxe* (Paris, 2011), 211–60; Ilmakunnas, 'Luxury shopping experience', 124–5; Fontaine, *Moral Economy*, 70–94.

[68] P. Edwards, 'Decline of an aristocratic stud: Edward, Lord Harley's stud at Welbeck 1721–1729', *Economic History Review* (forthcoming).

[69] See Finn, *Character of Credit*, 96.   [70] Eland, *Purefoy Letters*, no.104.

18 May 1792 and their bill was paid on 30 June.[71] Second, and most common, were consolidated but occasional bills for goods supplied over a period of time and often settled only after a considerable delay. Extreme examples are the bills for furniture, upholstery, and wallpapers presented by Burnett, Gomm, & Co. and Bromwich and Leigh. These itemize goods and services mostly supplied between May 1763 and July 1764, albeit in fulfilling a single order, and were only finally settled in December 1765. Similarly, the silversmiths Gilpin and Makepeace both presented consolidated bills, as did the draper William Fell and the coachmaker James Cope. If not regular suppliers, these were people to whom the Leighs returned on a number of occasions, the consolidated bills representing strong and mutual ties of commercial credit. Finally, there were retailers and craftsmen with whom the Leighs had regular accounts, often over a number of years. These were mostly for lower-order goods and services, including groceries, meat, carpentry, and saddlery, but also personal services, such as tailoring, and even more costly items such as books. For example, Mary Leigh ran quarterly accounts with several Kensington retailers, including the butcher Roger Buckmaster, the coal merchant Samuel Kingston, and the chandler James Wheble.[72] These were the type of tradesmen who might be referred to as 'my butcher', 'my tailor', or 'my bookseller', much as Henry Prescott did in early eighteenth-century Chester.[73] Whilst the sources are not able to reveal this kind of familiarity, it is apparent that this was the type of stable relationship that Mary in particular had with many of her suppliers.

As with many other wealthy customers, the Leighs often took a further period of credit by delaying payment of the bill once it was presented. These delays could be extremely long. James Cope the coachmaker presented a consolidated bill for £255 6s. on or shortly after 27 June 1764 which included £130 for a new crane-neck chariot for Edward, fifth Lord Leigh, and £90 for a post coach for Mary. In February 1765, he received £100 on account, but had to wait until August for the balance to be paid. Even Josiah Wedgwood, who made much of dealing only in ready money, had to wait from 5 September 1786 to 15 January 1787 to receive payment for a large consignment of Greek Border china he had supplied to Mary.[74] Whilst Muldrew suggests that unpaid debts might create doubt about trust, there is no evidence that the relationship between the Leighs and their suppliers suffered in this way: their credit remained strong, despite delays in payment.[75] Indeed, it might be argued that the aristocracy were above such doubts or at least that their character was far less fluid than that of other consumers: their rank served as a bulwark against the doubts that assailed most consumers.[76] Certainly, there is little evidence that retailers tried to restrict credit or purchases in the manner often seen with less wealthy customers who failed to maintain their

---

[71] SCLA, DR18/5/4559; DR18/5/5975.

[72] For fuller discussion of these arrangements, see Stobart, 'So agreeable and suitable a place'.

[73] J. Addy and P. McGiven (eds), 'The diary of Henry Prescott, Vol.II', *Records Society of Lancashire and Cheshire*, 132 (1994), *passim*.

[74] SCLA, DR18/5/4350, DR18/5/5684.

[75] See Muldrew, *Economy of Obligation*, 173–95.

[76] Finn, *Character of Credit*, 102–3.

accounts.[77] That said, Sir Roger Newdigate was sufficiently alarmed by receiving a writ for an outstanding debt owed to his late coachmaker, Mr Leader, that he dashed off two hasty letters to his lawyers, instructing them to pay the debt with all speed. He noted that the bill was for:

> some small articles in preceding years, for which they never thought it worth while before to send a bill. The rest is an enormous charge for a very plain chaise & harness for four horses, which I do not believe any Jury would allow two thirds, but I do not think it worth my while to contest.[78]

Part of the reason for not quibbling over the sum is Newdigate's evident concern that this 'ill usage', as he described it, would undermine his honour.

One mechanism that provided security for both tradesman and customer was to make regular payments against substantial orders. Burnett's 1765 bill reveals not just the accumulation of goods supplied, but also a series of payments being made by Edward Leigh. Indeed, by the time the final bill was presented, there was a balance of just £652 16s. 3d. from a total of £3,383 3s. 5½d. The auditors' accounts drawn up in 1774 reveal similar arrangements with other tradesmen, including Gomm, Bromwich, Cope, and Gilpin, and demonstrate that even wealthy customers were drawn into close and mutual credit relationships with their most important suppliers.[79] But to what extent did those suppliers influence the character of the goods being chosen? This question is important, as it lies at the heart of arguments that the elite were qualitatively different from other consumers in that they possessed distinct and distinguishing notions of taste—something which drew them together as a coherent group, united across national boundaries, but distinct in social terms. It will be explored by looking at the relationship with four sets of professionals and tradesmen: architects; furniture makers, upholsterers, and wallpaper merchants; booksellers; and grocers and tea dealers.

MAKING AND SHAPING TASTE: THE ROLE OF SUPPLIERS

As Wilson and Mackley make clear, architects both reflected and shaped the taste of their patrons.[80] Sir Roger Newdigate was undoubtedly the prime moving force behind the Gothicization of Arbury Hall, but he drew on the advice and expertise of friends and a range of professionals. Amongst the latter, Henry Keene was particularly important in giving the changes greater historical authenticity. Keene was Surveyor to Westminster Abbey and the links between his two roles are clear from the drawings and casts he provided of monuments in the Abbey; in the decoration of the Parlour, which drew inspiration from Henry VII's chapel; and in the vaulting

---

[77] D. Alexander, *Retailing in England during the Industrial Revolution* (London, 1970), 174–85; Stobart, *Sugar and Spice*,154–5.

[78] WRO, CR136/B/2627[1], Letter, 20 May 1799. See also CR136/B2627[2], Letter, 10 June 1799.

[79] SCLA, DR18/31/461, Auditor's accounts.

[80] Wilson and Mackley, *Building of the English Country House*, 109–45. See also Vickery, *Behind Closed Doors*, 156–7.

Figure 7.1. The Saloon at Arbury Hall (1786–95), for which Henry Couchman provided sketches; a Gothic stove, possibly that provided by Oldham and Oldham of the Patent Stove Warehouse in Holborn can be seen in the background.
Reproduced by kind permission of Viscount Daventry.

in the Hall. Following Keene's death in 1776, Sir Roger turned to Henry Couchman, who had been clerk of the works at Packington Hall in Warwickshire. He also made sketches at Westminster Abbey and oversaw the initial remodelling of the Saloon (Figure 7.1).[81] The extent to which either of these men shaped the vision for Arbury Hall is unclear: in some ways, the building developed organically, with changes in emphasis apparently driven by the owner rather than his architects. And it was Sir Roger who provided the thread of continuity, work beginning before either had been engaged (see Chapter 2) and continuing after Couchman was dismissed in 1789 for being 'very unreasonable' about money.[82] He also provided many of

[81] See Nares, 'Arbury Hall', 1129, 1210–13, 1415–16.
[82] Tyack, *Warwickshire Country Houses*, 14.

the designs, using his architects to provide decorative detail, oversee the work, and, to some extent, manage the craftsmen who carried out the work. Sir Roger even drew designs for Gothic stoves for several rooms, initially ordered from Bent & Son and subsequently from the Patent Stove Warehouse in Holborn.[83]

Such pronounced and direct involvement on the part of the owner was unusual and reflects Newdigate's character as well as his deep interest in and knowledge of both Gothic and classical architecture. Arrangements at Stoneleigh Abbey were more typical, with the architect playing a more prominent role. The vast west range, built for Edward, third Lord Leigh, was designed and executed by Francis Smith, the leading architect-builder in the Midlands during the early eighteenth century. He was dismissed by some contemporaries because of 'a great sameness in the plans, which proves he had but little Invention', but he was capable of building in a wide variety of styles, perhaps, as Colvin argues, in response to his employers' tastes.[84] This may have been the case at Stoneleigh, but the evidence is equivocal: Edward clearly thought well enough of his architect to commission a painting of him which still hangs in the house today; yet the lack of urgency shown in completing the interiors beyond the Great Apartment and some of the other principal rooms suggests a degree of indifference on Edward's part. Despite this, it is clear that the west range was largely designed and built by Smith, and many of the craftsmen who executed the work were assembled by and had worked with Smith at other houses.[85] Trust in the workmanship was thus delegated to the architect, who, to judge from the absence of separate bills, may also have been responsible for contracting and paying these workmen.

After the death of both patron and architect, responsibility for completing the west range passed between various hands without a stable relationship being established. Stuccowork was undertaken in the chapel by John Wright in the 1740s and on the main staircase by his pupil and successor Robert Moore in the 1760s, but neither had a wider remit. Francis Smith's son William was commissioned to draw up plans for the Great Hall and William Hiorn completed a number of fireplaces for the west range, but again both had limited influence. Indeed, Edward, fifth Lord Leigh, doubted his integrity: a note in his own hand on a bill from 1764 reads 'Mr Hiorn, You are acquainted that my servants are never allow'd to take any money as vails, acknowledgements, or presents. Upon discovery of bribes both tradesman & servant will be turn'd off.'[86] This breach of trust was compounded by doubts over the quality of his workmanship; he was not deemed up to the task of making the best chimney pieces, the work being given instead to the London

---

[83] WRO, CR136/B/2635a, Letter from Bent & Sons, 1 February 1799; CR136/B/3048/a–g, Letters from Oldham & Oldham, 19 June 1801 to 8 December 1802.

[84] H. Colvin, *A Biographical Dictionary of British Architects 1600–1840*, 3rd ed. (New Haven, CT, 1995), 882–90. The quote is from the late eighteenth-century antiquarian, Daines Barrington (Colvin, *British Architects*, 883). For a more generous and much fuller view of his work, see Gomme, *Smith of Warwick*.

[85] Gomme, 'Abbey into palace', 83–4.

[86] SCLA, DR158/5/4192. In a note written the same day, Edward had given exactly the same warning to the carpenter Robert Keene—see SCLA, DR18/5/4191.

carver, Devereux Fox.[87] By this time, oversight of decorating and furnishing had passed to Timothy Lightoler, an accomplished architect, author of *The Gentleman and Farmer's Architect* (1764) and co-author of *The Modern Builder's Assistant* (1757), who had moved to Warwick in 1750. At Stoneleigh Abbey, he was responsible for many of the improvements both in the house, presenting designs for several of the principal rooms, and in the kitchen garden, stables, and 'other offices'.[88] His influence went further: the two chimney pieces in the hall, made by Bastard and Fox, were to his design (Figure 4.2), as was a rococo altar table for the chapel. He also placed an order on Edward's behalf for architectural books with Robert Sayer of London.[89] Here we have the kind of influence described by Wilson and Mackley, and yet this power was circumscribed by his employer's own tastes and desires: none of Lightoler's decorative schemes were adopted in full, although elements of several can be found on the staircase and in the hall, and an undated memorandum written by Edward himself notes that the study should be decorated 'according to Mr Lightoler's plan'.[90] There are hints of the Hercules story in one of Lightoler's drawings for the hall, but there was quite clearly a dramatic shift in terms of how the scheme would be executed as well as its scale.[91] Perhaps Edward himself was responsible for this change? He was certainly well versed in architecture and purchased a wide range of books on the subject, both practical and decorative, and he was capable of producing detailed architectural drawings (see Chapter 4).

There were others besides Edward whose voices and work put limits on Lightoler's influence. We have seen in Chapter 6 that the steward, Samuel Butler, had reservations about the cost of the architect's designs which may have resulted in their remaining unrealized.[92] More important, perhaps, was the impact of the tradesmen charged with refurbishing the west range. Leading furniture makers and upholsterers are often seen as playing a key role as tastemakers. In Paris, the best craftsmen and retailers wielded considerable influence: the most famous *marchands de modes* not only played a central role in remoulding the luxury trade around ideas of fashion, including the complex integration and blending of oriental and European styles, but they were also able to choose their clientele. Both directly and indirectly, then, they shaped taste and the nature of goods being bought.[93] In Britain, the direct influence which men like Chippendale, Hepplewhite, and Sheraton had on the purchases made by their patrons was magnified through the widespread copying of the designs published in their *Directors* and *Guides*.[94]

---

[87] SCLA, DR18/5/4176, DR18/5/4203. See also Gomme, 'Abbey into palace', 99–101.

[88] SCLA, DR671/33, Designs for Stoneleigh Abbey. See also Gome, 'Abbey into Palace'.

[89] SCLA, DR18/5/4203, DR18/5/4408, DR18/5/4209, DR671/33, Designs for Stoneleigh Abbey. Gomme, 'Abbey into palace', 97.

[90] SCLA, DR18/3/47/52/12, Memorandum, no date, c.1763.

[91] Gomme, 'Abbey into Palace', 105–14.

[92] SCLA, DR18/17/27/97, Letter, 11 February 1764.

[93] D. Goodman, 'Furnishing discourses: readings of a writing desk in eighteenth-century France', in M. Berg and E. Eger (eds), *Luxury in the Eighteenth Century. Debates, Desires and Delectable Goods* (Basingstoke, 2003), 71–88; Sargentson, *Merchants and Luxury Markets*, 44–97; N. Coquery, *L'Hôtel aristocratique: Le Marché du luxe à Paris au XIIIᵉ siècle* (Paris, 1998).

[94] See Cornforth, *Early Georgian Interiors*, 135–88; Beard, *Upholsterers*, 161–3, 223–5, 257–8; Edwards, *Turning Houses into Homes*, 38–74.

At Stoneleigh Abbey, the individuals engaged were a notch or two down from these national figures, but nonetheless were important metropolitan craftsmen who supplied a range of aristocratic properties. Perhaps most famous was Thomas Bromwich, one of leading wallpaper merchants of the middle decades of the eighteenth century.[95] He supplied Horace Walpole with wallpapers for Strawberry Hill in the 1750s and is recorded in the 1760s as having showrooms on Ludgate Hill. These became important venues for selecting wallpapers. Walpole's friend, the poet John Gray, wrote in the autumn of 1761 that he had unsuccessfully rummaged Bromwich's shop for Gothic wallpapers to his taste, although he returned a week later and bought various papers, describing in detail the range of Gothic, flock, and stucco papers available.[96] By this time Bromwich's papers were found in many country houses. Lybbe Powys noted his work at Fawley Court in Buckinghamshire, writing in 1771 that 'On the left hand of the saloon is a large billiard room hung with the most beautiful pink India paper, adorn'd with very good prints, the borders cut out and the ornaments put on with great taste by Bromwich.'[97] At Stoneleigh, he hung two bedchambers with 'Indian Taffaty paper' and 'Indian Birds and Flowers' along with painted papier-mâché borders; in the bedchamber of Mary Leigh there were seventeen 'Indian pictures in Party gold frames' and a total of 343 feet of papier-mâché borders, and for Edward's own room, Bromwich supplied '147 yards of painted paper to match a Chintz' that was being used for the bed hangings.[98] He thus drew Stoneleigh Abbey into the wider taste for chinoiserie that characterized many elite houses across Britain and Europe, the French being particularly fond of Chinese styles.[99] However, the prices charged for these papers suggest that, with the exception of the pictures in Mary Leigh's room, they were probably English or French rather than genuinely Chinese.[100] Moreover, most of the twenty-nine rooms itemized in his bill were furnished with less exotic styles: 'mock embossed', 'stucco', 'ground stucco', 'sprig', or 'embossed', all in keeping with established taste at this time and linking these interiors to a more conventional European material culture (Figure 7.2).[101] It is telling that these transnational cultures were accessed and filtered through a London merchant—the Leighs had no direct connections with East India traders or European markets.

The furniture maker William Gomm was less a prominent craftsman, but one with strong European connections. He had opened his workshops and showroom in Clerkenwell Close in 1736 and had close dealings with the German cabinet-maker Abraham Roentgen, who visited London in the 1730s to work with some

---

[95] A. Sugden and J. Edmundson, *A History of English Wallpaper, 1509–1914* (London, 1926), 73–86; G. Beard and C. Gilbert (eds) *Dictionary of English Furniture Makers, 1660–1840* (Leeds, 1986), 110.

[96] Sugden and Edmundson, *English Wallpaper*, 79.

[97] Climenson, *Diaries of Lybbe Powys* (1771), 147.

[98] SCLA, DR18/5/4402.   [99] De Bruijn, 'Consuming East Asia'.

[100] French chinoiserie papers could be bought for as little as 4 shillings per yard by 1749; Chinese papers might be as much as 63 shillings for a single panel—see Kennedy Johnson, 'Taste for bringing the outside in', 122–3.

[101] See Sugden and Edmundson, *English Wallpaper*; Vickery, *Behind Closed Doors*, 166–83.

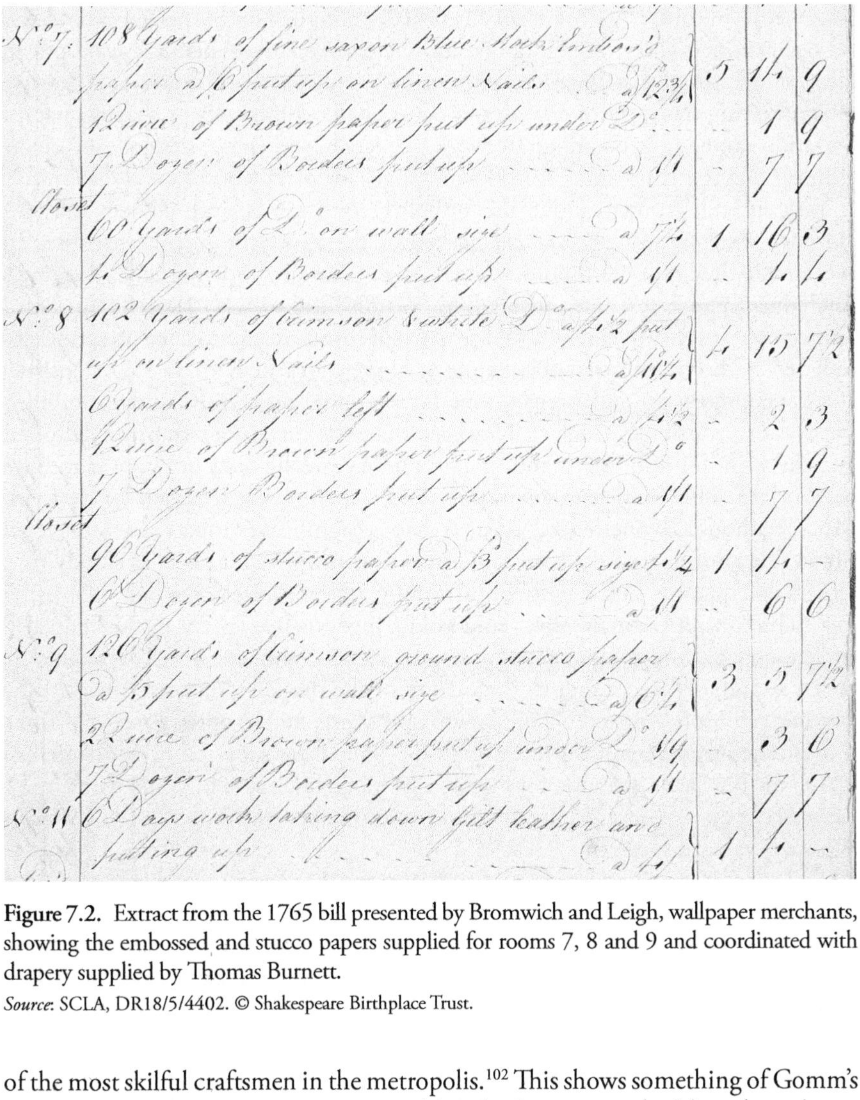

Figure 7.2. Extract from the 1765 bill presented by Bromwich and Leigh, wallpaper merchants, showing the embossed and stucco papers supplied for rooms 7, 8 and 9 and coordinated with drapery supplied by Thomas Burnett.

Source: SCLA, DR18/5/4402. © Shakespeare Birthplace Trust.

of the most skilful craftsmen in the metropolis.[102] This shows something of Gomm's reputation amongst contemporaries and he clearly prospered, although we know relatively little about his other commissions beyond sales to Richard Hoare in the 1730s and Sir Richard Worsley in 1778.[103] His work appears to have been heavily influenced by Chippendale, designs believed to be in Gomm's hand showing a strong resemblance to pieces in the *Director*, to which he subscribed in 1754. These included interpretations of Chippendale's Anglicized rococo, plus others in Gothic and Chinese style—broader international influences again coming to Stoneleigh

[102] L. Boynton, 'William and Richard Gomm', *The Burlington Magazine*, 122 (1980), 395. See also Beard and Gilbert, *English Furniture Makers*, 349–50.

[103] Boynton, 'William Gomm', 395–6.

via a mediated route.[104] Most of the furniture he supplied for Stoneleigh Abbey was for bedchambers and dressing rooms, and therefore relatively plain. It also came in fairly standardized sets for each room: a bedstead, chests of drawers, Pembroke table, dressing table, set of chairs, and occasionally commodes or shaving stands. Variation came in the detailing: fretwork cornices or serpentine designs, and chairs with various coverings and Chinese trunk, ogee, or plain feet.[105]

Very little is known about the upholsterers Thomas and Gilbert Burnett, although they were clearly well established by the 1760s. From their premises on the Strand they ran a substantial business, capable of supplying elite customers (including Peter Du Cane and Sir John Griffin Griffin) with large quantities of drapery and soft furnishings, as well as items of furniture and a range of upholstery services.[106] Thomas Burnett spent time at Stoneleigh Abbey in 1763, or possibly 1762, making notes and preparations for the large order subsequently fulfilled for Edward, fifth Lord Leigh.[107] However, once the furniture was being delivered and the work on upholstery and drapery under way, he does not appear to have been on site often and perhaps not at all, the work being overseen by his man, Mr Greenhouse. Nonetheless, Burnett had a significant impact on Stoneleigh Abbey. He coordinated the work of Gomm and Bromwich as well as supplying a remarkable quantity and quality of furnishing fabrics himself, the highlight being the 'rich crimson Genoan velvet' and gold fringe for seat covers in the chapel,[108] and he oversaw the construction of a series of bedchambers which were colour-coded and graded according to the quality of the drapery: Yellow Damask, Blue Morine, Crimson Worsted Damask, Wrought Work, and so on (Figure 7.3). These colour schemes were continued through the wallpapers supplied by Bromwich so that in the Blue Morine room, for instance, he hung 'fine saxon blue and white mock embossed' paper, whilst 'crimson ground stucco paper' was hung in the Crimson Worsted Damask room.[109]

This coordination and standardization suggests that Lord Leigh had opted for a series of standard types rather than impressing his own taste on every room. This would make a great deal of sense when furnishing a large number of bedrooms all at once, allowing work to progress quickly and yet giving each room a slightly different identity. But who was responsible for devising this decorative scheme? The obvious candidate is Thomas Burnett. We know that upholsterers produced such schemes elsewhere, Abner Scholes going a stage further and arranging his showroom in Chester into a series of 'rooms' comprising coordinated suites of furniture.[110] Moreover, Burnett was involved at Stoneleigh from an early stage: his 'Memorandum about furniture for the Rooms' is sketchy in detail and clearly

---

[104] The designs are held at the Henry Francis du Pont Winterthur Museum in Delaware, USA. See Boynton, 'William Gomm', 396.

[105] SCLA, DR18/5/4408.

[106] Beard and Gilbert, *English Furniture Makers*, 131–2.

[107] SCLA, DR18/3/47/52/14, Mr Burnett's Memorandum, no date; DR18/4/43, Inventory, 1774, with 1806 amendments.

[108] SCLA, DR18/3/47/52/15.   [109] SCLA, DR18/5/4402.

[110] CCA, WS Abner Scholes, 1736. See also Stobart, Hann, and Morgan, *Spaces of Consumption*, 128–9.

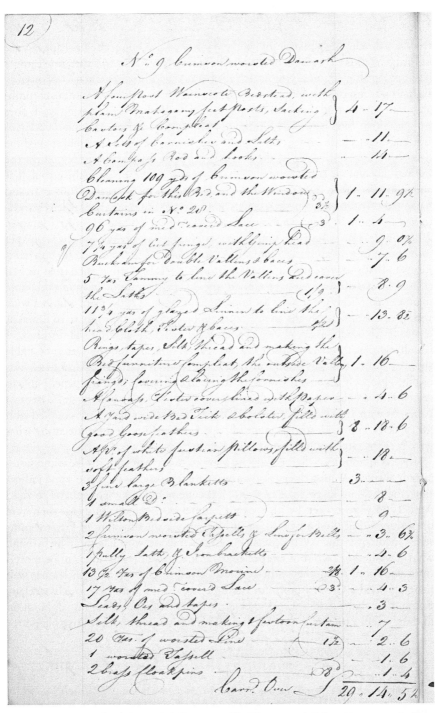

Nº 9 Crimson worsted Damask

	£	s	d
A four post Wainscote Bedstead, with plain Mahogany feet Posts, Sacking, Castors & Compleat	4	17	—
A Set of Cornishes and Laths	—	11	—
A Compass Rod and hooks	—	14	—
Cleaning 109 yds of Crimson worsted Damask for this Bed and the Window Curtains in Nº 28	1	11	9½
96 yds of med covered Lace	1	4	
7½ yds of cut fringe, with Gimp head	—	9	0½
Buckram for Double Vallens & laces	—	7	6
5 Yds Tammy to line the Vallens and cover the Laths	—	8	9
11¾ yds of glazed Linnen to line the head Cloth, Tester & laces	—	13	8½
Rings, tapes, Silk, thread and making the Bed furniture Compleat, the outside Vally fringe, Covering & lacing the Cornishes	1	16	—
A Canvass, Tester cover lined with Paper	—	4	6
A Yard wide Bed Tick & bolster, filled with good Goose feathers	2	18	6
A pr of white fustian pillows, filled with soft feathers	—	18	—
3 fine large Blanketts	3	—	—
1 small Do	—	8	
1 Wilton Bedside Carpett	—	9	
2 Crimson worsted Tassells & Line for Bells	—	3	6½
1 pully Lath, & Iron bracketts	—	4	6
13½ Yds of Crimson Moreen	1	16	—
17 Yds of med covered Lace	—	4	3
Leads, Oss and tapes	—	3	—
Silk, thread and making 1 festoon Curtain	—	7	
20 Yds of worsted Line	—	2	6
1 worsted Tassell	—	1	6
2 brass Cloak pins	—	1	4
Carried Over	29	14	5½

Figure 7.3. Extract from the 1765 bill presented by Thomas and Gilbert Burnett, upholsterers, showing the furniture and drapery supplied for room 9, coordinated with wallpaper supplied by Bromwich and Leigh.

Source: SCLA, DR18/5/4402. © Shakespeare Birthplace Trust.

records a developing situation in which many decisions about the final appearance of various rooms were still to be made. And it clearly predates by some time Butler's letter of April 1763 specifying which furniture could be dispatched.[111] Moreover, Burnett was responsible for communicating with Bromwich and Gomm and probably for coordinating their combined efforts.[112] However, coordinating work does not mean that Burnett was responsible for drawing up or even advising on designs. Indeed, there is little evidence to suggest that it was Burnett's taste that shaped the decoration and furnishing of the house.[113] In part, this might simply reflect the limited amount of correspondence that survives in the Leigh archive, but it is apparent that other craftsmen present at Stoneleigh in the early 1760s may also have had an influence on the designs for its refurbishment. Bromwich is mentioned by name in a memorandum dated 13 April 1763 and again in a letter of 27 April.[114] More telling, the same memorandum includes notes on the wallpaper to be hung in several of the rooms, the nature and colour of which broadly conforms to that subsequently supplied by Bromwich. It is possible, then, that he had offered advice on the most appropriate papers for each room in much the same manner that Vickery notes for Trollope & Sons in the 1790s, from whom a wide variety of customers sought advice on the type of papers appropriate to different rooms.[115] That said, as Bromwich's papers were matched with the bed furniture, it is unlikely that they were chosen first; so again it appears that this was a reputable supplier rather than an arbiter of taste. Indeed, it is likely that Bromwich was engaged precisely because he was a trusted source of fashionable wallpapers, able to match a broad suggestion of style or colour to a particular quality and design of paper. As with Trollope & Sons, his reputation for serving the gentry, coupled with his capacity to provide a wide range of papers, made him ideal for executing what were perhaps rather vaguely conceived designs.

The key question is whether Edward went to these men with his ideas and tastes already formed. Whilst categorical answers are impossible, there are some indications that Edward knew what he wanted: the memoranda in September 1762 and April 1763 were written by his steward Samuel Butler, indicating that they were drawn up within the household, most likely under the direction of Edward himself.[116] Moreover, the level of detail suggests someone who has thought through what is wanted in each room, especially as it includes notes on items to be moved from one room to another—the bedstead, window curtain, and gilt leather wall hangings in the Green Room, for example, were to be removed to Miss Leigh's Room. Elsewhere, details were sketchier: Burnett's memorandum noted 'Nothing fix'd on yet' in a total of ten rooms and Edward's own memoranda leave blanks for

---

[111] SCLA, DR18/3/47/52/14, Mr Burnett's Memorandum, no date.

[112] See, for example, SCLA, DR18/17/27/82, Letter, 27 September 1763, and DR18/17/27/84, Letter, 13 October 1763.

[113] On this role, see Edwards, *Turning Houses into Homes*, 38–74; Beard, *Upholsterers, passim*.

[114] SCLA, DR18/3/47/52/7, Memorandum, 13 April 1763; DR18/17/27/75, Letter, 27 April 1763.

[115] Vickery, *Behind Closed Doors*, 166–85.

[116] SCLA, DR18/3/47/52/6, Memorandum, September 1762, DR18/3/47/52/7, Memorandum, 13 April 1763. Burnett's notes are in a different hand—one that resembles that of his subsequent bill.

several rooms, especially on the attic storey.[117] This is perhaps unsurprising for what were working documents, rather than blueprints for all the improvements that were being planned, but the size and comprehensive nature of the orders being fulfilled by Burnett, Gomm, and Bromwich suggest that much of the detail was probably left up to the discretion of these trusted and reputable suppliers.

Trust in the judgement of craftsmen and suppliers was a key aspect of the relationship between them and their wealthy customers. At its foundation was the professional reputation of the tradesman, built on their training, perhaps through apprenticeship, and their experience and knowledge of the goods and ideas which they purveyed. In this sense, their attributes were akin to those of the gentlemen-scientists discussed by Shapin: integrity, credibility, and knowledge.[118] It was not simply goods that came from these tradesmen, but also an understanding of what was tasteful, appropriate, and practical. This is seen in the correspondence between Sir Roger Newdigate and the two London companies supplying him with Gothic stoves. Bent & Son wrote in 1799 with practical advice: 'we beg leave to submit that the ornaments would not be better of Teautenague [i.e. zinc] than Sheffield Plate & infinitely more durable'. Two years later, Oldham & Oldham were more concerned with taste and workmanship, writing to Sir Roger that 'the stove has been very much admired by different customers who have seen it in our warehouse and, though we cannot take any praise to ourselves in respect to the design, yet on account of the workmanship we hope to come in for our share'.[119] In both cases, there was deference to Newdigate's taste, but confidence in their knowledge and skills as craftsmen.

Many of the same qualities were on show in the relationship between Newdigate and metropolitan booksellers. He patronized many, but relied heavily on a handful of favoured booksellers, as did Edward, fifth Lord Leigh, who focused 90 per cent of his spending on just four men: James Fletcher, Thomas Payne, Paul Vaillant, and James Robson. These London tradesmen were particularly important in the supply of high-quality, foreign, and rare books (see Chapter 4). Buying this kind of book required more than a deep purse: it also involved the collector knowing what he wanted and having the right connections through which to realize his desires. Trust and reputation were again crucial, but the relative importance of the two varied from one bookseller to another. Trust was most evident in the long-term relationships built up with certain tradesmen, the patronage of whom fits Berry's suggestion that elite choices of supplier were predicated on personal acquaintance and credit.[120] James Fletcher, Thomas Payne, James Robson, John Shuckburgh, Thomas Cadell, and Benjamin White all fit into this category; but several of them had other merits that attracted wealthy bibliophiles. Payne's shop was a well-known focus for the metropolitan literati, the conviviality of which underlined his reputation as a

---

[117] SCLA, DR18/3/47/52/14, Mr Burnett's Memorandum, no date; DR18/3/47/52/7, Memorandum, 13 April 1763.

[118] Shapin, *Social History of Truth*, chapter 3.

[119] WRO, CR136/B/2635a, Letter from Bent & Sons, 1 February 1799; CR136/B3048b, Letter from Oldham & Oldham, 17 December 1801.

[120] Berry, 'Prudent luxury', 146.

well-connected and reliable tradesman. Much the same was true of Thomas Cadell, who, in addition to possessing about one quarter of copyrights owned by British booksellers, had a successful partnership with the printer William Strahan and a shop on the Strand which was a place to see and be seen in. James Robson, meanwhile enjoyed a reputation as a 'gregarious and learned bibliophile'.[121] In these shops, reputation and trusted familiarity combined to engender long-term relationships with both Leigh and Newdigate. The position with Paul Vaillant was rather different. Edward Leigh bought books from him on just two occasions, but acquired some very impressive and costly foreign books at a total of £217 9s.[122] Vaillant was of Huguenot extraction and, in addition to being magistrate and master of the London Stationers' Company, had excellent contacts with Europe. His status and networks were undoubtedly important in attracting Edward to his shop and making substantial purchases. Here reputation (and stock) trumped familiarity, not least because Vaillant was able to supply rare European books, of the type often acquired by Grand Tourists. Again, then, we have Lord Leigh accessing European goods and cultures of consumption via London tradesmen.[123]

In part, this relates to the nature of books as collectibles: particular volumes had to be sought out, which reinforced the need for a trusted bookseller who could access desirable volumes at the right price and quality, or they had to be acquired when the opportunity arose.[124] Ramsay notes that books sales were especially important in this regard, particularly when the library of an important collector came up for sale.[125] Auctions were often significant social events, but Sir Roger and Edward Leigh engaged booksellers to buy on their behalf rather than attending sales in person. In 1765, for instance, James Fletcher billed Edward for nineteen books 'from the sale', each with its lot number and price carefully noted. Sir Roger, meanwhile, was invoiced by John Shuckburgh for books bought over five days at 'Sir Baylis's Auction' (Figure 7.4).[126] In both instances, the booksellers were trusted to select books unseen by the customer, including a number of costly foreign volumes such as Overbeck's *Les Restes de l'ancienne Rome* and Montfaucon's *Antiquities,* French books which would have been difficult to acquire via other means.[127] From this, it is clear that trusted suppliers were able to anticipate and in some ways shape the taste of their customers. On one occasion, Payne wrote to Lord Leigh that 'I have made bold to send yr Lord^p Dionysius and Juston, they are good copies but if not approved of, shall be taken again. I am so much stuffed up with Books that

[121] J. Raven, *The Business of Books. Booksellers and the English Book Trade, 1450–1850* (New Haven, CT, 2007), 159–60, 189.

[122] SCLA, DR18/5/4202, DR18/5/4307.

[123] This point is made in relation to Edward's book collection in Purcell, 'A lunatick of unsound mind'.

[124] For discussion of the problems that could arise in terms of supply, see P. Beal, '"My books are the great joy of my life." Sir William Boothby, seventeenth-century bibliophile', *Book Collector*, 46/3 (1997), 350–78.

[125] Ramsay, 'English book collectors'. More generally, see R. Myers, M. Harris, and G. Mandelbrooke (eds) *Under the Hammer: Book Auctions since the Seventeenth Century* (New Castle, DE, 2001).

[126] SCLA, DR18/5/4319; WRO, CR136/B/2456a, Receipted bill, 21 May 1749.

[127] WRO, CR136/B/2638a, Receipted bills, various dates.

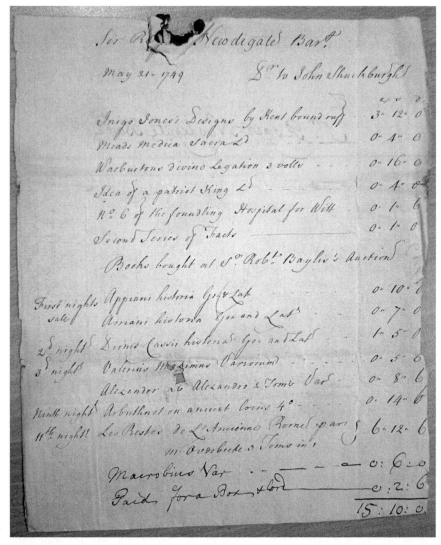

Figure 7.4. Receipted bill presented to Sir Roger Newdigate by John Shuckburgh in 1749, showing purchases at auction.

Source: WRO, CR136/B/2456a. © Warwickshire Record Office.

I am glad to send them out of my way.'[128] Significantly, Payne emphasized the quality of the copies rather than that of the books themselves—it was apparently taken as read that these texts would be worthy additions to Edward's library and the concern was more with their physical appearance.[129]

Although much could be achieved remotely, personal contact with books and people was also important. As with other luxury goods, reliable intermediaries were sometimes engaged, their knowledge and links with suppliers being drawn on to extend a consumer's own networks.[130] For example, Edward Leigh was billed by William Hayes, the Oxford Professor of Music, for books supplied by a certain Mr Warren and for busts from Campione—presumably those subsequently placed in the library at Stoneleigh Abbey.[131] However, both he and Sir Roger Newdigate visited book shops in person. A note attached to Paul Vaillant's bill of October 1764 seeks to explain a discrepancy in the following terms: 'When My Lord chose books at my Shop he took the trouble to enter down in his pocket book the titles & prices of all but One, which he bespoke a day or two afterwards.'[132] This shows that Edward was browsing in Vaillant's shop and perhaps others as well, seeing what was available, noting prices, buying some items, and returning with further orders. It also reveals he was assiduous in noting down prices and was thus able to question the bookseller's bill. Again, the professional knowledge of the tradesman was combined with the taste and judgement of the customer in a relationship of mutual trust and dependence.

Was the same true of those who supplied provisions? Vickery suggests that there was a particularly close relationship between Sir John Hynde Cotton and his wine merchant, recorded in the account book simply—or 'chummily'—as 'Charlie'.[133] Perhaps Cotton was unusual in this regard or maybe this chumminess is more assumed than real: whichever is the case, there is little to suggest this level of familiarity between the Leighs or the Newdigates and their wine merchants, despite the outlay of substantial sums of money. The Gibbards enjoyed a close personal friendship with their London tea merchant, Charles Hancock, who wrote to Mary Gibbard on a number of occasions, both to discuss her order and exchange news of their respective families. He was also entrusted with resolving some of the Gibbards' financial matters in London.[134] This level of familiarity was unusual: such tradesmen were normally valued for their skills and knowledge, rather than their friendship. Knowledge was imparted in many ways, but most often in notes appended to their bills. In this manner Joshua Long informed the Norfolk landowner Sir Martin Foulkes in February 1775 that 'teas are a great deal dearer' and chocolate 'much better' than they had previously been, whilst Wilson, Thornhill, and Wilson perfunctorily noted on their bill to Mary Leigh that 'the season for Prunellas and Gamaroons is now over, we have none that we can recommend & have therefore omitted them'.[135] Writing to Sir Roger Newdigate, William Coplin advised that the present crop of hops was selling 'exceedingly quick at advancing prices' and that 'it will be right for every Consumer to lay in sufficient for at least a

[130] Walsh, 'Shops, shopping'.   [131] SCLA, DR18/5/4517, DR18/5/4542.
[132] SCLA, DR18/5/4202.   [133] Vickery, *Behind Closed Doors*, 114.
[134] Bedfordshire and Luton Archives and Records Service (BLARS), GA93, Letters, 15 January 1824 and 15 September 1827; GA25/35, Letter 21 January 1819. See also Bailey, 'Maintaining status', 23, 51, 58.
[135] NoRO, MC50/23/5—17 February 1775; SCLA, DR18/5/5992.

Year & a half'.[136] However, this was essentially market information rather than an attempt to shape preferences: indeed, the customer's tastes and standards remained paramount. Thus, we see Hancock commending Mary Gibbard on her being 'a lady of excellent taste and judgement and an ornament to the tea table', whilst Richard Twining wrote to Newdigate agreeing to replace a consignment of 6s. souchong with another 'of the finest sort @ 8/-'.[137] The asymmetries of power that existed between tradesmen and their wealthy customers was apparent in all dealings, but appears to have been especially strong with those supplying more mundane goods, and their scope to influence taste was accordingly relatively limited.

CONCLUSIONS

Wealthy landowners were involved in a wide range of different relationships with their suppliers. Some were engaged ad hoc or on a one-off basis, but most were patronized on a number of occasions, sometimes over a long period of time. The balance varied between generations and different types of supplier, and there were diverse arrangements for billing and payment which signalled a similar diversity in relations between supplier and customer. The straightforward emphasis of familiarity through regular patronage identified by Berry was present, but formed just part of a more varied set of relations.[138] Of course, Berry was only looking at a small subsection of elite spending: the complex combination of intensive and extensive networks of supply is to be expected given the wide-ranging consumption that characterized the country house and closely resembles the web of suppliers drawn on by elites elsewhere in Europe.[139] Exploring these relationships in detail has provided fresh insights into the organization of supply to the country house, but also into the nature of trust within commercial relationships in eighteenth-century England. Some supplier relationships were inherited, but others had to be built from scratch—another instance of old and new combining in the country house. In both cases, trust was essential in cementing the bond between tradesman and customer, assuring the former of payment and the latter of good-quality goods and services. Along with everyone else, then, the elite were embroiled in constantly assessing and reassessing reputation and personal character in order to maintain a reliable supply network. They were thus an integral part of Muldrew's economy of obligation, but within this they held a particular and privileged position. One distinction came in terms of their ability to establish trusting relationships via intermediaries and over great distances. To

[136] WRO, CR136/B/2625, Letter from William Coplin, 7 September 1803.

[137] BLA, GA93, Letter, 15 September 1827; WRO, CR136/B/2625, Letter from Richard Twining, 14 February 1803.

[138] Berry, 'Prudent luxury'.

[139] Coquery, *Tenir boutique à Paris*; Ilmakunnas, 'Luxury shopping experience'; Chatenet-Calyste, 'Feminine luxury in Paris'; U. Ijäs, 'Favourites of fortune: the luxury consumption of the Hackmans of Vyborg, 1790–1825', in D. Simonton, M. Kaartinen, and A. Montenach (eds), *Luxury and Gender in European Towns, 1700–1914* (London, 2015), 190–205.

an extent, this removed them from the familiarity and sociability that Muldrew argues lay at the heart of credit relationships; or rather it recast them in epistolary form.[140] Another difference was that the elite customer was almost invariably in control—a reflection of the power relations that came with rank and title. Trusting relationships with tradesmen also helped to shape choices about spending and in some instances the definition and execution of taste. This again reminds us that taste was not forged in isolation, but was made and deployed in negotiation and partnership with others, through sociability with peers and commercial transactions with tradesmen. Here, the status of the seller was important, but so too was the product: choices of furniture, for example, being more influenced by the tradesman than those of groceries. In some ways, this was a consequence of the different order of these goods, groceries perhaps being less important in shaping identity and certainly less costly. However, there is a close parallel between the trust placed in Thomas Burnett to provide tasteful furniture and Richard Twining to provide good-quality tea: failure by either led to rebuke, complaint, and a loss of trust.

Overall, the complex and multilayered character of credit and trust is apparent, but so too is the powerful position held by titled landowners. Their engagement in what Fontaine styles a capitalistic merchant culture of credit was thoroughgoing, and again reveals their engagement with modern modes of consumption; yet they were largely, though not totally, immune from the fluidity of identity that required most people to engage in a constant round of assessing and reassessing personal character and credit.[141] Rank and title were relative constants that anchored their credit and character, despite the shifting sands of contemporary social distinctions.

---

[140] Muldrew, *Economy of Obligation*, 148–57.
[141] Fontaine, *Moral Economy*, 268–96; Finn, *Character of Credit*, 102–3.

8

Geographies of Consumption
Hierarchies, Localities, and Shopping

INTRODUCTION

London is often seen as having an overweening importance in the lives of the English elite. The lure of the metropolis was firmly established by the reign of Elizabeth, with historians agreeing on its status as the 'centre of conspicuous consumption', not least because of the feverish competition for status amongst Elizabethan nobles.[1] The elite made more frequent and protracted stays, despite royal proclamations ordering their return to the provinces, and a London season was firmly in place by the 1620s.[2] London's attractions were many and increased further through the seventeenth and eighteenth centuries. The draw of the royal court may have become weaker during the Georgian era, but it remained important to those with social ambitions. Parliament, meanwhile, grew as an attraction, with lengthening sittings helping to extend periods of residence and thus lengthening the London season. The Inns of Court were important for the education of country gentlemen and as a focus for litigation, and there was an ever expanding array of infrastructure for polite sociability, including pleasure gardens, theatres, concert rooms, and clubs. As Britain's main port, London was the place where new goods were first available and its extensive luxury trades further extended the range of goods on offer.[3] London shops were viewed with amazement by foreign visitors, who commented not only on the goods available but also on the magnificence of the shops themselves; and shopping as a pleasurable pastime had become firmly established by the mid-seventeenth century. Initially centred on the shopping galleries built into London's exchanges, the geography of leisure shopping spread to the West End, especially Oxford Street and later Regent Street.[4]

[1] F. J. Fisher, 'The development of London as a centre of conspicuous consumption in the sixteenth and seventeenth centuries', in E. M. Carus Wilson (ed.) *Essays in Economic History*, vol. 2 (London, 1962), 197–207. See also McCracken, *Culture and Consumption*, 11–12; L. Stone, *The Crisis of the Aristocracy 1558–1641* (Oxford, 1965), 186, 387.

[2] Whittle and Griffiths, *Consumption and Gender*, 55–7.

[3] R. Porter, *London. A Social History* (Harmondsworth, 1994), 131–59; Peck, *Consuming Splendor*, 25–72; Berg, *Luxury and Pleasure*, 247–78.

[4] Peck, *Consuming Splendor*, 42–5; C. Walsh, 'Social meaning and social space in the shopping galleries of early-modern London', in J. Benson and L. Ugolini (eds) *A Nation of Shopkeepers. Five Centuries of British Retailing* (London, 2003), 52–79; K. Morrison, *English Shops and Shopkeeping* (London, 2003), 36–40; A. Adburgham, *Shops and Shopping, 1800–1914* (London, 1964), 1–12.

The social and shopping attractions of London were often seen as particularly appealing to women. James I argued in Parliament that it was they who nagged their menfolk to 'bring them up to London; because the new fashion is to bee had nowhere but London' and who consequently marred their reputations and robbed their husbands' purses. This prejudice continued into the eighteenth century with frequent critiques appearing in print which lambasted female shoppers for wasting the retailers' time as well as hard-earned money.[5] Men could legitimately be in London on business or at Parliament, but their wives and daughters, it seems, had no right to be there. Despite this moralizing, large numbers of elite families chose to keep town houses, a trend that encouraged and fed off the residential development of aristocratic estates in Mayfair. Many more corresponded with family and friends in the capital, seeking updates on political life, news of the latest fashions, or society gossip.[6] Conversely, London was seen as a stamp of quality on a wide variety of goods, as a marker for all that was fashionable, and also as the benchmark in competitive pricing. It was a frequent point of reference for provincial advertisers who sought to add burnish to their goods and their reputation.[7]

The importance placed on London by both contemporaries and historians is paralleled by a corresponding emphasis on the dominance of metropolitan centres elsewhere in Europe, with Paris in particular being highlighted as the principal locus of European elite consumption.[8] Yet this emphasis has overshadowed the role played by other places in supplying the country house. Food and drink, building materials, and even some furnishings were produced on the estate, but few houses were self-sufficient, even in terms of basic provisions. Gifts might also be an important source of food, as Whittle and Griffiths demonstrate for the Le Strange family in Hunstanton. Most families, however, were dependent on supplies from a range of retailers and tradespeople in the neighbouring or local towns.[9] This links closely with the idea of elite landowners and their country houses being deeply embedded in their locality. The landowner was employer, patron, and patriarch, cementing social ties and obligations with tangible economic links, and local tradesmen often relied upon demand from the big house for their prosperity.[10] Indeed, the absence of this patronage was seen as injuring not just the local economy, but also the social and political influence of the landowner. Writing to his master in 1716, Ralph Verney noted that 'certainly Warwick

---

[5] James I, *The Works*, 567–8, quoted in Whittle and Griffiths, *Consumption and Gender*, 56; Walsh, 'Shops, shopping'; J. Stobart, *Spend Spend Spend! A History of Shopping* (Stroud, 2008), 94–6.

[6] See, for example, Vickery, *Gentleman's Daughter*, 168–72; M. Port, 'West End palaces: the aristocratic town house in London, 1730–1830', *London Journal*, 20/1 (1995), 17–46.

[7] N. Cox and K. Dannehl, *Perceptions of Retailing in Early Modern England* (Aldershot, 2007), 128–43; Stobart, 'Selling politeness'.

[8] See, for example, Coquery, *L'Hôtel aristocratique*; Ilmakunnas, 'Luxury shopping experience'; Chatelet-Calyste, 'Feminine luxury in Paris'; Finn, 'Swallowfield Park'; Clemente, 'Luxury and taste in eighteenth century Naples'.

[9] Whittle and Griffiths, *Consumption and Gender*, 72–84. See also Bailey, 'Consumption and status'; Vickery, *Gentleman's Daughter*, 168–72; Stobart, Hann, and Morgan, *Spaces of Consumption*, 53–4.

[10] Bailey, 'Squire, shopkeeper and staple food'.

must resent Lord Brooke's absence, he having often promised them to reside there when married, and the contrary must lose him good interest'.[11]

This chapter focuses on the ways in which metropolitan, regional, and local retailers and tradespeople were drawn upon to supply the country house. We begin by outlining the geographies of supply and assessing the extent to which there was a hierarchy of goods that mapped onto a hierarchy of centres, London being the source of luxury goods whilst local centres supplied everyday needs. This kind of rational behaviour underpins classical models of retail location, but is often distorted by different levels of personal mobility and particular preferences of the individual consumer.[12] We thus build our analysis by assessing patterns of supply in relation to seasonal and life-cycle changes in residence and exploring the broader relationship that existed between elite consumers and particular towns. Finally, we focus more closely on the geography of London shopping and examine the ways in which this was shaped by place of residence in the metropolis, but also by age and gender, and the nature of the individual's engagement with London. Of particular interest here is the possibility of identifying a shared geography of shopping—one that was distinctively aristocratic.

GEOGRAPHIES AND HIERARCHIES OF SUPPLY

In general terms, the geographical distribution of suppliers was relatively straightforward. London dominated in terms of both the number of suppliers and the overall amount spent (Tables 8.1 and 8.2). At Stoneleigh Abbey, the capital accounted for around three times as much spending as all other places put together, and at Arbury Hall the proportion was even higher. To an extent, this is a reflection of the relative ease of identifying London tradesmen amongst the records: many small-scale local suppliers are far more difficult to definitely identify or to confidently attribute to a particular place. However, even if we assume that all the tradesmen and women for whom a location could not be determined came from elsewhere, London still accounted for around one-third of total spending by the Leighs. This is much higher than the 10–20 per cent that Whittle suggests the Le Strange family spent in London in the early seventeenth century and may indicate a growing reliance on London by elite consumers.[13] It certainly confirms the general impression of eighteenth-century elite families showing a preference for metropolitan goods, especially when making large-scale purchases.[14] Of the twenty largest bills paid by the Leighs, seventeen were presented by London tradesmen; with Newdigate the figure is only slightly lower (fifteen of the twenty largest bills), in part because of substantial purchases of books, sculpture, and pictures that he made

---

[11] Quoted in P. Borsay, 'The landed elite and provincial towns in Britain', *Georgian Group Journal*, 13 (2003), 287.

[12] For a summary of these ideas, see Stobart, Hann, and Morgan, *Spaces of Consumption*, 38–49.

[13] J. Whittle, 'The gentry as consumers in early 17th-century England', in J. Stobart and A. Hann (eds), *The Country House: Material Culture and Consumption* (Swindon, 2015), 29.

[14] Vickery, *Gentleman's daughter*, 164–83; Berry, 'Prudent luxury'.

Table 8.1. Purchases of the Leighs of Stoneleigh by location of tradespeople, 1738–1806

	retailers								spend							
	1738–62		1762–85		1786–1806		total		1738–62		1762–85		1786–1806		total	
	No.	%	No.	%	No.	%	No.	%	£	%	£	%	£	%	£	%
Coventry	17	14.3	23	12.4	24	15.7	56	13.7	1054	25.3	719	5.0	831	7.8	2604	8.9
Kenilworth	0	0.0	2	1.1	2	1.3	3	0.7	0	0.0	36	0.3	419	3.9	455	1.6
Kensington	0	0.0	0	0.0	13	8.5	13	3.2	0	0.0	0	0.0	1120	10.5	1120	3.8
Lichfield	0	0.0	2	1.1	0	0.0	2	0.5	0	0.0	1	0.0	0	0.0	1	0.0
London	81	68.1	125	67.6	80	52.3	254	62.1	2492	59.8	11,607	80.7	7264	68.0	21,363	73.1
Oxford	1	0.8	6	3.2	1	0.7	8	2.0	1	0.0	92	0.6	22	0.2	115	0.4
Stoneleigh	4	3.4	9	4.9	17	11.1	27	6.6	71	1.7	1334	9.3	223	2.1	1628	5.6
Warwick	12	10.1	12	6.5	15	9.8	35	8.6	283	6.8	401	2.8	797	7.5	1481	5.1
Others	4	3.4	6	3.2	1	0.7	11	2.7	266	6.4	198	1.4	0	0.0	464	1.6
	119		185		153		409		4167		14,388		10,676		29,231	

Source: SCLA, DR18/5—bill series.

Note: 'Others' include all locations where purchases were made from single suppliers: Bedworth, Birmingham, Bristol, Canterbury, Cheltenham, Chipping Norton, Cubbington, Daventry, Hardacre, Wednesbury, and Woodstock.

Table 8.2. Purchases of Sir Roger Newdigate of Arbury Hall by location of tradespeople, 1747–96

| | retailers | | | | | | | | spend | | | | | | | |
| | 1747–62 | | 1763–80 | | 1781–96 | | total | | 1747–62 | | 1763–80 | | 1781–96 | | total | |
	No.	%	No.	%	No.	%	No.	%	£	%	£	%	£	%	£	%
Atherstone	1	1.1	2	2.5	2	3.3	4	2.3	1	0.0	55	0.7	122	1.7	178	0.9
Bath	11	12.1	3	3.7	0	0.0	14	8.0	227	5.1	497	6.5	0	0.0	724	3.7
Birmingham	0	0.0	2	2.5	1	1.6	2	1.1	0	0.0	27	0.4	60	0.8	87	0.4
Coventry	8	8.8	8	9.9	9	14.8	18	10.2	204	4.6	209	2.7	402	5.6	815	4.2
London	58	63.7	59	72.8	47	77.0	122	69.3	3661	81.8	6000	78.2	6037	84.0	15,698	81.2
Nuneaton	2	2.2	1	1.2	1	1.6	2	1.1	36	0.8	432	5.6	479	6.7	947	4.9
Oxford	3	3.3	4	4.9	0	0.0	5	2.8	132	2.9	271	3.5	0	0.0	403	2.1
Warwick	3	3.3	0	0.0	1	1.6	4	2.3	98	2.2	0	0.0	88	1.2	186	1.0
Others	5	5.5	2	2.5	0	0.0	5	2.8	116	2.5	183	2.4	0	0.0	299	1.6
	91		81		61		176		4475		7674		7188		19,337	

Source: WRO, CR136/V/136, Account books.

Note: 'Others' include all locations where purchases were made from single suppliers: Bedworth, Daventry, Essex, Leicester, and Winchester.

on the Grand Tour. That said, Newdigate's spending in London remained at a consistently high level throughout the second half of the eighteenth century, whereas that of the Leighs varied over the years: it dipped dramatically through the years of Edward and Mary's minority in the 1750s and when the estate was managed by Committee during Edward's lunacy, and peaked when Edward was refurbishing the house following his coming of age in 1763.

Apart from London, and the local suppliers that are so difficult to trace through the records, the Leighs and Newdigates turned most often to tradesmen in nearby Warwickshire towns, mostly accessible in journeys of an hour or two at the most. Arbury Hall is situated within a mile or so of Nuneaton and, although the number of suppliers identified in the town is very small, they accounted for a growing proportion of spending at the house, especially in terms of hardware and candles. The closest town to Stoneleigh Abbey is Kenilworth, but it appears to have played no role in supplying the house before the 1760s and only became significant in the 1780s, when the draper William Butler was favoured with regular and substantial orders. Overall, the town accounted for less than 1 per cent of suppliers and 2 per cent of purchases, suggesting that proximity was not an overriding factor in choosing suppliers in the local area. Looking slightly further afield, Coventry formed a far more substantial service centre and unsurprisingly accounted for about 14 per cent of suppliers to the Leighs, although many of these were for small amounts. For example, in 1738 the china dealer John Taylor presented three bills totalling £4 19s. 5½d., whilst, fifty years later, purchases of skins and gloves from Stephen Pollard amounted to just 16 shillings.[15] Altogether, Coventry traders commanded less than 9 per cent of the total spent by the Leighs, their importance declining markedly after the 1750s (Table 8.1). For the Newdigates, Coventry was always more marginal as a retail centre, but the number of tradespeople patronized grew steadily and the overall level of spending was higher at the end of the century than it had been in the 1740s. This contrasting trajectory suggests that change was a reflection of shifting demand at the two houses and the choices being made by the Leighs and Newdigates, rather than a result of changes in the strength and diversity of retailing in the town. Indeed, it is clear that Coventry's retailing was developing rapidly during the second half of the eighteenth century, despite the variable industrial fortunes of the town. Warwick retailers appear to have been patronized by the Leighs less often than their Coventry counterparts, despite the house being equidistant between the two towns. They accounted for barely half the level of expenditure, probably a result of the more limited retail provision in the town—in 1785 its shopkeepers paid only £37 in shop tax compared with £105 by those in Coventry.[16] They certainly had little to do with the supply of Arbury Hall, some 20 miles distant. Indeed, the county town appears to have lain largely outside the retail and perhaps also the social horizon of Sir Roger Newdigate. Aside from Nuneaton and

---

[15] SCLA, DR18/5/2111, DR18/5/2058, DR18/5/2191, DR18/5/5845, DR18/5/5860a.

[16] TNA, E182, Shop Tax, Coventry 1785 Exchequer Accounts. For more detailed discussion of retailing in Coventry and Warwick, see V. Morgan, 'Producing consumer spaces in eighteenth-century England: shops, shopping and the provincial town' (unpublished PhD thesis, Coventry University, 2003), 96–106, 114–28.

Coventry, he looked mostly to Atherstone; Birmingham, by some distance the most substantial retail centre in the county by this time, also was largely insignificant.[17]

Between them, these Warwickshire towns accounted for barely 15 per cent of spending at Stoneleigh Abbey and 12 per cent at Arbury Hall, levels which underline the complaints of contemporaries that local tradesmen were being overlooked in favour of London retailers. As an early nineteenth-century correspondent with *Blackwood's Edinburgh Magazine* put it, great landowners 'spend only the most contemptible portion of their incomes in the country... the best of his groceries, &c. he perhaps gets from London'.[18] Such sentiments echo those vocalized by many critiques of luxury across Europe, that it took money out of the country by focusing spending on imported luxuries, scaling these down to the level of the individual house and its locality.[19] Local spending was further undermined by outlays made whilst travelling. Few purchases were made in Paris, often seen as the centre of elite consumption in the eighteenth century and the destination for a growing number of shopping trips in the early nineteenth century. The latter were sometimes undertaken by returning nabobs, such as the Russells of Swallowfield Park, arguably as part of an agenda to add European lustre to their Anglo-Indian material culture; but many English families also indulged in similar spending sprees.[20] Sir Roger acquired a small quantity of books in Paris—part of the £1,026 laid out on books, paintings, and marble whilst on his 1774–6 Grand Tour. He spent a further £724 on accommodation and a range of durable goods at Bath in the 1750s and 1770s (Tables 8.2 and 8.3).[21] Similarly, Mary Leigh's patronage of retailers in the streets surrounding her house in Kensington Gore amounted to over 10 per cent of spending between 1786 and 1806; this formed an important fillip to businesses in these localities, no doubt partly at the expense of Warwickshire tradespeople, but also as an alternative to London retailers.[22] Undoubtedly, both families spent locally; they formed part of the group later identified by Flora Thompson as 'the rich who spent only part of the year at the country houses' but who 'believed it to be their duty to give the local tradesmen a turn'.[23] Yet, it seems clear that these local tradesmen enjoyed only a small proportion of the overall spending of the landowning classes.

One striking feature about the non-metropolitan geographies of supply to Stoneleigh Abbey and Arbury Hall is the lack of overlap between the two. The only town which served both houses to any significant extent was Coventry, and even there the number of suppliers serving both houses was remarkably small. From a

[17] Stobart, Hann, and Morgan, *Spaces of Consumption*, 42–3.

[18] 'English and Irish Land-Letting', *Blackwood's Edinburgh Magazine*, 17, 101 (June 1825).

[19] See, for example, Clemente, 'Luxury and taste in eighteenth-century Naples'.

[20] Finn, 'Swallowfield Park'. See also S. Garland, 'The use of French architectural design books in de Grey's choice of style at Wrest Park', in J. Stobart and A. Hann (eds) *The Country House: Material Culture and Consumption* (Swindon, 2015), 57–8; *Mistress of Charlecote. The Memoirs of Mary Elizabeth Lucy, 1803–1889* (London, 1983), 61–72.

[21] WRO, CR136/B/2638b—Books, marbles, etc.

[22] See Stobart, 'So agreeable and suitable a place'.

[23] F. Thompson, *Lark Rise to Candleford* (London, 1939), 462. See also Bailey, 'Squire, shopkeeper and staple food'.

total of sixty-four Coventry tradespeople listed in the Stoneleigh Abbey bills or Arbury Hall account books, only ten appear in both; just half of these were regular suppliers—a draper, Robert Hughes; two grocers, William Leaper and Lilley Smith; an ironmonger, Richard Steane; and a nurseryman, John Whittingham. That two substantial houses situated just 18 miles from each other could have such separate networks of supply says much about the range and quality of shops in Warwickshire, and their ability to meet at least some of the needs of aristocratic consumers. In London too, the Newdigates and Leighs operated in largely separate spheres, sharing just 29 suppliers from a total of 347. Given the huge number of retailers and craftsmen in the capital, this is perhaps less surprising; yet it suggests that, in contrast with Paris, any development of a distinct and well-defined class of metropolitan tradespeople focused on serving the aristocracy was distinctly limited at this time.[24] To be sure, there were individual retailers who appear in the records of several aristocratic and gentry families. Blakiston and Myles, for example, supplied groceries to the Leighs and Newdigates, and also to Judith Baker in County Durham and to the Leigh's cousin, James Leigh of Adlestrop in Gloucestershire.[25] Some London tradespeople deliberately targeted this group of elite customers. Josiah Wedgwood is perhaps the most famous example, with his finely grained differentiation in product and pricing, careful choice of showrooms, and assiduous cultivation of patronage.[26] Both the Leighs and Newdigates bought considerable quantities of porcelain from Wedgwood, but even so he was by no means the only supplier of such goods. In the period when he was making purchases from Wedgwood, Newdigate also bought china from at least five other London retailers (W. Parker & Co. of Fleet Street, Jonathan Collett of Cockspur Street, Lambden and Woods of Poultry, Colebron Hancock of Charing Cross, and Duesbury of Henrietta Street), only one of whom was also patronized by the Leighs. More generally, the two families looked to different suppliers for major purchases of durable goods. For example, furniture for Stoneleigh Abbey mostly came from William Gomm and Thomas & Gilbert Burnett, and later from Daniel Frost and Michael Thackthwaite, and silverware came from Thomas Gilpin and then Robert Makepeace; Newdigate went most often to Thomas Gillow, Edward Hirst, or William Yeard for furniture, and to Edward Ellicot, Pickle and Rundle, or Parker and Wakelin for silverware.

Behind a shared reliance on London, therefore, the regional and micro-geographies of supply to these two country houses varied quite considerably. Understanding these shared and diverse patterns involves looking more closely at the kinds of goods bought in different places. At first glance, the pattern again seems quite straightforward and rational: luxury goods were bought in the capital and everyday items were acquired locally, thus minimizing the effort required to access the full range of goods. This dichotomy characterized the supply of the Ardernes and Leghs in Cheshire, who looked to London for wines, silver plate, and books, but

---

[24] See Coquery, *Tenir boutique à Paris*; Chatenet-Calyste, 'Feminine luxury in Paris', 175–6.

[25] Berry, 'Prudent luxury'; SCLA, DR18/5/3702, DR18/5/3393, DR18/5/3466, DR18/5/3498.

[26] Berg, *Luxury and Pleasure*, 134–9, 145–53. For a French comparison, see Sargentson, *Merchants and Luxury Markets*, esp. 113–42.

purchased groceries, ironmongery, shoes, cloth, and the like in Manchester and Stockport. It can also be seen in the ways the Le Strange family used Kings Lynn, Norwich, and London suppliers.[27] As would be expected, then, the Leighs and Newdigates looked to retailers in London for all their silverware, paintings and prints, and coaches, and for the vast majority of their books, furniture, and decorative ware. Items such as the silver 'thread tea vase' bought by Mary Leigh from Robert Makepeace of Terle Street or the 113-volume set of the publications of *L'Académie des sciences* bought from Thomas Payne of St Martin-in-the-Fields by Edward, fifth Lord Leigh, or the painting by Terriers that he had from Edward Scarlett could scarcely have been acquired outside London.[28] At the other end of the scale, fresh produce would invariably be acquired locally, often by the housekeeper, whose periodic accounts, discussed in Chapter 6, reflect the combined efforts of a large number of local producers and suppliers which together formed an intense network of local supply.[29] Even in Kensington, Mary Leigh drew on local retailers to provide meat, fish, candles, coal, and bread.[30] Similarly, the day-to-day maintenance of the house and estate buildings was generally entrusted to local craftsmen. Thus we see Thomas Howlett, a blacksmith from Stoneleigh village, presenting a total of twenty-two bills to the Leighs between 1764 and 1792; meanwhile, Sir Roger Newdigate made payments to an Atherstone glazier named William Cobbett every year through the 1760s and 1770s. Arguably, it was simply not worth engaging tradespeople from further afield for this kind of mundane work.

Whilst this duality of supply works up to a point, the consumption practices of the Leighs and Newdigates reveal a far more nuanced system of supply. In addition to everyday goods, local towns provided a wide range of luxuries which underpinned the construction and operation of the country house as a symbol of elite power and taste. At Stoneleigh Abbey, the design and construction of the grand west range was the work of the Warwick man, Francis Smith, then the leading architect in the Midlands.[31] To carry out the work, he employed the same local craftsmen that he is known to have used elsewhere, including the joiner George Eborall and the carver Benjamin King, both of Warwick, the Birmingham locksmith John Wilkes, and John Wright, a stuccoist from Worcester. The building was completed by 1726, but the interiors were still unfinished at Smith's death in 1738 and remained so for a further twenty-five years. When work recommenced in the early 1760s, the job was entrusted to another Warwick-based architect, Timothy Lightoler, with much of the construction work being carried out by William Hiorn, also of Warwick. His 1764 bill itemizes a number of ornate marble chimney pieces and several designs in his hand survive for both these and a broader decorative scheme for the hall.[32] Partly from a desire for better-quality workmanship

---

[27] Mitchell, *Tradition and Innovation*, 109–10; Whittle and Griffiths, *Consumption and Gender*, 58–64.

[28] SCLA, DR18/5/5858, DR18/5/4482, DR18/5/4493.

[29] See also Whittle and Griffiths, *Consumption and Gender*, 88–97.

[30] For detailed discussion of this provisioning, see Stobart, 'So agreeable and suitable a place'.

[31] Gomme, 'Abbey into palace', 82–3. See also Gomme, *Francis Smith of Warwick*.

[32] SCLA, DR18/5/4192, DR631/33, Designs for Stoneleigh Abbey. See also G. Beard, *Decorative Plasterwork in Great Britain* (London, 1975), 57–8; Gomme, 'Abbey into palace', 97–9.

or the kudos of metropolitan associations, subsequent and more ornate chimney pieces were made by the London partnership of Bastard and Fox, Hiorn's work being relegated to lesser rooms.[33] And yet Warwick craftsmen continued to play a role in fashioning the fabric of the Abbey: in 1763 Robert Moore was paid £75 13s. 10d. for plasterwork and in 1789 Richard Bevan presented a bill for painting, varnishing, and gilding which amounted to £299 5s. 10d.[34] Similarly, at Arbury Hall, Sir Roger Newdigate employed David Hiorn (William's father) from the 1740s onwards to construct several garden buildings, lay out gravel walks, undertake some carving work, and, most importantly, fit up Lady Newdigate's dressing room in the Gothic style, for which he was paid £71. Work has also undertaken by Robert Moore and Benjamin King, mostly to the designs of Sanderson Miller, a pioneer of the Gothic revival who lived at Radway Grange in south Warwickshire (see Chapter 6).[35]

The picture of Warwick that emerges from the bills and account books is of a specialist centre—the focus of a dense network of skilled craftsmen who worked together on houses across the Midlands. Coventry tradesmen were largely missing from this structural and decorative work, although Newdigate employed a Coventry mason, John Alcott, in the 1790s.[36] More significant was the town's role in supplying a range of luxury consumables and manufactured items. In the 1760s, the nurseryman John Whittingham was the Leighs' chief source of trees, plants, and seeds for both the kitchen and ornamental gardens. His stocklist was extensive: a printed catalogue from 1764 ran to four pages and comprised 427 separate items, including 44 varieties of rose, and he supplied clients over a wide area—down to Ralph Sneyd of Keele Hall.[37] Around the same time, William Allen supplied the Leighs with china and earthenware, Abel Gravenor sold them imported wines and spirits, and Lilley Smith supplied groceries, including five different grades of tea.[38] Specialist and luxury textiles were bought from Robert Hughes, who dealt with the family for nineteen years, supplying over £250 of goods, most notably the mourning clothes following the death of Edward, third Lord Leigh in 1738. These included 'rich black velvet', 'fine broadcloth', 'rich silk hatbands', and a 'best crape scarf'.[39] The growing literature on retailing has alerted us to the widespread availability of such goods in provincial shops, but it is nonetheless striking that the extremely wealthy Leighs saw these local retailers as perfectly capable of meeting many of their needs.[40]

---

[33] Gomme, 'Abbey into palace', 99.   [34] SCLA, DR18/5/4070, DR18/5/5864.

[35] Tyack, *Warwickshire Country Houses*, 11–12; WRO, CR136/V,156, Account book, entry for 1752.

[36] Tyack, *Warwickshire Country Houses*, 12.

[37] K. Goodway, 'Landscapes and gardens at Keele, 1700–1900', in C. Harrison (ed.) *The History of Keele* (University of Keele, 1986), 7–8. See also R. Barbour, 'John Whittingham: Coventry nurseryman, diarist, Catholic apologist and political activist', *Warwickshire History*, 16/1 (2014), 8–25.

[38] SCLA, DR18/5/4171, DR18/5/4140, DR18/5/4177. See also Mui and Mui, *Shops and Shopkeeping*, 29–48, 221–48; Stobart, *Sugar and Spice*, 50–5, 208–10.

[39] SCLA, DR18/5/2110. See also DR18/5/2129, DR18/5/2210.

[40] See, for example, Cox, *Complete Tradesman*, 76–115; Berg, *Luxury and Pleasure*, 247–78; Mitchell, *Tradition and Innovation*, 37–60; Bailey, 'Consumption and status'.

Conversely, London was the source for many non-luxury goods which were available and purchased from provincial retailers. Sometimes, distinctions can be drawn in terms of the quality or variety of goods being purchased, as with the Persian and Italian silks purchased from Sarah Gunter in the 1730s or the best plain chocolate, fine green tea, fine souchong tea, fine green souchong, fine congou, and best turkey coffee bought from Thomas Thompson thirty years later.[41] However, there were also very mundane groceries bought in London which were comparable to the kinds of commodities being purchased from Lilley Smith and suggest considerable overlap in the systems of supply that serviced elite consumers. It is possible that part of the attraction was the keener prices supposedly offered by London retailers (many provincial advertisements noted that the shopkeeper sold at the best price 'as in London'[42]), but far more significant was the fact that many country house owners spent a large amount of time living in London, making metropolitan shopping simple and expedient. In this sense, London retailers became local, at least for the season.

SEASONALITY, LOCALITY, AND CHOICE

The impact of changing seasonal residence on elite consumption practices has rarely been discussed. Many elite consumers lived far away from centres of metropolitan supply. Like the Swedish nobility who relied on friends or diplomats in Paris to acquire for them the pick of French fashions or the merchants of Vyborg who drew on their trading contacts or made infrequent trips to St Petersburg, a large proportion of gentry families in provincial England received goods from London and made short visits, but did not spend prolonged periods in the capital.[43] For those who did, we find that their everyday routines of shopping and supply were profoundly affected. Sir Roger Newdigate had a London house in Spring Gardens, near St Martin-in-the-Fields, where he lived during much of the parliamentary season. For several months in the year, therefore, buying from London shops would have been the most convenient means of acquiring all manner of goods. Something of this can be seen in the seasonality of his purchase of books. Through much of his life, much of Newdigate's book buying took place in the spring, at the end of the parliamentary season. After his retirement from politics he spent relatively little time in London and dealt with metropolitan booksellers via correspondence; his spending on books quickly became more even through the year, August emerging as a particularly important month.[44]

---

[41] SCLA, DR18/5/1858, DR18/5/2105, DR18/5/4692.

[42] For fuller discussion, see Stobart, 'Selling (through) politeness'; Mui and Mui, *Shops and Shopkeeping*, 221–48.

[43] Ilmakunnas, 'Luxury shopping experience'; Ijäs, 'Favourites of fortune', 190–205; Vickery, *Gentleman's Daughter*; Berry, 'Prudent luxury'.

[44] See the following receipted bills from booksellers: WRO, CR136/B/2456b, CR136/B/2466a-j, CR136/B/2467a-g; CR136/B/2635j; CR136/B/2638a.

His diaries make clear that Newdigate visited shops as part of his daily routine. On 7 March 1759, for example, he started at home and 'walked to Lowes, Jones's, bespoke a Tea Vase, Deards—House till 4'; seventeen years later and by then aged fifty-seven, he was still energetically striding the London streets: 'walked to Ellicot, left watch to clean, over Blackfriars and Westminster Bridge to H[ouse of Commons]'.[45] Being in London also made it easy for tradesmen to wait on Newdigate at home. Thus, on the day following his visit to Deard's shop whilst on his way to Parliament, the silversmith called at Spring Gardens, where Newdigate 'bespoke a Tea Kettle and Lamp and Coffee pot'.[46] The routinized nature of these activities indicates how deeply embedded even seasonal residents could become in London's supply systems. Moreover, Newdigate not only took the opportunity to acquire goods whilst in the capital; he also maintained relationships with suppliers when he returned to his country residence. This involved both continued patronage of London booksellers, grocers, tea merchants, and many others beyond his retirement from politics, and the dispatch of goods from London during the summer months spent at Arbury Hall.

The impact on the geography of supply of both season and life cycle becomes clearer still in the shopping practices of Mary Leigh. As a young woman in the 1750s and 1760s she lived near Hanover Square and patronized retailers in the fashionable shopping streets of London's West End (see below). These were local suppliers, within easy walking distance, but the same could also be argued of the numerous shops she bought from in the City, just a mile or so to the east. This congruence of London and local changed markedly in 1774 when her brother, Edward, fifth Lord Leigh, was declared insane and especially after his death in 1786. At this point Mary inherited a life interest in the Stoneleigh estates and also acquired the lease on Grove House in Kensington. For the last twenty years of her life, then, she split her time between Grove House (where she spent around nine months each year, from November to June or July), Stoneleigh Abbey (two months in the summer), and Cheltenham (usually several weeks in October).[47] Local could thus mean one of three places, depending upon the time of year. Given that London was a short carriage ride away, it is also possible to view the West End and even City shops as local to her Kensington home. However, it is no surprise that Kensington shopkeepers dominated the provision of fresh foods, as well as the coal and candles that were central to day-to-day life in the capital. The consolidated bills from a set of local retailers, including the butcher Richard Buckmaster, the fishmonger John Loader, the baker William Simpson, and the coal merchant Samuel Kingston, represent a constant flow of goods to Grove House through the winter months. These were supplemented by a steady, but seasonal stream of food sent up to Kensington from Stoneleigh Abbey; few goods were sent in August, September, and October, when Mary was away from Grove House, but otherwise

[45] WRO, CR136/A/582, Diaries, 7 March 1759, 15 March 1776.
[46] WRO, CR136/A/582, Diaries, 8 March 1759. The corresponding entry in Newdigate's account books records the cost as £7 10s.—see WRO, CR136/V/136, Account book, entry for 1759.
[47] For a fuller discussion of these arrangements, see Stobart, 'So agreeable and suitable a place'.

the supply was regular and on a substantial scale.[48] In 1794, thirty-one different types of food were sent: fruit and vegetables, including cucumbers, peaches, French beans, melons, and mushrooms; domestically-reared meat such as fowl, ducks, pork, and turkeys; and game, comprising rabbits, hares, wildfowl, and fourteen whole deer. There was thus an important flow of fresh food into London from the country house which ran counter to the more general stream in the opposite direction. This was significant in terms of metropolitan dining and gift giving, venison in particular being used to cement patronage, but also in the economics of supply. As Sir John Williams noted in a letter to his daughter, newly ensconced at Charlecote House: 'you ought to have a first class gardener who will produce for you plenty of fruit and have it sent up to you in London where it will be extravagantly dear'.[49]

The seasonality of Mary's shopping in the 1780s and 1790s was underlined by purchases made whilst in Cheltenham in the autumn. Provisions and some durable goods were undoubtedly consumed whilst at the spa, but other goods followed Mary when she moved on to Kensington for the winter. The exact nature of these goods is mostly obscure, appearing only as payments for the carriage of hampers recorded in the Grove House daybook, but on one occasion Miss Baker, a friend or acquaintance at Cheltenham, acted as intermediary in the supply of bespoke silk shoes made by a Mr Townsend. Purchases of this nature were unusual and seem to have been linked to the fact that Townsend was a trusted supplier, able to supply shoes that were particularly comfortable.[50] Long-distance links to such favoured tradespeople were not uncommon: Lady Chester of Hams Hall near Coleshill, for example, bought cloth from a Stafford draper, Elizabeth Sneyd, despite the geographical distance, intervening opportunities, and disagreements over the quality of goods supplied.[51] However, they were the exception. Sir Roger Newdigate's purchases in Bath were more conventional. During his regular visits in the 1740s and 1750s with his first wife Sophia, the principal outlays after housekeeping bills were to Dr Morley for medicines, Dr Moysey for 'physic', and Mr Pearce for medicine and bleeding. Whilst at the spa, they also bought teacups to the value of £1 12s. and other china costing £1 13s., a greatcoat for £2 9s., a leather cloak bag costing 1 guinea, and boots, again costing 1 guinea. They also visited the millinery shop of Anne Walton on at least three occasions, being charged a total of £10 9s. 6d. for a range of haberdashery. None of these outgoings were extravagant and probably few were planned purchases, but it is clear that the Newdigates, like most other visitors to Bath, took advantage of the retail opportunities available in the town whilst visiting for ostensibly different reasons.

The same might also be argued for Sir Roger's spending in Italy whilst on his two Grand Tours (1739–40 and 1774–6). Much of the outlay was on travel and

[48] SCLA, DR18/31/655, Account of Sundries from Stoneleigh Abbey, 1793–8.

[49] *Mistress of Charlecote*, 40. On the gifting of venison, see S. Whyman, *Sociability and Power in Late-Stuart England. The Cultural Worlds of the Verneys, 1660–1720* (Oxford, 1999), 23–7.

[50] SCLA, DR18/31/656, Daybook for Grove House, 1793–8, 17 October, 1791; SCLA, DR18/17/30/35, Letter from Miss Baker, 19 April 1796.

[51] Staffordshire Record Office, D1798, HM37/36, Papers of Mrs Elizabeth Sneyd of Stafford (1713–52).

accommodation: his account book contains a summary of the costs of his travel for the second trip, which amounted to £2,257 10s., including £22 10s. for the final leg from London to Warwickshire 'in deep snow'.[52] A note of expenditure in 1739 includes the cost of inns and for post-horses and postilions; but there are also payments for entrance to various palazzos and cathedrals, and for consumables such as chocolate, coffee, and wine.[53] As at Bath, these costs were inevitably incurred and disbursed locally, but like many other tourists he also bought a range of books, statuary, medals, and marble which were carefully itemized before being shipped home. The prices paid for objects acquired on his first tour is not noted in the surviving records, but a list of purchases made on his second tour itemizes the sums spent on a range of objects and in a number of places (Table 8.3).[54] This large outlay underlines Newdigate's spending power, but also the importance of location: here, it was the opportunity to acquire goods largely unavailable at home that engendered this surge of place- and time-specific spending. Place mattered because it was only in Florence, Venice, Naples, and especially Rome that classical antiquity could be experienced first-hand, and it was in these same places that the various trophies of the Grand Tour were most easily acquired. Whilst the sums involved were impressive, Newdigate's spending on his Grand Tour was modest in comparison with other British collectors, such as Charles Townley, Henry Blundell,

Table 8.3. Summary of spending in Italy on art and books by Sir Roger Newdigate, 1774–6 (£ s.)

	Florence	Rome	Naples	Venice	Vicenza	France	Unspecified	Total
Books	48-16	148-3	47-12	9-10	3-4	149-15		407
Marbles, Vases, Tables		329-11						329-11
Paintings	25-5	59-9					23-10	108-4
Drawings, Cameos, Medals							62-17	62-17
Intaglios, 'Pictrelle', etc.							58-3	58-3
Casts in plaster	43-15	16-1						60-6
	117-16	553-4	47-12	9-10	3-4	149-15	144-10	1,026-1
Packaging and embarking								89-0
Freight, custom house & duties								331-1
Total								1,446-2

Source: WRO, CR136/B/2368b, Books, marbles, etc.

[52] WRO, CR136/V/136, Account book, entries for 1774–6.

[53] WRO, CR136/B/2510a-e, Accounts of costs incurred on the Grand Tour, 1739.

[54] WRO, CR136/B/2368b, Books, marbles, etc. Sir Roger's spending on books and art is discussed more fully in Chapter 4.

William Windham, and the first Earl of Leicester, and was dwarfed by the ruinous spending of men like Jorgen Scheel, who incurred massive debts whilst on an extended European tour in the 1790s.[55]

The geographical mobility of elites thus made 'local' temporally contingent: it could mean London, the environs of the country house or the suburban villa, a provincial spa or an Italian city visited on the Grand Tour. Despite this complexity, hierarchies of supply retained an essentially rational underpinning, reflecting choices made on the basis of convenience, cost, reputation, and status. It is dangerous, though, to read all elite consumption in such rational terms. We have already noted the lack of overlap between the supply systems serving Stoneleigh Abbey and Arbury Hall; different patterns reflected both the large number of suppliers from which the elite consumer could choose, but also the preferences of the two families for both specific suppliers and particular places. This is best illustrated through two examples: Oxford and Atherstone.

Personal factors were perhaps most obvious in the links with Oxford enjoyed by Edward, fifth Lord Leigh, and Sir Roger Newdigate. Edward was a student at Oxford and retained links with the university in later life, being elected High Steward in 1767 (see Chapter 4). His spending whilst a student is recorded in bills for battels at Oriel College and for servants, but also in others for items such as stockings and shoes, purchased from William Thorpe and Sandra Bennett respectively, and a watch and chain, bought from Henry Medcalfe on an outing to Woodstock in the spring of 1763.[56] Such local spending is unsurprising for a resident student, but Edward continued to draw on individuals in Oxford after he moved to Stoneleigh Abbey. Many of his early purchases of books were from James Fletcher, whom he probably got to know during his time as a student there, although the geography of this relationship is complicated by the fact that Fletcher also had a shop in London from which some of Edward's bills were sent.[57] The Oxford connection was also apparent in the bills paid to William Hayes, the Oxford Professor of Music. The earliest of these was for 205 music lessons, given between October 1762 and May 1764, and for supplying a range of books and music, some of which came from Hayes's own collection. Other books followed and in December 1766 Hayes presented a bill for books supplied by Mr Warren and for busts from Campione—presumably those subsequently placed in the library at Stoneleigh Abbey.[58] For Edward, then, Oxford remained a useful source of books and art, even when his main suppliers were to be found in London.

As MP for the University, Sir Roger Newdigate's largesse was considerable. Most famously, he set up an annual poetry prize of 21 guineas which still bears his name today, but he also contributed much to the fabric of the university and his alma mater, University College. Two candelabra from Hadrian's villa, which he purchased in Rome, were given to the Radcliffe Library and his accounts also record £200 of 'Books, Prints, Marbles, Casts, Medals &c, bt in Tour to Rome. Presents

[55] R. Guilding, 'Robert Adam and Charles Townley', *Apollo*, 143 (1996), 27–32; Christie, *British Country House*, 184–5; Wilson and Mackley, *Building of the English Country House*, 70–8.
[56] SCLA, DR18/5/4017.   [57] Raven, *Business of Books*, 154–92; SCLA, DR18/5/4283.
[58] SCLA, DR18/5/4173, DR18/5/4517, DR18/5/4542.

to Univ^y of Oxford and University College'.[59] In addition to these artefacts, he donated a further £2,000 to pay for the removal to the university of the famous Arundel collection of marbles (now held in the Ashmolean Museum). His accounts also include a 1766 bill for a 'large Gothic Chimney piece, set up in University College Hall' costing £150 and a £100 donation to Queen's College in 1780 to assist in 'rebuilding after fire'.[60] These major contributions to the material culture of the university were supplemented by regular payments towards the running of University College. These included sums of between 14s. and £4 11s. 9d. paid to a butcher, Patrick Musgrove, for supplying brawn and other meat in the 1750s and 1760s, and the regular payment of battels to the College, which continued through the 1780s, even after he had retired from Parliament. Beyond the university, however, Sir Roger appears to have made relatively few purchases for his own use. He paid 5 guineas for the bells of five churches to be rung during a 'Visit of Thanks to the University' made in 1776 following his re-election as the MP for the university and his wife was a subscriber to a girls' school in the city, making annual donations of 2 guineas through the 1770s. In terms of tangible goods, he bought small quantities of stationery from Daniel Prince in the 1770s, and there were purchases of wine 'from Oxford' in the 1760s.[61]

Sir Roger's reasons for donating so generously to the university were undoubtedly linked to his status as its MP, but this did not translate into regular visits to the city or patronage of its tradesmen. In contrast, his frequent presence in Atherstone was matched by a surprising range of goods being purchased from tradesmen in the town. Sir Roger was an active member of the town's circulating library, from which he borrowed and occasionally purchased books. He also visited periodically to play bowls.[62] Being in Atherstone and patronizing shops in the town did not necessarily mean multipurpose visits; indeed, it is doubtful that he would have dealt directly with the glazier William Cobbett or the breeches maker William Nuthall, who between them appear twenty-nine times in the account books. However, regular social engagements in the town appear to have encouraged a much fuller patronage of suppliers than might be expected—certainly much beyond that found with Birmingham, where his social ties were far weaker, amounting to little more than attending annual dinners of the Bean Club, a loyalist association in which leading townsmen and the rural gentry mixed freely.[63] This underlines the importance of personal preferences in determining the geography as well as the composition of spending. Eighteenth-century consumers, as much as those today, were influenced by a wide range of factors when determining

[59] WRO, CR136/B/2638b, Books, marbles, etc.; CR136/V/136, Account book, entry for 1776. It is unclear whether the candelabra are counted amongst the gifts noted in the account book, but their apparent cost of £227 10s. suggests that they were additional items.

[60] WRO, CR136/B/2424, Receipted bill, 22 March 1771; CR136/V/136, Account book, entry for 1780.

[61] WRO, CR136/V/136, account book, *passim*.

[62] WRO, CR/A/582, Diaries, 4 January 1751, 21 June 1751, 23 August 1751, 20 September 1751. The shop tax returns for 1785 indicate that Atherstone retailers paid £14 of tax, a modest sum, but the fourth-highest total in the county. Clearly the town was a significant local centre.

[63] WRO, CR136/A/582, Diaries, 17 July 1752, 29 July 1754.

where to buy things: they were not simply rational beings who weighed up the economics of distance, quality, and price.[64]

GEOGRAPHIES OF LONDON SHOPPING

London was consistent in its importance to elite consumption, the preferred source for a wide range of goods; but the space economy of metropolitan retailing was complex and changing. Traditionally, the key concentrations of shops had been on the main thoroughfares of the City, most notably Cheapside. A series of exchanges, built in the late sixteenth and seventeenth centuries, and each with its own 'shopping gallery', both marked and encouraged the gradual shift of fashionable metropolitan shopping westwards along the Strand. This drift continued in the eighteenth century with the building boom in Soho and north of Piccadilly—an area now referred to as the West End.[65] By the end of the century there was still a variety of specialist retail districts, including the booksellers of St Paul's Churchyard and the furniture makers of Long Acre; but these did not operate in isolation from each other. In 1803, *The Picture of London* informed its readers that the capital's key shopping streets were arranged in two lengthy east–west axes.[66] One ran from Leadenhall Street through Cheapside in the City, along Fleet Street and the Strand to Charing Cross. The other went from Shoreditch through Newgate Street and along Holborn and Oxford Street. Intersecting these ran a number of important cross streets including Gracechurch Street, Covent Garden, Piccadilly, and New Bond Street. These axes thus linked together older shopping streets within the City and burgeoning areas further west, combining them in mile after mile of opportunities to view, browse, and purchase a huge range of goods. It is remarkable, then, that we know relatively little about how elite shopping practices meshed with this retail geography or about the role of gender, life cycle, residential location, or personal preference in shaping these practices. The kind of detailed analysis of shops and elite shopping offered by Coquery's studies of Paris would help us to understand precisely where people shopped, how often, and for what. This would provide a deeper understanding of the spatial processes and practices of consumption which linked supplier and consumer.[67]

The spatiality of the shopping practices of Edward, fifth Lord Leigh, his sister Mary Leigh, and Sir Roger Newdigate all broadly conformed to London's retail

---

[64] Stobart, Hann, and Morgan, *Spaces of Consumption*, 52–4. See also D. Miller, *A Theory of Shopping* (Cambridge, 1998).

[65] V. Harding, 'Shops, markets and retailers in London's Cheapside, c.1500-1700', in B. Blondé, P. Stabel, J. Stobart, and I. Van Damme (eds) *Buyer and Sellers. Retail Circuits and Practices in Medieval and Early Modern Europe* (Turnhout, 2006), 155–70; Walsh, 'Social meaning and social space'; Morrison, *English Shops*, 31–40.

[66] *The Picture of London* (1803), quoted in Adburgham, *Shops and Shopping*, 5.

[67] See, for example, N. Coquery, 'Shopping streets in eighteenth-century Paris. A landscape shaped by historical, economic and social forces', in J. H. Furnée and C. Lesger (eds), *The Landscape of Consumption. Shopping Streets and Cultures in Western Europe, 1600–1900* (Farnham, 2014), 57–77. These arguments are developed more fully in Coquery, *Tenir boutique à Paris*.

geography as outlined in *The Picture of London* (Figures 8.1–8.5). For each, the southern axis was by far the most important, Fleet Street and the Strand forming a key link between the City and the burgeoning shopping streets of Westminster. Moreover, it is clear that the City itself remained an important locus of shopping, especially for Sir Roger. Whilst the bright lights of the West End dazzled many visitors, it is apparent that shops across the capital offered a spectacular display of goods and fittings. The German visitor Georg Lichtenberg noted in the 1770s that the shops from Cheapside to Fleet Street 'seem to be made entirely of glass; many thousand candles light up silverware, engraving, books, clocks, glass, pewter, paintings, women's finery, modish and otherwise, gold, precious stones, steel-work, and endless coffee-rooms and lottery offices. The street looks as though it were illuminated for some festivity.'[68] This splendour was reflected in the habits of elite shoppers who looked eastwards from their Westminster homes for a wide variety of luxury and everyday goods. Within the overall distribution of suppliers, certain specialist areas stand out: booksellers on Fleet Street and the Strand; coachmakers on Long Acre; and drapers, mercers, haberdashers, and the like around Covent Garden and Bond Street. More striking, however, is the spread of most types of suppliers across the capital: furniture, for example, came from craftsmen in Ludgate Hill and Liquorpond Street in the City; Clerkenwell to the north; St Giles and the Strand; Charing Cross, Cockspur Street, and Piccadilly; and Hanover Square, Oxford Street, and Marylebone Street in the west. These patterns reveal a high degree of mobility amongst elite shoppers as they chose favoured suppliers from amongst the dozens, even hundreds of possibilities available to them in metropolis. Yet the Leighs and Newdigates made different choices and shopped in different places, a reflection of varied and shifting priorities of status and identity.

Mary Leigh's shopping in the 1750s and 1760s shows a distinct preference for the West End (Figure 8.1), a distribution that suggests she shopped most often in the immediate vicinity of her home in Hanover Square or went to the fashionable streets around Covent Garden. This pattern is exactly what we might expect of a young and well-to-do London resident and reflects quite closely the behaviour of other elite women, including the Durham gentlewoman Judith Baker, who made annual shopping trips to the capital around this time. Lodging with family near Grosvenor Square, she shopped in nearby New Bond Street, Hanover Square, and Berkeley Square, slightly further afield in Jermyn Street and Coventry Street, and more occasionally about 2 miles distant on the Strand and Holborn. This geography was constrained in part by Baker's apparent reluctance to hire coaches to take her further afield but also by her preference to deal with a closer circle of known and trusted suppliers to whom she returned year after year.[69] As this suggests, the distribution of suppliers presents only a partial picture. Mary's West End suppliers, in the streets of Mayfair and St James's, were the most numerous, but the size of individual bills and total amount spent were generally modest (Table 8.4).

[68] Quoted in Porter, *London*, 145. For further discussion of the attitudes of von le Roche and others, see D. Davis, *A History of Shopping* (London, 1966), 181–98; Cox, *Complete Tradesman*, 12, 90–3.

[69] Berry, 'Prudent luxury', 143–52.

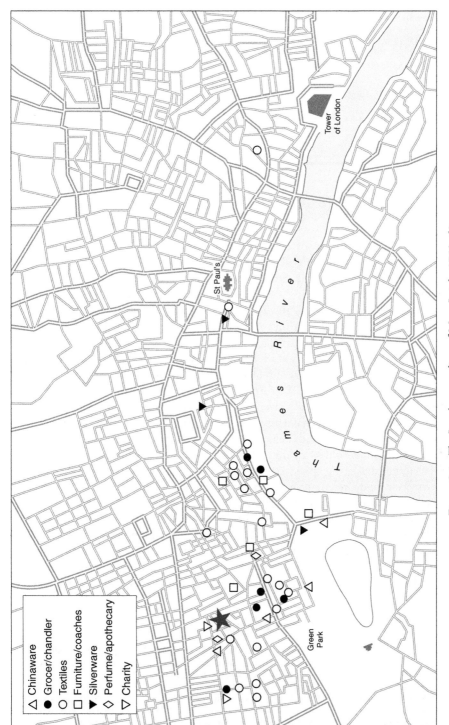

Figure 8.1. The London suppliers of Mary Leigh, 1750–69.
Source: SCLA, DR18/5/—.

Table 8.4. The distribution of London retailers supplying Mary Leigh, 1750–1806

	1750–69			1786–1806		
	No. of bills	Total (£ s. d.)	Mean (£ s. d.)	No. of bills	Total (£ s. d.)	Mean (£ s.)
Holborn & City	18	267-12-11	14-17-0	60	2,502-10-11	41-14-0
Strand & Covent Garden	47	466-18-5	9-18-0	18	506-3-0	28-2-0
Mayfair & St James	67	147-18-9	2-4-0	62	796-18-9	12-17-0
Charing Cross & Soho	88	17-15-8	1-8-0	36	1,460-2-8	40-11-0

Source: SCLA, DR18/5—bill series.

For example, the New Bond Street china dealer Edward Fogg and Samuel Brunt, whose Water Warehouse was on Saville Street, presented nine bills between them with a total value of just £3 17s. 4d.[70] Such purchases were most likely part of Mary's social round, the kind of leisure shopping described by Walsh.[71] The same may have been true for the knife cases, earrings, buckles, snuffboxes, garter buckles, and patch boxes bought over the course of seven visits to Peter Russell at Charing Cross in the early 1750s. But Russell had a reputation as the most fashionable toyshop in London at this time, so visits here were probably a key part of any expedition rather than a passing fancy.[72]

Such behaviour was important in shaping Mary's identity as a wealthy and titled young woman, not least in terms of the amount of her time that it occupied. However, the bright lights of West End shops did not dominate her shopping: the Strand and the streets around Covent Garden were far more important. It is here that we find some of her major suppliers, including the Long Acre coachmakers Thomas and James Cope and the mercers Croft and Hinchcliff of Henrietta Street, who between them sold Mary over £365 of goods.[73] Both the nature of the goods and the amounts being spent mark the importance of these suppliers in Mary's construction and presentation of herself as a person of rank. In this, they were joined by retailers located further towards the City of London. Most important in this respect were the partnership of Carr, Ibbetson, Bigge, Packard, & Gibson, at the Queen's Head in Ludgate Hill. They billed Mary on ten occasions, to a total value of £195 7s., and supplied the highest-quality dress materials, which allowed Mary to use fashion as a mark of her rank and dignity.[74] Costly brocades and silks created an impressive public appearance which was augmented by jewellery, largely

---

[70] See, for example, SCLA, DR18/5/3986, DR18/5/4252.

[71] Walsh, 'Shops, shopping'.

[72] SCLA, DR18/5/4252, DR18/5/4263, DR18/5/4264, DR18/5/3180, DR18/5/3334, DR18/5/3402, DR18/5/3565, DR18/5/3620. On Russell, see V. Brett, 'Derided and enjoyed: what was a toy—what was a toyshop', *History of Retailing and Consumption*, 2 (2015), 83–8.

[73] See, for example, SCLA, DR18/5/3738, DR18/5/3062.

[74] SCLA, DR18/5/4303, DR18/5/4441. Importantly, these textiles were bought in 21- and 23-yard lengths; those from Croft and Hinchcliff were in 12- and 16-yard lengths, suggesting more complex and elaborate dresses. See A. Buck, *Dress in Eighteenth-Century England* (London, 1979).

acquired from Thomas Gilpin of Serle Street, near Lincoln's Inn Fields, another of Mary's major suppliers.[75]

Mary's inheritance of the Leigh estates and the consequent growth and change in her spending towards estate and household management (discussed in Chapter 5) were associated with a geographical shift in her London shopping (Figure 8.2). The West End remained important, with over sixty shopkeepers from Mayfair and St James's sending bills during this period; but they were mainly occasional or minor suppliers, with average bills amounting to less than £13—comparatively small given Mary's considerably increased spending by this time (Table 8.4). Given that Mary no longer lived in the district and was probably making most of her visits by coach, it is likely that she combined trips to favoured shops with social calls.[76] Shopping in this manner retained the advantage of being able to browse and discover unexpected novelties or acquire broader knowledge of goods or fashions; it also held the possibility of companionable trips with friends. These were favoured practices amongst many female shoppers, despite a growing critique which highlighted the problem of so-called tabbies who took up a good deal of the retailer's time without any intention of making purchases.[77] However, it is clear that a large amount of Mary's shopping involved sending others to or, more often, corresponding with shopkeepers and having goods delivered either to Kensington or Stoneleigh.[78] In 1803, for instance, she was corresponding with John Taylor, a stay maker on Charles Street, about the 'thread satin' needed for lining her stays. He wrote that he had tried the silk mercers from whom he had previously acquired the cloth, but 'they had Disposed of the Remaines of the piece, and do not have any more made their [*sic*] being so Little Call for it, I have seach[t] all Silk Mercers that I can think on, for it, and Cannot get it, they told me it is quite out of date'.[79] Quite apart from the suggestion that, in common with many older women, Mary was no longer following the latest vogues in fabrics and probably in styles of clothing, this letter reveals much about the reliance placed upon suppliers to work remotely and on their own initiative to fulfil the orders placed by elite customers.[80]

Correspondence shopping was commonplace amongst the provincial gentry and aristocracy, and involved the acquisition of a wide range of everyday and luxury goods, even jewellery,[81] but it is revealing that metropolitan residents were also engaged in similar practices. For Mary, this allowed greater geographical flexibility, marked by the growing importance of major suppliers in the City or in Holborn. By

[75] Greig, *Beau Monde*, 99–130; SCLA, DR18/5/3136a. For a fuller discussion of the importance of jewellery, see M. Pointon, 'Jewellery in eighteenth-century England', in M. Berg and H. Clifford (eds), *Consumers and Luxury. Consumer Culture in Europe, 1650–1850* (Manchester, 1999).

[76] At least one of her friends, Miss Mary Parker, lived on Piccadilly—see SCLA, DR671/52, Letter, 23 March 1791.

[77] See Cox, *Complete Tradesman*, 139–45; Walsh, 'Shops, shopping'.

[78] The daybook for Grove House (SCLA, DR18/31/656) includes numerous payments for servants to travel into London and for the carriage of groceries and other goods back to Kensington.

[79] SCLA, DR18/17/27/31/15c, Letter from John Taylor, 31 December 1803.

[80] On the relationship between age, status, and adherence to fashion in clothing, see Vickery, *Gentleman's Daughter*, 175–8; Chatenet-Calyste, 'Feminine luxury in Paris', 181–5. On the customer–shopkeeper relationship, see Cox, *Complete Tradesman*, 116–45; Eland, *Purefoy Letters, passim*.

[81] See, for example, Pointon, 'Women and their jewels', 16–17.

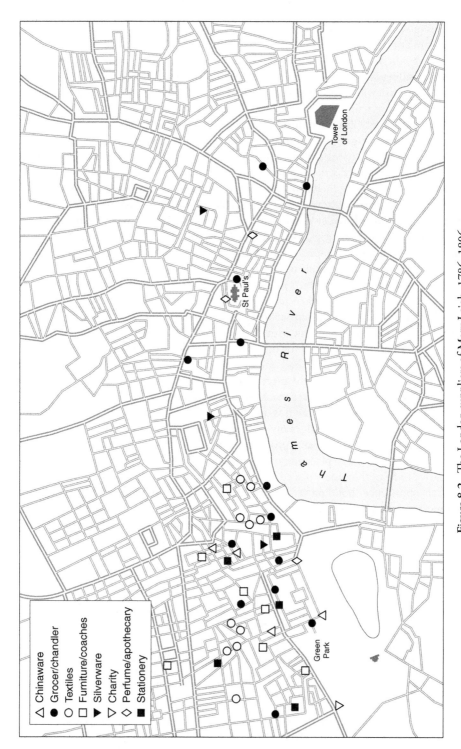

Figure 8.2. The London suppliers of Mary Leigh, 1786–1806.

Source: SCLA, DR18/5/—.

the 1790s, this area was by far the most important in terms of both volume and value of transactions, despite housing just nine of Mary's suppliers (Table 8.4). They included grocers, drapers, and silversmiths who sold the goods which were becoming increasingly central to Mary's consumption practices (see Chapter 5). Fine culinary groceries came from Frances Field of Holborn, and North, Hoare, & Hanson on New Bridge Street, just west of St Paul's, who together billed Mary on twenty-seven occasions and for a total of £736 11s. 8d. of goods.[82] Silverware amounting to £1,518 11s. 11d. was supplied by Robert and Thomas Makepeace, counted amongst the leading silversmiths in London and located on Terle Street in an area traditionally associated with such trades.[83] The engraved waiters, tureens, beef dishes, toast trays, tea vases, coffee pots, and candlesticks that would have adorned her table and side-board were important in the creation of Mary's self-image as a wealthy land owner. So too was livery acquired from the Fells of St Martin's Lane. Their nine bills amounted to over £1,110, making them second only to Makepeace in their impor-tance to Mary's material culture. In part, this growth helps to explain the decline in importance of Covent Garden retailers as London's retailing moved inexorably west-wards. Also important, though, was the marked shift in Mary's spending away from clothing for herself. In the 1760s, Covent Garden stood out in terms of bills for drapery and haberdashery; by the 1790s and 1800s, there was only one retailer in the area serving this need: the laceman, R Bentley & Sons of Bedford Street.[84]

Mary Leigh's London shopping thus changed in geography as its character shifted from the preoccupations of a young and wealthy woman to the responsibilities of a major and extremely rich landowner. Sir Roger Newdigate experienced less dra-matic shifts in his personal circumstances, his shopping patterns being shaped instead by the changing character of his engagement with the metropolis. As an active MP, Newdigate was frequently in London and it is no surprise that many of his suppliers were found in the streets around his house in Spring Gardens (Figure 8.3). Thomas Payne's bookshop in Leicester Fields, Collett's china shop on Cockspur Street, and Parker and Wakelin, the renowned silversmiths on Panton Street, were all within a brisk five-minute walk and all received his custom. Despite such easy access, this geographical clustering around his home did not form the most important shopping area for Newdigate in terms of the number and size of transactions (Table 8.5). Instead, it was Holborn and especially the City that took the greatest share of his spending in London, accounting for more than all the other areas combined. Like Mary in her later years, the City was a major source of food and drink, Bridget and Alexander Allan, wine merchants on Mark Lane, and James Bennett, a grocer on Fenchurch Street, both appearing in the account books each year from the 1750s to the 1770s and between them supplying well over £1,700 of goods. But Newdigate also looked to the City for regular and sustained supplies of

---

[82] See, for example, the large consolidated bills from Francis Field: SCLA, DR18/5/5865. For fuller discussion of the kind of groceries supplied by Field, see Stobart, *Sugar and Spice*, 50–5.

[83] SCLA, DR18/5/5809; H. Clifford, *Silver in London: The Parker and Wakelin Partnership 1760–1776* (New Haven, CT, 2004).

[84] See, for example, SCLA, DR18/5/6040, DR18/5/6181. Lace was an old luxury, again marking Mary's conservative taste.

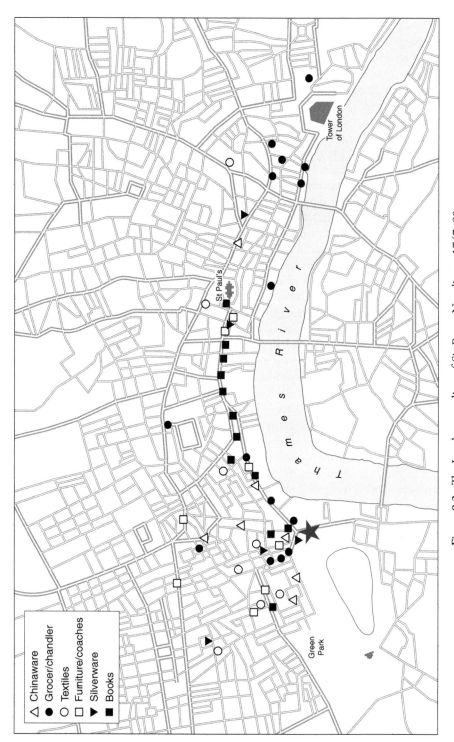

Figure 8.3. The London suppliers of Sir Roger Newdigate, 1747–80.

Source: WRO, CR136/V/156, CR136/V/136.

clothing fabrics and haberdashery, livery, books, and silverware. The retailers that he patronized there were thus central to constructing and maintaining his status as a wealthy landowner, London resident, and MP. That said, the same was true of tradespeople on St Giles and the Strand (where he acquired his coach and bought books), around Charing Cross and Soho (where he patronized a wine merchant, oilmen, and a tea merchant in addition to the silversmith, bookseller, and china dealers noted above), and even in Mayfair and Piccadilly (whence came linen, hosiery, and china, as well as much of his furniture, courtesy of J. Glover on Piccadilly and Thomas Gillow on Oxford Street). If Newdigate was constructing his identity through his consumption, he was doing so on the basis of purchases from across the metropolis, although some areas were financially more important than others.

Goods for his households came from across the city space, a reflection in part of the need to service two substantial households and improve two houses, but some of Newdigate's personal tastes were catered for by retailers in well-defined areas. This is most clearly seen in the distribution of his booksellers, the majority of whom were located along Fleet Street and the Strand (Figure 8.3). These were important streets in the London book trade, housing many of the key publishers and printers as well as a large number of booksellers. However, it is striking that he only occasionally ventured into other strongholds of the book trade, such as St Paul's Churchyard and Paternoster Row, or patronized any of the up-and-coming traders in Mayfair.[85] That said, his most important supplier during this period was Thomas Payne, with whom he spent £133 13s. 9d. between 1754 and 1778. It is impossible to know whether this concentration of spending reflected the conviviality of the shop, the reputation of the tradesman, or the range of stock on offer. Newdigate's personal preferences clearly played a role, his ability to choose between suppliers and patronize a wide range of shops being underpinned by his enthusiasm for walking London's streets. The walk to Deard's shop noted earlier would have involved a round trip of about 2 miles, but his visit to Ellicot to have his watch cleaned meant walking over 5 miles. The route which he took is also significant. From Spring Gardens, he would have walked along the Strand, Fleet Street, Ludgate Hill, St Paul's Churchyard, and onto Cornhill, exactly the southern axis of retailing described later in *The Picture of London*. This would provide ample opportunity to view at least the windows of a huge number of premises, thus broadening his awareness of and access to London's shops.[86]

The ability to visit shops in person and interact directly with tradesmen and their wares declined markedly when Newdigate resigned as an MP in 1780. He retained his London house through the 1780s and 1790s, and his spending remained at a high level, but he spent less time in the metropolis and patronized fewer London tradespeople. The geography of his shopping also changed, the earlier clusters thinning to leave a more even distribution of suppliers in which food and drink retailers were most numerous (Figure 8.4). In some ways, this resembles

---

[85] Raven, *Business of Books*, 158–92.

[86] On the importance of browsing in shaping shopping behaviour, see Cox, *Complete Tradesman*, 139–45; Berg, *Luxury and Pleasure*, 257–70; Walsh, 'Shops, shopping'; Stobart, *Spend Spend Spend!*, 93–5, 108–9.

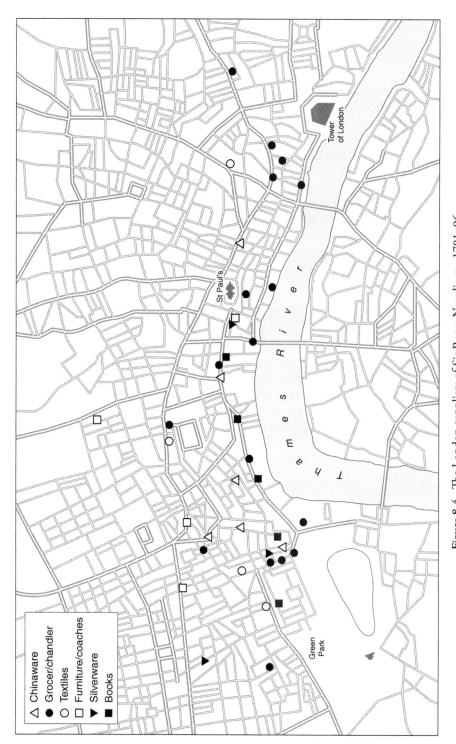

Figure 8.4. The London suppliers of Sir Roger Newdigate, 1781–96.
Source: SCLA, WRO, CR136/V/136.

Legend:
△ Chinaware
● Grocer/chandler
○ Textiles
□ Furniture/coaches
▶ Silverware
■ Books

Tower of London

St Paul's

Thames River

Green Park

Table 8.5. The distribution of London retailers supplying Sir Roger Newdigate, 1747–96

	1747–80			1781–96		
	No. of account entries	Total (£ s. d.)	Mean (£ s. d.)	No. of account entries	Total (£ s. d.)	Mean (£ s.)
Holborn & City	207	3,635-14-0	17-2-0	105	2,622-8-0	25-0-0
Strand & Covent Garden	47	603-2-0	12-16-0	30	425-1-0	14-8-0
Mayfair & St James's	89	832-16-0	9-6-0	52	718-8-0	13-16-0
Charing Cross & Soho	148	1,721-16-0	11-12-0	115	1,624-16-0	14-2-0

Source: WRO, CR136/V/136, Account books.

the shifts seen in Mary Leigh's shopping patterns, but with Newdigate the relative importance and role of different districts remained more or less steady. The area around Spring Gardens was still a significant source of various goods, from books, silverware, and china, to oil, candles, tea, and wine, in part because he remained loyal to suppliers used in earlier decades: Payne was still his principal bookseller, Wakelin his favoured silversmith, and Rutton his main source of tea. But the City was still the most important area in terms of spending (Table 8.5), particularly in terms of groceries, wine, and tailoring. Perhaps the most striking change was the transfer of business from Osman Adkins, who appears to have ceased trading in 1784, to William Leader of Liquorpond Street, from whom Newdigate purchased a new chaise in 1786 and a new coach the following year.[87]

The overall impression is that Newdigate had thinned out his network of suppliers, perhaps because, like Judith Baker, he was happier dealing with a smaller set of known and trusted tradespeople.[88] Certainly, his reduced time in London meant that more of his purchases were made remotely, arranged through correspondence with suppliers. This is true of books, but also of a range of other goods, including tea from Richard Twining on the Strand, clothing from Stephen Penny of King Street, fire irons and register stoves from William Bent & Sons of St Martin's Lane, scagliola columns from Joseph Alcott of Southampton Place, chimney pieces from William Stalker of Mortimer Street, and a 'gothic stove' from Oldham & Oldham of Holborn.[89] Newdigate was in correspondence with all of these tradesmen through the 1790s and early 1800s, often about the means by which goods would be delivered. For example, Barlo Valle wrote in December 1802 that a consignment of groceries had been delayed because 'owing to some dysfunction upon the Canal, they declined taking charge of the above at the Castle Inn, Wood Street, he therefore

[87] The total cost of these two vehicles was £297 10s.: WRO, CR136/V/136, Account book, entries for 1784 and 1786.
[88] Berry, 'Prudent luxury', 143–52.
[89] WRO, CR136/B/2625a, Letter from Richard Twining (tea); CR136/B/2635a, Letter from Bent & Sons (register stove and fire irons); CR136/B/3048a–g, Letters from Oldham & Oldham (Gothic stove); CR136/B/3049b, Letter from Penny & Son, 10 December 1801; CR136/B/2635e–g, Receipted bills, various dates (scagliola columns); CR136/B/2635b, Receipted bill, 16 November 1797 (chimney pieces).

forwarded them yesterday by Boonham's Atherstone waggon'.[90] Shopping remotely also required detailed instructions to be given to the tradesman in terms of both the character and quality of the goods being provided. Henry Purefoy came unstuck shopping in this way, the cut of this new waistcoat being wrong so that 'it gapes so intolerably before at the bottom, when I button it at ye wastbone of my breetches & stand upright it gapes at the bottom beyond my breetches & everybody takes notice of it'. Newdigate was clearly very exact about such things, his tailor Stephen Penny writing in 1801 that 'I hope your Breeches are right about the Pockets as my foreman says they are made exact in that as your last Breeches (and I have made them larger in the knee).' Yet things could still go awry; Penny's following letter included a lengthy apology for the poor fit of his servants' livery, which he blamed on having been sent the wrong measurements.[91]

For much of his long life, Sir Roger Newdigate had the benefit of a London house and took full advantage of the opportunities this afforded for visiting shops and nurturing bonds of trust with particular tradespeople. Edward Leigh was less fortunate in this regard, there being little to suggest that he had a town house from which to orchestrate his London shopping. This goes some way in explaining the lack of clustering of his suppliers, who were fairly evenly distributed between St Paul's and New Bond Street, again with the Strand as the key east-west axis (Figure 8.5). So too does the limited extent to which he appears to have shopped in person. He went to Vaillant's bookshop on the Strand and probably visited other booksellers and perhaps also his tailor, Edward Fell on St Martin's Lane; but he also dealt with Vaillant via correspondence,[92] and his engagement with upholsterers, furniture makers, and the like was mostly organized remotely or via his steward (see Chapters 6 and 7). Although this occasioned problems similar to those encountered by Newdigate and others, it released Edward to choose from tradespeople across the city. His engagement with booksellers is revealing in this context. Whereas Newdigate's suppliers were spatially concentrated, Edward's patronage spread from James Fletcher on St Paul's Churchyard, Joseph Graham on Fleet Street, and Paul Vaillant on the Strand to Thomas Payne in Leicester Fields and James Robson on New Bond Street. The last of these is particularly interesting, as his shop lay within what Raven calls 'the fast-growing western neighbourhoods [which] housed fashionable and controversial booksellers'. Robson counted amongst the former and had a reputation as a 'gregarious and learned bibliophile', which placed him on a similar footing to Payne and made his shop attractive not simply for the breadth and variety of stock.[93]

Whilst Edward ranged across established and up-and-coming retail areas, it was the former that accounted for the bulk of his spending, especially when it came to

[90] WRO, CR136/B/2625a—receipted bill. Use of the Atherstone wagon would further strengthen Newdigate's links with the town.

[91] Eland, *Purefoy Letters*, No.437; WRO, CR136/B/3049b, Letter from Penny & Son, 10 December 1801, CR136/B/3049c, Letter from Penny & Son, 3 February 1802. For more general discussion of the problems of remote shopping, see Stobart, Hann, and Morgan, *Spaces of Consumption*, 162–3.

[92] See, for example, SCLA, DR18/17/27/149, Letter from Paul Vaillant, 10 July 1766.

[93] Raven, *Business of Books*, 188–9.

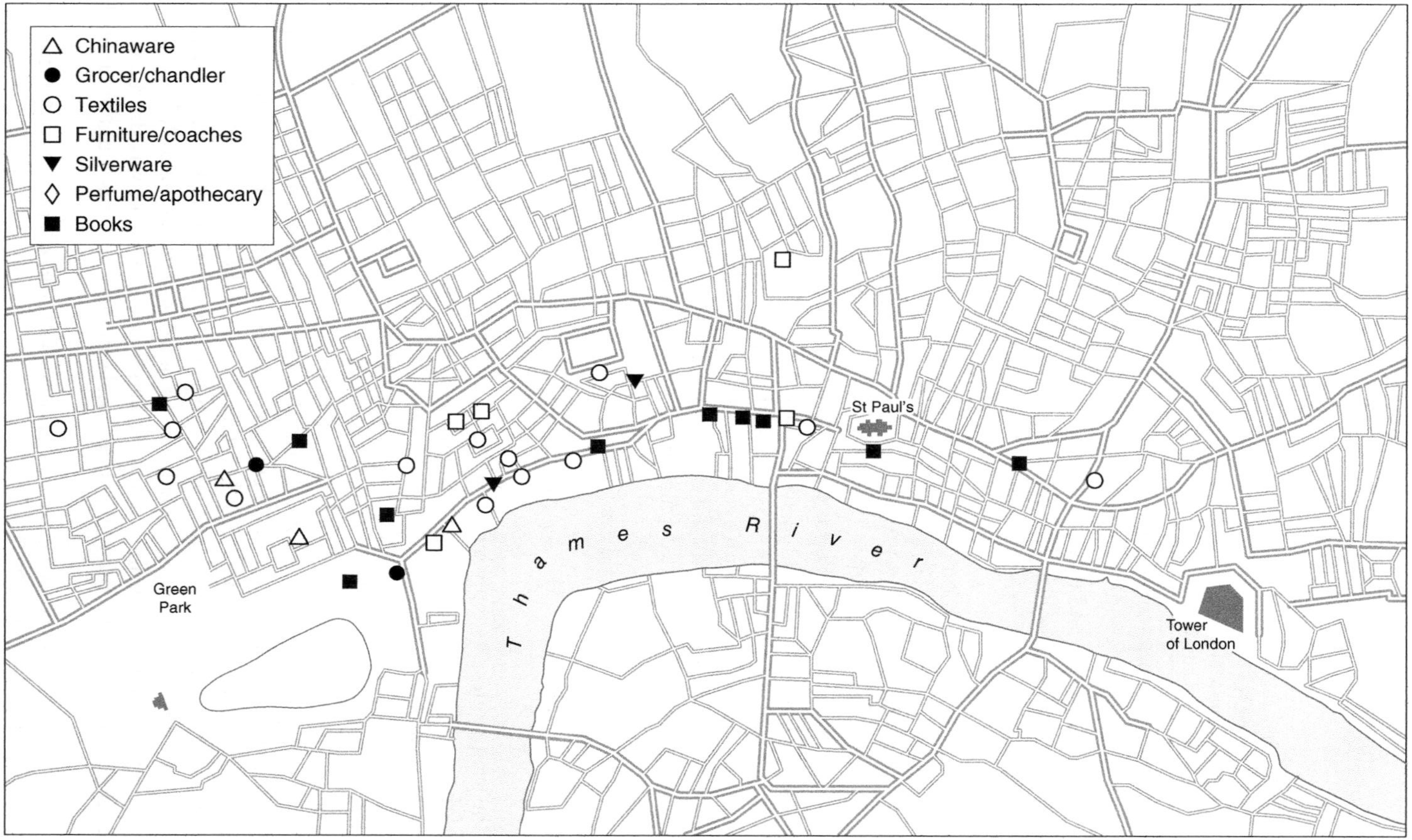
Chinaware
Grocer/chandler
Textiles
Furniture/coaches
Silverware
Perfume/apothecary
Books
St Paul's
Thames River
Green Park
Tower of London

Figure 8.5. The London suppliers of Edward Leigh, 1763–8.
Source: SCLA, DR18/5/—.

Table 8.6. The distribution of London retailers supplying Edward Leigh, fifth Lord Leigh, 1750–86

	No. of bills	Total (£ s. d.)	Mean (£ s. d.)
Holborn & City	27	2,874-19-2	106-8-0
Strand & Covent Garden	18	3,964-9-2	220-4-0
Mayfair & St James's	19	480-1-10	25-6-0
Charing Cross & Soho	19	736-4-1	38-14-0

Source: SCLA, DR18/5—bill series.

acquiring furniture and decorative items for his Warwickshire house (Table 8.6). These patterns were skewed somewhat by some extremely large bills, most notably that for £3,383 3s. 5d. from Thomas and Gilbert Burnett, upholsterers, on the Strand; nonetheless, it is readily apparent that retailers in traditional areas were central to the construction of Edward's identity as a wealthy and tasteful member of the aristocracy. There were substantial bills from Thomas Gilpin of Terle Street (£779 4s. 3d. for silverware), William Gomm of Clerkenwell (£818 9s. for furniture), Bromwich and Leigh (£356 7s. for wallpaper), and Jordan Biggar of Leadenhall Street (£329 19s. for table and bed linen).[94] This underscores both the inertia of London's retail geography and the concern of elite customers for the reputation of the tradesperson as well as the quality of their wares. As Davis has noted, a City shopkeeper 'with a good reputation in London and a sound connection among country gentry … still did a bigger trade than his more showy colleague in Oxford Street who depended much more on what was contemptuously called a 'dropping trade'.[95]

CONCLUSIONS

The geographies of supply servicing the country house, and the needs and desires of their owners, were both straightforward and complex. Although our sources mask many local supplies coming from the estate and the surrounding villages, they reveal a hierarchy of centres servicing Arbury Hall and Stoneleigh Abbey. London was dominant, both in both quantitative and qualitative terms: it attracted the largest amount of elite spending and was the chief source of luxury goods. However, local towns were the source of a remarkable range of goods, from groceries and livery, to glasses and clocks, and there was considerable overlap in the categories of goods purchased locally and from London. We cannot be certain about the precise motivations underpinning the consumer behaviour recorded in bills and account books. Considerations of quality, choice, and reputation were undoubtedly important, especially when buying from London retailers, but convenience was also a consideration. It made good sense to buy from local suppliers, and this could mean both

[94] See, for example, SCLA, DR18/5/4251, DR18/5/4408, DR18/5/4402, DR18/5/4028.
[95] Davis, *History of Shopping*, 196–7.

the towns and villages around the country house and the streets around a London residence. Seasonal or life-cycle mobility strengthened the influence of London and thus undermined any regional culture of consumption, there being relatively little overlap in the supply networks of the two houses. The Leighs and Newdigates were certainly not part of London's Beau Monde, nor did they show any interest in this metropolitan elite; but they were firmly within a London sphere. This was moderated by the personal preferences and loyalties of individual consumers, sometimes linked with leisure activities (Bath or Atherstone) and sometimes with earlier place associations (Oxford); yet London was central in shaping their purchases, their consumption, and their identities. Certainly, it was far more important, and exerted its influence more directly, than European centres of supply, which were the source of a remarkably small quantity of goods. Any broader, cosmopolitan cultures of shopping fed through to the consumption practices of the Leighs and Newdigates primarily through their interaction with London society and London suppliers.

Within London, patterns of supply were multivalent, different kinds of goods requiring different modes of shopping. This produced several overlapping geographies of aristocratic shopping, which suggest greater spatial flexibility than was apparent in elite shopping in Paris.[96] There were shops that were visited casually, perhaps as part of the social round. Most obvious amongst these were the mercers, milliners, and toyshops of Mayfair and St James's, visited by the youthful Mary Leigh and central to her identity as a wealthy young woman. There were others that were also the object of browsing, but which were linked more to the conscious construction of self. Sir Roger Newdigate and Edward, fifth Lord Leigh, both used bookshops in this way, shaping their identity as learned gentlemen and knowledgeable collectors through their visits to and patronage of key suppliers across the metropolis. A third geography of shopping focused on the enhancement of rank and status through the provision of luxury goods for the home: silverware, furniture, upholstery, wallpaper, chinaware, and the like. The shops and warehouses of these trades were visited purposely rather than casually, but they were certainly places to which the elite could and did go. Wedgwood's York Street showrooms are most famous in this respect (indeed, he positioned his premises both geographically and symbolically to make them a place of resort for the wealthy, not least by calling them 'Portland House'[97]), but the warehouses of Thomas Burnett and Thomas Leigh on the Strand were also visited by wealthy customers, as were the shops of toymen and silversmiths—a point made clear in the trade card of Phillips Garden.[98] A fourth set of shops, epitomized by grocers and wine merchants in the City, were places from which goods were dispatched, but to which elite customers rarely if ever ventured. Yet these were still important in servicing elite lifestyles and rank amongst those retailers patronized most regularly by country house owners.

[96] See Coquery, *Tenir boutique à Paris*; Chatenet-Calyste, 'Feminine luxury in Paris'.
[97] Morrison, *English Shops*, 36–7; Berg, *Luxury and Pleasure*, 146–7.
[98] British Museum, Heal, 67.156.

Combined, these overlapping geographies represent a set of behaviours that were shaped by and in turn moulded the retail geography of London.

Shopping also reflected and formed the needs and character of elite consumers. We see this in the variety of goods purchased and shops patronized—a reflection of the complexity of supplying the country house, but also the personal preferences and practices of the shopper. Whilst visiting shops was certainly an important pastime for the leisured classes, especially in London, this was not simply a frivolous activity; it provided opportunities to acquire useful knowledge about the character and attributes of goods. Berg makes this point in relation to the products of the 'industrial enlightenment', but it was just as true of traditional markers of status and everyday provisions—as the actions of Edward and Mary Leigh and Sir Roger Newdigate make clear.[99] Knowledge of this type was layered with information concerning price, quality, and the reputation of retailers, which was built into a bank of practical 'social knowledge' that could be deployed in deciding between myriad suppliers.[100] As we have seen in earlier chapters, especially Chapter 7, such knowledge was built up over time and shared across several members of the elite household. The geographies of supply that serviced the country house thus reflected the combined knowledge and experience of the consuming household, as well the tastes and preferences of the individual landowner.

[99] Berg, *Luxury and Pleasure*, 268.
[100] On social knowledge, see P. Jackson and N. Thrift, 'Geographies of consumption', in D. Miller (ed.) *Acknowledging Consumption* (London, 1995), 204–38.

Conclusions

For most people today, guidebooks and websites are often the first port of call when planning a visit to a country house: the information provided is thus central to decisions about where to go and what to look for. These guides tend to focus on the large-scale luxury and splendour of country houses, the things that made them exceptional both then and now. In *Hudson's Historic Houses*, the entry for Stoneleigh Abbey tells us that it contains 'magnificent state rooms', an '18th century Baroque West Wing', and '690 acres of grounds and parkland'. At Arbury Hall, we can expect to see 'a fine collection of both oriental and Chinese porcelain, portraits by Lely, Reynolds, Devis and Romney', along with 'soaring fan vaulted ceilings' and 'a most breathtaking and complete example of Gothic Revival architecture'.[1] Many of these features were planned, selected, purchased, and installed by the owners we have discussed in this book, people such as Sir Roger Newdigate and Edward, fifth Lord Leigh. The architectural exceptionality of country houses and the luxurious objects and artwork they contained were important signifiers of the power and identity of landowners, reflecting their distinctive elite status through conspicuous displays of wealth and taste. The sheer scale and the complexity of country houses, and the emphasis placed on luxury, suggest that these alone are what defined them. The reality was far more complex. Focusing on the magnificence of houses and their glittering contents masks the networks, relationships, and nuances of identity that we have explored in this book: the 'everydayness' of functional and lived environments that flowed beneath the surface of these projections of power and wealth. The surface details obscure the layering of spending, from the bedrock of everyday household running costs to the more conspicuous items of expenditure. Getting behind the facades of the country house has so much to tell us about them, their owners and the history of consumption.

MOTIVATIONS, IDENTITIES, AND MATERIAL CULTURE

In many ways, luxury was central to the meaning and form of the country house. The wealth of the landowning elite gave them much greater scope to indulge in spending on a wide range of luxuries, and their motivation for doing so is deceptively simple: to display their wealth and status. This conspicuous consumption is evident in the acquisition of positional goods, the price and scarcity of which

---

[1] *Hudson's Historic Houses and Gardens; Castles and Heritage Sites* (Banbury, 2000), 312, 308.

signalled the wealth of their owners: Sir Roger Newdigate's Italian marbles, the fifth Lord Leigh's rich crimson drapery, and Mary Leigh's gifts of venison. It was perhaps most obviously expressed in the size and fabric of the country house itself, which, as Girouard noted, was the ultimate marker of its owner's ambition.[2] These might be seen as the traditional markers of elite status: they were 'old luxuries' that aimed at social distinction. Yet they were symbols available to others as well, the nabob being the archetypal 'other' against which the established elites defended their status and defined their identity. In this context, taste was a weapon in defensive consumption, delimiting membership of the elite in terms of a certain hard to define but unmistakable quality. It defined the Beau Monde of eighteenth-century London and the Parisian elite of the 1950s, in part as a means of tempering the excesses of luxury and fashion—a trap into which the unwary could easily fall.[3] This is familiar enough, but our analysis nuances this in two important ways. Firstly, taste expressed in the form of collections could encourage excess and thus drove consumption in complex ways. This problem was familiar to bibliophiles, who spent considerable amounts of time and money pursuing particular volumes. The activities of Edward, fifth Lord Leigh, are particularly striking in this regard, especially given the pace at which he assembled his impressive library; but it might also be seen in Sir Roger's purchases in Italy. Whilst these could be justified in terms of taste and virtue, they might also be seen as excessive and obsessive, though by no means ruinous. Secondly, the conspicuous consumption of luxury was also moderated by other motivations: conservatism, rank, family pedigree, comfort, and thrift. The blending was different with each house and each individual, but they shaped the consumption of all three families. Standing as they did at the crossroads of dynastic identity, syncretic family relationships, the exigencies of financial and estate management, and everyday human needs and desires, the aristocracy illustrate the complex interaction of conspicuous consumption with broader sets of values and norms. It went some way to defining them, marking them out, but it was not their only or even their primary source of identity.

Perhaps most striking is the way in which the landowning elites studied here mixed the materiality and motivations of old and new luxury. Sir Roger Newdigate invested in the exclusive language of architecture, but also purchased the equipage of polite dining and tea drinking and engaged in the sociability of circulating libraries; Edward, fifth Lord Leigh, decorated his hall with allusions to classical mythology and acquired large quantities of engraved silverware, and at the same time demonstrated virtuous consumption in the form of books, music, and scientific instruments, later shared with his alma mater; and Elizabeth and Sir John Turner Dryden retained the symbols of family pedigree at Canons Ashby whilst relegating tapestries to marginal spaces and creating tasteful settings for informal sociability. Alongside their range of lavish spending, the Leighs and Newdigates engaged in productive investment—a key marker of the different priorities of new luxury. Just as Clemente argues, then, the dividing lines between old/traditional

---

[2] Girouard, *English Country House*, 1–12.
[3] Greig, *Beau Monde*; Bourdieu, *Distinction*; Berg, *Luxury and Pleasure*, 40–3.

and new/modern, which appear very clear and definite in rhetorical terms, can become blurred in the reality of material lives.[4]

In some ways, this questions the usefulness of old and new luxury as analytical categories, and perhaps also the broader distinction between traditional-aristocratic and commercial-urban modes of social engagement made by Fontaine.[5] Certainly, it challenges the assumption that the elite were somehow left behind by an increasingly bourgeois culture of consumption that emphasized different priorities and objects. The point here is fourfold. First and foremost is the reality of elite engagement in the ideology and practices of new luxury: the values expressed through the ownership of new luxuries were as important as the objects themselves. Second, this engagement was central to elite identity: Lord Leigh was defined as much by the mahogany backgammon table in his breakfast room, the flock wallpapers in his guest rooms, and the books and music in his library as he was by his showy carriage, engraved silverware, and splendid gilt furniture inherited from his grandfather. In short, old and new luxury came together in particular ways to define elite identities. Third, elites were central rather than marginal to the cultural and material currency of new luxury. Indeed, whilst undoubtedly more accessible, many of the manifestations of new luxury were made attractive by the example set by the wealthy elite, a reality to which contemporaries were very much alive. Fourth, the heterogeneity and variety of new luxury—which were, as Berg argues,[6] central to its accessibility to different social groups—also opened up the potential for displays of wealth and distinction in a manner more akin to the logic of old luxury. Taking the example of tea drinking, this allowed endless opportunities to show superior taste and status in terms of the quality of the tea and the porcelain, the deployment of significant quantities of silverware, the elegance of perfect white hands, and, of course, the exclusivity of the company invited to share the ritual. This does not mean throwing away the entire conceptual framework of old and new luxury—there was undoubtedly an important set of mental and material changes taking place through the early-modern period which involved shifting priorities and practices of consumption. However, it does mean nuancing its binary distinctions and being more attuned to the ways in which the impetus and spread were not necessarily linked to new social groups. The cultural influence of the elite did not cease with the emergence of new luxury.

That said, defining material culture in terms of luxury, in its various forms, is in many ways misleading. There is a need to recalibrate our perspective on the country house in particular, balancing conspicuous against everyday consumption. Large amounts of the spending of the Leighs, Newdigates, and Drydens were directed at maintaining, cleaning, heating, and lighting their homes, and feeding families, servants, and visitors. This mundane spending is often overlooked, largely because it lacks the obvious drama of paintings by old masters or furniture by Chippendale. Yet is was not only necessary in the upkeep of lifestyles embodied in

---

[4] De Vries, *Industrious Revolution*, 44–5, 57–8; Clemente, 'Luxury and taste in eighteenth-century Naples'.

[5] Fontaine, *Moral Economy*, esp. 70–94.   [6] Berg, *Luxury and Pleasure*.

the country house, but also helped to define those lifestyles: ample lighting was central to sociability in the evenings, and wax candles spoke of wealth and adherence to proper social standards; clean and crisp table linen spoke volumes of respectability and control; and fires, lamps, and servants allowed physical comfort and convenience.[7]

These priorities were shared with a broader set of polite and respectable households; so too was a concern for family. Our analysis confirms Lewis's argument that family and the material reminders of family offered emotional comfort; it also demonstrates the continued importance of rank and pedigree.[8] These were written into the fabric of the building and stamped onto material objects in the form of crests, coronets, and coats of arms in a manner that distinguished the elite from other social groups. Pedigree was also apparent in the presence of inherited furniture, galleries of portraits, and boxes of archives, even if Elizabeth Dryden had mixed feelings about the last of these. The middle ranks may have been increasingly engaged in constructing a diachronic sense of family through journals and letters, as Harvey argues, but this was still an essentially elite culture.[9] The patina glow of history was something that was difficult to create: its emphasis by all three families reflects its importance as a form of defensive consumption, but also as a defining element of the elite. Indeed, family was central to elite culture. Children ensured the future of the estate, but having ancestors who mattered, especially in the form of rank and title, made the elite distinct and shaped their self-identity. This linked to consumption in terms of choices about what to retain and how to present these things within the house. The pictorial family tree created by Henrietta Cavendish was exceptional, even excessive, but it was echoed in the preservation of the Great Apartment at Stoneleigh Abbey, in the reimagining of the Great Hall at Canons Ashby, and in the funeral arrangements of Edward, fifth Lord Leigh, where the symbols of rank and title were combined with an entourage comprising peers, the household, and key tradesmen. The fact that those seeking to gain acceptance within the established elite sometimes attempted to construct these material signs of pedigree, as the Russells did at Swallowfield Park when assembling a gallery of family portraits, demonstrates their cultural currency.

Constructing identity through consumption was, of course, a complex and multifaceted process which involved individuals shaping themselves in alignment with several different and sometimes competing character types. Exploring masculinity through the lens of consumption demonstrates how it was constructed materially as well as discursively: through the ownership of horses, paintings, books, and scientific equipment, as well as the pages of conduct literature and personal correspondence. Whilst this is well recognized in some senses, there has been a reluctance to look much beyond the showy extravagances of carriages and fine clothes or the apparent obsession with saddlery and tackle.[10] Sir Roger Newdigate and Edward, fifth Lord Leigh, were men of a different cut, cultivating an air of polite

---

[7] See Crowley, *Invention of Comfort*, 171–200, but also Chavasse, 'Material culture and the country house', 123–69.

[8] Lewis, 'When a house'.   [9] Harvey, *Little Republic*, 172–3.

[10] See Hussey, 'Guns, horses and stylish waistcoats'; Vickery, *Behind Closed Doors*, esp. 124.

learning, through both the possessions they acquired and the ways in which they related to other people, displaying taste and virtue, and exercising control of self and others. These men conformed to broader ideals of masculinity, whether that was the polite scholar or the heroic horseman, but just as they chose from a range of goods, services, and suppliers, so they also constructed their identities by selecting from a complex palette of gender archetypes.

Female consumption is also revealed as far more nuanced than is often recognized. To an extent, the role of the wife was defined in relation to her husband, which in Hester Newdigate's case, as with the married couples studied by Vickery, meant responsibility for the day-to-day management of the household.[11] But this is too limited a view of a wife's role in consumption and in shaping aristocratic identities: the elite women studied here enjoyed considerable scope for spending, even when married, as the outgoings on clothing for both of Sir Roger's wives attest. Moreover, they shared interests with him, making it more difficult to disentangle causality in terms of spending patterns: Sophia's travel journal makes clear her interest in architecture and especially the Gothic, and the catalogue of Hester's books reveals the size and diversity of her library. Equally, a wife's interests might be complementary, Sophia having a passion for gardening, revealed in detailed lists of flowering plants that noted their location in the garden, that is not readily apparent in Sir Roger at this time.[12] These reinforce and add further depth to the picture painted by Vickery of female consumption and feminine taste. Studying elite single women takes us beyond this and questions their experience as characterized by crisis and unhappiness. Singleness brought independence, especially when it was coupled with wealth, allowing Mary Leigh to spend freely. Yet her restraint is in line with that of her male counterparts and her spending patterns increasingly resembled those of other landowners. Female identity was thus overlain with that of the landowner, complete with its emphasis of family and rank. Whilst Elizabeth Dryden was heavily circumscribed by her husband's debts, she maintained a rhetoric of status and independence. For both these women and for the elite more generally, family remained an important touchstone, even in the absence of close living relatives.

How far did these particular motivations and identities make the country house a distinctly aristocratic space? Horrell, Humphries, and Sneath have recently examined the extent to which the poor of London shared in an eighteenth-century shift in consumption, but the elite have rarely been assessed in relative terms.[13] We have already noted that they were not defined by unswerving adherence to old luxury, although this was important in distinguishing them from the nouveau riche and the rising middling sort. The possession of tapestries, silverware, carriages, and the like was therefore not, as de Vries implies, a carry-over from an earlier material culture now devoid of its moral compass or its power to stimulate

---

[11] Vickery, *Behind Closed Doors*, 106–28.

[12] See WRO, CR136/V/166, Catalogues of Lady Newdigate's Books, 1798; CR136/71, Trees & shrubs at Arbury, 1753.

[13] Horrell, Humphries, and Sneath, 'Consumption conundrums unravelled'.

imitation and perhaps even emulation.[14] Rather, they were central to the character and identity of the elite, symbols of established rank and status that retained meaning for the elite and for wider society. Set alongside more novel and fashionable goods and within the changing structures and material cultures of the country house, their meanings shifted and morphed, but they provided a reference point for permanence in a new world of consumerism. We have also seen that taste was not the only restraint on the excess of luxury, important thought this was in defining the character and consumption of men like Edward, fifth Lord Leigh. Family was also critically important in shaping the materiality of the country house, being manifest in portraits, coats of arms, and rooms of inherited goods. Heritance and pedigree could be married into (a process which often linked new money and old title) and sometimes painstakingly recreated, but could not be purchased via the market like a carriage, a set of Chippendale furniture, or even an estate. The status and respectability that they brought was increasingly colonized by the nineteenth-century bourgeoisie, in a process that underpins the continued relevance of the elite as leaders of wider changes in domestic material culture.[15] In these ways, elite material culture was linked to, yet distinct from, that of the middle ranks, differentiated by qualitative as well as quantitative differences. Most obviously, the books, portraits, and sculpture accumulated in varying degrees even by those some distance below the great collectors like the first Earl of Leicester or the first Duke of Bedford, spoke of refined taste and deep pockets; fashionable interiors showed awareness of prevailing modes of decoration and entertainment; and the blending of this with old goods and older systems of taste demonstrated the pedigree and permanence of the family.

Examining the country house through the lens of consumption thus offers many new insights. The house was more than an elegant box filled with fine *objets d'art*, the character and provenance of which holds the key to our understanding of the house and its owner. Of course, such art historical perspectives are useful, but they often miss the broader picture: the meanings accorded to a whole range of goods, from candles to carriages, and from bohea tea to books. All these things were chosen, acquired, and used in ways that consciously or often subconsciously shaped elite identity and material culture. Seeing aristocratic landowners as consumers is in some ways anachronistic, but it invites us to think about their motivations rather than simply attribute these to notions of 'taste' that hide much more than they reveal. Moreover, it places elite material culture in a relational context, linking it to the needs and influences of the household, and to broader shifts in material culture. Here the country house offers a useful control against which to assess any transformation to a so-called new material culture. With money no object, this transformation should be complete. As we have already noted, however, change was partial and contingent: the inertia of existing material objects and of the house itself acted as a break on transformation and called into question the

---

[14] De Vries, *Industrious Revolution*, 45.

[15] See C. Edwards and M. Ponsonby, 'The polarisation of the second-hand market for furniture in the nineteenth century', in J. Stobart and I. Van Damme (eds) *Modernity and the Second-Hand Trade: European Consumption Cultures and Practices, 1700–1900* (Basingstoke, 2011), 105–6.

unthinking assumption that change necessarily signals progress. More generally, the everyday spending of the elite, so meticulously recorded in account books and receipted bills, added very significantly to the impact of domestic consumption as an economic driver. Enthusiasm for McKendrick's consumer revolution as a stimulus for industrialization may have wavered, but spending on the home undoubtedly stimulated considerable trade.

SPATIALITIES, PRACTICALITIES, AND SUPPLY

The country house was not an undifferentiated space. More than ordinary homes, its size and scale made it a collage of related and differentiated rooms, the arrangement of which reflected shifts in fashion and function, most obviously seen in the transformation from formal to social house identified by Girouard.[16] In both of these forms, rooms were arranged in a sequence that contextualized and gave additional meaning to their contents, and structured how they were accessed and by whom. However, these were ideal types to which none of the study houses conformed in any straightforward manner: attempts to construct an enfilade at Canons Ashby were compromised by scale and by variable and changing room use (and floor height); Arbury Hall worked more as a series of set pieces; and Stoneleigh Abbey was characterized by a pairing of formal state apartment with a suite of rooms designed more for informal sociability. In the last of these especially, there was a clear link between function and materiality, the furnishing of the two sets of rooms being strikingly different, both in their form and their resistance to change; but the distinction resists any simple differentiation between public and private or front and back stage. This does not mean that these distinctions were meaningless to contemporaries or useless as analytical devices for historians today; rather, it reveals how the form and function of space within the country house were contingent. In practical terms, this is usually associated with the differential access afforded to different parts of the house. Privacy, as Vickery notes, was a relative idea, varying according to the time of day and the relationship between people.[17] The focus here is on the movement of people through the house and the factors that influenced their ability to enter different spaces. However, as our analysis of Stoneleigh Abbey and Canons Ashby makes clear, goods also moved through the house, most notably in terms of periodic rearrangement of furniture. This impacted on the meanings held by goods and rooms, as well as their use: family portraits in the breakfast room at Stoneleigh Abbey carried different messages from those in the picture gallery, and tapestries relegated to a garret lost much of their power to communicate status. Goods, then, gained meaning from their context. This might be seen in the way imagined by Diderot, with assemblages resisting change or the imposition of discordant objects, or it might be understood in more

[16] Girouard, *English Country House*, 119–62, 181–212.
[17] A. Vickery, 'An Englishman's home is his castle? Thresholds, boundaries and privacies in the eighteenth-century London house', *Past and Present*, 199 (2008), 147–73.

practical terms, the silk-covered walnut chairs in the lumber room at Stoneleigh being 'cooled' before their removal to back rooms or disposal from the house.

In conceptual terms, there is an important distinction between the country house as a representation of space and as a lived space. The architect's plans and the craftsman's toil might be directed at producing spaces that communicated the power and good taste of the owner; but these meanings were overlain by the ways in which space was produced through everyday life. Both as stages for the performance of power and status, and as lived spaces constructed through sociability and everyday life, the various rooms of the country house were produced by and, in turn, helped to shape aristocratic identity. Focusing on lived space might direct our attention to some of the more mundane areas—the servants quarters, kitchens and bedrooms—but it also reminds us that the complex meanings of the country house were created through practice as well as plans.[18] The appearance of unity is, then, misleading and diverts from the truth that country houses as *habitus* were a collage of overlapping spaces and identities.

Beyond its walls, the country house was embedded in a series of spatial contexts. Links to the local area are most frequently emphasized, with patronage of tradesmen being part of a more general obligation that involved a range of paternalistic charitable donations. All these dues were carefully noted in Sir Roger Newdigate's accounts, along with his liabilities for taxes, tithes, and the like. If ideas of *noblesse oblige* were becoming less tenable in the eighteenth century, they continued to play an important part in the relationship between the big house and its locale, as the inclusion of tradesmen in Edward Leigh's funeral procession makes clear. However, our analysis has highlighted the contingent nature of 'local' and of these obligations. Sir Roger's patronage was directed towards Oxford University as well as the villages on and around his estate in Warwickshire, and Mary Leigh gave to London churches as well as those in Stoneleigh and its environs. More importantly, perhaps, their purchases came not just from tradesmen local to Arbury and Stoneleigh, but also those local to their houses in London and Kensington, where they spent several months each year. The level of spending recorded for the Kensington retailers supplying Mary Leigh reveals the extent to which country tradesmen lost out as spending was directed elsewhere: the economic losses occasioned by absence of the owner from their country house were substantial and tangible. Even the presence of the owner did not guarantee patronage, as the elite could choose between suppliers—a reality made clear through the lack of overlap in Warwickshire retailers sending goods to Arbury Hall or Stoneleigh Abbey.

The country house and its owner also stood on a national stage. In political terms, we see this in Sir Roger Newdigate's role as an MP, which took him to London, linked him to Oxford, and drew him into national debates and controversies. That said, the Leighs' unwillingness to involve themselves in politics, even at a local level, serves as an important reminder that not all landowners held strong

---

[18] This idea has particular significance in the light of current attempts, by the National Trust in particular, to present houses as if they were lived in: clothes draped over chairs in dressing rooms, newspapers on the side table, and dining tables laid for dinner.

political ambitions. Even so, their horizons were by no means narrow, and their reliance on London retailers was a striking feature of the supply network that serviced Stoneleigh Abbey, just as it was for Arbury Hall. In part, this reflected a periodic presence in London, but it also reveals much about the character of the English retail system at this time. London retailers were seen as offering the best quality and choice, but also the keenest prices, transport costs doing much to explain the often slightly higher prices charged by provincial and especially rural shops. If many consumers, even those of the middle ranks, relied on local shops for most of their purchases, the wealthy elite could short-circuit hierarchical supply chains by buying directly from London. Wealth was thus able to overcome the tyranny of space, not least because transport costs were often internalized or formed only a small proportion of the overall bill, especially for large orders—a point which came to the surface in the discussions of the shoddy furniture supplied to Lord Leigh by Thomas Burnett. At the same time, however, it is clear that the wealthy provincial landowner fed off and into an integrated retail system, a caveat on the usually stark distinctions made between 'metropolitan' and 'provincial' elites.

The focus of supply and retail networks on the metropolis was compounded by London's importance as the seat of fashionable taste, as is apparent in retailers' advertisements and the choices made by these elite consumers. Yet London was not the only point of cultural reference, nor the only source of exclusive goods. International links came indirectly in the form of imported goods, including the groceries, textiles, wines, tropical hardwoods, and books supplied by retailers and craftsmen. This gave the elite consumer a material cosmopolitanism that served to underline their cultural and social status. The growing world of goods, opened up by colonial trade and imperial connections, had a profound impact on the fabric and contents of many country houses, as Barczewski has argued.[19] However, the extent and character of this influence were highly varied. In contrast with the houses studied as part of the *East India Company at Home* project, where the study families had direct links with India, oriental goods were far from being central in shaping the material culture of our families.[20] There was the chinoiserie of several bedchambers at Stoneleigh Abbey, a range of 'Indian' screens, cabinets, and boxes, and mahogany everywhere; but explicit references to empire were largely absent. Moreover, there is little to suggest that these goods tied the mental allegiances and horizons of our families to the imperial project: they were tasteful and exotic decorative objects more than symbols of empire.

Europe formed a more important cultural context for these families, both explicitly and in their broader tastes in decorative schemes and consumer goods. Elites across the continent are often seen as sharing a collective European identity—a cosmopolitanism that linked to enlightenment thinking and fed into their social distinction.[21] Although none of our families were strongly tied to pan-European

---

[19] Barczewski, *Country Houses and the British Empire*.
[20] See the various case studies at <http://blogs.ucl.ac.uk/eicah/case-studies-2/>.
[21] See Clemente, 'Luxury and taste in eighteenth-century Naples'; B. Naddeo, 'A cosmopolitan in the provinces: G. M. Galanti, geography, and Enlightenment Europe,' *Modern Intellectual History* 10 (2013): 1–26.

social and political networks, the importance of Europe as a point of cultural and social reference is apparent in the Grand Tours undertaken by Edward, third Lord Leigh, Sir John Turner Dryden, and Sir Roger Newdigate. The last of these was clearly inspired by the ruins, buildings, and landscapes that he saw on his travels and he also brought home significant quantities of books, paintings, statues, and the like—typical souvenirs which set Arbury Hall into a European material culture, despite its consciously English Gothicism. Here we see the way that experiences intended to shape the individual in terms of social polish and correct forms of gender could reflect onto the canvas of the country house in complex and indirect ways. Even in the absence of a direct European experience, Edward, fifth Lord Leigh, was clearly influenced by broader cosmopolitan tastes when it came to assembling his library, purchasing books published in and discussing the architectural and artistic treasures of Europe.

Forging relationships with a varied set of suppliers across Britain and Europe involved country house owners in networks that were socially as well as geographically and economically complex. Choosing between potential suppliers was a key skill—just as important to consumers as the ability to select items of the right quality and price in an age before goods were standardized. As Berry argues, these choices were based on the reputation of the tradesman, but making these judgements across hundreds of suppliers inevitably took the Leighs and Newdigates beyond established personal relationships of mutual trust. Unable to visit all their suppliers in person, as Judith Baker did on her London trips, they relied instead on assessing the character and credit of the supplier through personal recommendation, their geographical location and regular correspondence.[22] These processes tied the elite consumer into the same webs of credit, trust, and obligation that enmeshed everyone who bought or sold. Their wealth and rank gave them a powerful position, not least in gaining credit and delaying payment; but they were just as exposed as everyone else. Indeed, their geographical dislocation from many of their suppliers brought additional risks in making informed judgements. Inevitably, then, mistakes were sometimes made: trust in Burnett was tested by the episode involving shoddy furniture, and Newdigate had cause to complain about the quality of his tailor's workmanship. More important, though, is the fact that these were commercial relations; far from being part of a traditional system of regard and obligation, as Fontaine implies, the aristocracy were integral to England's 'capitalistic merchant culture'.[23] That some of these relations were mediated by senior servants in no way obscures the integration of the elite into commercial systems.

Within these processes, retailers were far from passive. They had less scope to lead or mould elite taste—a role which is often accorded to them in their dealings with the middle ranks—but many were trusted to advise on and execute designs or to supply goods that matched up to expectations, even when these were ill-defined in advance. In effect, the aristocrat and the artisan were mutually dependent and both played a role in shaping the country house. Conversely, as prime consumers,

---

[22] Berry, 'Prudent luxury'; Bristol, 'Between the exotic and the everyday'.
[23] Fontaine, *Moral Economy*, 70–94.

the aristocracy played a key role in shaping systems of supply. The amounts laid out each year were enormous: Sir Roger's annual expenditure of £2,885 (excluding taxes, interest payments, and the like) was the equivalent to the annual wages of 144 of his highest-paid servants in the 1770s or to the amount they could earn in perhaps four lifetimes of work. His spending spread wealth and supported the livelihoods of scores of trades people, making his patronage an important prop to the businesses across the country. Whilst we need to guard against notions of benign altruism—the correspondence of the widowed Elizabeth Dryden makes clear the extent and impact of delayed payments to tradesmen—the economic impact of the country house is readily apparent. Equally, such relationships provide us with new layers of understanding of aristocratic status beyond 'master–servant' or 'political patron': counted in pounds, shillings, and pence, they are more tangible and nuanced than the more abstract notions of 'loyalty' or 'deference.'

CONSUMPTION AND THE COUNTRY HOUSE

Our aim in this book has been to examine the country house through the lens of consumption and to reflect on what this tells us about elite identity, material culture, and lifestyle, reconnecting them to their houses and tying their houses more firmly into the social, economic, and spatial contexts in which they were located. Due to their exceptional scale and complexity, country houses may seem on the surface to be 'traditional', but they were the product of modern forces and were ever-changing. Focusing on consumption helps to animate the country house, shifting our attention from the end product and onto the process. Rather than being a static set piece, comprising carefully orchestrated spaces, artefacts, and decorative themes, it becomes alive with flows of goods, people, and ideas—a dynamic system that is in constant flux as new goods are added, tradesmen and owners come and go, furniture is rearranged, and relationships are made and remade. This shift in perspective in some ways reflects that advocated by transnational historians, who remind us that focusing on place can obscure the multiple and complex networks and relationships that produced those spaces. Just as they argue for a break from national histories, we make a break from a historical obsession with the country house as a static space.[24] This affords important new insights into the ways in which old and new combine; luxury rubs shoulders with the mundane, and space is differentiated and integrated through daily life. All these things are important in providing a fuller understanding of the country house, but they are true of any house. Equally, the complex mixing of motivations that underpinned the behaviour of our three families—displays of magnificence and taste, assertions of family and pedigree, a desire to be comfortable and to express something of one's identity—are by no means unique to the aristocracy. Their wealth

[24] For a very useful entry point to discussions of transnational history, see C. A. Bayly, S. Beckert, M. Connelly, I. Hofmeyr, W. Kozol, and P. Seed, 'AHR conversation: on transnational history', *American Historical Review*, 111/5 (2006), 1441–64.

and status, however, afforded them greater opportunity to express these through material culture and to deploy that materiality to distinguish themselves in social and cultural terms.

Did this involve the construction of a distinct material culture? In some ways, it did. The country house—for all its variety in scale, form, and content—was qualitatively different from other places. It signalled the importance and ambition of the owners, but much more importantly it demonstrated their belonging to a particular social group. The identity of the elite was, therefore, not simply a question of openness to new blood or closure through strict settlement and entailed estates; nor was it produced by collections of art or the treasures from a Grand Tour, or the virtue of great architecture. Rather, it was expressed through the lived spaces of the country house and the particular combinations of artefacts, relations, and values that these embodied. What these expressions of identity and belonging provide us with is a new understanding of the basis of the permanence of the aristocracy and of the country house that goes beyond the structural forces of land, agriculture, and the family settlement. All of these were important, but discretionary spending— the choices they made as individuals and families—tells us far more about the identities of elites and their role in the eighteenth century. In a changing world of consumption and desire, the aristocracy in some ways formed an inertial force, but as progressive and enlightened consumers they remained relevant to the forces of modernity.

Family Trees

SIMPLIFIED FAMILY TREE FOR THE LEIGH FAMILY OF STONELEIGH ABBEY, WARWICKSHIRE

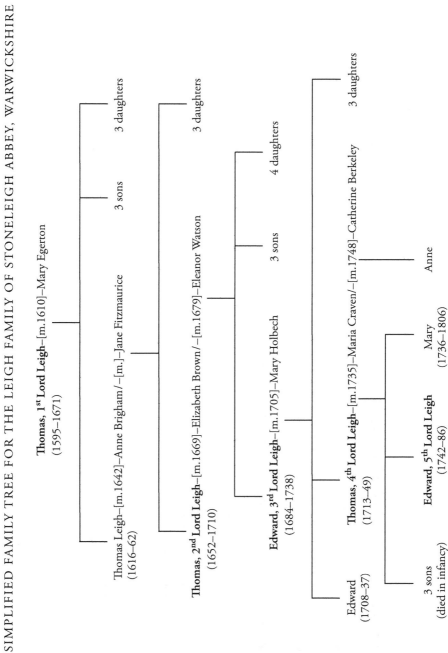

Thomas, 1st Lord Leigh–[m.1610]–Mary Egerton
(1595–1671)

3 sons   3 daughters

Thomas Leigh–[m.1642]–Anne Brigham/–[m.]–Jane Fitzmaurice
(1616–62)

3 daughters

Thomas, 2nd Lord Leigh–[m.1669]–Elizabeth Brown/–[m.1679]–Eleanor Watson
(1652–1710)

3 sons   4 daughters

Edward, 3rd Lord Leigh–[m.1705]–Mary Holbech
(1684–1738)

Thomas, 4th Lord Leigh–[m.1735]–Maria Craven/–[m.1748]–Catherine Berkeley
(1713–49)

3 daughters

Anne

Edward
(1708–37)

3 sons
(died in infancy)

Edward, 5th Lord Leigh
(1742–86)

Mary
(1736–1806)

SIMPLIFIED FAMILY TREE FOR THE NEWDIGATE FAMILY OF ARBURY HALL, WARWICKSHIRE

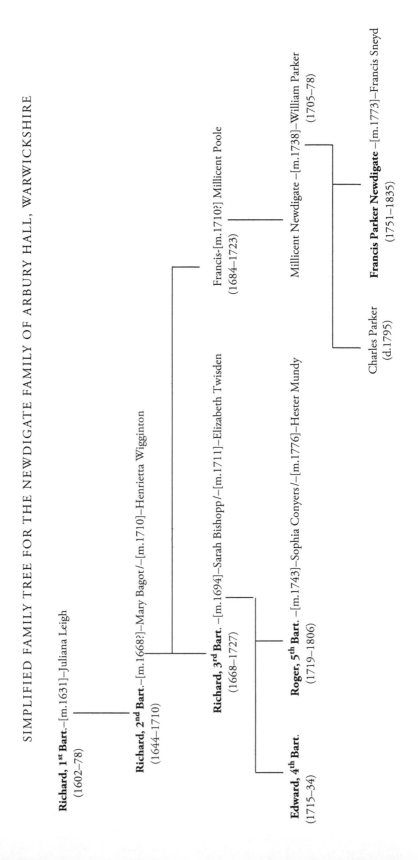

Erasmus, 1st Bart. –m– Frances Wilkes
(1553–1632)

John, 2nd Bart. –m– Honor Bevill (third wife)
(c.1580–1658)   (d.1654)

Erasmus –m– Mary Pickering

William –m– ???
(d.1654)

Robert, 3rd Bart.
(c.1638–1708)

Elizabeth Luck –m– John, 4th Bart.
(c.1635–1710)

Erasmus, 6th Bart. –m– Elizabeth Martin
(1638–1718)

John –m– Lady Elizabeth Cecil
(1631–1700)

Erasmus Henry, 5th Bart.
(1669–1710)

Edward –m– Elizabeth Allen
(d.1717)

John, 7th Bart. –[m1724]–Frances Ingram/–[m.1726]–Elizabeth Rooper
(c.1740–70)   (d.1725)   (c.1706–91)

Bevill –m– Mary Dubber
(1713–58)   (d.1791)

(adopted)

John Turner (Dryden),1st Bart by second creation–[m.1781]–Elizabeth
(1752–97)   (1753–1824)

John Edward, 2nd Bart.
(1782–1818)

Henry, 3rd Bart.
(1787–1837)

Caroline Julia
(1789–1872)

Leopold Erasmus
(1792–1846)

Lempster George Gregiry
(1794–1866)

3 daughters & 1 son
(died in childhood)

Bibliography

ARCHIVAL SOURCES

Bedfordshire Local Archives
GA25/35, Letter from Charles Hancock to Mary Gibbard, 21 January 1819.
GA93, Letters from Charles Hancock to Mary Gibbard, 15 January 1824, and 15 September 1827.

British Museum
Heal, 67.156, Trade card of Phillips Garden, goldsmith, of London (no date).
1871,0812.4497, Rowlandson, T., *The Comforts of Matrimony—A Good Toast,* 1809.
1985,0119.115, Sayer, R., *The Comforts of Matrimony—A Smoky House and Scolding Wife,* 1790.

Chester and Cheshire Archives
WS Abner Scholes, 1736.

Hertfordshire Archives and Local Studies
AH/2348, Bond of John Turner to George Brooks, 18 February 1783.
AH/2349, Insurance Policy, 2 April 1783.

Musée national des châteaux de Versailles et de Trianon
MV 5718, Brun de Versoix, L.-A., Portrait équestre de la reine Marie-Antoinette (*c.*1783).

The National Archives
E182, Shop Tax, Coventry 1785 Exchequer Accounts.
PROB 11/1448, Will of Mary Leigh, 1806.

Norfolk Record Office
WKC 7/21/15, Letter to Ashe Windham, 5 May 1708.
MC50/23/517, Bill from Joshua Long, February 1775.

Northamptonshire Record Office
Accounts and valuations
D(CA) 311, Sir John Dryden's expenses at Oxford, 1719–23.
D(CA) 322, Lady Dryden's account book, 1770–90.
D(CA) 364/2, Valuation of the Dryden estates, no date (1797).
D(CA) 364/10, Statement of the Affairs of Miss Dryden, 7 February 1810.
D(CA) 364/11, Statement of Affairs of Lady Elizabeth Dryden as they related to Sir G. D., no date.

Receipted bills
D(CA) 41, Goods purchased by Edward Dryden, 1 November 1708.
D(CA) 129, Bill from Thomas Phill, 30 April 1716.
D(CA) 1011, Receipt for cost of servants during the award ceremony, no date (1793).

Inventories of Canons Ashby

D(CA) 49, Inventory, 1708; D(CA) 901, Inventory, 1717; D(CA) 902, Inventory, 1756; D(CA) 201, Inventory, 1770; D(CA) 903, Inventory, 1791; D(CA) 904, Inventory, 1819.

Journals and diaries

D(CA) 347, John Turner Dryden's Tour of France, 1774.

Letters from William Peacock to Lady Elizabeth Dryden

D(CA) 360: 31 January 1804, 13 March 1804, 27 March 1804, 2 April 1804, 20 April 1804, 27 July 1804, 14 January 1805, 26 February 1805, 12 March 1805, 1 April 1806, 10 May 1808, 6 June 1809, 21 March 1809, 28 March 1809,11 April 1809, 18 April 1809.

Letters from Elizabeth Dryden to Mrs Steele

D(CA) 361: 26 September 1809, 3 November 1810, 26 May 1812, 19 July 1813, 28 January 1814, 20 October 1814, 28 December 1816, 8 January 1819, [no date] April 1819, 2 June 1819, 22 November 1819, 14 December 1823.

Correspondence concerning the upbringing of Elizabeth Dryden

D(CA) 1032, 6 April 1761; D(CA) 1035, 18 June 1761; D(CA) 1037, 6 October 1761; D(CA) 1081, 4 May 1761.

Correspondence between Elizabeth Dryden and creditors

D(CA) 364/13, 14 April 1805; D(CA) 364/17, 15 June 1799; D(CA) 364/22, 7 July 1800; D(CA) 364/31, 6 July 1797; D(CA) 364/32, 17 July 1797; D(CA) 364/35, 7 April 1798; D(CA) 364/37, 15 March 1804; D(CA) 1021, 26 March 1795.

Other correspondence

D(CA) 903b, Letter from Elizabeth Dryden, 13 January 1817.

D(CA) 971, Letter from Rev. D. Burton, 1764.

Miscellaneous

D(CA) 207, Commission as captain in the Oxfordshire Militia, 30 September 1782.

D(CA) 219, Commission in the Northamptonshire Yeomanry, 9 May 1794.

D(CA) 222, Memorial enrolled at Chancery of a bond, warrant, and indenture, 22 April 1790.

D(CA) 536, Marriage settlement of Godfrey Scholey and Dame Elizabeth Dryden, 19 March 1805.

IL 3902, Isham papers.

Shakespeare Central Library and Archives

Accounts and valuations

DR18/29/6 Box 1, Pocketbook of Edward, 3rd Lord Leigh, 1702.

DR18/1/815, Goods bought and remaining at Stoneleigh, 1738.

DR18/31/457, Miscellaneous accounts, 1735–44.

DR18/31/458, Stoneleigh estate accounts, 1744–6.

DR18/17/4/1, Account of Thomas Clarke, 1746–9.

DR18/17/4/3, Statement of accounts of Lord Leigh, 10 March 1749.

DR18/17/4/7, Robert Hughes's Account to Lord Craven, 1749–52.

DR18/17/4/8, Account of Christopher Wright, 1749–53.

DR18/17/4/19, Schedule of bills paid by William Craven, no date, *c*.1754.

DR18/17/4/22, Arrears of rent received and unreceived, not date, *c*.1754.

DR18/17/4/23, Lady Leigh's (Dowager) Accounts to the Executors of Lord Leigh, 1754.

DR18/31/548, Account of stores expended every half year, Adlestrop, 1757–61.

DR18/17/4/10, Account of South Sea Annuities purchased by Mr Hill, 1761–2.

DR18/31/461, Auditor's Accounts, 1763–74.

DR18/31/18, Household accounts, 1774.

DR18/31/22, Household accounts, 1778–9.

DR18/17/32/186, List of pictures bought at auction, 1788.

DR18/31/655, Account of Sundries from Stoneleigh Abbey, 1793–8.

DR18/31/656, Daybook for Grove House, 1793–8.

DR671/101, Account of the Personal Estate of Mary Leigh, 1822.

DR18/4/66, Valuation of Lady Barbara Leigh's pictures (no date).

Receipted bills

DR18/5/—, Main series of receipted bills and vouchers.

DR18/3/47/55/5, John Wright's bill for plasterer's work done in Stoneleigh Chapel, 29 September 1744.

DR18/3/47/55/6, An account of the workmen's bills at Stoneleigh, 12 January 1745.

DR18/3/47/55/7, William Smith's bill for work and materials at Stoneleigh, 12 January 1745.

DR18/3/47/52/15, Bill from Thomas Burnett, 14 December 1765.

Inventories

DR18/4/9, Inventory, 1738.

DR18/4/25, Inventory of goods remaining at Stoneleigh, 1749.

DR18/4/27, Inventory, November 1749.

DR18/4/26, Inventory, 1750.

DR18/18/3/4, Inventory of paintings from Leighton Buzzard, no date (1765).

DR18/4/75, List of books at Stoneleigh Abbey, 1766 and 1785.

DR18/4/43, 1774 inventory with 1806 amendments.

DR18/4/69, Inventory, 1786.

DR18/4/59, Inventory, 1806.

Letters from Samuel Butler, steward of Stoneleigh Abbey

DR18/17/27/75, Letter, 27 April 1763.

DR18/17/27/82, Letter, 27 September 1763.

DR18/17/27/84, Letter, 13 October 1763.

DR18/17/27/85, Letter, 27 October 1763.

DR18/17/27/91, Letter, 8 January 1764.

DR18/17/27/96, Letter, 1 February 1764.

DR18/17/27/97, Letter, 11 February 1764.

DR18/17/27/88, Letter, 13 February 1764.

DR18/17/27/98, Letter, 13 February 1764.

DR18/17/27/101, Letter, 25 March 1764;

DR18/17/27/107, Letter, 21 April 1764.

DR18/17/27/108, Letter, 3 June 1764.

Correspondence with Joseph Hill

DR18/1/27/52, Letter from Joseph Hill, 19 December 1761.

DR671/77, Letters from Mary Leigh: 22 August 1790, 27 March 1791, 12 September 1791.

Letters from tradespeople

DR18/17/27/149, Letter from Paul Vaillant, 10 July 1766.

DR18/17/30/35, Letter from Miss Baker, 19 April 1796.

DR18/17/27/31/15c, Letter from John Taylor, 31 December 1803.

Memoranda and Orders

DR18/17/4/28, Memorandum relating to Lord Leigh's Affairs, no date, 1749.

DR18/17/4/5, Orders Made by the Trustees of Edward, Lord Leigh, 18 September 1750.

DR18/17/4/9, Orders made by the Trustees of Edward, Lord Leigh, 11 October 1754.

DR18/3/47/52/6, Memorandum, 2 October 1762.

DR18/3/47/52/7, Memorandum, 13 April 1763.

DR18/3/47/52/12, Memorandum, no date, *c*.1763.

DR18/3/47/52/11, Memorandum, 22 July 1764.

DR18/3/47/52/14, Mr Burnett's Memorandum, no date.

Wills and settlements

DR18/15/11, Indenture Quadripartite between Arden Bagot of Pipe Hall, Esq. and the Hon. Mary Bagot, his wife, 27 May 1678.

DR18/9/1/2, Marriage Settlement of Theophilus Leigh and Elizabeth Craven, 1 December 1679.

DR18/13/1/15, Settlement between Thomas, Lord Leigh, and Catherine, 16 January 1747.

DR18/13/7/13–4, Will and codicil of Edward, Lord Leigh, 1767.

Other Correspondence

DR18/17/25/24, Letter from Lord Edward Leigh to Elizabeth Verney, 15 December 1727.

DR18/18/3/3, Letter from John Franklin, 24 December 1765.

DR18/18/3/5, Letter from John Franklin, 26 December 1765.

DR18/8/6/29, Letter from John Turner Dryden, 3 April 1792.

DR18/17/31/11, Letter from Mary Leigh, 24 October 1804.

Miscellaneous

DR631/33, Designs for Stoneleigh Abbey.

DR671/43, Directions for Edward Leigh's funeral, 1786.

DR18/29/6/Box 1, Vault at Stoneleigh, no date.

Staffordshire Record Office

D1798, HM37/36, Papers of Mrs Elizabeth Sneyd of Stafford (1713–52).

Warwickshire Record Office

Accounts

CR136/B/2510a–e, Accounts of costs incurred on the grand tour, 1739.

CR136/V/156, Accounts, 1747–62.

CR136/V/136, Accounts, 1763–96.

CR1841/14, Housekeeper's accounts, 1766–70.

CR1841/10, Housekeeper's accounts, 1770–4.

CR136/B/2638b, Books, marbles, medals, casts, etc. purchased from Italy, July 1774 to Jan 1776.

CR1841/29, General Account Book for Arbury Hall.

Receipted bills

CR136/B/2456a, 21 May 1749 (books); CR136/B/2456b, no date 1751 (books); CR136/B/2424, 22 March 1771 (chimney); CR136/B/2461e, 10 April 1771 (books); CR136/B/2635j, 2 August 1796 (books); CR136/B/2635b, 16 November 1797 (chimney); CR136/B/2635e–g, various dates (scagliola); CR136/B/2466a–j, various dates (books); CR136/B/2467a–g, various dates (books); CR136/B/2638a, various dates (books); CR136/B/31, 4 November 1803 (tea urn).

Inventories and lists
CR136/A/565, Books received at Arbury, from 1783.
CR136/A/47, Notes of persons coming to dinner; beer and ale brewed and wines ordered, 1798.
CR136/V/166, Catalogues of Lady Newdigate's Books, 1798.
CR1841/57, Shelf catalogue of the library at Arbury, *c*.1810.

Letters from Sir Roger Newdigate
CR136/B/4577, 21 August 1738; CR136/B/4578, 27 August 1738; CR136/B/4579, 8 September 1738; CR136/C/3298a, 19 March 1747; CR136/B/5270, 25 April 1748; CR136/B/1574, no date, January 1750; CR136/B/1530, 28 January 1750; CR136/B/4640, 18 March 1750; CR136/B/1874, 24 November 1750; CR136/B/2979, 13 February 1755; CR691/152/4, no date, 1761; CR691/152/7, 10 March 1761; CR691/B/152/14, no date, 1761; CR136/B/4592, 17 October 1762; CR136/B/1860, 19 October 1764; CR136/B/1833, 23 October, 1765; CR136/B/2331a, 7 October 1767; CR136/B/2333, 11 December 1767; CR136/B/2341, 11 January 1771; CR136/B/4046/e, 25 March 1773; CR1368/V/33, 6 December 1774; CR136/B/2010, 6 May 1775; CR136/B/1835, 5 May 1780; CR136/B/2012, 1 June 1780; CR136/B/2120, 17 October 1784; CR136/B/1687, 21 August 1786; CR136/B/1688, 4 September 1786; CR136/B/2145, no date, June 1793; CR136/B/2014, 29 April 1795; CR136/B/2439b, 14 June 1796; CR136/B/1970, 27 November 1797; CR136/B/2627[1], 20 May 1799; CR136/B/2627[2], 10 June 1799; CR136/B/3431, 7 June 1803; CR136/B/3522b, 24 January 1805; CR136/B/4050b, 24 May 1805; CR136/B/3576, 7 November 1805; CR136/B/4082, 5 July 1806.

Journals and diaries
CR1841/7, Lady Newdigate's tour in the south of England (1748).
CR136/A/248, Notebook of Sophia Newdigate, containing a list of trees and shrubs at Arbury, 1753.
CR136/A/582, Sir Roger Newdigate, Diaries.

Letters from tradesmen
CR136/B/2416, Letter from Wedgwood & Co, 17 April 1778.
CR136/B/2635a, Letter from Bent & Sons, 1 February 1799.
CR136/B/3048a–g, Letters from Oldham & Oldham, 19 June 1801 to 8 December 1802.
CR136/B/3049b, Letter from Penny & Son, 10 December 1801.
CR136/B/3049c, Letter from Penny & Son, 3 February 1802.
CR136/B/2625, Letter from William Coplin, 7 September 1803.
CR136/B/2625a, Letter from Richard Twining, 14 February 1803.

Miscellaneous
CR136/B/2803, Letter from Hester Newdigate, 5 October 1781.
CR764/214, Sketch of chair ordered from Gillows (1805).
CR1368, Vol. 4/57, Mordaunt Family Letters.

PRINTED PRIMARY SOURCES

Addy, J. and McGiven, P. (eds), 'The diary of Henry Prescott, Vol.II', *Records Society of Lancashire and Cheshire*, 132 (1994).
Austen, J., *Emma* (London, 1815; London, 1985).
Austen, J., *Northanger Abbey* (London, 1817; Oxford, 1998).
Betham, W., *The Baronetage of England* (London, 1803).
Blackwood's Edinburgh Magazine (June 1825).

Burke's Landed Gentry (London, 1847).

Burke's Peerage, Baronetage and Knightage (London, 1852).

Chippendale, T., *The Gentleman and Cabinet-maker's Director* (London, 1762).

Climenson, E. J. (ed.), *Passages from the Diaries of Mrs Philip Lybbe Powys, of Hardwick House, 1756–1808* (London, 1899).

Cowper, W., *The Task*, Book 1: 'The Sofa' (London, 1785).

Diderot, D., 'Regrets on parting with my old dressing gown', in *Rameau's Nephew and Other Works by Denis Diderot* (New York, 1964).

Eland, G. (ed.), *Purefoy Letters, 1735–1753* (London, 1931).

Gazetteer and New Daily Advertiser, Tuesday 30 May, 1786.

Gentleman's Magazine, The.

Harrison, W., *The Description of England* (London, 1587).

Housekeeper's Accompt-Book, The (Bath, 1797).

Mistress of Charlecote. The Memoirs of Mary Elizabeth Lucy, 1803–1889 (London, 1983).

Ramsay, A., *A Dialogue on Taste* (London, 1762).

Repton, H., *Fragments on the Theory and Practice of Landscape Gardening* (London, 1816).

Sachse, W. (ed.), *Diary of Roger Lowe of Ashton in Makerfield, Lancashire, 1663–74* (London, 1938).

Smith, A., *The Wealth of Nations* (London, 1776; Oxford, 1976).

Stout, W., *Autobiography of William Stout of Lancaster, 1665–1752* (Manchester, 1967).

Thompson, F., *Lark Rise to Candleford* (London, 1939).

Whitbread, H. (ed.), *I Know My Own Heart: the Diaries of Anne Lister, 1791–1840* (London, 1988).

SECONDARY SOURCES

Adburgham, A., *Shops and Shopping, 1800–1914* (London, 1964).

Alexander, D., *Retailing in England during the Industrial Revolution* (London, 1970).

Alm, G. and Plunger, M. (eds), *Kina Slott* (Stockholm, 2002).

Andersson, G., 'A mirror of oneself: possessions and the manifestation of status among a Swedish local elite, 1650–1770', *Cultural and Social History*, 3 (2006), 21–44.

Appadurai, A., 'Introduction: commodities and the politics of value', in A. Appadurai (ed.) *The Social Life of Things: Commodities in Cultural Perspective* (Cambridge, 1986), 3–63.

Arnold, D., 'The country house: form, function and meaning', in D. Arnold (ed.), *The Georgian Country House: Architecture, Landscape and Society* (Stroud, 1998), 1–19.

Arnold, D., 'Defining femininity: women and the country house', in D. Arnold (ed.), *The Georgian Country House: Architecture, landscape and Society* (Stroud, 1998), 79–99.

Arnold, D., *The Georgian Country House: Architecture, Landscape and Society* (Stroud, 1998).

Arnold, J. H. and Brady, S., *What is Masculinity? Historical Dynamics from Antiquity to the Contemporary World* (Basingstoke, 2011).

Aslet, C., 'Stoneleigh Abbey, Warwickshire', *Country Life*, (13 December 1984), 1847–8.

Austen-Leigh, W., Austen-Leigh, R., and le Faye, D., *Jane Austen: a Family Record* (London, 1989).

Bailey, L., 'Maintaining status: consumption in the nineteenth-century gentry household' (unpublished MA thesis, University of Northampton, 2010).

Bailey, L., 'Consumption and Status: Shopping for Clothes in a Nineteenth-Century Bedfordshire Gentry Household', *Midland History*, 36/1 (2011), 89–114.

Bailey, L., 'Squire, shopkeeper and staple food: the reciprocal relationship between the country house and the village shop in the late Georgian period', *History of Retailing and Consumption*, 1 (2015), 8–28.

Baird, R., *Mistress of the House. Great Ladies and Grand Houses, 1670–1830* (London, 2003).

Barbour, R., 'John Whittingham: Coventry nurseryman, diarist, Catholic apologist and political activist', *Warwickshire History*, 16/1 (2014), 8–25.

Barczewski, S., *Country Houses and the British Empire, 1700–1930* (Manchester, 2014).

Barnett, A., 'In with the new: novel goods in domestic provincial England, c.1700–1790' in B. Blondé, N. Coquery, J. Stobart, and I. Van Damme (eds) *Fashioning Old and New. Changing Consumer Patterns in Western Europe, 1650–1900* (Turnhout, 2009), 81–94.

Bayly, C. A., Beckert, S., Connelly, M., Hofmeyr, I., Kozol, W., and Seed, P., 'AHR conversation: on transnational history', *American Historical Review* 111/5 (2006), 1441–64.

Beal, P., ' "My books are the great joy of my life." Sir William Boothby, seventeenth-century bibliophile', *Book Collector*, 46/3 (1997), 350–78.

Beard, G., *Georgian Craftsmen and their Work* (London, 1966).

Beard, G., *Decorative Plasterwork in Great Britain* (London, 1975).

Beard, G., *Upholsterers and Interior Furnishing in England 1530–1840* (New Haven, CT, 1997).

Beard, G. and Gilbert, C. (eds), *Dictionary of English Furniture Makers, 1660–1840* (Leeds, 1986).

Beard, M., *English Landed Society in the Twentieth Century* (London, 1981).

Beckett, J., 'The pattern of landownership in England and Wales, 1660–1800', *Economic History Review*, 37 (1984), 1–22.

Beckett, J., *The Aristocracy in England, 1660–1914* (Oxford, 1986).

Bennett, J. and Froide, A. (eds), *Singlewomen in the European Past, 1250–1800* (Philadelphia, 1999).

Berg, M., 'Women's consumption and the industrial classes of eighteenth-century England', *Journal of Social History*, 30 (1996), 415–34.

Berg, M., 'New commodities, luxuries and their consumers in eighteenth-century England', in M. Berg and H. Clifford (eds), *Consumers and Luxury. Consumer Culture in Europe, 1650–1850* (Manchester, 1999), 63–85.

Berg, M., *Luxury and Pleasure in Eighteenth-Century Britain* (Oxford, 2005).

Berg, M. and Clifford, H., 'Selling consumption in the eighteenth century: advertising and the trade card in Britain and France', *Cultural and Social History*, 4 (2007), 145–70.

Berg, M. and Eger, E., 'The rise and fall of the luxury debates', in M. Berg and E. Eger (eds), *Luxury in the Eighteenth Century: Debates, Desires and Delectable Goods* (Basingstoke, 2007), 7–27.

Berger, R. M., *The Most Necessary Luxuries: the Mercers' Company of Coventry, 1550–1680* (University Park, PA, 1993).

Berry, C., *The Idea of Luxury. A Conceptual and Historical Investigation* (Cambridge, 1994).

Berry, H., 'Prudent luxury: The metropolitan tastes of Judith Baker, Durham gentlewoman', in R. Sweet and P. Lane (eds), *Women and Urban Life in Eighteenth-Century Britain: 'On the Town'* (Aldershot, 2003), 130–54.

Berry, H., 'Soul, purse and family: middling and lower-class masculinity in eighteenth-century Manchester', *Social History*, 33 (2008), 12–35.

Bianchi, M., 'The taste for novelty and novel tastes', in M. Bianchi (ed.) *The Active Consumer: Novelty and Surprise in Consumer Choice* (London, 1998), 64–86.

Bickham, T., 'Eating the empire: intersections of food, cookery and imperialism in eighteenth-century Britain', *Past and Present*, 198 (2008), 71–109.

Black, J., *France and the Grand Tour* (Basingstoke, 2003).

Black, J., *Culture in Eighteenth-Century England: A Subject for Taste* (London, 2006).

Blondé, B., 'Conflicting consumption models? The symbolic meaning of possessions and consumption amongst the Antwerp nobility at the end of the eighteenth century', in B. Blondé, N. Coquery, J. Stobart, and I. Van Damme (eds) *Fashioning Old and New, Changing Consumer Patterns in Western Europe, 1650–1900* (Turnhout, 2009), 61–80.

Blondé, B. and Laet, V. de, 'New and old luxuries between the court and the city. A comparative perspective on critical material culture changes in Brussels and Antwerp, 1650–1735', in J. Ilmakunnas and J. Stobart (eds) *A Taste for Luxury in Early-Modern Europe: Display, Acquisition and Boundaries* (London, forthcoming).

Blondé, B. and Van Damme, I., 'Retail growth and consumer changes in a declining urban economy: Antwerp 1650–1750', *Economic History Review*, 32 (2010), 638–63.

Borsay, P., *The English Urban Renaissance. Culture and Society in the Provincial Town, 1660–1770* (Oxford, 1989).

Borsay, P., 'The landed elite and provincial towns in Britain', *Georgian Group Journal*, 13 (2003), 281–94.

Bourdieu, P., *Distinction: A Social Critique of the Judgement of Taste* (London, 1984).

Boynton, L., 'William and Richard Gomm', *The Burlington Magazine*, 122 (1980), 395–400.

Brears, P., 'Behind the green baize door', in P. Sambrook and P. Brears (eds), *The Country House Kitchen, 1650–1900* (Stroud, 1996), 30–76.

Brears, P., 'The Ideal Kitchen in 1864', in P. Sambrook and P. Brears (eds), *The Country House Kitchen, 1650–1900* (Stroud, 1996), 11–29.

Brears, P., 'Kitchen fireplaces and stoves', in P. Sambrook and P. Brears (eds), *The Country House Kitchen, 1650–1900* (Stroud, 1996), 92–115.

Brears, P., 'The pastry', in P. Sambrook and P. Brears (eds), *The Country House Kitchen, 1650–1900* (Stroud, 1996), 144–56.

Brett, V., 'Derided and enjoyed: what was a toy—what was a toyshop', *History of Retailing and Consumption*, 2 (2015), 83–8.

Brewer, J., *The Pleasures of the Imagination: English Culture in the Eighteenth Century* (Chicago, 1997).

Brewer, J. and Porter, R. (eds), *Consumption and the World of Goods* (London, 1993).

Bristol, K., 'Between the exotic and the everyday: Sabine Winn and Nostell Priory, West Yorkshire, 1765–1798', in J. Ilmakunnas and J. Stobart (eds) *Taste for Luxury in Early-Modern Europe: Display, Acquisition and Boundaries* (London, forthcoming, 2016).

Buck, A., *Dress in Eighteenth-Century England* (London, 1979).

Burke, P., *The Historical Anthropology of Early Modern Italy* (Cambridge, 1987).

Butler, J., *Gender Trouble: Feminism and the Subversion of Identity* (London, 2000).

Campbell, C., *The Romantic Ethic and the Spirit of Modern Consumerism* (Oxford, 1987).

Campbell, C., 'The desire for the new: its nature and social location as presented in theories of fashion and modern consumerism', in R. Silverman and E. Hirsch (eds), *Consuming Technologies: Media and Information in Domestic Spaces* (London, 1992), 93–105.

Campbell, C., 'Understanding traditional and modern patterns of consumption in eighteenth-century England: a character-action approach', in J. Brewer and R. Porter (eds), *Consumption and the World of Goods* (London, 1993), 40–57.

Cannadine, D., *Lords and Landlords: The Aristocracy and the Towns 1774–1967* (Leicester, 1980).

Cannadine, D., *The Decline and Fall of the British Aristocracy* (London, 1990).

Cannadine, D., *Aspects of Aristocracy: Grandeur and Decline in Modern Britain* (Harmondsworth, 1995).

Cannadine, D., 'After the horse: nobility and mobility in modern Britain', in N. Harte and R. Quinault (eds), *Land and Society in Britain 1700–1914: Essays in Honour of F. M. L. Thompson* (Manchester, 1996), 211–35.

Cannon, J., *Aristocratic Century: The Peerage of Eighteenth Century England* (Cambridge, 1984).

Carter, P., *Men and the Emergence of Polite Society, Britain 1660–1800* (Harlow, 2001).

Chard, C., 'Grand and ghostly tours: the topography of memory', *Eighteenth Century Studies*, 31 (1997), 101–8.

Chatenet-Calyste, A., 'Feminine luxury in Paris: Marie-Fortunée d'Este, Princesse de Conti (1731–1803)', in D. Simonton, M. Kaartinen, and A. Montenach (eds), *Luxury and Gender in European Towns, 1700–1914* (London, 2015), 171–89.

Chavasse, H., 'Fashion and "affectionate recollection": material culture at Audley End, 1762–1773', in J. Stobart and A. Hann (eds), *The Country House: Material Culture and Consumption* (Swindon, 2015), 63–73.

Chavasse, H., 'Material culture and the country house: fashion, comfort and lineage' (unpublished PhD thesis, University of Northampton, 2015).

Christie, C., *The British Country House in the Eighteenth Century* (Manchester, 2000).

Clay, C., 'Property settlements, financial provisions for the family and the sale of land by the great landowners 1660–1790', *Journal of British Studies*, 21 (1981), 18–38.

Clemente, 'Luxury and taste in eighteenth century Naples: representations, ideas and social practices at the intersection between the global and the local', in J. Ilmakunnas and J. Stobart (eds) *A Taste for Luxury in Early-Modern Europe: Display, Acquisition and Boundaries* (London, 2016).

Clifford, H., 'A commerce with things: the value of precious metalwork in early-modern England', in M. Berg and H. Clifford (eds) *Consumers and Luxury. Consumer Culture in Europe, 1650–1850* (Manchester, 1999), 147–68.

Clifford, H., *Silver in London: The Parker and Wakelin Partnership 1760–1776* (New Haven, CT, 2004).

Clifford, H., '"Conquests from North to South": the Dundas property empire. New wealth, constructing status and the role of "India" goods in the British country house', in J. Stobart and A. Hann (eds) *The Country House: Material Culture and Consumption* (Swindon, 2015), 123–33.

Cohen, M., *Fashioning Masculinity: National Identity and Language in the Eighteenth Century* (London, 1996).

Cohen, M., 'The grand tour: language, national identity and masculinity', *Changing English*, 8 (2001), 129–41.

Cohen, M., '"Manners" make the man: politeness, chivalry and the construction of masculinity, 1750–1830', *Journal of British Studies*, 44 (2005), 312–29.

Colvin, H., *A Biographical Dictionary of British Architects 1600–1840*, 3rd ed. (New Haven, CT, 1995).

Connell, R. W., *Masculinities* (Cambridge, 1995).

Cooper, J. P., 'Patterns of inheritance and settlement by great landowners', in J. Goody, J. Thirsk, and E. P. Thompson (eds), *Family and Inheritance: Rural Society in Western Europe, 1200–1800* (Cambridge, 1976), 192–328.

Cope, K. L. and Cahill, S. A. (eds), *Citizens of the World. Adapting in the Eighteenth Century* (Lewisburg, PA, 2015).

Coquery, N., *L'Hôtel aristocratique: Le Marché du luxe à Paris au XIII᷑ siècle* (Paris, 1998).

Coquery, N., Tenir boutique à Paris au XVIII᷑ siècle: Luxe et demi-luxe (Paris, 2011).

Coquery, N., 'Shopping streets in eighteenth-century Paris. A landscape shaped by historical, economic and social forces', in J. H. Furnée and C. Lesger (eds), *The Landscape of*

Consumption. Shopping Streets and Cultures in Western Europe, 1600–1900 (Farnham, 2014), 57–77.

Corfield, P. J., 'Class by name and number in eighteenth-century Britain', in P. J. Corfield (ed.), *Language, History and Class* (Oxford, 1991), 101–30.

Cornforth, J., *English Interiors 1790–1848: The Quest for Comfort* (London, 1978).

Cornforth, J., 'The backward look', in G. Jackson-Stops (ed.) *The Treasure Houses of Britain. Five Hundred Years of Private Patronage and Art Collecting* (New Haven, CT, 1985), 60–9.

Cornforth, J., 'How French style touched the Georgian drawing room', *Country Life* (6 January 2000), 52–3.

Cornforth, J., *Early Georgian Interiors* (New Haven, CT, 2004).

Cowan, B., *The Social Life of Coffee. The Emergence of the British Coffeehouse* (New Haven, CT, 2005).

Cox, N., *The Complete Tradesman. A Study of Retailing, 1550–1820* (Aldershot, 2000).

Cox, N. and Dannehl, K., *Perceptions of Retailing in Early Modern England* (Aldershot, 2007).

Crowley, J., *The Invention of Comfort. Sensibilities and Design in Early-Modern Britain and Early America* (Baltimore, MD, 2001).

Crowley, J., 'From luxury to comfort and back again: landscape architecture and the cottage in Britain and America', in M. Berg and E. Eger (eds), *Luxury in the Eighteenth Century: Debates, Desires and Delectable Goods* (Basingstoke, 2007), 135–50.

Cruikshank, D., *The Country House Revealed: A Secret History of the British Ancestral Home* (London, 2011).

Dalkeith, Earl of, Fitzpatrick, G., Lister, C., and Adams, M., *Boughton. The English Versailles* (Derby, 2006).

Davis, D., *A History of Shopping* (London, 1966).

de Bruijn, E., 'Consuming East Asia: continuity and change in the development of chinoiserie', in J. Stobart and A. Hann (eds) *The Country House: Material Culture and Consumption* (London, 2015), 95–104.

de Bruijn, E., Bush, A., and Clifford, H., *Chinese Wallpaper in National Trust Houses* (London, 2014).

de Vries, J., *The Industrious Revolution. Consumer Behaviour and the Household Economy, 1650 to the Present* (Cambridge, 2008).

Dickson, P. and Beckett, J., 'The finances of the Dukes of Chandos: aristocratic inheritance, marriage and debt in eighteenth-century England', *Huntingdon Library Quarterly*, 64 (2001), 309–55.

Dolan, B., *Josiah Wedgwood, Entrepreneur to the Enlightenment* (London, 2004).

Dooley, T., *The Decline of the Big House in Ireland: A Study of Irish Landed Families* (Dublin, 2001).

Douglas, M. and Isherwood, B., *The World of Goods* (New York, 1979).

Duncan, A., '"Old Maids": Family and social relationships of never-married Scottish gentlewomen, *c.*1740–*c.*1840' (PhD, Edinburgh 2013).

Edwards, C., *Turning Houses into Homes. A History of the Retailing and Consumption of Domestic Furnishings* (Aldershot, 2005).

Edwards, C. and Ponsonby, M., 'The polarisation of the second-hand market for furniture in the nineteenth century', in J. Stobart and I. Van Damme (eds) *Modernity and the Second-Hand Trade: European Consumption Cultures and Practices, 1700–1900* (Basingstoke, 2011), 93–110.

Edwards, P. 'Decline of an aristocratic stud: Edward, Lord Harley's stud at Welbeck 1721–1729', *Economic History Review* (forthcoming).

Elias, N., *The Court Society* (Oxford, 1983).

Elton, A., Harrison, B., and Wark, K., *Researching the Country House. A Guide for Local Historians* (London, 1992).

English, B. and Saville, J., 'Family settlement and "the rise of the Great Estates"', *Economic History Review*, 33 (1980), 556–8.

Epp A. and Price, L., 'The storied life of singularized objects: forces of agency and network transformation', *Journal of Consumer Research*, 36 (2010), 820–37.

Feijfer, J. and Southworth, E., *The Ince Blundell Collection of Classical Sculpture* (Liverpool, 1998).

Ferguson, P., '"Japan China": taste and elite ceramic consumption in eighteenth-century England: revising the narrative', in J. Stobart and A. Hann (eds) *The Country House: Material Culture and Consumption* (Swindon, 2015), 113–22.

Finn, M., 'Men's things: masculine possessions in the consumer revolution', *Social History*, 25/2 (2000), 133–55.

Finn, M., *The Character of Credit. Personal Debt in English Culture, 1740–1914* (Cambridge, 2003).

Finn, M., 'Colonial gifts: family politics and the exchange of goods in British India, c.1780–1820', *Modern Asian Studies*, 40 (2006), 203–31.

Finn, M., 'Swallowfield Park, Berkshire', *East India Company at Home* (February 2013), <http://blogs.ucl.ac.uk/eicah/case-studies-2/swallowfield-park-berkshire/>.

Fisher, F. J., 'The development of London as a centre of conspicuous consumption in the sixteenth and seventeenth centuries', in E. M. Carus Wilson (ed.) *Essays in Economic History*, vol. 2 (London, 1962), 197–207.

Fletcher, A., 'Manhood, the male body, courtship and household in early-modern England', *History*, 84 (1999), 419–36.

Fontaine, L., 'The circulation of luxury goods in eighteenth-century Paris: social distribution and an alternative currency', in M. Berg and E. Eger (eds), *Luxury in the Eighteenth Century. Debates, Desires and Delectable Goods* (Basingstoke, 2007), 89–102.

Fontaine, L., *The Moral Economy. Poverty, Credit and Trust in Early Modern Europe* (English edition, Cambridge, 2014).

Fowler, J. and Cornforth, J., *English Decoration in the Eighteenth Century* (London, 1974).

Foyster, E., '"Boys will be boys"? Manhood and aggression 1600–1800', in T. Hitchcock and M. Cohen (eds), *English Masculinities 1600–1800* (Harlow, 1999), 151–66.

Foyster, E., *Manhood in Early Modern England: Honour, Sex and Marriage* (Harlow, 1999).

French, H., *The Middle Sort of People in Provincial England* (Oxford, 2007).

French, H. and Rothery, M., *Man's Estate: Landed Gentry Masculinities, 1660–1900* (Oxford, 2012).

Frew, J. and Wallace, C., 'Thomas Pitt, Portugal and the gothic cult of Batalha', *The Burlington Magazine*, 128 (1986), 582–5.

Garland, S., 'The use of French architectural design books in de Grey's choice of style at Wrest Park', in J. Stobart and A. Hann (eds) *The Country House: Material Culture and Consumption* (Swindon, 2015), 56–63.

Garrett, O., *Calke Abbey* (London, 2000).

Gemmett, R., '"The tinsel of fashion and the gewgaws of luxury": the Fonthill sale of 1801', *The Burlington Magazine*, 150 (2008), 381–8.

Gerard, J., *Country House Life: Family and Servants* (Oxford, 1994).

Gilbert, C. and Wells-Cole, A., *The Fashionable Fireplace, 1660–1840* (Leeds, 1985).

Girouard, M., *Life in the English Country House* (New Haven, CT, 1978).

Girouard, M., *Life in the French Country House* (London, 2000).

Gittings, C., *Death, Burial and the Individual in Early Modern England* (London, 1984).

Glennie, P. and Thrift, N., 'Consumers, identities and consumption spaces in early-modern England', *Environment and Planning A*, 28 (1996), 25–45.

Glover, K., *Elite Women and Polite Society in Eighteenth-Century Scotland* (London, 2011).

Goffman, E., *The Presentation of Self in Everyday Life* (New York, 1956).

Goldthwaite, R., *Wealth and the Demand for Art in Italy, 1300–1600* (Baltimore, MD, 1993).

Gomme, A., 'Stoneleigh after the Grand Tour', *The Antiquaries Journal*, 68 (1988), 265–86.

Gomme, A., *Smith of Warwick* (Stamford, 2000).

Gomme, A., 'Abbey into palace: a lesser Wilton?', in R. Bearman (ed.) *Stoneleigh Abbey. The House, Its Owners, Its Lands* (Stratford-upon-Avon, 2004), 82–115.

Goodman, D., 'Furnishing discourses: readings of a writing desk in eighteenth-century France', in M. Berg and E. Eger (eds), *Luxury in the Eighteenth Century. Debates, Desires and Delectable Goods* (Basingstoke, 2003), 71–88.

Goodway, K., 'Landscapes and gardens at Keele, 1700–1900', in C. Harrison (ed.) *The History of Keele* (University of Keele, 1986), 67–102.

Goody, J,. Thirsk, J., and Thompson, E. P. (eds), *Family and Inheritance: Rural Society in Western Europe, 1200–1800* (Cambridge, 1976).

Gregson, N. and Rose, G., 'Taking Butler elsewhere: performativities, spatialities and subjectivities', *Environment and Planning D: Society and Space*, 18 (2000), 433–52.

Greig, H., 'Eighteenth-century English interiors in image and text', in J. Aynsley, C. Grant, and H. McKay (eds), *Imagined Interiors: Representing the Domestic Interior since the Renaissance* (London, 2006), 102–27.

Greig, H., *The Beau Monde. Fashionable Society in Georgian London* (Oxford, 2013).

Guilding, R., 'Robert Adam and Charles Townley', *Apollo*, 143 (1996), 27–32.

Habakkuk, H. J., 'English landownership 1640–1740', *Economic History Review*, 10 (1940), 2–17.

Habakkuk, H. J., 'Marriage settlements in the eighteenth century', *Transactions of the Royal Historical Society*, fourth series, 32 (1950), 15–30.

Habakkuk, H. J., *Marriage, Debt and the Estate System: English Landownership 1650–1950* (Oxford, 1994).

Hall, M., 'Arbury Hall', *Country Life* (7 January 1999), 30–5, (14 January 1999), 40–3.

Hammond, P. and Hammond, C., *Life in an Eighteenth-Century Country House* (Stroud, 2012).

Harding, V., 'Shops, markets and retailers in London's Cheapside, *c.*1500–1700', in B. Blondé, P. Stabel, J. Stobart, and I. Van Damme (eds) *Buyer and Sellers. Retail Circuits and Practices in Medieval and Early Modern Europe* (Turnhout, 2006), 155–70.

Harris, J., *The Design of the English Country House, 1620–1920* (London, 1985).

Harvey, K., 'The history of masculinity, circa 1650–1800', *Journal of British Studies*, 44 (2005), 296–311.

Harvey, K., 'Men making home: masculinity and domesticity in eighteenth-century England', *Gender and History* 21/3 (2009), 520–41.

Harvey, K. *The Little Republic: Masculinity and Domestic Authority in Eighteenth-Century Britain* (Oxford, 2012).

Harvey, K. and Shepard, A., 'What have historians done with masculinity? Reflections on five centuries of British history', *Journal of British Studies*, 44 (2005), 274–80.

Haskell, F., 'The British as collectors', in G. Jackson-Stops (ed.) *The Treasure Houses of Britain. Five Hundred Years of Private Patronage and Art Collecting* (New Haven, CT, 1985), 50–9.

Hayes, J., 'British patrons and landscape painting', *Apollo*, 185 (1991), 254–60.

Heal, F. and Holmes, C., *Gentry in England and Wales, 1500–1700* (London, 1994).

Hilton, M., 'Consumer movements', in F. Trentmann (ed.) *The Oxford Handbook of the History of Consumption* (Oxford, 2012), 505–20.

Hirsch, F., *The Social Limits to Growth* (London, 1977).

Hitchcock, T. and M. Cohen, M. (eds), *English Masculinities, 1660–1800* (Harlow, 1999).

Hollingsworth, T. H., 'A demographic study of the British ducal families', *Population Studies*, 11/1 (1957), 4–26.

Hollingsworth, T. H., 'The demography of the British peerage', *Supplement to Population Studies*, 18/2 (1964), 20–46.

Horrell, S., Humphries, K. and Sneath, K., 'Consumption conundrums unravelled', *Economic History Review* 68 (2015), 830–57.

Houlbrooke, R., *Death, Religion, and the Family in England, 1480–1750* (Oxford, 1998).

Howard, M., *The Vyne* (Swindon, 1998).

Hudson's Historic Houses and Gardens; Castles and Heritage Sites (Banbury, 2000).

Hunt, M., *The Middling Sort: Commerce, Gender and the Family in England, 1680–1780* (London, 1996).

Hussey, D., 'Guns, horses and stylish waistcoats? Male consumer activity and domestic shopping in late-eighteenth and early-nineteenth century England', in D. Hussey and M. Ponsonby (eds), *The Single Homemaker and Material Culture in the Long Eighteenth Century* (Aldershot, 2012), 47–72.

Ijäs, U., 'Favourites of fortune: the luxury consumption of the Hackmans of Vyborg, 1790–1825', in D. Simonton, M. Kaartinen, and A. Montenach (eds), *Luxury and Gender in European Towns, 1700–1914* (London, 2015), 190–205.

Ilmakunnas, J., 'The luxury shopping experience of the Swedish aristocracy in eighteenth-century Paris', in D. Simonton, M. Kaartinen, and A. Montenach (eds), *Luxury and Gender in European Towns, 1700–1914* (London, 2015), 115–31.

Ilmakunnas, J., 'To build according to one's status: a country house in late 18th-century Sweden', in J. Stobart and A. Hann (eds) *The Country House: Material Culture and Consumption* (Swindon, 2015), 33–42.

Impey, O., 'Eastern trade and the furnishing of the British country house', in G. Jackson-Stops, G. J. Schochet, L. C. Orlin, and E. B. MacDougall (eds), *The Fashioning and Functioning of British Country Houses* (New Haven, CT, 1989), 177–92.

Jackson, P. and Thrift, N., 'Geographies of consumption', in D. Miller (ed.) *Acknowledging Consumption* (London, 1995), 204–38.

Jackson-Stops, G., 'Petworth House, Sussex, NT', *Country Life* (4 September 1980), 798–9, (25 September 1980), 1030–1.

Jenkins, P., *The Making of a Ruling Class: The Glamorgan Gentry 1640–1790* (Cambridge, 1983).

Jervis, S., 'The English country house library: an architectural history', *Library History*, 18/3 (2002), 175–90.

Johnson, M., *Housing Culture: Traditional Housing in an English Landscape* (London, 1993).

Kelch, R. A., *Newcastle, A Duke Without Money: Thomas Pelham-Holmes, 1693–1768* (London, 1974).

Kennedy Johnson, E., 'The taste for bringing the outside in: nationalism, gender and landscape wallpaper (1700–1825)', in J. Batchelor and C. Kaplan (eds), *Women and Material Culture, 1660–1830* (Basingstoke, 2007), 119–33.

Kenny, R., '"Apartments that are not too large": pastel portraits and the spaces of femininity in the English Country House', in G. Perry, K. Retford, and J. Vibert (eds), *Placing Faces:*

The Portrait and the English Country House in the Long Eighteenth Century (Manchester, 2013), 143–61.

Klein, L. E., 'The third Earl of Shaftesbury and the progress of politeness', *Eighteenth-Century Studies*, 18 (1984–5), 186–214.

Klein, L. E., 'Politeness and the interpretation of the British eighteenth century', *The Historical Journal*, 45 (2002), 869–98.

Kowalski-Wallace, E., *Consuming Subjects: Women, Shopping and Business in the Eighteenth Century* (New York, 1997).

Kuchta, D., *The Three-Piece Suit and Modern Masculinity: England 1550–1850* (London, 2002).

Ladd, F., *Architects at Corsham Court* (Bradford-on-Avon, 1978).

Langford, P., *A Polite and Commercial People: England 1727–1783* (Oxford, 1989).

Langford, P., 'The uses of eighteenth-century politeness', *Transactions of the Royal Historical Society*, 6th series, 12 (2002), 311–31.

Larsen, R. (ed.) *Maids and Mistresses: Celebrating Three Hundred Years of Women and the Yorkshire Country House* (Castle Howard, 2004).

Larsen, R., 'For want of a good fortune: elite single women's experiences in Yorkshire, 1730–1860', *Women's History Review*, 16/3 (2007), 387–401.

Lefebvre, H., *The Production of Space* (Oxford, 1991).

Lehmann, G., *The British Housewife: Cookery Books, Cooking and Society in 18th Century Britain* (Totnes, 1999).

Lemire, B., 'An education in comfort: Indian textiles and the remaking of English homes in the long eighteenth century', in J. Stobart and B. Blondé (eds) *Selling Textiles in the Long Eighteenth Century. Comparative Perspectives from Western Europe* (Basingstoke, 2014), 13–29.

Lewis, J., 'When a house is not a home: elite English women and the eighteenth-century country house', *Journal of British Studies*, 48 (2009), 336–63.

Linström, D., 'Maids, noblewomen, journeymen, state officials and others: unmarried adults in four Swedish towns, 1750–1855', in J. De Groot, I. Devos, and A. Schmidt (eds), *Single Life and the City, 1200–1900* (Basingstoke, 2015), 93–113.

MacArthur, R., 'Material culture and consumption on an English estate: Kelmarsh Hall 1687–1845' (Unpublished PhD thesis, University of Northampton, 2010).

MacArthur, R. and Stobart, J., 'Going for a song? Country house sales in Georgian England', in J. Stobart and I. Van Damme (eds), *Modernity and the Second-Hand Trade: European Consumption Cultures and Practices, 1700–1900* (Basingstoke, 2011), 175–95.

McCants, A., 'Poor consumers as global consumers: the diffusion of tea and coffee drinking in the eighteenth century', *Economic History Review*, 61 (2008), 172–200.

McCarthy, M., 'Sir Roger Newdigate and Piranesi', *The Burlington Magazine*, 114 (1972), 468–72.

McCarthy, M., *The Origins of the Gothic Revival* (New Haven, CT, 1987).

McCormack, M., 'A Man's Sphere?: British politics in the eighteenth and nineteenth centuries', in S. Brady, C. Fletcher, R. Moss, and L. Riall (eds), *The Palgrave Handbook of Masculinity and Political Culture in Europe: From Antiquity to the Contemporary World* (forthcoming).

McCracken, G., *Culture and Consumption. New Approaches to the Symbolic Character of Consumer Goods and Activities* (Bloomington and Indianapolis, IN, 1988), 3–30.

MacDonald, M., '"Not unmarked by some eccentricities": the Leigh family of Stoneleigh Abbey', in R. Bearman (ed.), *Stoneleigh Abbey: The House, Its Owners, Its Lands* (Stoneleigh, 2004), 131–62.

McDowell, S., 'Shugborough: seat of the Earl of Lichfield', *East India Company at Home* (April 2013), <http://blogs.ucl.ac.uk/eicah/shugborough-hall-staffordshire/>.

McKendrick, N., 'The consumer revolution of eighteenth-century England', in N. McKendrick, J. Brewer, and J. H. Plumb (eds), *The Birth of a Consumer Society* (London, 1982), 9–33.

McKendrick, N., 'Josiah Wedgwood and the commercialization of the potteries', in N. McKendrick, J. Brewer, and J. Plumb (eds) *The Birth of a Consumer Society* (London, 1982), 100–45.

Mandler, P., '"From Almack to Willis": aristocratic women and politics, 1815–1867', in A. Vickery (ed.), *Women, Privilege and Power: British Politics 1750 to the Present* (Stanford, CA, 2005), 152–67.

Mathias, P., 'The social structure in the eighteenth century: a calculation by Joseph Massie', in P. Mathias, *The Transformation of England: Essays in the Economic and Social History of England in the Eighteenth Century,* (London 1979), 171–89.

Miers, M., *The English Country House. From the Archives of Country Life* (New York, 2009).

Millar, O., 'Portraiture and the country house', in G. Jackson-Stops (ed.) *The Treasure Houses of Britain. Five Hundred Years of Private Patronage and Art Collecting* (New Haven, CT, 1985), 28–39.

Miller, D., *A Theory of Shopping* (Cambridge, 1998).

Mingay, G. E., *English Landed Society in the Eighteenth Century* (London, 1963).

Mingay, G. E., *The Gentry: The Rise and Fall of a Ruling Class* (London, 1976).

Mitchell, D. M., 'Fine table linen in England 1450–1750: ownership and use of a luxury commodity' (Unpublished PhD thesis, University of London, 1999).

Mitchell, I., '"Old books—new bound"? Selling second-hand books in England, *c.*1680–1850', in J. Stobart and I. Van Damme (eds), *Modernity and the Second-Hand Trade. European Consumption Cultures and Practices, 1700–1900* (Basingstoke, 2010), 139–44.

Mitchell, I., *Tradition and Innovation in English Retailing, 1700 to 1850* (Farnham, 2014).

Morgan, V., 'Producing consumer spaces in eighteenth-century England: shops, shopping and the provincial town' (unpublished PhD thesis, Coventry University, 2003).

Morrall, A., 'Ornament as evidence', in K. Harvey (ed.), *History and Material Culture* (London, 2009), 47–66.

Morrison, K., *English Shops and Shopkeeping* (London, 2003).

Mui, H.-C., and Mui, L., *Shops and Shopkeeping in Eighteenth-Century England* (London, 1989).

Muldrew, C., *The Economy of Obligation. The Culture of Credit and Social Relations in Early-Modern England* (Basingstoke, 1998).

Musson, J., *Up and Down Stairs: The History of the Country House Servant* (London, 2010).

Myers, R., Harris, M., and Mandelbrooke, G. (eds), *Under the Hammer: Book Auctions since the Seventeenth Century* (New Castle, DE, 2001).

Naddeo, B., 'A cosmopolitan in the provinces: G. M. Galanti, geography, and Enlightenment Europe', *Modern Intellectual History* 10 (2013): 1–26.

Nares, G., 'Arbury Hall', *Country Life* (8 October 1953), 1126–9; (15 October 1953), 1210–13; (29 October 1953), 1414–17.

Nenadic, S., 'Middle-rank consumers and domestic culture in Edinburgh and Glasgow 1720–1840', *Past and Present,* 145 (1994), 122–56.

Overton, M., Dean, D., Whittle, J., and Hann, A., *Production and Consumption in English Households, 1600–1750* (London, 2004).

Page, N., *The Language of Jane Austen* (Oxford, 1972).

Paston-Williams, S., *The Art of Dining. A History of Cooking and Eating* (Oxford, 1993).

Peck, L., *Consuming Splendor: Society and Culture in Seventeenth-Century England* (Cambridge, 2005).

Pennell, S., 'Material culture of food in early-modern England, *c.*1650–*c.*1750' (Unpublished DPhil thesis, University of Oxford, 1997).

Pennell, S., '"For a crack or flaw despis'd": thinking about ceramic durability and the everyday in late 17th- and early 18th-century England', in T. Hamling and C. Richardson (eds) *Everyday Objects: Medieval and Early Modern Material Culture and Its Meaning* (Farnham, 2010), 27–40.

Pennell, S., *Making the British kitchen, c.1600–1850* (forthcoming).

Phillipps, K. C., *Jane Austen's English* (London, 1970).

Phillips, C. and Wilson, G., *The Stately Houses, Palaces and Castles of Georgian, Victorian and Modern Britain* (London, 2011).

Pickles, J. D., 'Cotton, Sir Vincent, sixth Baronet (1801–1863)', in B. Harrison (ed.), *The Oxford Dictionary of National Biography* (Oxford, 2004), <http://www.oxforddnb.com/view/article/6427>, accessed 5 Jan. 2016.

Plumb, J. H. and Weldon, H., *Royal Heritage. The Story of Britain's Royal Builders and Collectors* (London, 1977).

Pointon, M., 'Jewellery in eighteenth-century England', in M. Berg and H. Clifford (eds), *Consumers and Luxury. Consumer Culture in Europe, 1650–1850* (Manchester, 1999), 120–46.

Pointon, M., 'Women and their jewels', in J. Batchelor and C. Kaplan (eds) *Women and Material Culture, 1660–1830* (Basingstoke, 2007), 11–30.

Ponsonby, M., *Stories from Home. English Domestic Interiors, 1750–1850* (Aldershot, 2007).

Port, M., 'West End palaces: the aristocratic town house in London, 1730–1830', *London Journal*, 20/1 (1995), 17–46.

Porter, D., 'A wanton chase in a foreign place: Hogarth and the gendering of exoticism in the eighteenth-century interior', in D. Goodman and K. Norberg (eds), *Furnishing the Eighteenth Century* (New York, 2007), 49–60.

Porter, D., *The Chinese Taste in Eighteenth-Century England* (Cambridge, 2010).

Porter, R., *London. A Social History* (Harmondsworth, 1994).

Pred, A., *Lost Words and Lost Worlds: Modernity and the Language of Everyday Life in Late Nineteenth-Century Stockholm* (Cambridge, 1990).

Purcell, M., '"A lunatick of unsound mind": Edward, Lord Leigh (1742–86)', *Bodleian Library Record*, 17 (2001), 246–60.

Purcell, M., 'The country house library reassess'd: or, did the "country house library" ever really exist?', *Library History*, 18 (2002), 157–74.

Ramsay, N., 'English book collectors and the salerooms in the eighteenth century', in R. Myers, M. Harris, and G. Mandelbrooke (eds), *Under the Hammer: Book Auctions since the Seventeenth Century* (New Castle, DE, 2001), 89–110.

Raven, J., *The Business of Books. Booksellers and the English Book Trade, 1450–1850* (New Haven, CT, 2007).

Retford, K., *The Art of Domestic Life: Family Portraiture in Eighteenth-Century England* (New Haven, CT, 2006).

Retford, K., 'Patrilineal portraiture? Gender and genealogy in the eighteenth-century English country house,' in J. Styles and A. Vickery (eds), *Gender, Taste and Material Culture in Britain and North America 1700–1830* (New Haven, CT, 2006), 315–44.

Richter, A. N., 'Spectacle, exoticism and display in the gentleman's house: the Fonthill auction of 1822', *Eighteenth-Century Studies*, 41/4 (2008), 543–63.

Robinson, J., *Regency Country House* (London, 2008).

Robinson, J. M., *James Wyatt (1746–1813): Architect to George III* (New Haven, CT, 2012).

Roebuck, P., *Yorkshire Baronets, 1640–1760* (Oxford, 1980).

Ronnes, H., 'A sense of heritage: renewal versus preservation in the English and Dutch palaces of William III in the 18th century', in J. Stobart and A. Hann (eds), *The Country House: Material Culture and Consumption* (Swindon, 2015), 74–83.

Roper, M. and Tosh, J., *Manful Assertions: Masculinities in Britain since 1800* (London, 1991).

Roscoe, I., 'The decoration and furnishing of Kirtlington Park', *Apollo*, 111 (1980), 22–9.

Rothery, M., 'The reproductive behaviour of the English landed gentry, 1800–1939', *Journal of British Studies*, 48 (2009), 674–94.

Rothery, M. and French, H., *Making Men: the Formation of Elite Male Identities in England, c. 1660–1900* (Basingstoke, 2012).

Rothery, M. and Stobart, J., 'Inheritance events and spending patterns in the English country house: the Leigh family of Stoneleigh Abbey, 1738–1806', *Continuity and Change*, 27/3 (2012), 379–407.

Rothery, M. and Stobart, J., 'Merger and crisis: Sir John Turner Dryden and Canons Ashby, Northamptonshire, in the late eighteenth century', *Northamptonshire Past and Present*, 65 (2012), 19–30.

Rowell, C. (ed.), *Ham House: a History* (New Haven, CT, 2013).

Rubinstein, W. D., 'New men of wealth and the purchase of land in nineteenth-century Britain', *Past and Present*, 92 (1981), 125–47.

Russell, F., 'The hanging and display of pictures, 1799–1850', in G. Jackson-Stops, G. J. Schochet, L. C. Orlin, and E. B. MacDougall (eds), *The Fashioning and Functioning of the British Country House* (New Haven, CT, 1989), 133–53.

Sambrook, P., 'Larder and other storeplaces for the kitchen', in P. Sambrook and P. Brears (eds), *The Country House Kitchen, 1650–1900* (Stroud, 1996), 184–6.

Sambrook, P., *Keeping their Places: Domestic Service in the Country House* (Stroud, 2009).

Sambrook, P. and Brears, P. (eds), *The Country House Kitchen, 1650–1900* (Stroud, 1996).

Sargentson, C., *Merchants and Luxury Markets: The Marchands Merciers of Eighteenth-Century Paris* (London, 1996).

Saumarez Smith, C., *Eighteenth Century Decoration: Design and the Domestic Interior in England* (London, 1993).

Savage, M., 'Status, lifestyle and taste', in F. Trentmann (ed.), *The Oxford Handbook of the History of Consumption* (Oxford, 2012), 557–67.

Schivelbusch, W., *Tastes of Paradise. A Social History of Spices, Stimulants and Intoxicants* (New York, 1993).

Schutte, K., *Women, Rank and Marriage in the British Aristocracy, 1485–2000: An Open Elite?* (Basingstoke, 2014).

Scitovsky, T., *The Joyless Economy: An Enquiry into Human Satisfaction and Consumer Dissatisfaction* (New York, 1976).

Shapin, S., *A Social History of Truth. Civility and Science in Seventeenth-Century England* (Chicago, 1995).

Sharp, K., 'Women's creativity and display in the eighteenth-century British domestic interior', in S. McKellar and P. Sparke (eds), *Interior Design and Identity* (Manchester, 2004), 10–26.

Sharpe, P., 'Dealing with love: the ambiguous independence of single women in early modern England', *Gender and History*, 11 (1999), 209–32.

Shepard, A., 'Manhood, credit and patriarchy in early-modern England *c*.1580–1640', *Past and Present*, 167 (2000), 75–106.

Shepard, A., *Meanings of Manhood in Early Modern England* (Oxford, 2003).

Shepard, A., 'Minding their own business: married women and credit in early eighteenth-century London', *Transactions of the Royal Historical Society*, 25 (2015), 53–74.

Smith, K., 'Englefield House, Berkshire: processes and practices', *East India Company at Home* (March 2013), <http://blogs.ucl.ac.uk/eicah/englefield-house-berkshire/>.

Smith, K., 'Warfield Park: longing, belonging and the country house', *East India Company at Home* (April 2013), <http://blogs.ucl.ac.uk/eicah/warfield-park-berkshire/>.

Smith, K., 'In her hands. Materializing distinction in Georgian Britain', *Cultural and Social History*, 11/4 (2014), 489–506.

Smith, K., 'Manly objects? Gendering armorial porcelain wares', *East India Company at Home* (June 2014), <http://blogs.ucl.ac.uk/eicah/armorial-porcelain/>.

Smith, W., *Consumption and the Making of Respectability, 1600–1800* (London, 2002).

Soja, E., *Thirdspace* (Oxford, 1996).

Sombart, W., *Luxury and Capitalism* (Munich,1913; English edition, Chicago, 1967).

Spring, D., 'Aristocracy, Social Structure and Religion in Early Victorian England', *Victorian Studies*, 6/3 (1963), 263–80.

Stafford, W., 'Gentlemanly masculinities as represented by the late Georgian *Gentleman's Magazine*', *History*, 93 (2008), 47–68.

Stobart, J., 'Clothes, cabinets and carriages: second-hand dealing in eighteenth-century England', in B. Blondé, P. Stabel, J. Stobart, and I. Van Damme (eds) *Buyers and Sellers: Retail Circuits and Practices in Medieval and Early Modern Europe* (Turnhout, 2006), 225–44.

Stobart, J., 'Selling (through) politeness: advertising provincial shops in eighteenth-century England', *Cultural and Social History*, 5 (2008), 309–28.

Stobart, J., *Spend Spend Spend! A History of Shopping* (Stroud, 2008).

Stobart, J., 'Gentlemen and shopkeepers: supplying the country house in eighteenth-century England', *Economic History Review* 64 (2011), 885–904.

Stobart, J., 'Inventories and the changing furnishings of Canons Ashby, Northamptonshire, 1717–1819', *Regional Furniture*, 27 (2013), 1–43.

Stobart, J., *Sugar and Spice. Grocers and Groceries in Provincial England, 1650–1830* (Oxford, 2013).

Stobart, J., 'The luxury of learning: books, knowledge and display in the English Country House', in A. Bonnet and N. Coquery (eds), *Commerce du luxe* (Lyons, 2015), 243–8.

Stobart, J., '"So agreeable and suitable a place": the character, use and provisioning of a late eighteenth-century suburban villa', *Journal of Eighteenth Century Studies*, (2015).

Stobart, J., Hann, A., and Morgan, V., *Spaces of Consumption. Leisure and Shopping in the English Town, c.1680–1830* (London, 2007).

Stobart, J. and Rothery, M., 'Fashion, heritage and family: new and old in the Georgian country house', *Cultural and Social History*, 11/3 (2014), 385–406.

Stoker, D., 'The ill-gotten library of "Honest Tom" Martin', in R. Myers and M. Harris (eds), *Property of a Gentleman: The Formation, Organisation and Dispersal of the Private Library 1620–1920* (Winchester and Newcastle, DE, 1991), 91–111.

Stone, L., *The Crisis of the Aristocracy 1558–1641* (Oxford, 1965).

Stone, L. and Fawtier Stone, J. C., *An Open Elite: England 1540–1880* (Oxford, 1984).

Styles, J., *The Dress of the People. Everyday Fashion in Eighteenth-Century England* (New Haven, CT, 2007).

Sugden, A. and Edmundson, J., *A History of English Wallpaper, 1509–1914* (London, 1926).

Summerson, J., *Architecture in Britain 1530–1830* (London, 1953; New Haven, CT, 1993).

Summerson, J., Colvin, H., and Harris, J. (eds), *The Country Seat: Studies in the History of the British Country House* (London, 1970).

Sweet, R., *Antiquaries: The Discovery of the Past in Eighteenth-Century Britain* (London, 2004).

Sweet, R., *Cities and the Grand Tour. The British in Italy, c.1690–1820* (Cambridge, 2012).

Tadmor, N., *Family and Friends in Eighteenth-Century England: Household, Kinship and Patronage* (Cambridge, 2000).

Tague, I., *Women of Quality, Accepting and Contesting Ideals of Femininity in England, 1690–1760* (London, 2002).

Thompson, F. M. L., *English Landed Society in the Nineteenth Century* (London, 1963).

Thompson, F. M. L., *Gentrification and the Enterprise Culture: Britain 1780–1980* (Oxford, 2001).

Tinniswood, A., *The Polite Tourist: Four Centuries of Country House Visiting* (New York, 1999).

Tosh, J., *A Man's Place: Masculinity and the Middle-Class Home in Victorian England* (London, 1999).

Tosh, J., 'Masculinities in an industrialising society: Britain 1800–1914', *Journal of British Studies*, 44 (2005), 330–42.

Trentmann, F., 'Introduction', in F. Trentmann (ed.), *The Oxford Handbook of the History of Consumption* (Oxford, 2012), 1–19.

Tyack, G., 'Country house building in Warwickshire, 1500–1914' (BLitt thesis, Oxford University, 1970).

Tyack, G., *Warwickshire Country Houses* (Chichester, 1994).

Vaizey, M. and Gere, C., *Great Women Collectors* (London, 1999).

Veblen, T., *The Theory of the Leisure Class: An Economic Study of Institutions* (Basingstoke, 1912).

Veeckman, J. (ed.), *Majolica and Glass from Italy to Antwerp and Beyond. The Transfer of Technology in the 16th–early 17th century* (Antwerp, 2003).

Vickery, A., 'Women and the world of goods: A Lancashire consumer and her possessions, 1751–81' in J. Brewer and R. Porter (eds) *Consumption and the World of Goods* (London, 1993), 274–301.

Vickery, A., *The Gentleman's Daughter: Women's Lives in Georgian England* (New Haven, CT, 1997).

Vickery, A., 'An Englishman's home is his castle? Thresholds, boundaries and privacies in the eighteenth-century London house', *Past and Present*, 199 (2008), 147–73.

Vickery, A., *Behind Closed Doors. At Home in Georgian England* (New Haven, CT, 2009).

Wainwright, C., *The Romantic Interior. The British Collector at Home, 1750–1850* (New Haven, CT, 1989).

Walker, S., 'Identifying the woman behind the "Railed-in Desk": the proto-feminisation of bookkeeping in Britain', *Accounting, Auditing & Accountability Journal*, 16/4 (2003), 606–39.

Walker, S., 'Accounting histories of women: beyond recovery?', *Accounting, Auditing & Accountability Journal*, 21/4 (2008), 580–610.

Walsh, C., 'Shop design and the display of goods in eighteenth-century London', *Journal of Design History*, 8 (1995), 157–76.

Walsh, C., 'Social meaning and social space in the shopping galleries of early-modern London', in J. Benson and L. Ugolini (eds), *A Nation of Shopkeepers. Five Centuries of British Retailing* (London, 2003), 52–79.

Walsh, C., 'Shops, shopping and the art of decision making in eighteenth-century England', in J. Styles and A. Vickery (eds) *Gender, Taste and Material Culture in Britain and North America* (New Haven, CT, 2006), 151–77.

Walsh, C., 'Shopping at first hand? Mistresses, servants and shopping for the household in early-modern England', in D. Hussey and M. Ponsonby (eds), *Buying for the Home: Shopping for the Domestic from the Seventeenth Century to the Present* (Aldershot, 2008), 13–26.

Weatherill, L., *Consumer Behaviour and Material Culture in Britain 1660–1760* (London, 1988).

Wees, B. C., *English, Irish and Scottish Silver* (Easthampton, ME, 1997).

Westman, A., 'A bed in burnished gold', *Country Life*, (4 May 2000), 128–9.

White, A. W. A., *The Correspondence of Sir Roger Newdigate of Arbury Warickshire* (Hertford, 1995).

Whittle, J., 'The gentry as consumers in early 17th-century England', in J. Stobart and A. Hann (eds), *The Country House: Material Culture and Consumption* (Swindon, 2015), 26–34.

Whittle, J. and Griffiths, E., *Consumption and Gender in the Early Seventeenth-Century Household. The World of Alice Le Strange* (Oxford, 2012).

Whyman, S., *Sociability and Power in Late-Stuart England. The Cultural Worlds of the Verneys, 1660–1720* (Oxford, 1999).

Whyman, S., *The Pen and the People: English Letter Writers 1660–1800* (Oxford, 2009).

Williams, J. D., *Audley End: the Restoration of 1762–97* (Colchester, 1966).

Williams, J. D., 'The noble household as a unit of consumption: the Audley End experience, 1765–1797', *Essex Archaeology and History*, 23 (1992), 67–78.

Wilson, C. A., 'Stillhouses and stillrooms', in P. Sambrook and P. Brears (eds), *The Country House Kitchen*, 1650–1900 (Stroud, 1996), 129–43.

Wilson, M., *The English Country House and its Furnishings* (London, 1977).

Wilson, R. and Mackley, A., *The Building of the English Country House, 1660–1880. Creating Paradise* (London, 2000).

Wood, A., 'Diaries of Sir Roger Newdigate, 1751–1806', *Birmingham Archaeological Society*, 78 (1960), 40–54.

Worsley, L., 'Female architectural patronage in the eighteenth century and the case of Henrietta Cavendish Holles Harley', *Architectural History*, 48 (2005), 139–62.

Websites
<http://blogs.ucl.ac.uk/eicah/case-studies-2/>.
<http://www.bonhams.com/auctions/15270/lot/107/>.

Index